to Al
fr.
A. v A.

INVENTING
EUROPE

INVENTING EUROPE

THE RISE OF
A NEW WORLD
POWER

JAMES LAXER

LESTER PUBLISHING

Canadian Cataloguing in Publication Data

Laxer, James, 1941-
   Inventing Europe: the rise of a new world power

ISBN 1-895555-00-0

1. European Economic Community.   2. Europe 1992.
I. Title.

HC241.2.L3 1991   382'.9142   C91-094732-5

Lester Publishing Limited
56 The Esplanade
Toronto, Ontario
M5E 1A7

Printed and bound in Canada.

91 92 93 94 5 4 3 2 1

CONTENTS

★ ★ ★ ★ ★ ★ ★ ★ ★ ★ ★ ★

To Sandy, Michael, Kate, Emily and Jonathan

INTRODUCTION

★ ★ ★ ★ ★ ★ ★ ★ ★ ★ ★ ★

TEN YEARS AGO IT SEEMED IMPOSSIBLE, BUT IN 1991, WITH A UNITED Germany at its head, Europe is fast coming together as a new kind of superpower. What Europeans are establishing is much more than the world's largest single market, although that is of great importance. They are inventing a new kind of federation, a post-national state, which currently consists of twelve member states with a population of 340 million people. Over the next decade, the European Community (EC) will almost certainly take in up to ten new states, including not only such countries as Austria and Sweden, which will fit relatively easily into its existing structure, but also such countries as Hungary, Czechoslovakia, and Poland, which will pose a completely new kind of challenge for the community.

The "invention" of Europe has vast implications for the whole international economic and political order. The completion of the EC's "1992" program and the steps beyond that towards a European central bank and common currency will force changes on the global operations of multinational corporations and on the international trading system. It will alter the economic relationships among the world's leading states. Since economic power serves as the basis for other forms of power, the emergence of Europe as the world's largest integrated market has implications for the political and military position not only of the declining Soviet Union, but of the United States as well.

For Europeans, this is a perplexing era in which a new European identity and very old regional identities are in the ascendancy, fusing to challenge the paramount position of national identities, and with them, the continent's system of nation-states.

The transformation of Europe involves much more than the decisions of political and economic élites, important though they are. It is the consequence of a long historical process that has resulted in altered relationships among Europeans at many levels. The origins of the New Europe in some respects lie in traditions that are centuries old, and in spite of setbacks, I believe the EC is poised on the threshold of establishing a European federal state.

No question has been more endlessly controversial than whether a federal state will be the ultimate consequence of the movement for European union. Long periods of Euro-pessimism have succeeded bouts of Euro-optimism as the probabilities of the outcome of the European venture have seemingly tilted, at some moments towards success, at other moments towards failure. The controversy is very much alive today. Throughout Europe, the speculation about where European union will lead is more intense than ever. Everywhere there are optimists and pessimists. In Britain, the nay-sayers, those doubting the wisdom of the movement for European union and its prospects, have always been more numerous than in any other major country. This situation has coloured the perspective of the wider English-speaking world as it has sought to make sense of European developments.

Recognizing the strength of some of the arguments of those who believe that European union will never lead to the creation of a European federal state, I none the less number myself decidedly in the camp of the optimists. The movement for European union has survived many hazardous passages, and it is my conviction that, despite its present daunting challenges, success in the achievement of a European federal state is much more likely than failure. In my opinion, therefore, the course of wisdom for those outside Europe is to prepare to deal with an economically and politically united Europe.

The conviction that the prospects for European union are bright does not rest on the assumption that Europe's future will be tranquil. Far from it. In the summer of 1991, the Yugoslavian crisis and the failed coup in the Soviet Union were clear evidence that the death pangs of the old Communist order would continue to generate crises affecting the whole of Europe.

For me, the writing of *Inventing Europe* has been a personal as well as an intellectual odyssey. In the early 1980s, my attention shifted away from the study of Canadian political economy to work on the changing global economy. In 1986–87, while living in France, I wrote *Decline of the Superpowers*, a study of the economic strategies of the leading industrial nations. In 1988, when I began writing this book, the idea was to analyse the project of Western European economic and political union. It was already evident then, in the era of Gorbachev's *perestroika*, that the relationship between Western Europe and the Communist states of the East was rapidly altering. The "German question" was returning to the top of the European agenda well before the opening of the Berlin Wall. I was fortunate enough to be based in Europe in 1989–90 during the great years of its transformation, and to see that transformation firsthand.

In this book, I have chosen to survey the subject from a very broad perspective, making use of personal interviews, wherever possible, with politicians, businesspeople, trade unionists, and other Europeans from many walks of life and in many parts of the continent. I conducted approximately three hundred such interviews in the course of my research. As I watched and recorded the transformation of Europe, my own perspective on key questions of our age having to do with the role of nation-states, nationalism, and the possibility of the pooling of sovereignty among states was subjected to rethinking and change.

Inventing Europe does not provide a comprehensive record of all of the major economic and political events in contemporary Europe: no one book could do that. At its centre is the question of European union, its origins, and its viability. This book turns on that question, its likely outcome, and the implications not only for Europeans, but for the rest of us who must share the future with them.

Chapter One

BERLIN

★ ★ ★ ★ ★ ★ ★ ★ ★ ★ ★ ★

ERLIN IS A PHOENIX. A CITY OF ASHES AND RUINS AT THE end of history's greatest war, its destruction was brought on itself by a regime that planned conquests, concentration camps, and the Final Solution from its inner sanctums of power. Hitler's fondest dream was to crown his empire with a completely rebuilt Berlin, a city of enormous boulevards, massive structures, giant monuments — a totalitarian vision, a focus for the rule of a megalomaniac. Hitler's legacy, instead, was a destroyed Berlin rent in two, a partitioned Germany, and a divided Europe. In place of the demolished Nazi empire, two superpowers were to anchor their global systems in Berlin. During the decades of their Cold War rivalry, Berlin was the most intimate meeting ground for the United States and the Soviet Union, the most likely flashpoint should their deadly antagonism become uncontrollable. The city became the symbol of irreconcilable ideologies. For the capitalist world, West Berlin became an oasis, a materialistic temptress in the antechamber of Stalin's Communist empire. For the East, West Berlin was a choke-point, the target for skilful threats that could extract concessions elsewhere. Twice the Soviet Union tried to bring West Berlin to its knees. First, it used a strategy of annihilation when it closed off land routes to the city in 1948, forcing the West to supply the metropolis by air in the famed Berlin airlift. Second, it deployed a strategy of attrition when it placed the city under long-term siege with the building of the Berlin Wall in 1961. In both cases, West Berlin rebounded to become more brilliant, more culturally significant: because of the failure of the assaults, this city under siege was gaining the upper hand, negating the legitimacy of the East German system by its very presence. These assaults transformed the former Nazi capital into a symbol of freedom. As Berliners responded to menacing encirclement with grace under pressure, they started down the long road to rehabilitation in the eyes of the world. Time would be needed before other Europeans would again accept Berliners and other Germans simply as neighbours and not as invaders and murderers. Time would be needed for the Communist empire in the East to corrode.

In the end, West Berlin prevailed over its surrounding Communist hinterland. On the day the Berlin Wall was opened, November 9, 1989, the city celebrated as one. It would be whole again. The consequences were legion. Berlin was again the heart of Germany. Beyond that, it was the city around which the New Europe was to be constructed. The bipolar world of American and Soviet global power was in its twilight days. On November 9, it became clear that Europe as well as Berlin could be whole again. With Germany at its centre, Europe could become a vast and effective global power. The Berliners who celebrated that night as they danced by the Wall, popping champagne corks and shouting delirious cheers as bewildered East Germans crossed into West Berlin, were feting the coming together of their city. Their celebrations heralded the birth trauma of a new era of global power. Berlin, Germany, and Europe would no longer have their fate determined principally in Washington and Moscow, as had been the case since the end of the Second World War. The era in which the Germans were the losers of a global war was over. They would chart their own course, while an anxious world waited to see how they would use their new found power.

Those who revelled that night in Berlin could not escape the ghosts of history, nightmarish ghouls whose shadows intruded on the glittering celebrations. Just a few metres west of the Wall was the Reichstag building, reconstructed after the notorious fire of February 1933 that served as a pretext for the Nazis to tighten their dictatorship. Only a short distance from here, but on the other side of the Wall, was the Brandenburg Gate, the symbol of German unity. Not far away was the site of Hitler's destroyed bunker, where the Nazi leader took his own life. From the time before the Nazi era, were the ghosts of earlier days. It was down the Unter den Linden, the grand boulevard that passes around the Brandenburg Gate, that German officers drove their vehicles on August 1, 1914, as they exulted in the news that mobilization for war had been proclaimed. The echoes of Bismarck's triumphs were here, as were the memories of tragic Weimar, the febrile, ill-fated cultural capital of the world during the 1920s.

From the day the Wall was opened, the process of exorcizing the ghosts began. It was not that the past would ever be forgotten. Too many people, Germans and non-Germans, were determined never to lose the lessons of two world wars and the Holocaust for that to happen. Germany's most distinguished writer, Günter Grass, sounded a lonely protest against the creation of a single, powerful Germany: "no one of sound mind and memory can ever again permit such a concentration of power in the heart of Europe. Certainly the great powers cannot; nor can the Poles, the French, the Dutch, the Danes." Despite the eloquent warning, however, Berlin was moving ineluctably away from its past towards its future at the centre of the continent, with the potential to play a pre-eminent global role.

The exorcism took different forms. One was the sound of hammers ringing as enterprising Berlin students worked round the clock, chipping fragments from the Wall and selling them to passers-by for a few marks each. They were all too willing to stop their work to philosophize with astonished visitors about the future of their city and the future of Europe. "You foreigners are too worried about German reunification," one serious student told me as he chipped away at the Wall near the Brandenburg Gate. "We have learned our lessons, and it hurts us that we are still not trusted," he said, stopping to warm his hands. It made a great impression on me, this sober youth, the grandchild of those who had lost the war, reassuring an older visitor from one of the victorious countries. History had come full circle.

Just up the Wall from the serious young man, revellers in red and white Father Christmas outfits were singing carols to two bemused East Berlin border guards who stood atop an observation point, right beside the Wall. Not far from them, near the Reichstag building, simple memorials marked the places where people desperate to escape from East Berlin had been shot down by border guards. One person who would not be enjoying the revelling that night was a young man of twenty-two who had been killed at the Wall in February 1989. The words "Honecker Murderer" were scrawled across the memorial.

Exorcism took political forms as well. Just six weeks after the opening of the Wall, the West German Social Democratic Party held its national congress in West Berlin, having transferred it there from Bremen at the last minute. The congress opened on the seventy-sixth birthday of Willy Brandt, the former mayor of West Berlin, who had become the first Social Democratic chancellor of West Germany in 1969. Brandt was a special kind of godfather for German social democracy, indeed for German democracy as a whole. "Lieber Willy, dear Willy, we love you," said Herta Daubler-Gmelin as she opened the party congress, embracing Brandt and presenting him with a bouquet of roses. There was no artificiality in the gesture. Brandt had spent a lifetime fighting for German democracy and now he was there to preside over the exorcism of the past. He had gone into exile during the Nazi era. Mayor when the Wall was built, Brandt had stood at John F. Kennedy's side when the president delivered his famous "I am a Berliner" speech. Even in those tense days, Brandt had fought to keep up a modicum of communication with those on the other side. As chancellor, he had challenged Cold War orthodoxy with his *Ostpolitik*, his historic opening to East Germany and Eastern Europe. On November 10, 1989, he had stood by the newly breached Wall to proclaim: "What belongs together, grows together."

As long as the Germans were on the front lines of two geo-political systems centred elsewhere, they were safely contained. They were history's ultimate potential cannon fodder, all too aware that any war between the superpowers would begin with Germans killing Germans. Suddenly, the opening of the Wall made them no longer victims, but the most important political actors in Europe.

Berliners felt the change in the status of the Germans more acutely than anyone else. For more than four decades, Berlin was a city to which things were done. It was a crucial piece on the Cold War chessboard. It symbolized two social systems and, in a characteristically German way, managed to push both of them to their limits. No bureaucracy has ever made itself so coldly ugly as that in East Germany. Crossing by car from West Berlin to East Berlin was an education in itself. At Checkpoint Charlie, you would pass the small allied control hut without having to stop, and then encounter the East German bureaucratic maze on the other side of the Wall. Handing your passport and car-ownership papers to one guard after another, you would finally be motioned to stop and get out of your car to buy Ostmarks for Deutschmarks. Typically, the officials in the wickets were facing the other way and would turn to make the currency exchange only after interminable delays. At last, you were signalled to drive into East Berlin. The city was stilted and life-less in a way that had to be experienced to be believed. There was an emptiness at the heart of this metropolis that no perfectly preserved opera house or museum of German history could ever dispel.

West of the Wall, by contrast, was capitalism at its most orgias-tic. The matchless way to experience the full high of West Berlin was to set out by car from West Germany, passing through East Germany to reach the city. After the long journey that took you past the dreary, smoky East German towns and through the ugly checkpoints — if passport processing were a growth industry, this country's future would have been assured — the entry into West Berlin was mind altering. All at once you were cruising down the Kurfürstendamm. The brilliant lighting, the opulence of the breathtaking structures, the explosiveness of the contrast brought you fully alive to the oasis that was West Berlin. New York had nothing on the Kurfürstendamm, where capitalism felt as bright and new as it did on Tokyo's great thoroughfares. Here were the neon gods calling down the names of the world's great corporations from on high. On the street, the sleek Audis and Mercedeses swept past crowds of window shoppers.

Behind the façade, however, there was another story. The decades-long, Soviet-sponsored siege of West Berlin exacted a toll. Even though its symphony orchestra was probably the finest in Europe, and its museums, theatres, and nightclubs were without equal, West Berlin entered a period of long-term industrial and com-mercial difficulty as a consequence of the interminable Berlin crises and the building of the Wall. Over time, Berlin-based industries suf-fered decline, sometimes falling on hard times, closing their doors or moving elsewhere. The West Berlin economy became increasingly dependent on highly mobile multinational corporations whose com-mitment to the city was no greater than to any other specific loca-tion. In part as a consequence of the claustrophobia that went with living in a city under siege, many Berliners left for West Germany. The German-born population of West Berlin stagnated. The city came to have a much higher proportion of those over sixty-five and a much lower proportion of those under fifteen than did the cities of West Germany. Many of the newcomers were Turkish and Yugosla-vian guest workers, whose influx provoked a nativist reaction among some Berliners, fuelling the development of an important con-stituency for the extreme right wing. Many other newcomers were students from West Germany who often drank deeply at the well of Berlin culture and intellectual life and then took disturbing ideas back to the stolid West German communities from which they came. Hard-drug use was much higher in West Berlin than in the Federal Republic. The city became a spawning ground for a proliferation of subcultures and political protest movements. West Berlin became associated with violent demonstrations, the occupation of buildings by protesters, street battles involving the police, and terrorism. To help the city withstand the siege, the West German government poured money into it, setting up programs to entice people to move there from the Federal Republic. West German taxpayers ended up paying about $2 billion a year for the nurturing of West Berlin. Considering the long-existing feelings of estrangement between Berliners and other Germans, this tax was a very real irritant. Berliners had thought of themselves as more intelligent, more cultured, more alive than the comfortable burghers of other German cities and towns. For their part, other Germans often saw Berlin as a city of anarchists, drug pushers, and spawners of dangerous ideas.

Despite the costs extracted as a consequence of the siege, however, West Berlin sparkled, becoming ever more a jewel of freedom. In East Berlin, it was instantly obvious that a terrible social experiment had been carried out. And the Wall and the social corruption in East Germany made it evident that that experiment had been stillborn from the start. The regime that had gunned people down for attempting to flee to West Berlin ruled from behind an unchallengeable arsenal of Soviet weaponry. While its leaders were making the monstrous claim that East Germany was breeding the "new socialist man," they were themselves living luxuriously in perfumed villas north of Berlin, in secluded Wandlitz, where all the pleasures of the West were sumptuously present. The barbecues, double bathrooms, bars, aquariums, and satellite dishes were installed and serviced by West German workers so that East Germans would not be tainted by acquaintance with these luxuries. I could not help thinking of Wandlitz as I was driving across East Germany one rainy afternoon in early December, just weeks after the Wall had been opened. I stopped at what was called a restaurant, actually a trailer that served no coffee, only lemon tea as a hot beverage. What turned out to be quite good toffee was the only thing to eat. Posted up at this peculiar establishment was a sign warning parents to guard against the television advertising of the West and to take seriously the task of rearing socialist children. Along the side of the highway, people could often be seen working under the hoods of their Trabant cars, trying to coax a few more kilometres out of these two-stroke pollution-generating machines. The families sitting in them, often with their belongings on the roof or in the rear window, did not look like West Germans. They had that genuine proletarian appearance — old-fashioned moustaches, haircuts, and clothes that had long since disappeared in the West. These were characters out of a Steinbeck novel, for whom the phrase "the people" would not seem embarrassing or out of place. The leaders who had hidden out at Wandlitz had presided over a system that made people wait fifteen years for a Trabant. In the end, it was "the people" working in the most polluting factories in Europe who could stand it no longer. Even more than in relatively well-supplied East Berlin, in miserable, industrial Leipzig the implacable hatred for the regime had boiled over into the streets.

The regime had specialized in grand and petty tyrannies. Locking people up so they could not travel, and transforming their country into a prison where they could not speak or publish or meet freely, made East Germany a grand tyranny. Deciding how scarcity would be allocated so that the friends of the regime were more likely to be rewarded with consumer goods made it a petty tyranny.

One dissident who was finally expelled from East Germany in 1977, and now lives in West Berlin, where she is an author of children's books, told me how she explains the difference between the two Berlins to her youthful audience. Franziska Groszer recounted the story of buying food for her family. In East Berlin, she would have to spend an hour each day in long line-ups to purchase food. Occasionally, she would be lucky and buy a large fish. When she reached home, she would call her friends at once to make the fish the occasion for an instant party. In West Berlin, she would find the fish she wanted easily enough, but might have to go to five or six stores to find one she could afford, since she had no job.

As the story shows, neither social system seemed ideal to her. She had, however, the kind of appreciation for the freedoms of the West that only those who have lived without them can ever feel. In the East, her children's bookstore was closed on the order of the authorities, her efforts to publish or to present children's puppet shows blocked. In the maze of bureaucratic repression she experienced, she was never given the satisfaction of being told what rules of the East German state her cultural activities had violated. She was simply told that she could not continue them.

Her description of the dissident circle of which she was a part in the mid-1970s was a testament of hope and hopelessness. Her circle included thirty or forty people, for the most part intellectuals, who would gather in people's houses. While they had no concrete basis for optimism during what was the heart of the Brezhnev era, they tenaciously clung to a belief that someday something would have to give. Their main weapon against a system that enjoyed an overwhelming monopoly of coercive power was to try to raise the consciousness of people, to counteract the mind-numbing message of the regime that any well-being they could hope for came from an unassailable power above them. For the dissidents, reading to children and putting on puppet shows were acts of subversion, aimed at instilling the idea that people could be self-sufficient, that they did not depend on largesse from on high. During these years, Franziska Groszer would never go to see the Wall. She avoided it, always aware that it was there. She and her friends were well-informed, and knew a great deal about other countries. But they could not reach out to them. For her, the Wall meant the loss of the world. She felt diminished by it. Everything she lived was shrunken. While the Germans were clearly one people, it was evident that those who had survived the experience of being dissidents in East Germany had no intention of giving up the hard-won lessons of their experience. That experience would always mark them off from other Germans.

The euphoria, the sense of possibility that accompanied the opening of the Wall, was worth savouring. It would not last; the practical difficulties ahead, the calculations of the powerful, the dislocation of the powerless would foster new and often dark emotions. But, for those who experienced the opening of the Wall, the wonder of the moment could never be taken away. However briefly, people without positions of power had seized control of their fate and, in the process, they had toppled not only a local system of tyranny, but a world order: they had opened the way not only for a new Germany, but for a new Europe, a Europe that would be invented not only in the streets, but at the highest political levels.

Chapter Two

REBIRTH:
INVENTING EUROPE

★ ★ ★ ★ ★ ★ ★ ★ ★ ★ ★

At present there is and can be no Europe other than a Europe of the States —
except, of course, for myths, fictions, and pageants.
    — CHARLES DE GAULLE

General de Gaulle's proposals are based on notions that are out of date.
They forget the lessons of our most recent history. They completely ignore what
a series of failures has taught us: that it is impossible to solve Europe's problems
among States which retain full national sovereignty.
    — JEAN MONNET

Monnet has the great merit of having built Europe and the great
responsibility to have built it badly.
    — ALTIERO SPINELLI

WHEN VALÉRY GISCARD D'ESTAING RISES IN HIS PLACE in the front row of the chamber in Strasbourg to speak to the European Parliament (EP), everyone knows that his speech is but a single event in an election campaign scheduled to run until 1995. Giscard, the leader of the French liberals (Union pour la démocratie française), served as president of France from 1974 until he was defeated by François Mitterrand in the 1981 election. That defeat did not stop him. Assiduously, day after day, Giscard has carried on, hoping he will have a chance to win back the top job in French politics, even though he will be sixty-nine years old when the 1995 presidential election is held. When the European Parliament is in session, which it is one week each month, Giscard is a fixture in the institution. He speaks from the floor whenever he gets a chance, and holds press conferences almost on a daily basis. The performance in Strasbourg is very deliberate, as is everything the former French president does.

Strasbourg and the European Parliament suit Giscard to a tee. The parliament is for him an ideal "bully pulpit," a forum where he can feed his ideas to the French national media and to the rest of Europe. Giscard is not alone in understanding the institution that way, although there are few who excel him in carrying off such a use for it.

Jean-Marie Le Pen is also a member of the European Parliament. The pudgy-faced leader of France's Front National comes to Strasbourg as the most prominent and politically significant member of the European Community's far-right parties, to gain media access to his followers. Le Pen spends little time in the parliamentary chamber, listening to the debate. Nor does he show much interest in the work of parliamentary committees. Characteristically, he lunches in the dining-room just outside the chamber, slouched at the table, surrounded by half a dozen male cronies, with a goodly supply of wine on their table. When it is time for his speech, allotted to him as spokesman for the European Right, he rises in the chamber and begins speaking quietly, quickly working himself into the impassioned lather for which he is famous as Europe's leading demagogue. In the chamber, however, Le Pen is supported only by the tiny handful of extreme right-wing members. While they rise to cheer him lustily, the rest of the members, who detest him, sit in stony silence until his allotted time is up. Then, as the chairman gavels him to conclude his remarks, Le Pen reaches his foam-flecked, snarling conclusion while the rest of the chamber howls him down. The television cameras are taking it all in. Le Pen's perorations invariably extol the virtues of national sovereignty for the French and for other Europeans, warning of the dangers of immigration and European union. The job done, the television message complete, with the hope that a clip from it will appear on the French evening newscasts, Le Pen, the consummate professional, leaves the chamber to rejoin his cronies.

In their different ways, and with different political objectives, Giscard and Le Pen share a common appreciation of the extent to which the European Parliament has grown in prestige and importance, making it now the premier debating arena on the continent. The problem with the EP is that it is a parliament that has always had to fight for additional powers for itself, and remains the least powerful of the three key decision-making institutions in the EC, which include the European Community Commission and the Council of Ministers, in addition to the EP itself. Despite its limitations, however, the EP is a unique institution, and it has come a long way since the days when its members were appointed by member governments. Since 1979, the EP has grown enormously in stature because its members are elected by universal suffrage across the member states of the EC. In today's 12-state European Community, the EP has 518 members.

It is natural, and often misleading, to compare the EP with national parliaments. Unlike them, the EP cannot propose and pass legislation on its own. On paper, the most impressive power enjoyed by the EP is its right to dismiss the entire EC Commission from office, should the members lose confidence in the way the EC's executive branch is carrying out its duties. While this dramatic, albeit negative, authority ensures that members of the commission do not ignore the EP and are emphatic in taking the trouble to consult it, the removal of the commission is a drastic weapon that, not surprisingly, has never been wielded.

Despite its limitations, the EP has certainly emerged as an increasingly important and respected watchdog, carefully monitoring the exercise of executive power in the community. The EP must approve the budget of the EC, an authority that allows it to hold hearings on every aspect of the life of the community, and to be taken seriously in doing so. Here, the analogy with the evolution of national parliaments is more helpful. In numerous instances, including the classic case of the British House of Commons, the rise of national parliaments was precisely linked to their ability to control the purse strings of the state. Such authority, once established beyond dispute, enabled national parliaments to wrest other areas of power from the executive branch of government.

The budgetary authority of the EP automatically gives it a say in every aspect of the life of the EC. But, while its budgetary power is important, even in this critical field the institution shares power with the council, which, because of the nature of the budgetary process in the EC, still has greater influence.

In legislative matters, the EP plays an essentially advisory role vis-à-vis the more powerful commission (the EC's executive arm), which must draft proposed legislation in the first place, and the more powerful council (the senior legislative body), which must adopt it before it becomes EC law. In a large number of areas, the founding treaties stipulate that the EP must be consulted before legislation is finally adopted. In these fields, the parliament can propose amendments to draft legislation. In practice, the commission now brings all proposed legislation before the EP for an expression of its opinion, even though this procedure is not precisely required.

The adoption of the Single European Act (SEA), which came into effect on July 1, 1987, has resulted in a significant increase in the legislative authority of the EP. This seminal act has had the effect of altering the balance of authority among EC institutions, lending greater momentum to yet further initiatives in the area of Economic and Monetary Union (EMU) and political union. One power that the SEA conferred on the EP was the requirement that it approve the accession of new countries to the community, either as members or as associates. In a period when many such applications are virtually certain, the EP has thereby gained a new bargaining tool. It can push for new powers for itself, if it is to go along with the commission and the council in agreeing to their plans for the expansion of the community.

At a time when EC activities are quickly expanding and are having an increasingly observable impact on the social, economic, and environmental fabric of European life, the demand for additional powers for the EP, the only community body directly elected by the people of Europe, is gaining in force. The case has been effectively made that a so-called democratic deficit exists in which EC institutions are too remote from the people of Europe. Correcting that deficit means putting more power in the hands of the EP, spokesmen for the institution proclaim at every opportunity. In the critical early months of 1990, when German unification was becoming irreversible, Helmut Kohl placed his very considerable political clout behind expanded powers for the EP when he made a unique appearance on one of France's leading television programs, "L'Heure de la Vérité," in which he was cross-examined by three leading French journalists.

Despite its higher profile and increased powers, there is no doubt that the EP remains the junior partner in the legislative affairs of the community. The relationship between the EP and the council is the reverse of the more customary relationship within the national institutions of many countries. In the EC, the elected EP occupies a role typical of an upper chamber in a bicameral legislature, while the council, whose representatives are appointed by member governments, occupies the role normally played by more powerful lower houses.

Whatever its limitations in terms of legislative power, the EP is a potent lobby for Europe. More than any other institution, it throws people together on a large scale to work on an agenda of economic, social, and political problems, and to do so not in national, but in European terms. The physical layout of the parliament itself reinforces the tendency to "think European." In the Palace of Europe, the parliament is set out in a hemisphere — not like the British or Canadian parliaments, where a government and an opposition face each other at a distance of two sword lengths, but in the manner of the French National Assembly in Paris.

In the hemisphere at Strasbourg, the members' seats form a large fan, centring on the president's table at the front. Parliamentarians sit, not in national delegations, but in EC-wide political formations. On the president's left sit the Communists and Left socialists. Next to them are the members of the largest bloc in the current parliament, which was elected in June 1989, the Socialists, with 180 members out of the EP's total of 518. Behind the Socialists sit the Greens. Next to the Socialists, on the right, are the second-largest bloc in the current EP, the 121 members of the European People's Party (Christian Democrats). Next to them, on the right, are the Liberal and Democratic Group, whose most prestigious figure is Giscard d'Estaing. To the right of the liberals are the European Democratic Group (EDG), the EP name for the British Conservatives, a forlorn contingent, now more isolated than ever following their defeat at the hands of Labour in the EP elections in 1989. The long-term failure of the British Conservatives to come to terms with the Christian Democrats for important doctrinal reasons has cut them off from their natural allies on the continent and has rendered them politically ineffectual. Behind the EDG sit the far-right parties led by Le Pen for the Front National in France and Schönhuber for the Republicans in Germany, grouped together as the European Right.

On the extreme right of the hemisphere sit the members of the EC Commission. In the front row is the seat of Jacques Delors, commission president. On the far left of the hemisphere sit the representatives of the Council of Ministers. Council and parliament are natural adversaries in the system, since the council represents national power in the EC while the parliament is elected directly by the people of Europe. The institutional power struggle within the EC has tended to drive the parties in the European Parliament together, since most of them share a mutual desire to increase the powers of their institution vis-à-vis the council and the commission. In the current EP, while the Left has a very small working majority when the Socialists draw support from the Greens and a few other minor groups, in practice the Socialists and the Christian Democrats are typically able to come to terms on major issues, which means that, on most questions, the EP is dominated by a wide centre bloc that is able to pass resolutions by large majorities, giving the EP more clout against the council and the commission.

The political behaviour of parliamentarians in the EP is shaped by much more than a narrowly conceived struggle for greater influence for their own body. The very fact of the EP, with its assembly, its party caucuses, its committees, all working on a European and not on a national basis, has the effect of transforming the perspectives of EP members, making them different in their attitudes from the members of their sister national parties back home. Those differences can be seen across the mainstream of the political spectrum.

Physically, the EP hemisphere makes an awe-inspiring spectacle. The sight of parliamentarians from twelve countries, many of which have been bitter foes in the past, sitting side by side, participating in the creation of a European federal state, cannot help but provoke wonder. The translation facilities are a marvel. Nine languages are used in debates. When you look up above the floor of the chamber, you see that, all around the hemisphere, behind glass partitions, sits an army of translators.

If political figures like Giscard d'Estaing and Jean-Marie Le Pen make use of the EP as a forum to reach their target audiences, so too do the major political leaders of Europe and of the world. Mikhail Gorbachev, Pope John Paul II, and Nelson Mandela are among those who have addressed the EP in recent years, not to mention numerous figures from the emerging democracies in Eastern Europe, and, of course, all of the important leaders in Western Europe. Frequent addresses by top leaders have drawn a very large media contingent to the sessions of the EP in Strasbourg. Regulars from all of the quality daily newspapers in Europe and broadcasters from the continent's national television networks crowd the newsrooms at the EP to overflowing, particularly on days when a key speech is scheduled. The visit of President Mitterrand to the European Parliament in October 1989 produced the kind of media frenzy that surrounds major speeches to the EP. The visit created unusual interest for a number of reasons: France held the presidency of the EC (the presidency rotates from country to country every six months) at that particular time, making the French government, and ultimately Mitterrand, responsible for guiding the EC agenda; that agenda not only was crowded with progress reports on the "1992" program, but was further embroiled in two questions that divided the British government from those of the other eleven member nations — whether a social charter should be adopted to enshrine the rights of workers, communities, and women, etc., and whether the EC should move beyond "1992" towards Economic and Monetary Union (EMU), with the ultimate creation of a European central bank and common currency; as the EC was pushing ahead its own ambitious agenda, Eastern Europe was in turmoil, with the pressure building that forced the Communist regime in East Germany to open the Berlin Wall just over two weeks later.

The French president lived up to his billing as he compared the events in Eastern Europe to those during the French Revolution two hundred years earlier. Making it clear that he believed that the EC could not sit by while Eastern Europe was being remade, Mitterrand called for accelerated moves towards Economic and Monetary Union within the EC, hinting that, if necessary, those who were prepared to move should do so alone, leaving those unprepared for action out of the next steps towards European union — a warning shot directed at Margaret Thatcher.

Once the speech was over, the journalists and broadcasters from across Europe jammed the newsrooms and bars and, before filing their stories, engaged in that common pastime in the age of "pack journalism," endless dissections of what had been said. All of the British journalists insisted that the key point in the Mitterrand speech was the implied threat to proceed without Britain through the drafting of a new treaty, if necessary, to deal with Economic and Monetary Union and thereby to avert the threat of a British veto. French government officials were circulating among the journalists with their own, off-the-record interpretation of the meaning of the Mitterrand speech. They were saying that Thatcher's performance at the recent Commonwealth Conference, where she had joined a consensus on South Africa only to disown it later, had convinced Mitterrand that Thatcher simply could not be trusted to enter an agreement in good faith. Therefore, it made sense for the French to adopt a "get tough" posture as far as the British prime minister was concerned. The French officials punctuated their comments with the assertion that they had no intention of being "Kuala Lumpured" by Thatcher. (Kuala Lumpur, Malaysia, had been the site of the Commonwealth Conference.)

All of this — the "pack" journalism and the off-the-record briefings by officials — is the normal way that news is assembled in national capitals. What matters here is that these practices, commonplace in national journalism, are now being felt at the European level. The media, print journalists and television broadcasters, are themselves subjected to the cross-cutting influences that are the hallmark of the EP. The national styles of the media teams from different countries remain clear and observable. So, too, is the mingling, the sharing of stories, the personal contact that is transforming the perspective of this critical group from a largely national to an increasingly European one.

In the EP, from the sublime, it is never far to the ridiculous. Uncertainties about the final shape of the institution and severe growing pains result in various absurdities. Currently the EP meets in Strasbourg for eleven weeks of the year (one week a month, with August off). Eighty per cent of its staff is based in Luxembourg, a legacy of the Grand Duchy's position as the provisional capital of the European Coal and Steel Community (ECSC) from its inception in 1952. Staff members must travel to Strasbourg for the weeks when the EP is in session and to Brussels for periods when parliamentary committees are meeting. Committees meet in Brussels to be close to the EC Commission and the Council of Ministers, with their respective bureaucracies. Each member of the EP has three offices, one in his or her home constituency, one in Brussels, and one in Strasbourg. The travelling, the time spent in hotels, and the general madness involved in moving staff from one city to another mean that, apart from the French, who want to keep the EP in Strasbourg, virtually everyone looks forward to the day when the EP will move all or most of its sessions to Brussels, where a new hemisphere has been constructed by the Belgian government.

It is not accidental that the Euro-capitals that have so far emerged — Brussels, Luxembourg, and Strasbourg — are all on the "fault line," that ribbon of territory between France and Germany that has been a historic battleground. Now the essential union between France and Germany, which is at the very heart of the New Europe, is physically expressed in the emergence of capital cities in this critical region.

If the EP is the sounding-board of the New Europe, its nerve centre is the commission, which plans the EC's strategies, administers its policies, and proposes its line of advance. The commission is at the heart of Europe's nascent federalism. To describe the commission and the other institutions that make up the EC as the equivalent of a federal government, like those in the United States or Canada, over-states the case. However, to describe them as simply intergovernmental instruments whose purpose is to facilitate agreements among sovereign states is also misleading. The EC exists tantalizingly between the two. Given its trajectory since the mid-1980s, it can most accurately be understood as a European federal system in the making.

The commission has seventeen members, two each from the five largest states — Germany, France, Italy, the United Kingdom, and Spain — and one each from the seven smaller states — Denmark, Ireland, Holland, Belgium, Luxembourg, Portugal, and

Greece. Commissioners are appointed for four-year terms by member governments, and the appointees are ratified by the Council of Ministers. The president of the commission is picked by the council from among the seventeen commissioners. Once the commission has been constituted, its members convene and agree on how they will divide up responsibilities among themselves, with the president playing a key role in allocating what amount to cabinet posts.

When it comes to such appointments, informal political manoeuvring plays a key role. Next to the selection of Jacques Delors as president of the commission, which took office in 1985, the most important appointment was that of Lord Cockfield to undertake the development and launching of the "1992" project. Lord Cockfield told me candidly that theory and practice are not the same when it comes to the role a specific commissioner will play. "I was offered the chance to go in [to the commission]," he said. "In theory, portfolios are not discussed in advance of an appointment. In practice, they are."

In the fall of 1984, Lord Cockfield and Margaret Thatcher plotted strategy with Delors on what role Cockfield would play if appointed to the commission. "Margaret and I had dinner with Delors and made it clear to him that I was going to do the single market," he said.

Community legislation begins with the commission. Once the commission has worked up its proposals, the draft legislation proceeds through the system, going to the European Parliament for proposed changes and finally to the council, the supreme legislative body of the community, for adoption. The commission draws up action programs to implement EC policy.

In carrying out their work, the commissioners are backed up by a rather remarkable civil service, known invariably, negatively, and undeservedly as "Eurocrats." The term "Eurocrat" implies that there is a vast army of civil servants in Brussels administering the fiats of the EC. The reality is quite different. In comparison with the size of the civil service in member countries of the EC, the ranks of personnel of the commission are extremely modest. In the late 1980s, about 10,500 people worked for the commission. For such a tiny civil service to administer programs on behalf of 340 million people (including the 17 million people in eastern Germany) is a truly daunting undertaking, and reveals at once how far the EC remains from being a true European federal government. The commission and all its staff would be lost in a corner of official Washington, Ottawa, or London.

Since becoming president of the EC Commission in January 1985, Jacques Delors has dominated the current commission and the community as a whole in a fashion unequalled by any commission president in recent times. Delors is the ideal case of the right man being in the right place at the right time. He took over the presidency at a time when a series of new initiatives for European union were having their effect. Responding to political pressures for further steps towards union from within EC institutions and to the rising demand throughout Europe for a response to the economic pressures of globalization and, in particular, of competition from the United States and Japan, Delors launched the most important initiative since the founding of the community. "1992" turned out to be the key that opened the door not only to the economic integration of the community, but to sweeping institutional advances as well.

When Jacques Delors, Lord Cockfield, and the other EC commissioners rode the wave of opportunity created by these pressures, they were steering a unique political body that owes its allegiance to the community and not to the member states that make it up. Although commissioners are appointed by member governments, the governments that select them have no power to remove them from office once they have been appointed. The first act of duty of a commissioner is to make a solemn declaration that formally cuts any ties between him or her and any member government. The declaration begins: "I solemnly undertake: to perform my duties in complete independence, in the general interest of the Communities; in carrying out my duties, neither to seek nor to take instructions from any Government or body . . . ."

Naturally, the mere swearing of a declaration does not cut the emotional, intellectual, and political ties between an appointee and a government or a political past. But commissioners have shown themselves to be remarkably free of the governments that appointed them, often to the disgust of those doing the appointing. Of note have been the appointees of Margaret Thatcher. No more exacting taskmaster has existed at the top level of government in the West in recent decades than Thatcher. When she fell out with cabinet colleagues — such as Michael Heseltine, Geoffrey Howe, or Nigel Lawson — she did not hesitate to cut them down to size. When she disapproved of the behaviour of local governments, such as the Greater London Council, she did not hesitate to go to the extreme of abolishing them. Appointing EC commissioners was an immensely frustrating experience for Thatcher, however. She was up against a structure she could not control, against which she could not deal out retribution. And despite the care she exercised in picking ideologically compatible candidates, on reaching Brussels, they "went native." The appointment that rebounded most disastrously from her perspective was undoubtedly that of Lord Cockfield, who was, as we will see, instrumental in the "1992" project. Cockfield explains his split with Thatcher this way: "Where the divide came was over my belief that to do the job one had to do it completely and effectively."

What had tempted Thatcher to appoint Cockfield in the first place had been her realization that he would be immensely effective in pursuing the single market, and especially the single market in financial services, which she strongly favoured. What she did not understand was what many other British politicians had failed to understand, that the EC was much more than a pragmatic economic grouping, that it was committed to the long-term union of Europeans.

After her experience with Lord Cockfield, Margaret Thatcher appointed Sir Leon Brittan to sit on the commission that took office in 1989. A trusted former Tory cabinet minister who shared Thatcher's free-market passions, Sir Leon promptly went native, as had his predecessor. By the autumn of 1989, Thatcher found herself at odds with him on the issue of Britain's entry into the Exchange Rate Mechanism (ERM) of the European Monetary System (EMS), which he came to favour, while she continued to oppose it.

Understanding why commissioners go native helps us understand the magnetic power of the EC to pull people to the European ideal. A number of Brussels-based insiders have made the point to me that it is entirely natural for commissioners to go native. If they want to be effective in getting their jobs done and if they want to survive as political animals with clout in the institution, they are forced to make deals, to come up with solutions acceptable to others — in other words, they are required to operate within the rules of the game in which they find themselves. For this reason, being appointed to the EC Commission, an independent political posting, is entirely different from being appointed ambassador of one's country to a foreign capital, where one makes reports to one's home government and can be withdrawn by one's political masters at a moment's notice.

If the commission is beyond the control of national governments and is sometimes a source of frustration for them, the third major institution of the community, the Council of Ministers, is their creature. Lord Cockfield, who does not suffer slow procedures gladly, told me that, as far as he is concerned, the Council of Ministers should be known as "foot draggers anonymous." He has little regard for the way decisions are made in the EC's top legislative body, noting that the way things really work is that the commission "tells the heads of state what to think, and they then push the council." The council represents the voice of national governments in the EC. It is constituted of members who are appointed by national governments for specific purposes. Ministers of Agriculture will meet as the council when the subject is agriculture, ministers of Finance will meet to discuss economic and monetary affairs, and so on. The council is empowered to act on proposals from the commission and to reach conclusions that take the form of regulations, directives, decisions, recommendations, and opinions. Regulations are binding on all member states; directives are binding on member states where applicable, and are often acted on by member states through the passage of national legislation; decisions, which are binding, come from either the council or the commission, are derived from previous regulations or directives, and are aimed at member governments or corporate entities; recommendations and opinions, while expressing the view of the council, are not binding. Each national government maintains a permanent staff that prepares the national positions adopted on the decisions taken in the eighty or so annual meetings of the council.

Of critical importance to the functioning of the council is Coreper (an acronym deriving from the French initials for the Committee of Permanent Representatives). In Coreper, the top staff of the member countries meet at least once a week to work through proposals for presentation to the council itself. While those who meet in sessions of Coreper are on the level of senior ambassadors, a more junior body, Coreper II, is composed of deputies who thrash out proposals to be later dealt with at higher levels.

Depending on the subject, decisions are reached in the council by simple majority vote (for procedural questions), by qualified majority for those subjects so specified by the founding treaties and the Single European Act (SEA) — a qualified majority is now fifty-four votes out of seventy-six on the council — and by unanimity for certain specified questions. Chairing the council is a job rotated among the member countries every six months. The country in the chair for a given six-month period occupies what is called the presidency, so that presidencies are referred to as the "French presidency" or the "Italian presidency." "President of the Council" is the title held by the foreign minister of the country doing the job of steering the council during a particular six-month period. The country holding the presidency makes an effort to negotiate deals on major questions during its term of office. Its officials appear at the sessions of the European Parliament to provide information on the functioning of the council.

Since 1975, a new body has played a vital role in the EC, the so-called European Council. Formally, it is simply a meeting of the Council of Ministers at which the representatives are the heads of government. Until 1985, these sessions were held three times a year. Now they are held twice a year, so that a meeting of the European Council climaxes the six-month term of each country's presidency. While, in the early days of the community, the commission was the point of origin for EC initiatives, since its inception, the European Council has become another point where critical initiatives are made. Often, these initiatives first come from the commission, but then are directed to the European Council, because, at the level of heads of government, sufficient political clout exists for major departures to be taken. Formally, the European Council does not itself pass legislation. Following its deliberations, the Council of Ministers convenes a session in which it adopts the decisions that have been agreed upon by the heads of government.

Rounding out the major institutions of the EC is the European Court of Justice, whose thirteen judges (one from each member state, and one other, chosen by the Council of Ministers from nominations by member states) sit in Luxembourg. The body plays the role of a supreme court within the system. Its constitutional law is comprised of the treaties setting up the EC, the most important ones being the Treaty of Paris, which established the European Coal and Steel Community (ECSC); the Treaty of Rome, which established the European Economic Community (EEC); the treaty founding the European Atomic Energy Community (Euratom), and the Single European Act (SEA). For the EC, these treaties are the equivalent of the written constitution of a nation-state. While the supreme courts of most countries base their decisions on their national constitutions, the Court of Justice bases its decisions on treaties among member states. In its field of competence, the Court of Justice constitutes the highest court of appeal for member states; its decisions are final and binding on the community as a whole or on particular member states. Therefore, in addition to laws made by the Council of Ministers, the rulings of the court are important in establishing principles and practices according to which the community must operate.

In recent years, court rulings have had an increasing impact on the community, and not simply on economic issues. Water-purity standards, the rights of persons under arrest, and retirement-age provisions for women — such questions have come under the scrutiny of the court. As an agent for the advance of European federalism, the court is extremely potent. Such is the case because the treaties cover very wide ground in their economic and social objectives, and since the Court of Justice is the highest court of appeal in these matters, all national high courts and all national parliaments must act within the orbit established by the European court.

In the spring of 1990, this fact came home to the British, with their centuries-old tradition of an unwritten constitution, when a ruling of the Luxembourg court asserted that British courts were required to uphold the body of law established in the EC without waiting for cases to go to the European court. The consequence was a furious debate at Westminster in which both Conservative and Labour members warned against a loss of sovereignty by Parliament. Judicial review, well-known in countries with written constitutions, was coming to Britain via the EC. Christopher Prout, himself a solicitor and the leader of the British Conservatives (European Democratic Group) in the European Parliament, made precisely this point to me. He asserted that the EC "provides Britain with her first written constitution, something we haven't had for a thousand years."

The institutional structure of the EC makes clear two contradictory things: Europe has advanced far beyond the relationships that exist even among friendly nation-states to a nascent federalism; that system, however, has a long way yet to go before Europe becomes anything like a typical federal state with the member states equivalent to American states or Canadian provinces within a federal union.

The current state of European federalism is made clear when we look at the financing of the EC. The community budget makes up only about 3 per cent of the taxes paid by citizens of the member states. The EC's revenues come from a number of sources, and the system has changed since the community was first founded. One source is a levy on the production of coal and steel firms, a system that has been in place since the launching of the European Coal and Steel Community in 1952. Until 1970, EC revenues came mainly from contributions from member states, based largely on the relative size of their economies. Since then, the community has moved more towards a system where it collects its own revenues. Today, the financing of the EC comes from the following sources: the biggest source is a proportion of the Value Added Tax (VAT) — a tax, similar to a sales tax, that is collected at each stage in the creation of a good or a service, so that the EC now can collect up to 1.4 per cent of the final selling price of goods and services; the collection of customs duties on goods imported from outside the EC; levies raised on food imported from outside the EC to bring the price up to the community price level; and a contribution from member states based on the size of their economies, with this latter amount capped so that total EC revenue does not exceed 1.2 per cent of the EC's Gross Domestic Product.

Today, EC federalism remains strictly limited because 97 per cent of tax revenues go to other than the community level of government. This system makes the community by far the most decentralized federal system in the world. In terms of taxes and institutions, however, the EC is in transition. The integration of European economies, initially as a consequence of the removal of tariff barriers among them and now as a result of "1992," is creating ever-greater pressures for the mounting of Europe-wide social and regional policies to offset the uneven effects of market forces acting on Europe's development. At present, however, the regional policies of the EC, while they have been innovative in many respects, have been severely restricted as a result of the very limited revenues of the community. But, as we will see when we discuss the future movement of the EC towards Economic and Monetary Union, the pressures for a much larger community budget may well become unstoppable.

First, though, in order to understand where the community is likely to go, we need to see where it came from, to consider the broad sweep of European history of which it is a central part.

IN THE BEGINNING

Today's rapidly evolving European union is the product of many historical forces, one of them being the superpower rivalry that characterized the post-war world. That it arose in Western Europe during the decades following the Second World War, the part of Europe in which the United States enjoyed hegemonic influence, was critical to its development. Though the United States was not itself a partner in the movement for European union and can even be seen as its historical rival, the Americans, uniquely powerful in the early post-war years, played the indispensable role of sponsor. They did not believe in European union for its own sake, but saw it as a convenient way to shore up a critical front in the all-consuming struggle for global power with the Soviet Union.[1] They had come to the view that the Germans must become the key European bulwark against the Soviets. Since such a potent role for the Germans, while the memories of Nazi occupation were so fresh among Germany's neighbours, was bound to provoke apprehension and, potentially, division in the West, a way needed to be found to make the rebuilding of Germany palatable. European union was such a way. As long as the Germans were integrated into European structures, the unity of the West could be maintained, the Americans hoped.

Beyond taking a benign attitude to projects for European union, the Americans played an important role in buttressing the movement in specific ways. First, they provided capital through the Marshall Plan, the investment of American corporations in Western Europe, and U.S. defence spending in Europe — all of which were important to the relaunching of the economies of Europe, including that of West Germany. Second, the unmatched military might of the United States, symbolized by its possession of atomic and, later, hydrogen bombs, overcame the insecurities felt among Western Europeans about one another. The key institution for American involvement in Europe was to be the North Atlantic Treaty Organization (NATO), which was founded in 1949. Lord Ismay, the first secretary general of NATO, is supposed to have defined the three unstated objectives of NATO as "to keep the U.S. in, the Soviet Union out and Germany down."[2]

The third way the United States contributed to European union was through the position it occupied as a cultural and social role model in the post-war years. While more difficult to pin down than the economic and security contributions, it may well be that the most important way Americans drew Europeans together was through the export of their own powerful culture, which was to provide cement for the long-divided Europeans. American popular culture has been unique in the twentieth century in the universality of its appeal. The first to master the new technologies of radio, the movies, and, later, television, the Americans exported to the world a powerful message of corporate wealth and earthy populist appetite, an unmatchable combination for people in other countries who dreamed of a way to achieve the improvement of their own conditions, sensing that the American dream would take them much further than Marxist ideology.

While the British, unlike the Americans, were Europeans, they did not find it agreeable to think of themselves that way, and came at the issue of European union also as outsiders. Unlike the Americans, whose sense of their own power made them willing to pursue European union without the slightest thought that Europe might some day become their rival, the British, all too aware of their own increasing weakness, feared the idea of European union, seeing in it a threat to their already diminishing global role. Indeed, aside from rhetorical gestures, the British shied away from the movement towards European union. The British global outlook had two crucial features in the early post-war years: the transatlantic connection with the United States and the receding, but still important, connection with the Empire-Commonwealth. The continental connection was seen as problematic. The British did not want to regard themselves as a European power. Their rise to greatness had resulted from playing some Europeans off against others to allow Britain to focus its energies on building global power across the seas. Now, in the hour of their imperial decline, the British retained their almost instinctual antipathy to cross-Channel entanglements. The long-term rise of a European federation could only tend to marginalize Britain, and, while British leaders saw European union as only a dim possibility, they well understood its long-range implications. Enthusiasts for the idea of European union had initially vested large hopes in the participation of the British and of British personalities such as Winston Churchill, who had himself coined the memorable phrase "the United States of Europe."[3] It was not long, however, before they learned that the British were very chary of anything beyond elegant phrases.

While the Americans provided critical extrinsic support for European union and the British were to make repeated attempts to steer the movement off course, it was up to continental Western Europeans themselves to determine whether the movement for union would have enough substance for a genuine historical transformation to be achieved. The first steps towards European union came in the early post-war years when the pattern of relationships among European nations was hardening into place, following the vast upheaval of the war. The inspiration for European union, however, the true genesis of the movement, had come during the war itself. Among the resistance movements that grew up in opposition to Nazi occupation, a common critique of the nation-state system and its consequences was developed. So, too, was elaborated the idea that, to avoid yet further catastrophe in the future, the nation-state system must be superseded by the creation of a European federation once the war was over. This perspective was the hard-won lesson of the European tragedy. What is remarkable is that it evolved, not in concert, but in parallel among isolated resistance movements that had relatively little mutual contact. As far as the resistance movements were concerned, the fascist domination of Europe and the world war were the consequences of extreme nationalism. Under fascism, the nation–state system was pushed to the point where nations totally negated one another, shutting out the vast background of a common European civilization that formed the shared heritage of Europeans. Because the critique of Europe's catastrophe and the perspective on how to prevent its repetition were independently developed in a number of places during the war, it can truly be said that the modern movement for European union has no single source, but genuinely has multiple origins. A few examples make this point.

Jean Monnet was that rarity among statesmen, a major historical figure who eschewed the trappings customarily associated with statesmanship. Modesty and practicality, allied with visionary idealism, were the qualities he brought to his quest for European union. Contrasting Monnet with de Gaulle is unavoidable. In their divergent ways, they were the two greatest Frenchmen of the twentieth century, and, while Monnet was often able to work with de Gaulle, their visions of France and of Europe were basically at odds with each other. The general was tall, with striking features, a personage who towered over others and was born to rule, the ideal figure around whom the shattered French nation could ally after its catastrophic military defeat in 1940. While everything de Gaulle did was calculated to add to his effect, to his grandeur, Monnet was a study in understatement. A short, balding man without prominent features, Monnet would easily have been lost in a crowd. Far from drawing attention to himself, it was his lifelong method to bring people together and to arm them with ideas, concepts, and plans, which he was all too eager that they should claim as their own.

At first glance, it seems odd that the leading architect of European union, its "master builder," as he has been described,[4] should have been born in the little brandy-producing town of Cognac in the southwest of France, the heir to a long line of brandy merchants, and that his start in life should have come selling the world-famous product of his home town, in such out-of-the-way places as Winnipeg. In its own way, however, it was a most appropriate background. Monnet never suffered a crisis of identity. He was rooted in his native community. But it was a community whose fortune was tied to selling its product to the whole world. Local identity and global marketing were the twin principles of the merchants of Cognac, and those principles taught Monnet much about the world.

Monnet's conviction that a pooling of sovereignty was needed to solve Europe's problems had its origins during the First World War when he sought, largely unsuccessfully, to merge the supply strategies of the British and French governments so that they would have a coordinated approach to their mobilization for the war effort. That experience taught Monnet how much the concept of national sovereignty limited the quest for solutions to common problems among nations. After the war, Monnet worked for four years as deputy secretary general of the League of Nations, witnessing at close hand an experiment he later concluded "prefigured supranationality." His experience at the league brought him into intimate contact with the problems of post-war Central Europe, where the successor states to the Austro-Hungarian Empire foundered in their attempt to establish themselves as successful nation-states. In 1921, he advised Eduard Beneš, the Czechoslovakian foreign minister, to address the problem of the weakness of Central European economies by establishing a federation because the region formed "a natural economic unit."[5] With this background, it was not surprising that the supreme shock of the Second World War should lead Monnet on to a much deeper development of his views on European federation.

In London, in June 1940, as Monnet anxiously followed the news of the Nazi offensive rolling across France, he came up with the idea for one of the most dramatic initiatives of the war — Winston Churchill's appeal to the government and people of France to pool sovereignty with Britain, to form one state grouping the two peoples together, so that, even if France was occupied, it could count on its British partners to carry on the struggle until ultimate victory was won. Churchill's spectacular offer fell on the deaf ears of the defeated nation across the Channel. For Monnet, the lessons learned here would bear fruit later on. In 1943, writing on behalf of the French Committee of National Liberation, Monnet, for the first time, advocated the formation of a federation of European states to be established following the conflict.

Resistance to fascism similarly had a profound effect on the most illustrious Italian proponent of European federalism, Altiero Spinelli. Spending years in prison under the Mussolini dictatorship, Spinelli continued his political development while incarcerated. He abandoned his former commitment to communist ideas, and evolved his belief in European federalism, which was to become the centre-piece in his new political philosophy, which he characterized as "democratic radicalism."[6]

In 1941, Spinelli collaborated with a group of Italian federalists, the most important among them being Ernesto Rossi, to produce the so-called Ventotene Manifesto, one of the earliest resistance programs to be dedicated to the idea that Europe's future must lie in the creation of a European federation. In the manifesto, Spinelli made the critical point that the destruction of most European states had already "reduced most peoples of the Continent to a common fate" and that the consequence of their wartime experience was that people were "already much more favourable toward a new, federative European order."[7]

Among German opponents of the Nazi regime, there was a similar evolution towards the idea that the nation-state system lay at the root of Europe's problems and that it must be transcended and replaced by a European federal system if the continent's tragic history was not to be repeated in the future. Some of these opponents went into exile during the Nazi years, others were imprisoned and often killed, and still others entered a period of "internal exile," during which they remained in Germany while silently opposing the regime and thinking through their views on what should come after the destruction of Hitler's Germany. Although Willy Brandt was much younger than Monnet and Spinelli, his odyssey during the Nazi years provides an important indication of how thinking was evolving among anti-Nazi Germans. While in exile in Scandinavia, Brandt spent time thinking about the future relationship between Germany and the other peoples of Central Europe, reaching the conclusion that, both for economic reasons and to resolve the national tensions of the region, a Central European federation should be considered.[8]

Needless to say, all of these ideas, developed by the opponents of fascism, awaited the end of the war before they had any hope of becoming the basis for concrete political action. With the war over, Europe existed as an idea. The task now was to invent it as a reality. A beginning had to be made somewhere. Concrete initiatives had to be taken. Specific leaders and specific countries had to decide that it was up to them to speak for Europe and to undertake the daunting task of invention. As it turned out, "Europe" was too large and too amorphous, too ill-defined, for its invention initially to involve all of the countries of Europe, or, to be realistic, of Western Europe, for the continent was already divided into the spheres of the two superpowers by the end of the 1940s. Speaking for Europe and taking the first decisive steps towards European union in these critical years was a group of countries that came to be known as "Little Europe" or "The Six" — France, West Germany, Italy, and the Benelux countries (Belgium, the Netherlands, and Luxembourg). While The Six had played extremely different roles in the war, ranging from aggressor to victim, they shared the decisive fact that they had all ended up as losers in the war. For the post-war governments of these countries, ensuring that there would never be a repeat of the war was an overriding objective. Within The Six, however, there were also different and often contradictory objectives. Naturally, the Benelux countries and France wanted security from the threat of a revival of German nationalism and military power. For their part, the Germans and the Italians wanted international rehabilitation so that they could overcome their marginalized position as defeated powers.

Within The Six, one relationship was of supreme importance and, on it, the fate of European union ultimately turned, in the early post-war period and ever since — that between the French and the Germans. Franco-German enmity had been at the centre of the European tragedy from 1870 to 1945. The key to European union, therefore, and one of the most compelling motivations in favour of it, was to put that past to rest. Naturally, France and West Germany came at the problem from opposing vantage points.

The First World War had been followed by French efforts to restrict Germany's capacity for economic and military recovery. The Versailles regime was notorious as a cause of German revanchism, extreme nationalism, and ultimately the rise of Hitler and the Second World War. If holding Germany down would not work for the long term, Jean Monnet concluded, then France must join with Germany, merging both countries into a new European framework in which German power could be contained, indeed tapped, as a source of strength for Europe.

The Germans, of course, saw the problem the other way round. Their concern was to end their nation's isolation and gradually to win equality of status for the Federal Republic with its neighbours. The key figure in formulating and implementing this policy was Konrad Adenauer, the first chancellor of West Germany. Adenauer's fundamental goal was to integrate the Federal Republic into the Western world, not simply in matters of security and diplomacy, but also in terms of the very shape of the German economy, society, and system of government. For his country, which had been devastated not simply physically, but morally and spiritually, Adenauer sought a role model whose emulation would allow his people to undertake the wholesale re-creation of their society. So central was his belief in the need to make his country a part of the West that he was prepared to sacrifice indefinitely the Federal Republic's chief foreign-policy ambition — the unification of Germany — to that end.[9]

Between the French and the Germans, there was the neat fit, like a hand and a glove coming together. The French were attracted to European union precisely to limit German sovereignty by confining Germany firmly within a framework of European institutions. The Germans wanted to regain sovereignty through the achievement of equality with their neighbours.[10] What allowed these two agendas to be meshed was the fact that Adenauer was always comfortable with the idea of ceding German sovereignty to supranational institutions, but only on terms of equality with other states, as a way to achieve the rehabilitation of the Germans and to embed his people in the most complex possible interrelationships with other countries in the West. Given the history of the war, and the position of the Germans as the defeated people, it was naturally up to the French to take the initiative in the movement for European union.

However, standing in the way of a far-reaching breakthrough were not merely important concrete irritants, but the atavistic mind-set of national leaders, wherein suspicion was instinctual and the focus was on the quest for military advantage. An important obstacle to improved relations, which prompted an outpouring of the poisonous attitudes that had developed between the French and the Germans since 1870, was the fate of the Saar, a strategic coal- and steel-producing region west of the Rhine, on the doorstep of Lorraine. Indeed, the Saar was not a new source of conflict, since, for fifteen years following the signing of the Treaty of Versailles in 1919, the region had been placed under the auspices of the League of Nations. As that treaty had stipulated, the future of the region was to be determined by means of a popular referendum after a period of fifteen years. In 1935, the residents of the Saar voted overwhelmingly in favour of returning to Germany, making their choice a political triumph for Adolf Hitler's Third Reich.

At the end of the Second World War, the Saar formed a part of the French occupation zone in Germany. Influential French politicians hoped that the Saar could be economically linked with industrial Lorraine, and even that it would one day be annexed by France. The territory surrounding the Saar was heavy with tragic symbolism. It is but a short distance across the Rhine into the Saar. Beyond Saarbrücken, the region's major city, it is a series of short steps to the French border, and beyond the border to the remnants of the Maginot Line, the stark reminder of French military failure in 1940, and beyond that to Verdun, where the French and the Germans bled each other to death in 1917. The French who wanted to seize the Saar were expressing attitudes natural to people in thrall to the dreadful symbols of the past. At the end of each war, the victorious power seized strategic pieces of territory or resources from the other to capitalize on its momentary advantage, thereby inevitably creating an issue around which the defeated power's resentment would fester, thus putting the two countries on the road to their next military conflict. For Konrad Adenauer, the struggle to regain the Saar was a major preoccupation, and the controversy continued to be a serious irritant in Franco-German relations until 1955, when a referendum settled the future of the region. As in the referendum twenty years earlier, the residents of the area opted overwhelmingly to become an integral part of West Germany and rejected the novel proposal that they be governed as citizens of Europe, later to be joined by other regions and countries.

If haggling over the Saar expressed the worst instincts, those of a tortured past, they were not the only instincts, and happily not the dominant ones. In both countries, there were leaders who were determined to break the vicious cycle of the past. Goodwill, though it existed, was far from sufficient to guarantee success, however. If France and West Germany were to seek a new relationship, what kind of relationship should it be? Should a traditional arrangement be sought in which the two countries reached agreements in a number of important fields, while sovereignty was retained in watertight compartments in each country? Or should the quest be for an entirely novel international arrangement, in which sovereignty itself was ceded to a new entity created by the founding states, an entity that would be vested with the power to undertake important and binding initiatives within its field of competence? And if a merging of sovereignty was to be considered, where should it be begun — with a general political agreement or with practical economic undertakings? From the outset, people like Monnet in France and Adenauer in the Federal Republic were open to the more radical option, the merging of sovereignty.

While the critical actors in the creation of supranational institutions were the French and the Germans, the movement always involved other countries as well, and was therefore couched in European terms from the outset, rather than exclusively in Franco-German terms. Two approaches to the project of European union existed from the start, amounting to rival concepts among architects of how the new building should be constructed. There were those who wanted to sketch in the whole edifice of a united Europe from the start, beginning with the general notion of political union and moving from there to deal with specific aspects of union. For others, Jean Monnet being the most important among them, concrete parts of the building needed to be solidly constructed first, both to allow practical use to be made of the new facilities and to demonstrate that further steps were also feasible, so that one day the entire edifice would be completed.

Both approaches were tried. The first major initiative towards European union was the establishment, in May 1949, of the Statute of the Council of Europe through an agreement signed in London. The council illustrated perfectly both the strengths and the weaknesses of the general approach to the achievement of European union. Proponents of union wanted an organization with a strong supranational component that would represent the first stage in the founding of a European federal state. Those who were not prepared for federalism wanted the organization kept vague in its purposes and relatively powerless, so that it would be merely a forum for existing national governments. The structure of the council reflected this schizophrenia. The council's Committee of Ministers was a very traditional body, amounting to little more than a twice-annual meeting of foreign ministers. For most purposes, decisions of the committee could be taken only if they were unanimous, which meant that reluctant states were assured that they could veto any measures that did not suit them. There was here no crucial leap beyond the sovereignty of the nation-state, the very thing the enthusiasts for European union regarded as the key to the future.

If the Committee of Ministers was entirely traditional, the Assembly of the Council of Europe more clearly expressed the hope for a new kind of relationship among European peoples. Beginning in 1951, its members were appointed by the national parliaments of member countries. In the Assembly, there was the suggestion of a future European parliament. Enthusiasts for union looked forward to the day when the Assembly's members would be elected by Europe-wide universal suffrage, which would vastly enhance the body's prestige and political clout. As it turned out, the Assembly became a forum for high-flown speeches in favour of union. Possessing little power, however, it ended up more as a monument to the hope for union than as an important step towards its realization.

While it was a hopeful initiative, in the end, the Council of Europe did not lead on to greater things. Instead, the main line of advance has come from a second path, the functional approach to European union.[11] Its starting-point was an initiative that was, at once, pragmatic, to the point of being pedestrian, and idealistic, to the point of being visionary. Its goal was the creation of a supranational authority to oversee the French and German coal and steel industries and those of other European countries willing to join in the initiative. The idea was Monnet's. And more than anyone else, Monnet understood how to craft reforms that contained within them the germs of revolution, a revolution that would be realized, not at once, but over a long period of time, and through the taking of numerous other steps along the same path.

Although for many people, particularly in the English-speaking world, the European Community has been understood simply as the European Economic Community, or the Common Market, several decades further on, the actual launch of the community came seven years before the Treaty of Rome with the conference to establish the European Coal and Steel Community (ECSC) in 1950. All of the principles that have motivated the European Community were there at the start, expressed with remarkable clarity in that first initiative, which was, in the words of Jean Monnet at the time, to provide the "basis for the building of a new Europe."[12] That idea, the very kernel of the New Europe, was conceived in the thatched-roof country house of Jean Monnet, sixty kilometres from Paris, in April 1950. After having first put some ideas down on paper, Monnet worked with two close associates to produce the initial proposal, which was to see the light of day as the "Schuman Plan." Later, when European institutions became much more developed and complex, it was easy in the plethora of details to lose sight of the essentials. In that first initiative, the essentials were sparklingly clear, and in all that has come afterward they have stood the test of time. The European Community is based on the insight that France and Germany, as nation-states, have each served to thwart the other, have each played the role of nemesis for the other. Only by achieving a revolution in the relationship of these nations could this tragic history be prevented from reproducing itself. To achieve this end, sovereignty must be merged between the two formerly antagonistic nation-states. The result would be a federation, a supranational state embodying both France and Germany, a state that would make war between them impossible because it would transcend the conflicts that had divided them.

Romantic suggestions of a sudden step to complete Franco-German union had no hope of success, however. The long history of hostility between the two peoples and the jealous preservation of the sovereignty of nation-states would not yield easily. An opening had to be found to make that yielding possible. Jean Monnet found that opening, the idea on which the European Community would be based. The idea was that, if a practical project could be undertaken that could be the occasion for the merging of sovereignty between the two countries in a specific sphere of activity, a beginning would have been made.

A critical distinction must be drawn here, a distinction relevant to all the subsequent history of the European Community. There had been numerous examples of agreements among nations to cooperate to achieve specific ends. This kind of cooperation is called "intergovernmentalism." What was proposed here was not another example of intergovernmentalism, but rather an actual merging of sovereignty, what is called "supranationalism." A further distinction needs also to be drawn among the federalists, that between those who favoured broad political advances to European union and those who favoured piecemeal, pragmatic advances, the latter group being described as "functionalists."

As a starting-point, the creation of a supranational authority to govern the European coal and steel industries was ideal in 1950, for a number of reasons. It is easy to forget in today's world of microelectronics that, throughout most of the twentieth century, steel-producing capacity was considered the broadest measure of a nation's economic and military power. German steel and coal had provided the sinew for German power from the time of the rise of Prussian militarism in the 1860s. In 1950, the Cold War between the United States and the Soviet Union was heating up. While, at the end of the war in 1945, the Allies had been committed to restricting German industrial development as a guarantee against the military resurgence of the Germans, five years later the Americans saw German industrial development as a key to winning the Cold War. Chancellor Konrad Adenauer was determined both to pursue the goal of rapid economic and industrial development and to tie nascent West Germany to the West. In France, these developments were viewed with alarm. While France had been successful in restraining German steel-making in the early post-war years and in commandeering German coal and iron ore for its own use as part of Allied command of the defeated country, the days when such strategems could be effective were obviously coming to an end. And yet, to do nothing meant that France would watch as Germany inevitably made itself, once again, the industrial giant of Europe, with the inevitable result that it would once again have the potential to pose a military threat to France.

In April 1950, Jean Monnet and two close associates came up with a draft proposal for what came to be called the Schuman Plan, the establishment of a common market in coal and steel.[13] Monnet decided the most likely figure in the French cabinet to achieve success in the launching of the plan would be Robert Schuman, the foreign minister.

The Schuman Plan provoked a diplomatic revolution in Europe. With one stroke, it drew France and Germany together and pushed Britain to the margin of European affairs. All the initiatives for European union to come in the years and decades to follow were based on the principles established in this first initiative and, as with the first one, all the later steps developed around a Franco-German axis, with Britain on the sidelines. In his historic declaration of May 9, 1950, when Robert Schuman called for the creation of the European Coal and Steel Community, he reflected Monnet's conception of how Europe would be built when he proclaimed: "Europe will not be built all at once, or as a single whole: it will be built by concrete achievements which first create de facto solidarity."[14]

The ECSC was conceived as a way to rebuild a critical industry that had become internationally uncompetitive. The proponents of the ECSC hoped that, by establishing a common governing authority and market for coal and steel products, future war between France and Germany would become impossible. For the French, the ECSC was a way to ensure that the Ruhr would never again serve to arm German revanchism. For the Germans, the ECSC guaranteed that French hostility, and therefore the French desire to weaken and dismember the industrial regions of the Federal Republic, would be at an end. While, at one level, the ECSC constituted an economic agreement, it was established essentially for political reasons. The ECSC was a "politically driven" economic agreement, and not, as the British often thought, an "economically driven" agreement with political implications. For the British, who did not themselves feel the compulsion to union, this line of reasoning never made sense — and thus they guaranteed their own position as outsiders for the long term.

Schuman's declaration in May 1950 stressed that success depended on the inclusion of both France and West Germany in the scheme for a supranational authority for coal and steel. The door was open to Britain to join at the outset, however. Once British counter-proposals, which would have rendered the new body innocuous, were brushed aside, it was left to the governments of The Six to undertake a set of protracted negotiations. While the principles that were to be embodied in the ECSC were clear from the start in the initial document drafted by Jean Monnet and in the public declaration of Robert Schuman, winning a group of national representatives around to enshrining them in a concrete agreement proved a very onerous task. Even though Monnet urged the delegates from each of the six countries to put national interests aside and to consider the establishment of an authority to oversee the coal and steel industries only in terms of the problems of the two sectors, the adoption of such a common perspective turned out to be difficult. That this was so is not surprising. The whole experience of negotiating among sovereign states had always been based on the need to pursue national interests. To convince skilled national negotiators to think as Europeans was extremely difficult — and, indeed, from Monnet's perspective, it was the major point of the whole exercise. Employing the techniques for which he was well known, Monnet forced the delegates into an intimate set of interrelationships in which they worked together and ate together. Ultimately suspicions waned, and the original principles emerged relatively unscathed in the final draft agreement, which was then signed by the governments of The Six as the Treaty of Paris in April 1951.

At the end of the process, two events occurred that symbolized the realities of the Europe that was being created: Jean Monnet was the unanimous choice of the member countries to head up the new organization as president of the High Authority of the ECSC; and the successful work to launch the organization nearly foundered when it became impossible to choose a capital city out of which to organize its work. Monnet, the obvious choice for president, was so exasperated by the issue of the capital that he came close to refusing the post. All was saved at the last moment with the proposal that Luxembourg serve as the temporary headquarters of the Coal and Steel Community. The building of the New Europe was always to be like that: a noble step forward, quickly followed by stumbles caused by narrow national or regional preoccupations threatening to undermine the whole.

The ECSC aimed during a five-year period to eliminate tariffs and other barriers to trade among The Six in the coal and steel sectors. Along with the removal of these barriers, the ECSC set out to restructure the industries in the two sectors so that the cartels that had been so important in the past would be eliminated. While the goal was thus the creation of a competitive, market environment, the ECSC was by no means imbued with a simple laissez-faire philosophy. It was intended to be from the start, as it proved to be in practice, strongly interventionist, taking steps to promote the well-being of the European steel and coal sectors in the face of American and Japanese competition, steps that included the investment of public-sector capital to underwrite the upgrading of the industry. [15]

To govern the ECSC, a unique structure was established, a structure whose logic pointed far beyond the immediate experiment to the ultimate goal of a federal political system for Europe. The critical executive arm of the new body was the High Authority — the counterpart of the commission in the EC — which was composed of nine individuals, chosen for their competence by member governments, of whom not more than two could be from one country. To ensure continuity, selections for membership in the High Authority were made every two years, with one-third of the body being chosen at that interval. Under the Treaty of Paris, the ECSC gained the authority to intervene directly in the activities of steel and coal industries throughout the six member countries, giving it, in this limited but important respect, supranational power.

The High Authority was not alone as a governing body. There was a Special Council of Ministers, whose members were appointed directly by member governments. This body was, of course, the counterpart of the Council of Ministers in the EEC. And, as with the later EC, there was a popular component as well, the first step on the road to today's European Parliament, the Common Assembly of the ECSC. As is the case with the EP, the Common Assembly was granted the power to dismiss the High Authority as a group in the case of gross dissatisfaction with its performance (a power never used). Members of the Common Assembly were appointed by the parliaments of member countries, and the charter of the ECSC pointed the way to the future in a provision allowing for direct election by Europeans of those to sit in the Common Assembly. The ECSC was also equipped with its own Court of Justice — as is the EC's Court of Justice, it was empowered to rule on the actions taken by the authority under the terms of the Treaty of Paris. Member governments and coal and steel companies were enabled to appeal the actions of the ECSC to the Court of Justice. Also key to its existence as a body vested with elements of sovereignty was the fact that the ECSC was empowered to raise its own funds through direct levies on the coal and steel industry. When the organs of the new body are examined in their totality, it is evident that what was being established was a nascent federal structure for the six member countries. It was a limited cession of sovereignty on their part, to be sure, but what was accomplished was the first real step towards the creation of a federal Europe.

Naturally enough, the ECSC would be judged a success or failure in narrower terms, having to do with the fate of the coal and steel industries in the participating countries. By 1958, it was clear that the experiment had been a success in this sense. By then, trade barriers had been eliminated in the two sectors. Within the borders of the ECSC, trade in steel had increased by 157 per cent, and steel output had increased by 65 per cent.

While the ECSC had shown how national differences could be overcome through the creation of a supranational authority, nationalism, the deadly enemy of European union, was far from finished as a force. Success in the field of coal and steel was soon followed by rising expectations and then crushing failure in an area of great sensitivity where sovereignty was concerned — security and defence, and, dependent on that, political union.

Developments were triggered by the changing global military perspective of the United States, still the decisive actor in Western European affairs in the early 1950s. As we have seen, against the background of the rising Cold War with the Soviet Union, American policy makers concluded that West Germany must be integrated fully into the Western alliance, even if that meant rearming it. From the perspective of Washington, the most logical course was to bring the Federal Republic of Germany into NATO and to build a German military force under these auspices.

For Germany's neigbours, the proposal caused shock and distress. Memories of Hitler's occupation of these countries were far too fresh. Faced with what they most feared, a new German military force, and inspired by the example of the ECSC negotiations already under way, the French government came up with its own alternative scheme, the notion of a European Defence Community (EDC). The EDC, like the ECSC, would mean a transfer of sovereignty from the countries that joined it to a new supranational authority. Its principles and its governing structure were modelled directly on the coal and steel authority.

From the beginning, however, differences were evident in an attempt to establish a European union in the critical area of defence. Control over the means of coercion — the mounting of military

forces — constitutes the very heart of state sovereignty. While the
ECSC was fundamentally political, its creation, as we have seen, did not
attempt to remove from the nation-state the centre of its political
authority, not to mention its symbolic association with the past
history of the nation. Establishing a common European military force,
which would quickly become the European pillar of the Western
alliance against the Soviet Union, was an act so overtly political that
it was evident that it could not stand by itself. If the EDC was to work,
it was concluded, it must be capped by another structure, a European
Political Community (EPC), to oversee the whole. With the French
proposal for the EDC, called the Pleven Plan, after the French prime
minister who proposed it, the idea was that member countries would
each contribute a portion of their armed forces to the combined
entity. The motivation for the French was obvious. Rather than contributing their own military forces to NATO, the West Germans would
create a military force under the auspices of the EDC. Moreover, there
would be complete integration of German military personnel into EDC
units, which would include personnel from the other member countries as well. There would be no German military as such.

For a time, it appeared that the new proposal would go ahead,
just as the ECSC had. Once again, the British and the Scandinavians
proved unwilling to participate in the proposed defence venture,
because they were unprepared to compromise their national
sovereignty. In the spring of 1952, it was therefore the representatives
of The Six who met in Paris to sign the treaty setting up the EDC.

From this point, however, the paths of the ECSC and EDC
diverged radically. The defence proposal proved to be extremely
volatile and divisive, both in West Germany and in France. In West
Germany, public opinion and the major political parties were sharply
divided on the question of rearmament and involvement in the
Western alliance.

In France, the still potent force of nationalism manifested itself
on both the right and the left to threaten the new accord. On the
right, the forces of Gaullism and, on the left, the Communists were
bitterly opposed to the creation of a mixed military force that would
merge French with German units and place both of them under a
supranational European authority. While de Gaulle had regarded the
ECSC as an evil technocratic scheme, he saw in the EDC a threat to the
very survival of an independent and sovereign France, whose preservation had been the cause to which he had devoted his life. About the
ECSC, de Gaulle stated: "We're offered a mish-mash of coal and steel,

without knowing where we're heading, under some sort of cabal." On the EDC, he exploded in wrath: "Here is a crafty scheme for a so-called 'European' Army which threatens to put a legal end to France's sovereignty. It would make our Army disappear in a hybrid creation under the deliberately misleading label of 'Europe.'"[16] As far as de Gaulle was concerned, "Europe" was nothing more than a fiction, masking the truth of American domination. The new military arrangement would end up under the direction of Washington: "Since Europe does not exist as a responsible sovereign entity — because no one has done what is needed to create it — this force will be entrusted to the American 'chief.'"[17] De Gaulle, too, had a conception of "Europe" that he was fond of invoking, both in these years when he was out of power and later when he was president of the Fifth Republic. De Gaulle dreamed of a day when Europe would order its own affairs, free from the influence of "outsiders," the American and Soviet super-powers that had ended up controlling the continent's affairs as a con-sequence of the war. And de Gaulle conceived of a place for Germany in his Europe, but it was to be Germany as a junior partner to France, particularly in military matters. While his "Europe" sounded ambitious and forward-looking, in reality it was nothing more than the old Europe of the nation-states. His Europe would be organized around a loose confederation of nation-states, with France at its centre and the superpowers pushed back from their present paramountcy. Based in the past, Gaullism was capable of making trouble for the superpowers, but it was never capable of sponsoring a new European order. That, ironically, would be possible only through the establishment of the very supranational institutions de Gaulle disdained and feared.

De Gaulle and the French conservatives were not the only oppo-nents of the cession of sovereignty to supranational organizations. On the left, the powerful Communist Party, its political stock high in the post-war years as a consequence of its leading role in the French resis-tance, also stood against moves towards European union. Since a corollary of the movement towards union was the rehabilitation of West Germany, its reindustrialization and remilitarization under supra-national auspices, the Communists were bound to oppose such devel-opments, which would have the effect of strengthening the West and threatening the position of the Soviet Union on the continent.

At the end of a long and acrimonious debate, the French National Assembly voted down the EDC, thereby killing it.

The disintegration of the EDC stopped the progress towards union within The Six, which had begun so hopefully with the ECSC. The demise of the EDC meant, as well, the failure of the related project, the so-called European Political Community (EPC), which was to have stood at the apex of a new Western European federal system.

As far as defence was concerned, the collapse of the French-initiated EDC opened the door to an alternative British initiative. In 1955, British prime minister Anthony Eden proposed the establishment of a new structure, the Western European Union (WEU). Under his scheme, the signatories to the Brussels Treaty of 1948, an agreement among Britain, France, and the Low Countries to stand united against any renewed aggressiveness on the part of Germany, would now update their alliance to include West Germany in light of the present Soviet military threat to Western Europe. Under the WEU, the British agreed to maintain forces on the continent as long as their allies wanted them to do so, a proposal that was quickly accepted by West Germany, France, and the Low Countries.

The British willingness to commit forces to Europe's defence helped mollify French concerns about the other aspect of the new arrangement — the creation of a West German defence force under the auspices of NATO. In reality, the WEU amounted to little more than a diplomatic shell. The substantive element was NATO. With the assurance of American and British forces on the continent, France acquiesced in the rearmament of its German neighbour. The WEU was a typical British proposal, inasmuch as it amounted to a substitute for the creation of a supranational structure, always the British purpose during debates on European union. In this case, the British effort to substitute a traditional intergovernmental arrangement for supranationalism succeeded, because the French themselves proved unwilling to stand behind their own proposed creation.

Jean Monnet, watching the EDC débâcle from his post in Luxembourg as president of the High Authority of the ECSC, was alarmed. He decided that the cause of European union must be rejoined on a much broader front. He resigned his post, moved to Paris, and set up one of the most effective lobby groups in modern history, the Action Committee for the United States of Europe, whose purpose was to draw together the very considerable political, intellectual, and trade-union forces that favoured European union, and to focus this sentiment, to make it politically potent.

The Action Committee soon included leading figures from the Christian Democratic, Socialist, and Liberal political formations throughout the six member countries of the ECSC. Monnet enjoyed very broad support across the political centre in Europe. Then, as later, it was the centre of the political spectrum that was the fertile ground for European union. For six months, from the summer of 1955, Monnet drew on his immense contacts across Europe, the product of a lifetime of activity, to forge the new committee, which held its first formal meeting in Paris in January 1956.[18] Monnet's idea centred on the peaceful harnessing of atomic power. In the mid-1950s, the revolutionary new technology, which had opened the door to atomic weapons on the one hand, and to nuclear energy on the other, was monopolized by the superpowers. Monnet believed that, for Europe to regain its position in the world, it needed to avail itself of this new technology, for peaceful purposes, under its own auspices. With the aim of ensuring the energy security of Europe and its technological advancement, Monnet proposed the creation of Euratom (the European Atomic Energy Commission), to be a supranational authority based on the model of the ECSC.

His initial strategy was to create Euratom alone. It turned out, however, that the Germans were not much interested, since they calculated that they could do better in the field of atomic energy by making bilateral deals with other countries, such as the United States. Only when the concept was vastly broadened to involve the creation of a Common Market for all goods and services were the West Germans enticed to come on board, and to accept the Euratom proposal as a part of a much larger package. The concept of a Common Market was already very much in the air. Spurred on by the urgings of the Common Assembly of the ECSC, in June 1955, at Messina, the foreign ministers of The Six had established a committee under the forceful chairmanship of Paul-Henri Spaak, the Belgian foreign minister, to study the feasibility of a Common Market. The efforts of the Spaak Committee and of Monnet's Action Committee intertwined and intersected, since their initiatives drew on similar inspiration and personnel. Eventually, proposals from the Spaak Committee were approved by the foreign ministers of The Six and then were returned for public debate to the ECSC Common Assembly, where they were overwhelmingly supported.

Fruition was achieved with the signing of the Treaty of Rome on March 25, 1957, through which the governments of The Six established the European Economic Community (EEC). On the same day, another treaty was signed by The Six in Rome to establish Euratom. This time there was no repeat of the débâcle that had attended the launching of the EDC. All six governments, propitiously led by the French National Assembly, ratified the treaties, which came into effect on January 1, 1958.

The EEC, like the ECSC before it, was a "politically driven" undertaking. Its inspiration went back to Schuman's notion that economic union among the European states would make war between them impossible and, positively, would lead eventually to political union. If the EDC and EPC had represented the direct route to the goal of political union, the Common Market represented the indirect route. The long-range goal of the undertaking was clear enough, as the preamble to the Treaty of Rome attested with its commitment "to establish the foundations of an ever closer union among the peoples of Europe." [19]

The economic activities of the EEC involved the launching both of the Common Market and of the Common Agricultural Policy (CAP). Members of the Common Market undertook to eliminate tariffs between member countries over a ten-year transitional period. The Common Market had as a goal, for the economy as a whole, what had been achieved for coal and steel already. The founding of the EEC was based on an implicit deal involving industry and agriculture, West Germany and France. By 1957, when the Treaty of Rome was signed, the German economic "miracle" had already produced formidable results. It was, therefore, assumed that German industry would tend to enjoy a paramount advantage in the new market. Offsetting this advantage was the CAP. The goals of the CAP were to promote European agricultural production and to protect European farm communities. These goals were to be realized through the large-scale outlay of funds by the EEC to support the agricultural sector throughout the member countries. Indeed, CAP outlays constituted the large bulk of expenditures by the EEC.

With the establishment of Euratom and the EEC, which oversaw the CAP, Europe's supranational structures were proliferating in such a way as to make the emerging communities unwieldy. This problem was addressed through the adoption of a treaty that came into effect on July 1, 1967, through which the ECSC, Euratom, and the EEC were amalgamated to form the European Community.

A TIME OF TESTING

In an economic sense, the first decade after the signing of the Treaty of Rome was one of spectacular success for the Common Market. Twice the deadline for the removal of tariffs and quota restrictions among The Six was shortened so that this process was completed on July 1, 1968, eighteen months ahead of the original schedule. Despite the concerns that had existed at the launching of the Common Market that West Germany would leave its partners behind economically, the 1960s was the decade of the French and Italian economic "miracles." The economies of both France and Italy grew faster than that of the Federal Republic during the decade. Indeed, among the major industrialized countries, only Japan enjoyed steeper growth. Also during these years, the CAP was put into place, and was enormously successful in promoting increased efficiency in European agriculture, in raising living standards among farmers, and in assisting in the orderly process of the shrinking of Europe's farm population by two-thirds (over twenty years), while farm output increased to the point that the EC became self-sufficient in food production. Despite these gains, the negative consequences of the CAP were all too visible. Under the system, Europeans ended up paying higher-than-world prices for food at the same time as they shouldered major tax outlays to support the farm sector. In addition, the CAP generated friction with other major world food producers, particularly the United States, on the issue of protection and public support for European farmers, becoming the most serious trade irritant between the EC and the United States.

For a time, success in economic realms gave the impression that more sovereignty had been shifted to the EEC than was actually the case, an impression strengthened by the decisive management of the community by commission president Walter Hallstein, a former associate of Konrad Adenauer. A showdown was coming, however, over the issue of where power ultimately lay. The issue around which it developed was de Gaulle's vision of Europe and his attitude to British participation in the EEC. If de Gaulle was prepared to live with the economic activities of the EEC, this implied no alteration in his profound philosophical rejection of the very concept of supranationalism. De Gaulle wanted France to embrace West Germany as a partner, while it held Britain at arm's length as an interloper that was not truly European, and could be expected, in the French president's trenchant phrase, to act as a "Trojan horse" on behalf of the United States. At the first meeting between de Gaulle and Adenauer, shortly after de Gaulle's resumption of power, the relationship between the two leaders was described as "love at first sight." The reason for the close match between the two was that de Gaulle was prepared to support certain aspects of Adenauer's hard-line approach towards the Soviet Union, in return for the West German chancellor's acceptance of the French president's preference for "little Europe," in which EEC membership would be denied to the British.[20] Adenauer's line was attractive to de Gaulle because it seemed very unlikely to lead to German unification, and, with the British outside the EEC, France felt it could dominate the politics of The Six.

If the pyrotechnics of Gaullism were European, its essence remained the nation-state. Gaullism tested power relations and political attitudes in Europe in fundamental ways. It drove a wedge into the Western Alliance between the United States and France, and forced West German politicians into the uncomfortable position of having to choose between Paris and Washington. The splits created by Gaullism were reflected in the internal politics of the Federal Republic itself. The governing Christian Democratic Union/Christian Social Union in West Germany was split between Gaullist and Atlanticist tendencies, with Adenauer attracted to the Gaullists, and his successor, Ludwig Erhard, a firm Atlanticist. De Gaulle created expectations of the possibility of a new order in Europe and also provoked fears that what he was aiming for was the achievement of French hegemony within the "little Europe" of The Six.

De Gaulle's European vision ended by generating much more heat than light. Its tangible consequence was the creation of a committee to study the potential for various forms of political cooperation among The Six. This drive for closer political and foreign policy coordination drifted to an inconclusive result, however. Its only lasting effect was the eventual signing of a treaty of friendship between France and West Germany in 1963.

The most decisive effect of Gaullism was to keep Britain outside the EEC throughout the 1960s. Britain's initial response to the prospect of the Common Market had been to attempt to sidetrack the movement towards supranationalism, in favour of its own less far-reaching proposal. In place of the Common Market, the British proposed the less intrusive alternative of a European free trade area. The Six had not been tempted by the British alternative, concluding that the real purpose of the initiative was to steer the movement for European union back into the traditional channels of intergovernmentalism.

British failure to convince The Six did not end the matter. They set out to organize their own alternative to "little Europe," through the sponsoring of the European Free Trade Association (EFTA), which grouped together Sweden, Norway, Denmark, Switzerland, Austria, and Portugal, along with Britain. The EFTA model was quite different from that of the EEC. EFTA established a free-trade area, but with no supranational dimension. The creation of EFTA left Western Europe divided between two rival concepts enshrined in the Inner Six and the Outer Seven. Looking back on the rivalry between British conceptions of Europe and those of The Six, Jean Monnet concluded that "the British had persisted in the illusion of their power long after the nations of continental Europe had realized that they themselves were no longer a match for the modern world. When the British had ignored the European Community's appeals and tried to set up rival groupings, they had hurt and discouraged many of their friends." [21]

As far as the community was concerned, it was not to be long after the founding of EFTA in January 1960 that the British government of Harold Macmillan began the path to redemption. Macmillan's government reckoned that Britain could not afford to remain outside the EEC, whose market grouped together twice as many people as did that of EFTA. In July 1961, Britain applied for full membership in the EEC and was joined in its application shortly afterwards by Denmark, Norway, and Ireland. Protracted negotiations on the terms of British accession began in November 1961 — the British came with a very detailed list of concerns on the future of Commonwealth trade, relations with EFTA, and agriculture. The difficult talks between Britain and the EEC proceeded for over a year before President de Gaulle's underlying hostility towards the admission of an "Anglo-Saxon" country, which he did not regard as fully European, boiled to the fore.

At first glance, the reason for the blow-up was an unlikely one. In December 1962, Harold Macmillan met U.S. president John Kennedy in Nassau and decided to abandon the British Skybolt air-to-ground missile project as too costly, and instead to obtain Polaris missiles from the United States. In an extraordinary press conference a couple of weeks later, President de Gaulle stunned the world by announcing that France would not support Britain's admission to the EEC. He cited the British decision on defence as evidence that they had not yet chosen to become European, and that their American orientation made them unfit for membership. What was as stunning as the decision was de Gaulle's peremptory unilateralism, the assumption that it was appropriate for him to cut down a multilateral process of negotiations without warning, on grounds that, though extraneous to the matter at hand, appeared appropriate to him. For the other five members of the EEC who would have been happy with Britain's accession, de Gaulle's decision was a bitter blow. For a time, in the stormy aftermath, it appeared possible that the EEC itself might fly apart, but, in the end, the other members of The Six reckoned that, though the community would suffer because of the absence of Britain, it could not survive without France.

De Gaulle's second veto of a renewed British application for membership came in 1967, when the Labour government of Harold Wilson attempted to gain entry. In addition to keeping Britain out of the EEC against the will of France's other five partners, de Gaulle also challenged the supranational system of decision making within the community. In 1965, the transitional system of EEC decision making was nearing its projected end, and unanimity was due to be replaced by a system in which qualified majority voting in the Council of Ministers was to be used to reach a wide range of decisions. For de Gaulle, this transition was anathema, implying that France could find itself outvoted by its partners, without any ability to veto significant decisions. The crisis came in the summer of 1965 over a range of issues concerning the self-financing of the community and the financing of the Common Agricultural Policy. In the council, France found itself in a minority of one against its five partners on the issues. Unprepared to face the prospect of submitting to the will of the majority once the new system came into effect six months later, the French government simply withdrew its representatives from the council. This "empty chair" crisis went on until January 1966, when a deal was reached at a session in Luxembourg, and France resumed its participation in the council. The deal, known as the "Luxembourg Compromise," undercut the promise of supranationalism by asserting that, in the event that a situation arose that a member state believed raised "very important" issues for it, the council would attempt to reach a solution that would not override the position of that member. In other words, on such issues, qualified majority voting would not prevail, and the veto would continue. The Luxembourg Compromise meant that, henceforth, the commission would operate on a very short leash in making new proposals, and that the decision-making process in the council would be slow.

This showdown within the community was between the French government and the commission. It was also between two forceful personalities, de Gaulle and commission president Walter Hallstein. In the contest, de Gaulle easily prevailed and, shortly thereafter, Hallstein resigned his post. It would be a long time before a commission president would feel in a position to push ahead with European integration the way Hallstein had in the euphoric early years of the EEC. For a very long time, the Luxembourg Compromise produced exactly what de Gaulle wanted, a more intergovernmental emphasis within the community, in which the main lines of policy would be established in state-to-state agreements. The effects of his assault on the community were felt until the 1980s, when a new and powerful movement towards European union began. For fifteen years, however, the heavy hand of Gaullism appeared to have negated the hopes for a profound transfer of powers from nation-states to a supranational authority. Much of the intellectual energy and political vigour that had been such remarkable features of the early movement faded during these years. The theory of functionalism, the idea that a union that began in practical areas such as coal and steel, would later, to use the term employed, "spill over" into other areas of decision making, opening the path to wider and wider forms of integration, appeared to have lost its promise. Leading intellectuals who had promulgated the theory of functionalism later recanted, proclaiming that their previous hopes had been misplaced.

The long road to British membership in the community was resumed only when de Gaulle was no longer in office. A new Conservative government under Edward Heath undertook Britain's third bid for membership, and, through negotiations with France in 1971, cleared aside the French government's objections to membership. Finally, with de Gaulle dead and the French government won around, Britain became a full member of the community in 1973, along with Ireland and Denmark.

While British entry resolved the issue as far as Britain's continental partners were concerned, it did not resolve the issue within the country itself. The question continued to roil British politics for another generation, with passions raised to a high pitch around the holding of a referendum on British membership in the EEC in 1975, in which the electorate voted "yes" by a wide margin. Emotions were not permanently cooled, even by the referendum result, however.

REGAINING THE MOMENTUM

Recovery from the ravages inflicted by Gaullism was a long and arduous process for the EC and there were many false starts before the movement for European union once again achieved significant advance. Following de Gaulle's departure from office, the change in atmosphere that opened the way for British entry also made other gains possible.

As always in the history of the movement for European union, the critical relationship was that between France and West Germany, and the most important personal political relationship was that between the leaders of those two countries. In 1969, both France and the Federal Republic acquired new leaders, Georges Pompidou and Willy Brandt, who took centre stage in the affairs of the community. Of the two, Brandt was by far the more interesting figure, with a perspective on Europe that was much more penetrating than that of the cautious French president, whose world-view was bounded by the shibboleths of Gaullism. Brandt had gone into exile from Germany when the Nazis had taken power in 1933. In his memoirs, he wrote of the meaning of this exile for him: "I became aware before many others that this continent could not be rebuilt on the decayed foundations of the old order of things: the nation-state was a thing of the past." [22]

Brandt sought the Europeanization of Germany as a solution to the German question. While he was most famous for his *Ostpolitik*, his political opening to the East and to the Soviet Union, and his historic shifting of the Federal Republic's position on East Germany, his vision included Europe as a whole. Pompidou, by contrast, while not wedded to all of the dictums of his predecessor, was essentially a Gaullist none the less, and, as such, was unwilling to countenance any significant loss of French sovereignty. The new partnership came to fruition in 1969 with the Hague summit, where progress was made on the issues of monetary union and foreign-policy cooperation and where the mood turned hopeful again, for the first time since the disastrous struggles centring on de Gaulle.

Even more progress was made when there was a further change of leadership in both Paris and Bonn. This time the partners were Valéry Giscard d'Estaing and Helmut Schmidt, whose personal chemistry added to a philosophical commitment to furthering the cause of European union. Giscard's arrival was particularly important since he was not lumbered by the Gaullist terror of any loss of power by the French government to European institutions. The Giscard–Schmidt axis was indispensable to the advances made at the Paris summit of December 1974. The concrete achievements included the agreement that heads of government, accompanied by ministers of Foreign Affairs, would meet three times a year; an accord on the pursuit of an ever-more-closely coordinated foreign policy for the members of the EC; an undertaking that direct elections to the European Parliament would take place sometime after 1978; and the commissioning of Leo Tindemans, the Belgian prime minister, to submit a report before the end of 1975 on a comprehensive scheme of European union.

While progress was being made, it was progress endogenous to the workings of the community institutions themselves. Life was being breathed into the community from the summit of nation-state power, the very power the community had been established to transcend. Critical to decision making was the link between Paris and Bonn, and, from the time of the adhesion of Britain, to some degree between the other two capitals and London. This system of decision making, by definition, tended to shut Italy and the smaller partners out of the process. Not surprisingly, Italy and the others wanted to surmount this problem by infusing community institutions themselves, particularly the European Parliament and the commission, with enhanced powers.

When the Tindemans Report was received in December 1975, it proved a disappointment. While it was deliberately conceived as a way of achieving an advance in the direction of supranationalism and away from the predominant intergovernmentalism, indeed the bilateralism of France and West Germany, it shied away from the provocative word "supranational." In the end, the report contributed little to the advance of the cause of union since the member governments were simply not prepared to transfer additional power to the centre.

There was great risk in all of this, risk that Europe would founder in its failure to advance, that, without steps forward, there would be retreat. These risks even existed in the economic realm, the area where greatest progress had been made. The Common Market itself could be endangered. It could end up simply as a free-trade area, with all the grander notions of union pushed into an indefinite background. In fact, while the removal of all tariffs within ten years of the Treaty of Rome had been a substantial achievement, the world was entering a new economic age in the late 1960s and early 1970s. Beginning was the era of the non-tariff barrier characterized by the myriad of measures, apart from tariffs, adopted by governments to give their own industries protection at home or an advantage in markets abroad. The goal of the Single European Market appeared to yawn off into an indefinite future, and with it the hope of an economic union followed by a political union appeared to all but vanish.

But, finally, in 1979, the European Parliament was elected by universal suffrage for the first time. The mere creation of an elected parliament, however, was no guarantee of its being a powerful entity. National governments, as we have seen, had jealously kept most powers in their own hands in setting up the new body.

Despite its limitations, it was in its advocacy role that the EP was to prove most effective, taking a step in 1984 that was significantly to advance the cause of European union. Under the leadership of Altiero Spinelli, the almost legendary Italian who was the universally acknowledged leader of European federalism, the European Parliament passed a draft treaty for European union. In devoting what turned out to be the last years of his life to this latest crusade for European union, a cause he had championed for over four decades,[23] Spinelli brought together federalist-minded members of the European Parliament to form a concerted grouping on behalf of the cause. Spinelli's so-called Crocodile Group took its name from the site of its first meeting, the Crocodile Restaurant, an esteemed dining establishment in Strasbourg. The idea was to complete the political design for a united Europe, to replace the Treaty of Rome with a new treaty. When the parliament first voted in support of the draft treaty, it appeared to have little chance of success. This situation changed, however, as a result of the dramatic intervention of François Mitterrand in a speech to the European Parliament in Strasbourg in which he appeared to endorse the treaty (although a close reading of his text makes it clear that he by no means endorsed its details).

For Spinelli, the functionalist road to European union that had been championed by Jean Monnet had always been a false one that would ultimately peter out in disappointment. Spinelli saw the European Community that had been built to date as a brittle, technocratic structure, as not fundamentally answerable to the people of Europe and not prepared to rely on the popular will to further its aims. Such a structure, he believed, could never stand up in times of crisis to the entrenched power of its member nation-states. In the end, Spinelli's draft treaty proved to be a magnificent example of advocacy, but it could not itself gain the support among the member states it needed to be adopted.

The example of the treaty, however, helped serve as an inspiration to and a pressure on the leaders of the EC. As we will see, when the ground swell developed for the completion of the Single European Market (SEM), Jacques Delors insisted that the "1992" program must be accompanied by a political counterpart in the form of an addition to the founding treaties. That addition was the Single European Act (SEA), which made "1992" a fundamental goal of the EC. The SEA renewed the advance towards political union in important ways. Although it fell far short of the scheme for European political union favoured by Spinelli, its adoption owed much to the work of the great Italian federalist.

In the end, it was the "1992" project that decisively broke the log-jam and opened the way to a broad new advance towards European union. Once "1992" had gained the attention of the world and had been perceived throughout Europe as an irreversible process, optimism replaced the fatalism and pessimism that had existed for so long. However, "1992" did not long remain alone in the European spotlight. Although, in 1988, the project had enjoyed that monopoly of attention, by 1989, the historic revolutions in Eastern Europe and the looming question of German unification had taken centre stage. It has always been thus in the history of the community, which is itself only one of the major forces for change in Europe. Wider global developments, technological changes, the functioning of the international financial and economic systems, and the interactions of the superpowers — such phenomena bombard the community from the outside, continually redefining the context in which it operates. As in previous periods, the pressures exerted on the EC by major historical events were testing the architecture of the community and creating the conditions for further changes in its structure.

The challenge posed by the revolutions in Eastern Europe and German unification are of an entirely new kind in the history of the community, and, as we will see in subsequent chapters, they are leading the community into uncharted waters. Throughout its history, the community has developed as a Western European formation, itself the child of the Cold War and of the division of Europe. As Europe changes shape, as Germany emerges as a single state, no longer held down by the superpowers, the relationships within the EC itself are being subjected to tremendous strains of a qualitatively new kind. Will those stresses force Europe forward to deeper unity, towards the completion of a European federal state, or will they push Europe backwards in the direction of a renewed system of nation-states? Much depends on "1992."

Chapter Three
"1992" — UNDER CONSTRUCTION

★ ★ ★ ★ ★ ★ ★ ★ ★ ★ ★ ★

T
HE BERLAYMONT, THE HEADQUARTERS OF THE NEWEST
world power, is unlike the centre-piece of any other great
global capital. A glass-fronted office building, the Berlaymont was constructed in 1969 in Brussels to house the
commission, the executive body of the European Community.
Unlike the long-established capitals, this one has a completely unsettled feeling. The functional headquarters, actually rented rather than
owned by the EC, has none of the majesty of the sovereign state about
it. It could easily be the headquarters of a major insurance company.
Beside the Berlaymont is a giant construction site, the location of
future Euro-government structures. And yet, to these unlikely surroundings, the statesmen of the world, from their ornate official
edifices, must now make pilgrimages to the home of what is fast
becoming the world's largest single marketplace.

There is more than a little irony and a good deal of poetic
justice in the emergence of Brussels as the capital of the New Europe.
Brussels and Belgium have characteristically been the butt of jokes,
paternalism, and arrogant oversight on the part of Europeans from
neighbouring countries. The mere thought of being governed from
Brussels is so distasteful to some people in Britain that the Conservative party warned against a "diet of Brussels" as its main slogan in
the elections to the European Parliament in 1989.

Far from fearing rule from Brussels, the French tend to be paternalistic when the subject comes up. If you make the comment to a
French friend that Brussels is renowned for its restaurants, the retort
is likely to be that, while the food is not as good as in Paris, you will

get twice as much. The French specialize in Belgian jokes, relegating the Belgians to the position occupied by Newfoundlanders in Canadian humour.

Ask the neighbouring Dutch about Belgium and you will hear unfavourable comparisons of Brussels with Amsterdam. Even the Belgians themselves, linguistically divided as they are, often define themselves negatively. A Belgian humorist has portrayed the Walloons as too Anglo-Saxon to be Latin and the Flemish as too Latin to be Anglo-Saxon. In the end, Belgian national survival has been attributable to the fact that the territory Belgium occupies is simply too militarily strategic for its great neighbours to allow any one of them to occupy it. If the German invasion of Belgium was a crucial event in the First World War, it was not unique in that respect. The Battle of Waterloo was fought on Belgian soil in 1815 and the Battle of the Bulge, Hitler's last offensive in December 1944, was launched in Belgium. Sitting on a fault line between the great states of Western Europe, Brussels is a logical place to put the capital of the superstate that Europeans are now erecting.

Today, the Berlaymont is alive with the effort to pull the European Community forward from its ambiguous past, with its mixed record of successes and failures, towards a much more embracing form of European union, both economic and political. As we have seen, powerful impulses towards political union have been indispensable to the drive for economic union. Successes in the quest for economic union reinforce and add fresh momentum to the drive for political union.

The "1992" program is not an end in itself. Beyond the achievement of the single market, the door is being opened to yet more ambitious schemes for Economic and Monetary Union (EMU) and for political union as well. Before analysing "1992," it helps put the discussion in perspective to stand back and look at the EC in comparison with the other major states of the world today. Leaving aside, for the moment, the question of whether the quest for European union will ultimately succeed or fail, we need to consider the human and material potential of the EC as the base upon which a great state could, in principle, be erected. That way we can see just how large the stakes are in what is being undertaken by those who pull the levers in the Berlaymont.

The European Community is located in a compact region, with a mainly temperate climate, a relatively poor resource base, and a large, though ageing population, which enjoys what, by global standards, is a high standard of living. The 338 million people in the EC live on a land mass of 2 million square kilometres. Representing 7 per cent of the world's population, they occupy less than 2 per cent of its land mass. Their population density is 140 people per square kilometre, compared to a global average of 35.[1]

Compact though it is, the EC displays wide internal variations. Its twelve member states, from the largest to the smallest in millions of people, are the Federal Republic of Germany (78.5), Italy (57), the United Kingdom (56.3), France (54.8), Spain (38.5), the Netherlands (14.6), Portugal (10.3), Belgium (9.8), Greece (9.6), Denmark (5.1), Ireland (3.6), and Luxembourg (0.4). Some of these countries are relatively spacious, others very crowded. Ireland is the least crowded EC country, with 50 inhabitants per square kilometre; the Netherlands the most, with 345 people per square kilometre, making it more densely populated than Japan.[2]

In global terms, Europeans are prosperous, the Gross Domestic Product of the EC per capita being 270 per cent of the world average, in comparison with China's, at 30 per cent, and that of the United States, at 360 per cent. Within the EC, however, there are very wide regional disparities. A wealthy heartland comprising Paris and northeastern France, much of western Germany, southeastern England, parts of the Benelux countries, and northern Italy is surrounded by a poorer periphery, which includes the southern agricultural regions of Ireland, northern England, and Scotland. The richest of the European Community's 171 self-designated regions for the period 1986–88 was Groningen in the Netherlands, where the average per-capita income was 183 per cent of the average EC income. The poorest region was Voreio Aigaio in Greece, where the average per-capita income was only 39.9 per cent of the average EC income.[3] This very wide range, from the richest to the poorest region, reveals the immense diversity of the EC's social and economic landscape.

Europe's economy, like that of the United States and Japan, has been shifting away from industry and agriculture as a source of employment and towards services. In 1983, while 65 per cent of Americans worked in the service sector, the proportion in the EC was 58 per cent, and in Japan 56 per cent. In 1984, not counting intra-EC trade, the EC was the world's leading trading power, accounting for 22 per cent of global imports and 21 per cent of global exports, while the United States accounted for 21 per cent of global imports and 15 per cent of global exports, and Japan 9 per cent of global imports and 11 per cent of global exports.[4]

Although this profile points out the weaknesses of the EC, its relatively limited resource base and an ageing population, its enormous strengths shine through. What is clear is that, if the EC is successful in achieving a greater degree of economic and political union, it will be capable of wielding immense global power. Hans-Jorg Rudloff, chairman of Credit Suisse–First Boston in London, put it bluntly: "The European challenge is to restore the Europe of 1914 when Europe was the biggest economy in the world and had the best educated population."[5] Presiding over the effort to give Europe the unity it needs to become a formidable global power is a group of exceptionally talented bureaucrats who have piloted the European Community on a revolutionary course. Seizing on the opportunity presented by the creation of a new and very broad political consensus in favour of proceeding towards economic and political union, the EC leadership has come up with concrete initiatives to make a stunning advance possible.

At the beginning of the 1980s, few people would have predicted such a bold course for the European Community. Not only did the EC have to deal with the dispiriting atmosphere of global recession in the early 1980s, it had to deal with Margaret Thatcher. As we have seen, her election as Britain's prime minister in 1979 placed an implacable foe of the idea of European union at the head of one of the EC's major states. In an institution in which forward steps have been very difficult in the absence of unanimity among the major member states, Thatcher became an important obstacle to advancement. Instead of spending their time working out a strategy for the serious issues that confronted Europe — the burgeoning of non-tariff economic barriers among the member states of the EC that were undermining the achievements to date of the so-called Common Market, and the growing high-technology gap between Europe, on the one hand, and the United States and Japan, on the other — the leaders of the EC were spending their time fussing about the relatively petty sums of money Britain should or should not pay as a consequence of the EC's Common Agricultural Policy (CAP). Summit after summit of the EC was taken up with haggling over Thatcher's insistence that there ought to be a rebate to Britain since it was a relatively small agricultural producer, but a large consumer of farm products, and therefore was paying more into the EC coffers than it was getting in return for its contribution. For Thatcher, the most nationalist and anti-European of the EC's leaders, the furore over the CAP and the British rebate made sense because it was good, if cheap, politics with the British public. She could be seen to be beating bone-headed continental Europeans about the ears for the milk and wine lakes, the butter mountain, and the other excesses of surplus agricultural production in the EC that were underwritten by CAP subsidies. There was, however, a deeper underlying motive for Thatcher. If she could keep the EC fixated on issues of small change, she could thereby avert the threat of visionary steps towards tighter European union being contemplated and taken.

For several years, Thatcher succeeded in tying up the EC agenda. Beginning in 1984, however, the growing fury of her fellow leaders, the reality of Europe's pressing problems, and the rising conviction on the part of French president François Mitterrand that serious initiatives towards European union were needed, combined to break Thatcher's domination of the existing agenda and to achieve a new one that was to have immense implications for Europe and the world. Mitterrand's emergence as the key proponent of European union, midway through his first seven-year term, was the consequence of a conversion born of experience.

In 1981, François Mitterrand was elected president of France with a bold program to remake the country as a prosperous, socially transformed society. With flags flying and guns blazing, the new government of France launched its recovery program. Within two years, it was in full retreat. French imports had shot up. The government was going massively into debt. France had failed to develop new markets for itself abroad. The difficult lesson was learned. Even a country as large as France could not fight a world recession on its own. Once again the French were forced to look across the Rhine, not this time at a military adversary, but at a new kind of implacable economic foe, the Federal Republic of Germany.

By the 1980s, West Germany was the ageing wunderkind of the continent, its economy was a little paunchy around the middle, its growth rate a far cry from that of the glory days of the economic miracle of the 1950s, but still the strongest in Europe. Because the Common Market had succeeded in eliminating many of the barriers to trade (although not all), all members of the EC were greatly affected by the policies of West Germany, the single most powerful entity in their midst. For France, the frustrating result of stimulating internal demand on its own was to increase the opportunity for West German firms to make additional export sales to French consumers. This damaging leakage outward proved to be the undoing of the initial Mitterrand strategy.

In learning his lesson about the limitations of France's capacity to chart its own economic course in the world, Mitterrand drew the logical conclusion that getting the economic recovery he wanted would require changes at the European level. While France could not act alone, the EC taken as a whole, and including crucially important West Germany, certainly had the potential to act in concert with great effect. Since his conversion, Mitterrand has been the most important and consistent leader in the drive to deepen the unity of the EC.

During the first six months of 1984, a period when France held the six-month presidency of the EC, Mitterrand was determined to break the log jam created by Thatcher's obduracy on the issue of the CAP and the British rebate and to get the EC onto a more serious agenda. The climax came at a summit of the European Council (leaders of governments of the EC member states) in Brussels in March 1984. After two days of haggling over the size of the rebate due Britain, Thatcher found herself alone against the then nine other members. The figure she had in mind differed from the one being offered by France with the support of all the others, by £86 million, a trivial sum for the heads of ten governments to wrangle over. At 6:30 p.m., on March 20, the explosion came. Helmut Kohl, the West German chancellor, pushed back his chair, stood up, and announced that he was leaving. Caught off guard by this development, Thatcher immediately tried to meet her opponents halfway in an uncharacteristically conciliatory gesture.[6] It was too late, however. The chancellor was going home. Kohl's walk-out revealed the flaw in Thatcher's negotiating strategy. Her fellow heads of government were prepared to take steps forward without the British, if necessary.

Personal relationships among government leaders cannot be discounted in matters such as this. There was always a negative chemistry between Thatcher and Kohl, and Thatcher acknowledged her dislike for the German chancellor. In part, she was infuriated because Kohl, a conservative, aligned himself with Mitterrand, a socialist. Not to get on with socialists who are French and, therefore, prone to Latin excess was one thing. Not to get on with sensible German conservatives could only be interpreted as a betrayal. However, while relations between Kohl and Mitterrand have not been as personally warm as were those of their respective predecessors, Helmut Schmidt and Valéry Giscard d'Estaing, who enjoyed private conversations in which they spoke English to each other, they have been friendly. Indeed, when Mitterrand and Kohl were out for a stroll during one Franco-German summit, the chancellor took the French president's hand, and, for a time, they walked on, maintaining that gesture of national reconciliation, despite the fact that Kohl, who is close to six and a half feet tall, towered over the diminutive Mitterrand.

With Mitterrand and Kohl in agreement, the threat that the other EC members could rework the architecture of the EC without Britain had its effect. Having called Thatcher's bluff successfully, they developed a new weapon that was permanently to draw the fangs of the British prime minister. The idea was very simple. To outflank Mrs. Thatcher, her continental opponents threatened to seek agreements in critical economic and political spheres in which those agreeing would proceed, while those dissenting would be left out, thus giving rise to a "two-speed Europe." Proceeding this way would make European decision making even more structurally confusing than it already was. Messiness aside, however, its prospect had the desired effect of nullifying Mrs. Thatcher's veto.

Moreover, as British business, particularly its critical financial sector, came to believe that integration with Europe was essential, the nationalism of the British prime minister became increasingly anomalous. Having found the chink in the Iron Lady's armour, the other leaders of the EC were in a position to impose their new agenda.

The very top item on that new agenda was "1992," the completion of the single market of the EC. At the simplest level of economic necessity, the fact was that the European Common Market launched in 1958 had succeeded in establishing a customs union among its member states, but had failed to create a full economic union. The reason was that international trade and the role played by states in international trade had altered profoundly. As we have seen, in the 1950s, when the Common Market was set up, tariffs constituted the key barrier to trade. By the 1970s, non-tariff barriers had become much more significant than tariffs as impediments to trade.

The most common forms of non-tariff barriers included subsidies and tax breaks for a state's own producers, procurement policies on behalf of state agencies favouring national producers, national technical and safety specifications that often barred imports, and regulations for checking imports at frontiers. All such measures were trade-distorting, even though formally they usually had nothing directly to do with trade.

Over the past two decades, non-tariff measures have proved to be extremely hardy creatures. As quickly as states hunted them down through mutual agreements, they mutated, taking new and resistant forms. The reason for successful mutation was that states, which played a much greater role in the economy than they did in the 1950s, were determined to hold on to as much economic activity within their own boundaries as they could.

To some extent non-tariff barriers were in the eye of the beholder. One person's industrial strategy was another person's non-tariff barrier. The nation-states that made up the EC still saw economic development in national terms. The measures they took to enhance and protect economic activity at home unavoidably placed barriers in the path of economic integration with their EC partners. The EC was like the proverbial bicycle. If it did not keep going forward, it risked falling over.

At the same time as non-tariff barriers were threatening the degree of integration already achieved among European states, Europe was up against a rising external threat, particularly in the vastly important high-technology industries, where Japan and the United States enjoyed a significant lead. Having achieved an overall economic growth rate twice that of the United States during the first fifteen years after the launching of the Common Market, Europe was in the doldrums, particularly prey to long-term unemployment among its young. Playing in the same economic league as the Americans and the Japanese, hence completing the single market, became increasingly attractive. It was at this point that the particular genius of the leadership at the Berlaymont in Brussels had its telling effect.

In 1985, the moment when a bold initiative became politically possible, the EC was blessed with the inspired leadership of Jacques Delors, who had just been appointed president of the European Commission. Delors was that most unlikely of combinations, an intellectual and author who was also a very tough-minded economic manager, and who was given credit by almost everyone for charting France's economic course out of the shoals into which it had been steered by the original Mitterrand program of 1981. No one has ever accused Delors of being chummy or congenial with his socialist comrades. An impatient visionary, much more intellectual than most politicians, devoted to his own agenda, Delors is now universally known as "Mr. Europe." Reappointed to the commission for a second term, which began in 1989, Delors has remained in charge of what amounts to Europe's first real cabinet.

It is not that the world has never seen Delors before. For a long time it simply failed to recognize him. To illustrate, consider the official photograph that is taken each year at the annual economic summit of the seven major industrial powers. In the photograph, seven of the faces are well known: the presidents of the United States and France, the chancellor of West Germany and the prime ministers of Japan, Britain, Italy, and Canada. The eighth face is that of Jacques Delors. He has participated in the meetings in recent years with little attendant publicity. In fact, he appears destined to have more to do with reshaping the world of the 1990s than almost any of the others. Delors is religious, intensely cerebral, full of energy that is matched by a sense of human tragedy and perspective — highly unusual attributes in so public a man. One senior British trade-union official told me that Delors always clung to his own ideas whether they were popular or not, and that, in the end, when historic opportunity knocked, he knew what he wanted to do.

If Jacques Delors was well suited to steer the EC through the historic transformation of the move to the single market, he was ideally complemented by fellow commissioner Lord Cockfield, the British Tory appointee of Margaret Thatcher, who supplied the practical genius and indomitable energy to make "1992" a success. Although the goal of the single market had existed ever since the formation of the European Economic Community, the real launch of what became the "1992" program was at a meeting outside Paris on December 7, 1984, when Delors and Cockfield agreed broadly on how the single market was to be achieved.

Cockfield is a bulldog of a man. Short, but with a large upper body, he is pugnacious. He possesses that truly rare combination of qualities: the clarity and drive, precision, and directedness of the businessman, but allied with the vision of the statesman, understanding that the world does not consist of markets alone, and, rarest of all for an Englishman, appreciating that there is intelligent life beyond the Channel.

Still, Cockfield is the very embodiment of the English establishment. He took his first important post with the Inland Revenue in 1944. Later in his career, he was chief executive officer of Boots. He has been a lifelong Tory, an intimate of the power-brokers in the party for decades. He comes from the wing of the party known as the "wets," those who, while believing in the efficacy of the market, also advocate compassionate government through extensive social policies, a conviction that sets them apart from the Thatcherites. Cockfield was close to Ted Heath in the late 1960s, and played a role in the move that brought Britain into the EC in 1973. He entered the Thatcher government, first, in the treasury, later, in a cabinet position, as secretary of state for Trade. He was, therefore, actively involved in

European affairs throughout the period that preceded his appointment to the EC Commission.

When I interviewed him in the summer of 1990 in his office in the City of London, overlooking the Thames, Lord Cockfield had been out of the commission for a year and a half, not reappointed to his post by Margaret Thatcher, who was furious with him for having devoted himself to a transformation of Europe that would move much more power from the EC's nation-states to its centre. From the very start of their collaboration, as Lord Cockfield told me, he worked very well with Delors, who gave him his complete support. Delors and Cockfield realized that the program had to be both sweeping in its approach and very specific in its details and timetable. "Before I went to Brussels, I realized there was one way to go," Lord Cockfield observed. "My approach was to do the whole job. I knew from my experience in industry that the whole job had to be drawn up and then put in a time frame. I decided on the actual date for the program. Delors was thinking of January 1, 1992. I wanted December 31, 1992. That would give us the lifetime of two commissions. There was no way it could be done in four years in the life of one commission. And three commissions would have been hopeless because, during the first four years, nothing would have been done. Later commissions would have blamed their predecessors for handing down a mess."

The breadth of Cockfield's vision of Europe is evident in the way he sums up his goals: "I've always said the United States has had three great advantages: a single market; a single currency; and a single language. I said I would give them [the EC] a single market by 1993, a single currency by the turn of the century, but that I couldn't do anything about a single language." Then, in an aside: "There's a single language and it's English."

In characteristic form, Cockfield told his staff: "If we don't do the job, the first to be crucified will be ourselves." They then went away to carry out his orders, drafting a list of reforms whose wholesale adoption would result in the completion of the single market. When this task was completed, Lord Cockfield had in his hands a list of three hundred reforms. The 1992 target, to become the motto of the program, was first bruited to the public in a speech by Jacques Delors before the European Parliament on January 14, 1985.[7]

While it has often been observed that Delors and Cockfield were an "odd couple," what appears to have bound them together in their history-making venture was that each of them was solidly "his own man." In later years, Cockfield would have warm feelings for the socialist Delors, the man he credits with masterminding the successful U-turn in France's economy during his time as finance minister. "It is not France which is now the weak man of Europe with a currency no one trusts," remarked Cockfield in another critical aside regarding Thatcher's policies. When I put it to him that it was noteworthy that he could work so well with a socialist such as Delors, he replied: "He's not all that different from people like Rab Butler or Geoffrey Howe, in the centre of the Conservative party. He recognizes that all governments have a social duty as well as economic responsibility."

Both Delors and Cockfield were committed to the idea of a sound monetary policy and the need for social programs, and neither of them had any use for nationalization of industry. Beyond this philosophical compatibility, there was something more, in the personal dimension of the relationship. Cockfield told me: "At the end of the day, Delors trusted me to run the program. There was a bond between us. These things are important. He knew I would never do anything he did not agree with, without consulting him."

The formal political request for the program to complete the internal market came from the European Council in Brussels in March 1985. The initiative for it had come from Delors, who had determined that it was the major step towards European union that would command the broadest political and public support throughout the community. The approach taken by Lord Cockfield in 1985 turned out to contain a touch of genius. Had the European Commission come up with a prioritized list of twenty-five reforms, failure would have been virtually inevitable, as each member country fought for projects giving advantage over its neighbours. Instead, because the list was so lengthy, dealt with such a range of subjects, and was unprioritized, its breath-taking character had the effect of sweeping away immediate parochial doubts. The idea was so large that it initially made it difficult for national governments and their bureaucrats to define their own ground so that they could fight the turf wars for which they were so renowned.

The program cobbled together by Lord Cockfield aimed at the removal of "physical," "technical," and "fiscal" barriers that stood in the way of the creation of the Single European Market. At the end of June 1985, the Cockfield program, the White Paper entitled "Completing the Internal Market,"[8] was presented to the European Council in Milan, where it was adopted. (Speaking about the authorship of the White Paper, Lord Cockfield told me: "I physically wrote much of the White Paper myself. That's why it's in English.") Despite opposition from Margaret Thatcher,[9] her government eventually went along with the notion of an intergovernmental conference to be held in the second half of 1985, winning the concession that the work would take the form of revisions to the existing treaty and not a new treaty. This matter was important to the British because a new treaty could be implemented by those accepting it, while leaving out those rejecting it, and thus give rise to the dreaded "two-speed" Europe. The Intergovernmental Conference was to result in the drafting of the Single European Act (SEA) with the agreement of all twelve EC members. When the SEA had been passed into law by each member country, it came into force in 1987. It amounted to the most significant addition to basic EC law since the signing of the founding treaties in 1951 and 1957.

The SEA amended the founding Treaty of Rome by writing the achievement of the Single European Market by the end of 1992 into the basic purposes of the EC in the following terms: "The Community shall adopt measures with the aim of progressively establishing the internal market over a period expiring on 31 December 1992. . . . The internal market shall comprise an area without internal frontiers in which the free movement of goods, persons, services and capital is ensured in accordance with the provisions of this Treaty."[10] To ease decision making for the creation of a Europe without frontiers, the SEA altered the rules within the EC so that in most cases concerning "1992" weighted majority voting replaced the need for unanimity. This major step in the direction of European federalism removed the problem of a single member state playing the role of spoiler and blocking the taking of decisions. (In a number of important fields — professional qualifications, labour relations, and taxation — unanimity remained the rule.)

1992: ANATOMY OF THE PROJECT

The idea behind "1992" is very simple. It is a program for the removal of the non-tariff barriers that stand between the EC and the achievement of the single market. Its aim is to transform the EC into one large economic space, occupied by nearly 340 million people, in which separate national markets will no longer exist. If the program is fully implemented, here are some of the things Europeans can look forward to:

- A business based in Denmark will have as easy access to the Italian market as a business based in Massachusetts has to the market in Georgia.
- Accountants and engineers, graduated from a university in any EC country, will be able to practise their professions anywhere they like within the community.
- A family in France will be able to set out in the family car for neighbouring Luxembourg, make all the purchases they like, and drive back home, not having to stop at the border, either on leaving their own country or on returning to it, and not having to make any declaration on the purchases they have made.
- A customer in Germany will be able to purchase baby clothes from a mail-order firm based in Britain with no need to make any declaration to German authorities.

Prior to "1992," none of these things was possible. Indeed, some of them seem unlikely to be fully realized by the date on which the single market is supposed to be in effect, January 1, 1993. Watching the progress of the EC as it proceeds towards these apparently simple, but, in reality, profoundly difficult reforms allows us to measure the extent to which "1992" has succeeded.

The rationale for the move to the single market is that European states have been burdening their common economy with useless frontier controls, bureaucratic red tape, missed business opportunities, and lost incentives to economic expansion. If these are removed, it is hoped that the EC will simultaneously create hundreds of thousands of new jobs, expand overall economic output, reward European consumers with lower prices, establish conditions in which governments can reduce their deficits, and make Europe more competitive vis-à-vis the United States and Japan. Based on this reasoning, the "1992" program as set out in Lord Cockfield's White Paper, aimed to overcome what have been called "the costs of non-Europe" through the removal of physical, fiscal, and technical barriers among EC states.

The most important physical barriers were the frontier controls between EC countries, which acted as sticking-points in the way of the free flow of commerce. Indeed, the removal of customs posts became a symbol of "1992." The ambitious goal was the complete elimination of customs formalities between EC countries by January 1, 1993. Thus would be established a "Europe without frontiers" through which people and commerce would have the right to pass without hindrance. Opening the internal frontiers was essential to the inner promise of "1992," the transformation of the economic relationship among the member states of the EC from one of privileged trading partners to one in which they shared a single "home market" from which they could project their fused economic power onto the global stage.

Technical barriers were the rules and regulations that differentiated one national economic arena from that of its neighbours. These barriers included professional qualifications, industrial specifications, safety rules, environmental safeguards — the whole myriad of standards that exist in any industrial society and are policed by industry associations and government departments. Crucial to the success of this aspect of the program was the complete freeing of capital flows within the EC and the elimination of remaining foreign-exchange controls. Thus, Europe would be given a single capital market to match its immense economic weight. A unified capital market erected on an economy with an annual output of $5 trillion would indeed be ready to compete on equal terms with the Americans and the Japanese. Figuring out how to transform the regulatory environment is the very heart of the "1992" program.

Fiscal barriers were the plethora of tax mountains and valleys across Europe that made the economic landscape anything but uniform. To achieve the Single European Market, this landscape would have to be altered so that commerce would not flow in capricious ways from one country to another. The goal was for a large degree of harmonization of tax regimes so that, for example, commerce would not rush from France with its high Value Added Tax (VAT), to Luxembourg, with its much lower VAT.

To give the overall drive towards the single market coherence, it has been essential for the EC to keep the benefits of the larger goal in mind while driving forward through the minutiae of the individual reforms in each of the three aspects of the program. Lord Cockfield was well aware of that need from the start. In 1986, at the outset of "1992," he decided to undertake a major study of the impact of the single market. He placed the chairmanship of this unique endeavour in the hands of Paolo Cecchini, a former commission deputy director general, who assembled a talented team. Over the next two years, the team carried out a massive research project, which included twenty-eight studies of specific sectors and problems and a survey of 11,000 firms. In addition, it deployed a macro-economic model to corroborate and enhance the results of the

sectoral studies and the survey. The final result in 1988 was the publication of the Cecchini Report, which gave the commission a powerful analytical tool and an effective propaganda weapon.

It should be kept in mind that "1992" is not a single grand event
that takes effect on an appointed day. It is not a "Big Bang" like the
deregulation of a financial market. It is a vast process, relying on the
drafting of close to three hundred reforms by the EC Commission,
which then go as directives (EC draft legislation) to the EC Parliament
for advice and suggested revision, to the EC Council for adoption, and
finally to the governments of the twelve member states to be passed
into national laws. "1992" is happening. It is like a tide, pushing
forward, brushing barriers out of its path, changing its course when
it confronts more difficult obstacles. Long before the day the Single
European Market is supposed to be complete, most of the reforms
will have been implemented.

DISMANTLING FRONTIERS

Frontiers are much more than economic barriers. They are crucial
control points that regulate the passage of people. They are, above
all, the most visible symbols of the sovereign state, marking off the
territory of one state from another. Throughout history, tribes,
empires, and nations have measured their effectiveness as sovereign
entities through their ability to maintain their territorial integrity
against their neighbours. Between potentially hostile states, borders
are heavily fortified, with watchtowers and guards patrolling the frontier itself, and, farther back, with military units ready to move into
action in the event of a hostile incursion. The most heavily milita-
rized frontier in the world in the era after the Second World War was
that between West and East Germany. No one could reach the mid-
point between the border posts, without reflecting on the fact that
this was the focal point of the Cold War, that on either side of this
frontier there were hundreds of thousands of NATO and Warsaw Pact
troops, fighter bases, and thousands of nuclear missiles poised to go
into action should an assault across this space be mounted.

If this border between the two Germanys, which symbolized an
age now past, was the most menacing, even the frontiers between
friendly adjoining states are very important divisions that mark off the
limits of one sovereign power from that of its neighbour. Frontier
posts are important tools in the kitbag of the sovereign state. In the
typical case, a large number of government departments exercise

authority at border-control points, which makes their elimination a highly complex affair. In the case of Britain, for example, eight government departments are directly concerned.[11] Typically, officials at border posts of EC countries collect taxes, the most important being Value Added Tax, excise duties, and EC levies. They also monitor whether citizens exceed the duty-free allowances they are permitted. They enforce import controls on some traded products as well as restrictions on the import of banned drugs, weapons, explosives, pornography, toxic waste, and certain categories of animals, plants, and food. Exports are also controlled to conform to restrictions on the sale of high-technology products to non-EC countries, to prevent the loss of art treasures defined as a part of the national heritage, and to block the shipping abroad of dangerous chemicals and particular classes of arms and weapons. Currency controls, in the process of being abolished by EC member states, have also been monitored at border points. Transport checks are carried out to inspect the safety of vehicles, to monitor the respecting of weight limits, and to ensure that drivers are not working excessive hours. Border points also control the passage of people, a much more politically sensitive matter than the monitoring of the shipment of goods. At frontiers, people are sorted into categories: citizens of EC countries, tourists, migrant workers, refugees, asylum seekers. In the most extreme cases, border points are used as one tool in the battle against criminals and terrorists.[12]

Because border-control points distinguish, in a tangible way, between that which is domestic and that which is foreign, their removal is a radical step that transforms the relationship between the peoples formerly divided by them. If you can simply drive your car or pedal your bicycle across the Rhine from Strasbourg in France into Germany without having to stop and speak to customs officials, the distinction between two exclusive states has been modified and a new common social space created. The new space becomes much like that encountered in crossing from one Canadian province to another.

For some EC countries, a psychological change, the extension of that which is domestic to that which was foreign, was precisely what was wanted. France, West Germany, the Netherlands, Belgium, and Luxembourg signalled their desire for such a change when their governments agreed to do away with border controls among themselves by January 1, 1990. Officials of these five of the six original members of the EC met at the small town of Schengen in Luxembourg in June 1985 and decided to proceed in advance of the EC as a whole. As in all of the important moves to closer European integration since the late 1940s, France and West Germany were the key partners around whom the other states took their positions.

The Schengen experience — in Euro-speak the five partners are referred to as the "Schengen countries" or "Schengenland" — has been instructive for the EC as a whole, highlighting the advantages of a move beyond frontiers, but also the nagging difficulties. To compensate for the loss of control at borders, governments have been tempted or pressured to increase state vigilance everywhere throughout their territories, not necessarily a trade-off all citizens would want to see being made. In addition, the removal of border controls raised the question of how much cooperation among national police forces would be necessary to prevent the easy flight of criminals from one state to another. Anyone who has seen a Hollywood film in which bandits race across the state line to shake the state troopers off their trail will understand this issue.

Several approaches have been considered, including the creation of a federal European police force — invariably referred to as a European "FBI," an idea floated by Helmut Kohl in 1988. The idea of "hot pursuit" raised thorny issues. If the police of France were in hot pursuit of a criminal who drove across the open frontier into Germany, should the French police be allowed to continue the chase into German territory? Should they be required to call on the German police to take over once the suspects crossed the line? The issue of "hot pursuit" was extremely sensitive since it raised questions in a highly public way about the desirability of merging sovereignty with neighbouring countries. To date, Luxembourg and France have been prepared to contemplate hot pursuit, while doubts continued to be expressed by the other partners. Likewise, the idea of a European FBI was still thought of as somewhat visionary.

The Schengen countries have had to face the fact that relaxing border controls among themselves necessarily means coordinating the mutual hardening of their common external frontier against the outside world. For Schengenland to function as a domestic space unto itself, the partners needed to agree on common policies regarding outsiders, sensitive matters in an age of refugees, migrant workers, and drug smuggling. [13]

As it turned out, the flood of East Germans into West Germany in the closing months of 1989 delayed the full removal of intra-Schengen border controls until July 1, 1990. When I drove across France, the Benelux countries, and West Germany in July 1990, there were no stops at all at any of the borders. Psychologically, an enormous step towards European union had been taken. When Italy joined the Schengen countries in the autumn of 1990, the original six members of the community had achieved the most visible aspect of the move to a Europe without frontiers. It remained for the national parliaments of the participating countries to ratify the Schengen convention so that the removal of border checks and the establishment of police and judicial cooperation would be enshrined in the legislation of each of the six countries.

While the Schengen countries have for decades been in the forefront of the movement towards European union, those on the periphery that have had more doubts about union have balked at the idea of such a radical assault on national frontiers. The key doubter has been Britain. No country in Europe values its separateness, both physical and spiritual, the way Britain does, the manifestation of that peculiar consciousness known only to island peoples.

It is no accident, therefore, that the issue of the removal of customs posts in the United Kingdom should be linked inexorably to the building of the railway tunnel under the English Channel to provide a land link between England and France. The Channel Tunnel, the "Chunnel," which is now under construction, is expected to be open for traffic in 1993. The Chunnel will give Britain a land frontier with the continent for the first time in its history. The volume of traffic through the Chunnel will be so enormous that the customs procedures that have traditionally greeted entrants to Britain, by far the slowest and most elaborate for any EC country, will simply become impractical.

The way the British approach the Channel Tunnel reflects their general view of the relationship they want to have with the continent. The Chunnel's advantages are evident. If a high-speed train bed is laid between Dover and London, a rail trip between London and Paris should take just a shade over two hours, a far cry from the present six-hour journey that involves a shift from train to boat to train. The experience of rapid train travel in France suggests that a high-speed Paris–London rail connection will compete effectively with airlines, and can relieve pressure on already massively overcrowded air-terminal facilities at both ends. Even more important, from an economic standpoint, the undersea line promises to become the most utilized rail connection in the world for the shipment of commercial products. It will increase the speed and reduce the cost of goods shipments between Britain and the continent, leading to investments on both sides of the Channel aimed at responding to the new demand that will thus develop. A land boom already exists in the French countryside adjacent to the Chunnel terminal. English residents, attracted by large tracts of relatively cheap land, are hoping to move here, and to commute across the Channel to work in London.

The Chunnel has convenience and economic logic in its favour. Against it are arrayed the formidable forces of history and national identity, most important the notion that Britain's strength has depended on its status as an impregnable island. While few people in Britain will look you in the face and claim that they fear a hostile military invasion through the Chunnel, almost anyone you encounter will warn you of an invasion of a different kind — the incursion into England of rabid animals from France. For centuries the English and French have traded epithets concerning disease on each other's territories, so much so that venereal disease was known in France as the "English disease" and in England as the "French disease." Understandably proud of the fact that their country is rabies-free, the British require that animals brought to the United Kingdom be quarantined for a period of six months, before being allowed to rejoin their owners. When people warn of the risk of rabies entering England through the Chunnel, they are contemplating the possibility that an infected dog, fox, or rat could enter the tunnel in France and successfully migrate through it to emerge at the other side in England, ready to infect animals there.

And yet, despite the unlikelihood, it is almost impossible to discuss the Chunnel with anyone in England without having it indicted for threatening to import rabies into the country. Even a world-wise English publisher, with a summer home in Tuscany, told me that, while he favoured the Chunnel on balance, he feared the arrival of rabies in England. "The sort of thing the English have been adept at avoiding in the past," as he put it. These encounters recall Shakespeare's lyrical evocation of England:

> *This other Eden, demi-paradise,*
> *This fortress built by Nature for herself*
> *Against infection and the hand of war,*
> *This happy breed of men, this little world,*
>
> . . .
>
> *This blessed plot, this earth, this realm, this England.*

Margaret Thatcher made it abundantly clear that the completion of the Chunnel would not mean the elimination of border controls for travellers from Paris to London. Indeed, this normally parsimonious prime minister decided to construct a brand-new, and expensive, customs post in London at the terminus of the new line, a post that Lord Cockfield told me was like a "great mausoleum, a gift from Thatcher which would ensure that whatever time is gained by the fast train will be soaked up by the enforcement agents." The customs post reflected the British prime minister's general attitude to border controls. She had no intention of duplicating what she regarded as Schengenland foolishness. In her celebrated speech to the College of Europe at Bruges, Belgium, in September 1988, now a manifesto for Britain's nationalist anti-Europeans, the British prime minister said she did not favour the elimination of border controls for intra-EC border crossings: "It is a matter of plain common sense that we cannot totally abolish frontier controls if we are also to protect our citizens from crime and stop the movement of drugs, of terrorists and of illegal immigrants." This statement, in clear violation of the Single European Act, to which Thatcher's government had agreed, was immediately pounced on by EC officials.

The efforts of the Schengen countries and the contrasting reticence of Margaret Thatcher revealed the range of attitudes within the community on the issue of border controls. Aware that the credibility of "1992" rested on the creation of a Europe "without internal frontiers," the EC Commission had no intention of giving up on the goal of the complete elimination of border controls. Experience, however, has now shown just how difficult the full achievement of that goal will be. In practice, numerous steps towards the goal will be taken. Already, the EC has greatly speeded up truck traffic through border points by the establishment of the Single Administrative Document (SAD), which went into effect on January 1, 1988. Other reforms that make up parts of the technical and fiscal aspects of "1992" will also automatically lessen the need for border controls. Agreement on the range of Value Added Taxes and on how to distribute them throughout the community, the ending of all limits on the right to import goods duty-free across intra-EC frontiers, and the lifting of controls on capital flows are all measures that will reduce the official functions presently performed at intra-EC border posts. On January 1, 1993, the day the Single European Market is supposed to be in full effect, the EC will have taken major steps towards the elimination of border controls. In Schengenland, the full program will almost certainly be implemented. Even Britain, under the pressure of the impending Chunnel link, will have vastly speeded up its border processing, going over, in many cases, to the use of spot checks, the system already standard at non-Schengen intra-EC border points on the continent. Greece and Denmark, which also have some doubts about the complete elimination of border controls, may end up somewhere between the Schengen option and the British position.

How much will Europeans save if intra-EC border procedures are eliminated? According to the Cecchini Report, each year firms pay about 8 billion Ecu* in administrative costs and delays as a consequence of intra-EC customs formalities. In addition to these direct costs, Cecchini estimated that additional business in the range of 4.5 billion to 15 billion Ecu has been forgone annually as a consequence of these procedures. Finally, Cecchini reckoned that taxpayers paid out between 500 million and 1 billion Ecu each year to finance the customs operations, which were themselves the road-blocks in the way of intra-EC trade.[14]

REMOVING TECHNICAL BARRIERS

If dismantling border controls will give Europe the appearance of a single domestic space, removing technical barriers to the full flow of commerce among EC member states is much more important to giving it substance. The very heart of the Cockfield program comes under the heading of the removal of technical barriers, comprising, as it does, the free movement of goods, unimpeded by differing national standards; public procurement; free movement of labour, including the right of professionals to practise their professions throughout the EC; free movement of capital; and establishment of a common legal framework for the resolution of thorny problems such as the disposition of intellectual property. It is as we enter this realm that we appreciate that border controls are the mere ramparts of the state. Here we approach the very web at the centre of the state.

Sometimes in the history of statecraft, apparently trivial matters can be the occasion for important developments. Such was the case

* The Ecu, the European Currency Unit, is determined by a weighted basket of national currencies. Even though banknotes and coins are not issued in it — except for a commemorative offering in Belgium — companies often deal in it, governments use it as a reserve currency, bonds are issued in it, and travellers' cheques are denominated in it. It is the predecessor to a full-fledged EC currency. In May 1991, 1 Ecu was worth $1.21 U.S.

when a bizarre episode concerning the right to market French black-currant liqueur in West Germany led to a decision on the part of the European Court of Justice that helped move the EC forward to a critical new concept for handling national regulations. The case arose out of the attempt of a West German company, Rewe Zentral AG, to import Cassis de Dijon into West Germany. The import was blocked as a consequence of a German law that prohibited the sale of liqueurs with an alcoholic content of less than 25 per cent. Because Cassis de Dijon had an alcoholic content of between 15 and 20 per cent, its export to West Germany was blocked. [15] In the celebrated Cassis de Dijon case in 1979, the European Court of Justice, which sits in Luxembourg and rules on cases of EC law, ruled that where a product (an alcoholic beverage or foodstuff) is lawfully sold in one member state, its sale cannot be barred in another member state, except on the grounds of risk to public health. In this curious case, which was to lead to an important commercial innovation, the government of the Federal Republic of Germany argued that liqueurs with a low alcoholic content were insidious to public health because they tended to promote alcoholism. The court ruled against this argument, stating that most liqueurs are diluted when they are consumed. Whatever one thinks of the merits of this rather odd argument, the court concluded that it is not valid for another member state to use a technical barrier or standard to block the import of a product from the first state unless the barrier is objectively necessary to achieve some important end, such as the protection of public health.

Such reasoning pointed the way to an innovation central to the "1992" program. Instead of attempting to "harmonize" the tens of thousands of technical requirements for products across the EC, the Cockfield program invoked an alternative principle — "mutual recognition." Mutual recognition meant that EC member states would accept one another's rules for the production of commodities when it came to imports, provided these rules could be shown not to harm the public welfare. Mutual recognition meant that, provided that essential requirements for safety and durability were met, the differences in standards between one country and another within the EC would no longer constitute a barrier to trade. Mutual recognition would not entirely replace harmonization, but it would have the advantage of speedily removing barriers to trade. Harmonization would be kept as a principle for the long term, for the establishment of common standards to allow Europe-wide production of commodities that would be competitive in the global marketplace. For this purpose, two bodies have been set up, the European Committee for Standardization and the European Committee for Electrotechnical Standardization.[16]

Costs to the EC economy as a consequence of conflicting standards in key industries have been very large, as the following estimates from the Cecchini Report indicate:

- In the telecom sector, usually regulated closely by publicly owned authorities, which also operate the systems, the annual cost was estimated at 4.8 billion Ecu.[17] Barriers in this sector, which is now so crucial to operations of an information-based economy, include the pricing of telecom equipment — telephones, telefax, telex machines, wires, cables, and switching equipment — at between 30 per cent and 100 per cent more than competitive world prices.[18] Customers are directly affected in other ways, for example, by incompatibility of systems from one EC country with those of another. A business person using a car telephone on a journey from Germany through Belgium to Britain would have to have three different systems installed.[19]

- In the automobile industry, a critical one for EC employment, and a strategic sector, not least because the EC market constitutes 40 per cent of the global market for autos, the annual cost of barriers was put at 2.6 billion Ecu.[20] Differing technical standards from one EC country to another lead to sub-optimal production runs in the industry, dividing what ought to be the world's largest market into a series of smaller ones. Here are a few examples of differing standards: in France, yellow headlights are required; in Germany, reclining driver's seats are mandatory; in Italy, side repeater flasher lights are compulsory.[21]

- In the foodstuffs sector, the cost of barriers was estimated at between 500 million and 1 billion Ecu per year.[22] Germany's notorious beer-purity law keeps imports of beer into that country down to 1 per cent of the market, while protecting the 1,200 German brewers, three-quarters of the EC total, from outside competition.[23] Similarly a pasta-purity law in Italy helps keep competitors out of that country's pasta market.[24]

Overlapping in some important cases, particularly telecoms, with the technical barriers that stood in the way of a single market for key industries has been the major problem of public procurement.

The problem was very easy to define and very difficult to resolve. Governments in all modern industrial societies are by far the biggest spenders on goods and services. All of them make use of public-sector spending to help steer the market, even if, in theory, they do no such thing. In the countries that are the main competitors of the EC — the United States and Japan — government procurement has been utilized as an element in industrial policies, both acknowledged and unacknowledged, for the support of strategic national industries. In the case of the United States, the most notorious example is the defence budget, which is used on a massive scale to underwrite American industry, research, and development, and strategic high-technology sectors. In Japan, the Ministry of International Trade and Industry (MITI) has quarterbacked the effort of Japanese industry to achieve international competitiveness.

The Cecchini Report estimated that, in 1986, total purchasing by all levels of government within EC countries, including government agencies and enterprises, amounted to 530 billion Ecu, equal to 15 per cent of the total GDP of the community, an amount that exceeded the total value of intra-EC trade, which was valued at 500 billion Ecu. [25] While the report reckoned that much of this total comprised purchases that were necessarily local, often made in small amounts, none the less, it concluded that between 240 and 340 billion Ecu, 7 to 10 per cent of EC GDP, constituted public purchases capable of being made through open, public competition in the awarding of contracts. For this huge portion of public purchases where, in principle, contracts could go to companies from across the EC, the shocking conclusion of the report was that only 0.14 per cent of GDP was represented by such awarding of contracts, in which a public authority in one EC country made a purchase from an entity based in another EC country. [26] The importance of prying open the door of public purchases to make them an EC affair rather than the preserve of national fiefdoms was fully recognized in the Cockfield White Paper. [27]

The Cecchini Report concluded that enormous savings would be realized by the greater efficiencies that would result from the removal of the barriers to EC-wide purchasing by public-sector entities. For the five countries surveyed by Cecchini — Belgium, France, West Germany, Italy, and Britain — potential annual savings were estimated at between 8 and 19 billion Ecu. A very large "static trade effect" would be realized simply by having public entities purchase from the cheapest suppliers (within the EC), leading to savings put at between 3 and 8 billion Ecu per year. A further "competition effect" would flow from the downward pressure on prices as domestic firms responded to new EC-wide competition, a saving put at between 1 and 3 billion Ecu a year. In addition, a "restructuring effect" would result in the longer term from the achievement of improved economies of scale as a consequence of industrial reorganization (mergers, take-overs, consolidation) that would be prompted by making public procurement a truly EC-wide affair. A further benefit would be the lower prices private-sector buyers would pay for goods whose prices had been driven down as a consequence of the elimination of the restrictive trade practices of the public sector. Opening up public procurement would also have a long-term dynamic tendency to promote innovation, investment, and general economic growth. [28]

To achieve the goal of opening up public procurement, the EC Commission has developed proposals to close down loopholes in existing EC rules for the awarding of public contracts; give firms legal redress to challenge public authorities for failure to comply with the new rules; extend open awards procedures to critical sectors formerly excluded from them — energy, transport, telecommunications, and water supply. [29] The Cecchini Report holds out the carrot of spectacular potential price savings for important products as a consequence of all of the combined effects of opening up public procurement. Here are some examples:

- pharmaceuticals — 52 per cent price saving in Germany; 40 per cent in Britain;
- telephones — 20 per cent price saving in Belgium; 43 per cent in France; 39 per cent in Germany;
- automobiles (weighted average) — 13 per cent price saving in France; 4 per cent in Germany; 10 per cent in Italy; 9 per cent in Britain. [30]

If opening up public procurement involves reform at the heart of the state apparatus of a kind that is often not highly visible to the public, the next technical barrier to be assaulted is extremely visible — removing impediments to the right of citizens of EC countries to work anywhere they like in the community, and, in the case of professionals, to practise their professions. As in other parts of the "1992" program, this is not new ground for the community, but rather the completion of a process begun when the EEC was established.

A large degree of labour mobility had already been achieved by the mid-1980s. Lord Cockfield's White Paper pointed out that the right of citizens of one EC state to seek employment in another EC state was broadly established and that rulings of the Court of Justice had restricted the right of public authorities in EC countries to reserve posts for their own nationals. Even in this area, however, theory and practice often diverge. In the area of the south of France where I was living, friends told me that, if you were a foreigner from another EC country, the local rule was that to acquire a Carte de Séjour (a card giving you the right to live and work in France), you had to provide proof that you had a job. The problem was that, to get a job, you had to show your prospective employer your Carte de Séjour. Catch-22. It turned out that ingenuity usually helped you to overcome this apparently insoluble dilemma, not to mention the fact that French bureaucracy is usually much more forbidding theoretically than in practice, particularly in rural areas where rules are often ignored in the interests of practicality. The ideal, though, of universal, even-handed treatment of citizens of other EC countries by national author-ities has yet to be achieved. Members of the European Parliament have told me that they receive appeals for assistance from constituents who are not treated as they should be under EC law when it comes to working in another EC country. Glyn Ford, leader of the British Labour Group in the European Parliament, said that, in such cases, he writes on behalf of the complainant to the national government in question or, if necessary, to the EC Commission. Usually he has found such intervention effective.

Some of the problems encountered in the field of labour mobil-ity are clearly cultural in the sense that, in some countries, there is great hesitation about accepting the public practices that prevail in other EC member states. A conversation I had with an upper-class English intellectual who serves on the board of the British Museum underlined this point for me. Under EC law, the museum has no right to refuse to consider applications for employment from citizens of any EC member country. By the end of the "1992" process, any loopholes under which the museum might have sheltered in the past will plainly be gone. And yet, the hesitation remains. The board member told me that the British Museum has invaluable treasures, highly attractive targets for thieves. He put the problem bluntly: the museum would be loath to trust police files from across the EC since it is well known that governments such as those of Greece and Italy are riddled with corrupt officials and shoddy police records. How could you then trust such records when it came to vetting employee applications? Here the concern expressed was not about professional qualifications — the museum board member was delighted at the prospect of recruiting distinguished Greek and Italian scholars — it had to do with lower-level employees, the sphere in which the EC has, in principle, made the greatest progress in eliminating discrimination.

While the general right to work across the EC has already been established and is being steadily improved through rulings of the European Court of Justice, the area where important steps remain to be taken has to do with professional qualifications. Here the approach of the White Paper and of the EC Commission has been similar to that developed to deal with technical standards for products, where the principle of mutual recognition, rather than that of standardization, has proven so useful. The idea is that EC countries should recognize one another's university degrees and professional standards, with the result that professionals will have the right to work throughout the EC. In some cases, they will have to sit examinations to be allowed to practise in other EC countries. In principle, doctors, dentists, midwives, lawyers, architects, and pharmacists can already move freely from country to country within the EC to work.

Of immense importance to "1992" and also included under the heading of the removal of technical barriers, is the achievement of a single market across the EC for services, the most important of which is financial services. The EC, like the other industrialized parts of the world, has become a services-based economy. Services employ a majority of the European work-force and account for more of the EC's GDP than does manufacturing. Free trade in services was guaranteed in the Treaty of Rome, and yet a formidable range of barriers has stood between that aspiration and reality. In the process of European self-examination that preceded the single-market program, a central conclusion was that the EC would remain enfeebled in its competition with the United States and Japan as long as its financial-services market was divided among insufficiently large national components. The Cecchini Report estimated on the basis of a projection made from the cases of the eight countries studied — France, West Germany, Italy, Spain, Britain, and the Benelux countries — that gains resulting from integration of the three main areas of financial-services activity — banking and credit, insurance, and brokerage and securities — would be 22 billion Ecu for the EC.[31]

Citing the Cassis de Dijon case, the Cockfield White Paper attacked the problem of barriers in financial services by asserting the principle of mutual recognition, the notion that EC countries should accept one another's standards as the basis for allowing a cross-Europe exchange of "financial products." [32] Without the single market for these products, as the Cecchini Report revealed, there has been a shocking range of price differences in the community. Here are some examples of how much consumers have been charged in excess of a standard "money-market rate" already achieved in parts of the EC:

- In Germany, for a 500 Ecu consumer loan, customers have been charged an annual interest rate 136 per cent above the money-market rate.
- In Spain, based on a mortgage of 25,000 Ecu, the consumer paid an annual interest rate 118 per cent in excess of the money-market rate.
- In Belgium, the customer's cost for term life insurance was 78 per cent above the money-market rate. [33]

Moving towards an integrated market for services, particularly financial services, was linked to the removal of another key barrier: of the capital controls exercised by a number of EC states. The EC has taken substantial steps in this direction already. Britain and Denmark have removed exchange controls, while the Federal Republic of Germany and the Benelux countries permit the free movement of capital, merely retaining reporting and authorization procedures for some transactions. France and Italy have been dismantling their exchange controls, leaving Spain, Portugal, Greece, and Ireland operating with strict controls. To ensure the complete removal of barriers on the movement of capital as a part of the "1992" program, the EC Commission has adopted a strategy whose purpose is to see all remaining barriers removed by January 1, 1993.

Rounding out the "1992" program's assault on technical barriers are a number of other matters: the creation of a legal framework to facilitate EC-wide economic activity; the question of intellectual property; and the establishment of an EC set of rules to deal with competition policy and state aids to industry.

One of the key requirements for the smooth operation of business across the EC is the drafting of a statute for the incorporation of European companies. This area is thorny; much disagreement exists among member states, because the question of which model to follow in drafting the statute raises questions about the relationship between labour and management in the running of enterprises. Christian Democratic notions of worker participation in the management of corporations are anathema to British conservatives, and French socialists have their own ideas about how a company statute should be set up. The approach the EC Commission has taken has been to suggest that three possible models be established, allowing a European company to be incorporated under any one of them. The hope here is that this approach will prevent the whole idea of a European company statute from foundering as a consequence of ideological incompatibility.

In the area of intellectual property, a field being transformed and made more complex by technological revolution, the goal is to achieve agreement on the creation of an EC trademark, EC patents, and EC copyright.

REMOVING FISCAL BARRIERS

If much of the substance of "1992" is to be found under the heading of the removal of technical barriers, the third segment of the program, dealing with the removal of fiscal barriers, also covers important and difficult ground. Since the overall goal of the single market is to establish a European economic space in which access for business to the marketplace and the conditions under which business is conducted is reasonably uniform, the vexing subject of the tax regimes of EC countries necessarily comes into the equation. If the EC's twelve national tax systems differ significantly, the result will be that capital will flow capriciously from one country to another, upsetting the goals of the single market program and, indeed, threatening its survival. Despite this point, about which the EC Commission has no illusions, no subject threatens sensitivities about the erosion of sovereignty in national states more than the notion of coordinating tax regimes across the EC. Taxation is the most ancient prerogative of government. In many cases, democratic institutions themselves have evolved around the issue of who is to be taxed and by how much, and on what the money is to be spent. Needless to say, national governments and parliaments are extremely leery of having the EC tread too heavily on this sensitive terrain, and have run tax regimes that have bedevilled the workings of a supposedly "common market."

A telling illustration of this truth came home to a large group of Socialist members of the European Parliament in 1984, when their caucus decided to travel across the Rhine from Strasbourg, where they had been meeting in a parliamentary session, to Kehl. The social outing, whose purpose was dinner, turned out to be a lesson on the costs of "non-Europe." When the buses in which they were riding reached the German frontier post just across the Rhine, they were stopped by officials who announced that they intended to check the amount of fuel in each of the buses, which happened to be registered with a French bus company. It was the intention of the officials later to be able to collect the amount of Value Added Tax owing on the fuel consumed. Willy Brandt, former West German chancellor, climbed down from the bus he was riding in to speak to the customs officials, who, of course, immediately recognized him. Try as he might, however, he could not talk them out of the time-consuming, bureau-cratic exercise they had undertaken. "We realized then that something had to be done," Marijke Van Hemeldonck, the Socialist member of the EP for Antwerp, Belgium, told me, in recounting the story.

Doing something meant, for the EC, avoiding intruding directly into the tax territory of national governments. It meant becoming involved in tax matters almost entirely in the field of indirect taxation — customs duties (collected from imports from outside the EC), Value Added Tax, and excise duties (collected on products such as tobacco, alcohol, and gasoline).[34] It meant working on the levels of indirect taxes levied and on the creation of a system for allocating tax collected to the appropriate EC state in such a way that absurd incidents like the adventure of the delayed dinner, recounted above, would not recur.

In approaching the problem of how to prevent uneven indirect tax rates from subverting the single market, Lord Cockfield's model was the United States, where state governments levy their own sales taxes. The American model was reassuring because, while the sales-tax levels varied from state to state, the variation was seldom so much that it promoted the purchase of commodities across state lines.

When the authors of the Cockfield White Paper looked at the problem, they concluded that, in the field of indirect taxation, thorny difficulties stood in the path of achieving a regime across the EC that would not result in trade-distorting effects. The White Paper first examined the overall take from country to country from the VAT and excises. In 1982, the average take within the EC for these two items was 10.68 per cent of GDP. Most countries were not too far from the average, with the exception of Denmark, where the take was 15.71 per cent of GDP, and Ireland, where the percentage was 17.13.[35] However, while the average VAT yield per member state was 7.05 per cent of GDP, there was a significant range of yields among them, from

Britain at the low end, with 5.22 per cent of GDP collected, to France at the high end, at 9.19 per cent of GDP. Adding to the difficulty in any attempt to lessen differences among rates was the fact that VAT was collected in quite different ways from state to state. While Britain had only a single VAT rate of 17.5 per cent, and applied a zero rate to a wide range of goods and services, France had three sets of rates — a standard rate of 18.6 per cent, a higher rate at 33.3 per cent for so-called luxury goods, and two lower rates at 5.5 and 7 per cent. Italy also had three sets of rates, with its high rate at 38 per cent. A number of countries had two sets of rates, a standard and a lower rate.[36] When one examines these differing sets of rates, the problem becomes obvious. France charges its high rate, 33.3 percent, for cars. For neighbouring Luxembourg, the rate for the purchase of a car is only 12 per cent. While consumers will not travel far to save a few VAT points on a relatively inexpensive item, they will certainly travel far to save thousands of Ecu on the purchase of a new car. (If a French citizen could travel to Luxembourg to buy a Renault 21, at a price of approximately 11,000 Ecu, he or she would pay a VAT in France of over 3,600 Ecu, but, in Luxembourg, would pay only 1,320 Ecu, a differential that would definitely entice French citizens to travel major distances to buy their cars across the border. Autos, as we will see in a later chapter, are to be treated differently from other products in the move to the single market.)

If the case of autos illustrates the difficulties most dramatically, other sectors present serious problems as well. One of them is the sale of books. In Britain, books have had a zero VAT rate, which, naturally enough, British publishers have been determined to keep. This situation ran smack up against the starting position of the commission, which was to favour a reform of VAT rates so that the high rate would be eliminated, an agreed-upon range for a standard rate would be set up, and a low rate for a specified list of products would be established. Initially, there was little sympathy in the commission for the idea that, in some cases, such as books, there could be a VAT rate of zero. As she campaigned towards her third electoral victory in Britain in 1987, Margaret Thatcher pledged that she would "veto" any attempt by the commission to prevent zero rating by Britain,[37] a position that, predictably, was popular in Britain and presented the commission with a serious political difficulty.

After two years with little progress on the VAT issue, a more flexible proposal was put forward by Christiane Scrivener, a new French commissioner. The proposal was that there be a standard rate band for the VAT (between 14 and 20 per cent); a reduced band (4 to 9 per cent), with the right of countries to have a specified, and short, list of essential items at zero; and, in addition, the right to a high rate as well.[38] In practice, the Scrivener proposal meant that the commission was coming to see that the real weapon for driving rates closer together was the market itself, rather than a fiat from Brussels. If countries insisted on maintaining an excessively high VAT rate for some commodities, they would simply motivate their citizens to travel to neighbouring countries to make their purchases there. Countries like France, which have relied on VAT much more than have their neighbours, will be forced to undertake tax reform as a consequence. While the British income tax ends up collecting about 13 per cent of GDP, the French income tax nets only about 8 per cent.[39] Downward pressure on the high French VAT rate will doubtless result in upward pressure on French income tax rates, something that the French, notoriously resistant to income tax, will not find to their liking. In June 1991, it appeared that further progress was being made on the VAT issue when all EC finance ministers, with the exception of Britain's chancellor of the exchequer, agreed that beginning on January 1, 1993, there should be a minimum standard VAT rate of 15 per cent.[40]

In addition to reworking VAT rates, the EC has been challenged by the problem of how to allocate the VAT owing from state to state throughout the community. At present, countries allow a zero VAT rating on products exported to other EC states. They then refund to producers the VAT paid on each stage of production up until the point of export. The importing country then collects VAT at the border on the incoming product, and an additional sum when it is sold to the consumer. To move over to the new single-market system, zero rating will have to be abolished. Instead, VAT will be collected on each stage of production and will have to be allocated to the proper national authorities. To understand this, it must be realized that a VAT is not a sales tax, but a tax imposed on each stage in which value is added to a good or a service. Once zero rating for exports is abolished, it will be necessary to ensure that the right amount of tax ends up in the right coffers. The EC Commission has proposed a clearing system to achieve this goal, so that member states will figure out how much they owe one another at the end of each year. While, in an age of powerful computers, working out the sums will not be hard, such a system does require what technology cannot provide — honesty and mutual trust.

Progress on VAT has been slow, and many experts believe that a satisfactory arrangement will not be in place by the end of 1992. In the long term, agreement is expected, but it will likely not bring about as close an approximation of VAT rates as Lord Cockfield had initially wanted. The same is probably true of excise duties.

THE PROMISE OF "1992"

From this summary of the "1992" program, it is evident that its success depends not on any one overriding measure, but on the implementation of hundreds of measures, which, taken in combination, result in a commercial revolution. In spite of the dry technical terms, however, it is a gigantic gamble, the greatest in economic history, on the veracity of one notion, that the pooling of a series of smaller markets into one giant market is a formula for guaranteed economic success. If barriers can be removed, through a sustained, collective act of political will, the costs of "non-Europe" can be eliminated.

Underlying "1992" is a liberal faith in the efficacy of a market economy to deliver economic benefits. At the heart of it lies a great paradox. "1992" is the most ambitious attempt in the history of capitalism to launch a vast, open-market economy, as a consequence not of long, historical evolution but of political will. At the same time, the EC is laying the base not only for the world's largest single market, but also for a new global state, a state that, as we will see in a later chapter, may well have the power to control and direct the immense market so critical to its creation.

The Cecchini Report, like "1992" itself, despite all the research on which it is based, is also finally anchored on the theory of the efficacy of the single market to deliver economic gains. It reckons that, when all of the static and dynamic gains from the creation of the single market are totalled, the EC should stand to gain more than 200 billion Ecu in annual economic output if the "1992" program is fully implemented, lifting it onto a "higher plane of overall performance."[41]

According to the report, the achievement of the single market will produce the following immense gains for the EC economy over the medium term:

- trigger a major relaunch of economic activity, adding on average 4.5 per cent to EC GDP;
- simultaneously cool the economy, deflating consumer prices by an average of 6.1 per cent;
- relax budgetary and external constraints, improving the balance of public finances by an average equivalent to 2.2 per

cent of GDP and boosting the EC's external position by around
1 per cent of GDP;

- boost employment, creating 1.8 million new jobs, although
  unable of itself to make big inroads into the present stock of
  unemployment, the effect would none the less be to reduce
  the jobless rate by around 1.5 percentage points. [42]

These are extremely optimistic forecasts, predicting a significant
improvement in virtually every major realm of economic life. The
optimism does not end here. The report concludes that the completion of "1992" will give European policy makers greater room to
manoeuvre in seeking beneficial trade-offs between inflation, on the
one hand, and economic growth and job creation, on the other. If
this freedom of manoeuvre is utilized, through income-tax cuts and
increased public investment, among other things, then the EC countries can achieve even more favourable results. The Cecchini predic-
tion is that full use of this policy freedom would mean that, in the
medium term, the EC GDP would grow by 7 per cent, and that 5
million new jobs would be created.

Naturally, the optimistic forecasts in the Cecchini Report have
engendered some inevitable scepticism. The world has seen too many
one-sided forecasts in the past for such optimism simply to go unchallenged. Anyone who doubts that the experts can be wildly wrong is
invited to leaf through national or international forecasts for economic performance over the past couple of decades for a quick dash
of sobriety.

One widely voiced criticism of the Cecchini conclusions is
that the creation of the single market will necessarily involve vast dislocation as weaker firms, hitherto sheltered by national barriers, are
driven out of business or are taken over by the strong, with the shutting down of numerous production facilities and the loss of an
immense number of jobs. Sir John Harvey-Jones, former chairman
of the British-based ICI conglomerate, has said that he expects more
than half of Europe's plants to be closed over the next decade as a
consequence of rationalization. [43] Even the optimistic Cecchini
Report itself does not predict a pain-free process. The very large
gains it points to are to develop in the medium term. In the first year
of the process, the Cecchini Report forecasts a net loss of as many
as half a million jobs, as a consequence of the shutting down of the
operations of border posts (customs officials, etc.), the rationalization
of financial services across the EC, capital investments resulting in the

shedding of labour, and the rationalization of firms. However, it expects net gains in employment during the second year, and more after that. [44] Another concern often raised has been that "1992" will create a wealthy inner Europe surrounded by a much poorer outer Europe. The theory is that investment will stream towards the EC heartland — Paris and northeastern France; much of Germany, London, and the English southeast; parts of the Benelux countries and northern Italy. It will be in this privileged heartland, it is feared, that most of the best jobs will be created. The periphery, however, including most of the Mediterranean, western France, Ireland, northern England, Wales, and Scotland, will be left with high unemployment and deindustrialization. When I spoke to Bryan Gould, the British Labour Party's spokesman on trade and industry in September 1989, he gave strong voice to these concerns. Gould, who was born in New Zealand and who is often described by members of his own party as anti-EC, told me: "When we first joined the Common Market, everyone thought things would be wonderful, but, at first, British industry lost very substantially. In the present circumstances, large parts of British industry will be fighting for its life."

Those who doubt the risk of economic concentration at the centre point to the very strong economic record of Spain in the last few years, during which the Iberian country has had the most rapid rate of economic growth in the EC. Spanish growth, the doubters respond, is a consequence of attracting low-wage jobs from elsewhere in Europe, along with a sustained tourism boom. In the case of investment being drawn to Spain by cheap labour, the doubters fear the risk of "social dumping," the flight of business from high-wage centres, where strong social benefits exist, to low-wage centres, where social benefits are much less developed.

What is striking in the debate is not the presence of these doubts and criticisms, but how muted they have been. To an overwhelming degree, the logic of the Cockfield White Paper and the approach of the Cecchini Report have been accepted in Europe. The immense appeal of "1992" is revealed in the wide range of political support the program has received. Rich and poor countries, large and small, northern and southern, politicians from the moderate left to the moderate right, industrialists, bankers, and most trade unionists have lined up on the side of the Single European Market. Of immense significance, business, both European and global, has bought the idea of "1992," assumes that it is going to succeed, and is carrying out its own changes in marketing strategies and investments, as well as in mergers, acquisitions, and corporate alliances that have already gone a long way to making the single market a reality, even in advance of the completion of the program itself.

For the wide acceptance of "1992," while the genius of Delors and Cockfield is to be praised, the economic threat posed by the Americans, and especially the Japanese, has been the critical factor in driving such diverse people to seek shelter under the same tent. It seems that every political leader, business person, trade unionist, and regional spokesman has his or her own "1992." What this reflects is the conviction that the single market is a necessity, that only as "Europeans" can the citizens of the EC countries compete successfuly with the Americans and the Japanese. François Mitterrand, who has played a pivotal role in supporting "1992" and in giving this fundamentally capitalist program the adhesion of the left, put it succinctly: "Only the European dimension . . . can ensure competitiveness with Japan and the U.S. Only Europe can stand up to the other powers that dominate the world."[45] Even the British Trades Union Congress (TUC), once a hotbed of anti–Common Market sentiment, has come on board as a supporter of "1992," although it does not endorse every aspect of the program. When I met with David Lea, assistant general secretary of the TUC at its headquarters in central London, he reflected on the change: "The world has shrunk, so we just can't look inward. Everything doesn't finish at the White Cliffs of Dover. Now we're thinking European."

If the coalition for "1992" is surpisingly broad, within it there is passionate disagreement about the kind of Europe that ultimately is wanted. This is so because "1992" opens the door to a number of quite different possible futures. The single market can be seen as an end in itself, a tighter commercial union that does not lead to further economic and monetary union and does not challenge the political supremacy of the European nation-states. Alternatively, it can lead to complete economic union, including the establishment of a European central bank and common currency. Beyond Economic and Monetary Union (EMU), "1992" can open the door to political union, to the establishment of a full-fledged federal Europe — a "United States of Europe" — in which the European Parliament takes over many of the powers now wielded by national parliaments, and in which, one day, there may be an elected president of Europe.

Chapter Four

EUROPEANS:
ARE THERE ANY?

★ ★ ★ ★ ★ ★ ★ ★ ★ ★ ★

FRANK DESDEMAINES-HUGON IS AN ARTIST WHO LIVES IN the Périgord, a languorous region in the southwest of France where the shallow Dordogne River meanders through a verdant, hilly countryside of tall trees and chalk cliffs, past castles and ancient forts perched on high points, giving them a hawk's outlook over the valleys below. For Desdemaines-Hugon, this unique *paysage* is central to his career as an experimental "land artist," where his work integrates the land itself into his artistic statements. Deploying such homely industrial products as chicken wire in brightly coloured coils, he creates effects in which kaleidoscopes of light splash across a small pond or wooded area. These works can be photographed or visited. With his wife, Christine, who is of English origin and who is an expert on the prehistoric cave art of the Périgord, Desdemaines-Hugon lives in a traditional stone house that has been renovated to open it up for the admission of sunlight, normally not found in the fortress-like houses of the region.

A quiet man who is passionate about his art but who enjoys isolation, Desdemaines-Hugon owns a large parcel of land, on which he permits no hunting, an edict that has gotten him into considerable difficulty with many of his neighbours, engendering a conflict that has made him think hard about the region he lives in and its relationship to France and to Europe. Barring hunting in the Périgord amounts to a virtual declaration of war on a very large segment of the population, for whom hunting is a way of life. For Desdemaines-Hugon, however, a man who is extremely fit and who knows and works on the land on terms of intimacy shared by few, hunting is to be abhorred as a kind of substitute war; it is barbaric because its purpose is the death of a living creature. His reward for these views has been hostility from some of his neighbours, climaxed by a garish death threat, scrawled in red paint on a tree on the edge of his property. At about the same time, his two dogs were found poisoned, and, although he cannot prove it, he believes they were killed in retribution for his anti-hunting position. As a man of strong views who is very much a part of his society at the same time as he is at odds with it, Desdemaines-Hugon has found himself, rather against his will, thinking about politics and the political process. For him, the emerging federal Europe is a point of hope, for a broadening of social norms, for a counterweight against what he sees as the narrow ways of his own society and the suffocating centralism of his own country. For many who share his views on wildlife, the European Community, which has taken an increasingly active role in ecological questions, is now looked to for redress of the negative effects of too much hunting. Aware that Brussels is becoming involved in the issue of ecology and, therefore, of limits on hunting, the fierce opponents of people like Desdemaines-Hugon have also been taking an interest in European politics. In fact, in many parts of southern France, those who favoured hunting and fishing (*la chasse et la pêche*) organized and contested the elections to the European Parliament in 1989. In the area where Desdemaines-Hugon lives, the pro-hunting candidate placed second to the French liberals.

For Desdemaines-Hugon, the conflict with the hunters in his area has heightened his hostility to the conformity he associates with highly defined national cultures and their centralized systems of political power. He considers that, to its cost, France is such a country, with the result that too many of his countrymen remain strongly nationalistic, believing as a matter of course in the superiority of their own ways.

As an antidote to the overcentralized power of nation-states, he likes to think in European terms, favouring a "Europe of the regions" in which long-established regions with clear identities would enjoy considerable autonomy within an overall European system. For Desdemaines-Hugon, it makes sense that Europe and the regions go together as natural allies in the effort to lessen the power of nation-states. When one encounters people like this serious artist from the Périgord, the question is whether, in addition to being fascinating and unique individuals, they are also important transitional types — people who, while clearly part of a nation, are also becoming European, forging a second, but powerful new aspect of their identity.

A daunting problem confronts those whose ambition it is to build a European federal system. Are there any Europeans? Are people so deeply imbued with their distinguishing national characteristics that they simply cannot transcend them to embrace a new and common identity? If the answer to this latter question is yes, then is any effort to build a political structure where real power is exercised at the European level doomed to failure, because it can only be a rickety creation of political élites, incapable of enduring any significant crisis? Is political legitimacy inexorably tied to nationality, making nation-states the only enduring form of political structure?

Many people assume that nationality is the essential cornerstone of the political order, that nations are virtually a part of "nature," and that the nation-state system is, therefore, inherently rooted in essential reality in a way that no other system could be. In Europe, this set of notions has been the conventional wisdom. In everyday conversation, to an overwhelming degree, it still is the conventional wisdom. In any European country, you are regularly treated to stereotypical views of the people who live in neighbouring countries. Sometimes the stereotypes are complimentary, usually not. Stereotypes matter, not because they are accurate — usually, they aren't — but because they reflect an accumulation of popular wisdom.

The French are often described by other Europeans as brittle, sensitive, inward-looking, chauvinistic, and cold to foreigners, the last observation invariably being applied to Parisians. The British, in particular, seem to find it difficult to say complimentary things about their neighbours across the Channel. A favourite comment they often make, one I have also heard from other northern Europeans, is that France is a beautiful country unfortunately occupied by the French.

At a summer garden party at Notting Hill Gate, now a fashionable section of London where remodelled flats look out over large, luxuriant gardens, a solicitor from Britain's largest law firm was talking about the firm's decision to open a Brussels office. Sipping a glass of particularly vicious apricot punch, he reflected on his dealings with "people on the continent." For some reason, he said, the British and the French are perennially at loggerheads. It's always easier to get on with the Germans, maybe because of the ancient shared Anglo-Saxon inheritance, he mused. The claim that it is hard to deal with the French seems to grow out of a web of notions I have often encountered in conversations with the English. In Britain, one frequently hears that things do not work well in France, that the French are impractical and flighty, and that their inflexible bureaucracy imposes impossible rules on those who have the misfortune to deal with it.

One of the characteristics of popular stereotypes is their tendency to persist even if clear evidence indicates that they are mistaken. The idea that things work better in Britain than in France, that Britain is materially a more successful society, is flatly contradicted by cold statistical evidence, as well as by dispassionate observation. France passed Britain in per-capita income in the early 1960s and has stayed significantly ahead ever since, a fact that has made little impact on the British consciousness. (If you should ever have the misfortune to try to convince someone who is British that this is true and find it hard going, you can always add insult to injury by pointing out that, in 1987, Italy's economy passed Britain's in absolute size. This, you can be sure, will not be believed.)

For obvious historical reasons, the Germans are subject to the most relentless and critical stereotypes, stereotypes that one encountered with much greater frequency all over Europe during the months following the opening of the Berlin Wall, when it became apparent that German unification had become a virtual certainty. The impeccably tailored Rüdiger von Wechmar, the former West German ambassador to the United Nations, and now an FDP (German liberal) member of the European Parliament, talked with me about the problem of attitudes to the Germans on the part of other Europeans over a sandwich at the bar in the European Parliament in Strasbourg. Putting it with some delicacy, he said: "People tend to be more worried about German unification in the parts of Europe where the Germans were present during the war, and less worried where they were not present, such as in Spain and Ireland." A Christian Democratic Union member of the Bundestag (the lower house of the West German parliament) made the key point concerning attitudes to the Germans at a top level Anglo-German conference at Cambridge University in March 1990 when he quipped: "Germany doesn't have such a hot curriculum vitae."

Popular impressions of the Germans are very much shaped by memories of the Second World War. The Germans are seen as hardworking and efficient, positive qualities often depicted as having a dark side in ruthlessness and discipline. What other Europeans appear to fear most about the Germans is not their present demeanour, which is thoroughly democratic and non-militaristic, but the possibility that, as a consequence of some future crisis, perhaps a recession or international political turmoil, things could be otherwise. The Germans, many Europeans say, tend to push things to extremes, to take an idea that may not be too harmful in itself and then pursue it to the point where its consequences become ominous. This characteristic is often allied with the notion that Germans are easily led and risk becoming the followers of dangerous, fanatical leaders.

A social scientist of Scandinavian origin who lives much of the time in France insisted in conversation with me that a tendency to fanaticism, to push things to extremes, is a deeply ingrained feature of German culture. He recalled his boyhood trips to West Germany after the war, when, during hiking exercises in the woods and mountains, he was struck by the forcefulness, the single-mindedness, and strong character of his youthful German companions, in this case in a benign pursuit, but which, he feared, could, in other cases, be turned to dangerous ends. A Spanish physiotherapist who was born in Madrid, but now practises her profession in Paris, told me she is sceptical about the success of the project of European union because she believes the Germans will always be German first, and European second. She echoed the often-encountered perception that young Germans are different from their Latin counterparts because they are so disciplined. But, she insisted, they lack the initiative of the Latins. A successful French entrepreneur, whose oil business just outside Marseille is expanding its markets internationally, explained the economic success of the Germans as the product of their narrowness, their dedication to hard work, making them much the same as the Japanese and, for that reason, not sympathetic people. Another French businessman repeated for me an old joke motivated by the underlying anxiety that Germany's neighbours feel about the Germans: "Why do the French plant so many trees along the sides of the road? Because the Germans like to march in the shade."

In France, the French character is often contrasted favourably with the German. The Germans, one hears, are prone to follow charismatic leaders, devoting blind obedience to them, while the French are too individualistic ever to fall prey to such behaviour. The fact that the extreme right-wing Front National, led by Jean-Marie Le Pen, whose stock in trade is his visceral dislike of North Africans, commands the support of over 10 per cent of the French population does not do much to mute this happy self-assessment on the part of the French.

The stereotypes employed to describe the Germans are not exactly state secrets. They are well known, and the reasons for them are well understood. Many Germans are resigned to living with the stereotypes as the price their country inevitably has to pay for its crimes during the war. For other Germans, many of them two generations removed from those who fought the war, the burden of these negative perceptions can be a heavy one and is bitterly resented. In February 1990, Michael Naumann, the head of a publishing house based in Hamburg, came back from a trip to New York, where, as he put it, "they think we're about to reopen the concentration camps." He said this attitude abroad worried him greatly because it was capable of prompting a resurgence of the nationalism in Germany "that people of my generation fought so hard to get rid of." [1]

For other Germans, the fear of a united Germany that emerges in the stereotypes is not dismissed as groundless. By far the most eloquent exponent of this view has been Günter Grass, who is probably Germany's best-known contemporary writer. For him, the starting-point was learning the truth of what the Germans had done at Auschwitz. In lectures delivered in Frankfurt and East Berlin in the winter of 1990, he said: "Auschwitz speaks against even a right of self-determination that is enjoyed by all other peoples. . . . We have every reason to be afraid of overselves as a functioning unity. . . . We cannot get by Auschwitz. We shouldn't even try, as great as the temptation is, because Auschwitz belongs to us, is branded into our history." [2]

Klaus Harpprecht, a writer whose wife, Renate, is a survivor of the Nazi camps, disputes this interpretation: "I don't agree with Günter Grass that Auschwitz was a consequence of German unity, and have written him to tell him so. Renate, who survived Auschwitz and Bergen-Belsen, shares this view." [3]

On the critical point, whether the old dangerous Germany lurks beneath the new one — the point that underlies the stereotypes — one of Britain's most distinguished historians is guardedly optimistic. In March 1990, in an address to the House of Lords, Hugh Trevor-Roper, now Lord Dacre, made these comments:

> I believe there has been a fundamental change in German mentality since 1945. There was no such change in 1918, when the Germans did not believe that they had been fairly defeated. . . . I believe that there has been a fundamental change in German historical attitudes, historical teaching and historical tradition. . . . Although I realise that I am taking a great risk, I am prepared to trust the Germans. [4]

The stereotypes that depict the British are kinder than those about the Germans, but equally the product of history. The British tend to be seen as a people apart, as a strange, cold race of non-physical beings, with pale skins that turn pink in the sun, badly dressed, asexual, linguistically stunted, and with no ability to empathize with people from other cultures. They are not objects of fear, but more often of humour, the way one tends to think of people who were once formidable but now are past it.

The British are seen as not quite European, a perception that is not at all in conflict with the British self-image. This view of the British has a venerable pedigree. It derives from the British practice in centuries past of allying with one group of continental powers against another, to prevent the domination of Europe by a single state. As a consequence of their habit of switching alliances opportunistically and of financing the armies of their allies, the British developed a reputation for being eager to fight to the last continental.

Recently, the British image on the continent has been very much affected by the reputation of Margaret Thatcher. As always, she excites powerful emotions, positive or negative, in the heart of the observer. A few years ago, the popular French singer Rénaud wrote a song about "Madame Thatcher" that was so scurrilous that it is not quotable in decent company. By contrast, I have often heard unsolicited praise for Margaret Thatcher from the French, particularly from businessmen who admire her toughness, her crackdowns against the trade unions, and her success at whipping the British into line — something they, no doubt, wish would be done at home by François Mitterrand.

Other Europeans are also subject to stereotyping by their neighbours. The Swiss, about whom seldom a positive word is ever heard, are described as cold and calculating, and are berated for profiting very handsomely from the miseries of humanity because they provide a banking haven for dictators and drug pushers. The Swedes like to depict the Danes as self-satisfied, the Norwegians as boring, and the Finns as unpredictable and highly temperamental, leaving themselves as the golden mean among Scandinavians.

In Central Europe, now emerging from the ice age of Stalinist repression, long-obscured national rivalries, and their accompanying national stereotypes, have shown themselves to be robust organisms. In Hungary, I was particularly struck by the notion, often encountered, of some cultures in the region being "higher" than others, not a concept evident in everyday discourse in Western Europe. In Central Europe, the word *Kultur*, in the old odious sense in which it was employed in Germany in the decades before the Second World War, has retained its currency. Many Hungarians I met looked to the West, and particularly to West Germany, as their social role model. Hungarians do not fear Germans; for Hungarians, German is often a second language, the Deutschmark their preferred hard currency, and the West German "social market" economy the one most often chosen as an object of praise.

If the dream of the inhabitants of Budapest is to live the life of the Viennese, they have quite different feelings about their other neighbours. Hungarians still look back with emotion on the loss of national territory at the end of the First World War to neighbouring Czechoslovakia and Romania, a loss that placed millions of ethnic Hungarians under foreign rule. In recent years, thousands of ethnic Hungarians fled across the wooded boundary into Hungary, some of them shot down by Romanian border guards, the survivors welcomed as heroes when they crossed the border. A teacher of English, whom I spoke to in her apartment in the hills of Buda, high above the Danube, expressed the often-heard view that the problem in Transylvania was that the Hungarians represented a higher level of culture than the Romanians, and were resented and hated for it. Though the Hungarian-Romanian hostility has been explosive in recent years, it is only one of many festering ethnic tensions in Central Europe, where Croats and Slovenes fear and resent Serbs, Slovaks speak of Czech domination, Poles fear German intentions east of the Oder-Neisse, and everyone looks down on the Russians, the former occupiers from the East who are universally thought to represent a "lower" culture by the people of this region.

Everywhere in Europe, then, national stereotyping of neighbours is a common practice. From this the conclusion could be drawn that, in the presence of such clearly demarcated national groups, and in the absence of "Europeans," the idea of establishing a polity that groups Europeans together must be doomed to failure.

Despite the immense body of evidence one can amass to support this conclusion, it represents only one part of a much more complex reality, strands in a tapestry that reveals other striking patterns when seen in its totality. National stereotyping gives rise to two immensely important distortions. It vastly exaggerates the homogeneity of Europe's nation-states, and, in highlighting national differences, it fails to take account of what the peoples of Europe have in common, characteristics that are becoming more, not less, pronounced in the present historical period.

Europe's nation-states were as much "inventions" in the era of their evolution as the "invention" of Europe is today. It is easier to see that nations are inventions when we make a crucial distinction. The nation is far from being the immediate community people encounter in their everyday lives and therefore forms their natural point of reference. All people, whether they live in towns, cities, or the countryside, do indeed have an immediate community, which may consist of their urban neighbourhood or the hills and valleys surrounding them. Such a tangible point of reference has always existed for people, providing them with a sense of their being that does not involve abstraction. Once we move beyond the level of this community directly at hand, however, we enter the realm of abstraction, of invention. Nations are large entities. Attachment to the national community is a cultural inheritance, the result of learning, of deliberate teaching. There is nothing natural about it. I was especially struck by the fact that the nation is an invention when I heard a teenage French girl tell me how beautiful she thought the shape of France was on the map. The shape of France is an icon that depicts something that has powerful meaning for her. She did not invent the icon. Everywhere she goes, it is presented to her. On the French ten-franc coin, the icon, the silhouette map of France, is depicted. On the television weather forecasts, the map of France is shown, abstracted from the rest of Europe, with showers in Normandy, clouds over Strasbourg, and sun over the Côte d'Azur, as though all this exists by itself, forming the whole and not simply a part of reality.

Europe's nation-states were constructed over a period of centuries and were the outcome of extremely complex interrelated processes: dynastic struggles; military alliances; victories and defeats in wars; the ebb and flow of Catholicism and Protestantism; and the advance of technology, which had the effect of promoting agricultural and industrial revolutions, helping create ever-larger economic units. Europe's states can be likened to geological formations, continental plates, that, over the centuries, have rubbed up against each other along fault lines, producing tension, heat, and conflict. Around the evolving national centres, peripheral regions have been absorbed, lost, fought over, and sometimes regained.

Everywhere one looks, the nation-states of Europe give evidence of the processes of their formation. National uniformity, the kind that warms a patriot's heart, has rarely been the result. Europe's nation-states, with their half-digested disparate regions, are the product of real history, not of an idealized version of history whose preordained purpose is national self-determination. To understand what Europe is capable of becoming, the place to start is with a consideration of the untidiness of Europe's regions — an untidiness left over from the past, which is pregnant with meaning for the future.

FRANCE: THE VERY IMAGE OF THE NATION-STATE

No country has an image of greater centralization than France. It is popularly thought to be the very model of the nation-state. With its neatly established, highly uniform administrative units, all of them fiefdoms of Paris, here is a country that carries out the will of the consuls and proconsuls of its cultural and political metropolis. There is much truth in the image. The rail and highway systems of the country, its airline routes, its national newspapers, its national television channels — all of these radiate their influence outward to the corners of France from Paris. And yet, the image of centralization, of France the nation-state, misses much of the reality of a country that is astonishingly complex in its regional make-up. France, the nation-state, comprises only one layer of the country, which is also France, the regional kingdom.

Provence, so called because it was the first Roman province in Gaul, is the natural place for me to think of in France since I lived there for two years. In the small rural community of Beaumont-du-Ventoux, where I was a resident, everyone over the age of sixty speaks Provençal, a language spoken in the region north and west of Marseille. Provençal is not a dialect of French. It is a separate Romance language, whose vocabulary resembles Latin and Italian as much as it does French. My neighbours have told me that Provençal is closer to Catalan, spoken in the region of northeastern Spain centred on Barcelona, than it is to French.

Before the Second World War, when the population of Beaumont was several times its present level of about 250 people, and when the major crop in the fields was grain, since replaced with grapevines, fruit trees, and olive trees, the everyday language at home and in the fields was Provençal. French was the language of the state and of the national school system. The children learned it, not at home, but in the classroom. One is reminded of this evolution at the annual gathering of the townspeople several days before Christmas each year. The children, under the direction of the schoolteacher, perform plays and recite poetry in French, and, reflecting the trend towards European integration and the fact that a woman from

England now teaches the children English once a week, they sing songs in English as well. Sitting in the front row of the audience are the people of Beaumont who are over eighty years of age. When the children's performance is over, the mayor, who is in his fifties, presents Christmas gifts to each of the children and to each of those over eighty. On such occasions, he has been known to recite poetry in Provençal.

The region around Avignon became definitively a part of France just over two centuries ago, at the time of the French Revolution, having previously been a papal territory controlled by the Church. For a time in the fourteenth century, the papacy itself was located in Avignon. In Provence, where local custom is strongly entrenched, the word *étranger* (which means both *stranger* and *foreigner*) is applied as much to Parisians as it is to those from outside France. Indeed, transplanted Parisians have complained to me that it is easier to be accepted in the region if you are a real foreigner than it is if you are from the much-resented metropolis of France. While Provençal is spoken east of the Rhône, west of the river another regional language, similar to Provençal, is spoken over a wide area.

East of the region where Provençal is spoken is France's Côte d'Azur, which takes in the territory along the Mediterranean coastline to the Italian border. It was only in 1860 that Napoleon III acquired Nice and Savoy, from the Kingdom of Sardinia, the Italian kingdom then involved in promoting Italian unification under the leadership of Count Cavour. Nice, a city whose inhabitants speak a unique dialect of French, was at one time a part of the territory of Monaco, the tiny principality that still retains its independence as it devotes itself to gambling, race-car driving, and the memory of Princess Grace.

Once when I was en route from France to Italy via the highway tunnel (twelve kilometres in length) under Mont Blanc, I stopped for a few hours in the mountain town of Thônes in Haute Savoy, not far from Annecy. The mountain food, the local songs performed at outdoor festivals, the style of dress, and the local accent marked the region off abruptly from the rest of France. Here one is only two hours driving time from the rolling fields of Burgundy, with their vineyards, cattle, contrasting architectural style — altogether a different way of life, a different sensibility. In Thônes, one is closer in spirit to other alpine regions in Switzerland, in Italy, and in Austria than to most of France.

Whereas Savoy is the region of France just south of Switzerland and bordering Italy, Alsace is just north of Switzerland, bordering the

Rhine and Germany. The fate of Alsace and the fate of Europe have been very much intertwined since 1870 when the Prussian army swept to a stunning victory over the French army in the Franco-Prussian War. In the peace treaty of the following year, Alsace and neighbouring Lorraine were annexed by the newly formed German Empire. A trip to the region explains part of the reason for the annexation. The blue hills of the Vosges range run down the length of Alsace. The German military, always thinking ahead to the next war, coveted this natural fortress position west of the Rhine, giving little thought to the fact that the seizure of the province would actually make the next war much more likely. The two provinces became the symbol of lost French greatness. "Think of it always; speak of it never" was the French statesman Léon Gambetta's advice to his people on the subject of the two lost provinces and the determination to get them back when the opportunity presented itself. [5]

Alsace had been traded back and forth between the French and the Germans for centuries before it became a part of France in 1648 as a result of the Treaty of Westphalia, at the conclusion of the Thirty Years War.

Mention of Alsace still evokes emotions about the conflicts this province has engendered for France. Once I provoked mild offence from an elderly Parisian, a former schoolteacher, when I described an ancestor of mine who had left Alsace to settle in Canada in 1835 as a "German from Alsace." In addition to French, Alsatians speak their own language, which is remote from French and is, indeed, a German dialect. Those who speak it are perfectly capable of understanding German. However, Alsatians are French, not German, and, in the months following the opening of the Berlin Wall, there were reports of particular unease in the region concerning the prospect of German unification.

If the loss of Alsace-Lorraine in 1871 became a later cause of the First World War, the experience of life in the provinces for those who were in the very vortex of European militarism helped point the way beyond the chain of wars in which each one served as a cause of the next. The astonishing life and career of Robert Schuman, who was born in Lorraine, provides testimony to this fact. At the time of Schuman's birth, Lorraine was German territory. Naturally, he grew up speaking fluent German as well as French. During the First World War, Schuman served in the German army. Later, when the region was returned to France as a consequence of the peace treaty of 1919, Schuman became a French citizen and entered French politics. After one more world war had been fought, he emerged as a major French statesman, serving as foreign minister of France. As we have seen, it was the "Schuman Plan" that brought France and West Germany together, along with Italy and the Benelux countries in the establishment of the European Coal and Steel Community. For Schuman, whose life had been spent as a witness to the consequences of war along the Rhine, the common market in coal and steel was much more than an economic arrangement — its goal was to make war between the two former enemies impossible, by merging the heavy industries of the two countries into a common unit so that they would never be used again for hostile remilitarization by either the French or the Germans.

In western and southwestern France are two further examples of peoples who fit no neat stereotype of the French. Living in their isolated western peninsula are the Bretons, a seafaring people, whose country and way of life are reminiscent of those of the Celts of the British Isles. In the remote parts of Brittany, some inhabitants still speak a Gaelic language close to the indigenous languages spoken in Ireland, Wales, and Scotland. A small but noisy terrorist organization, the Breton Republican Army, dedicates itself to the battle for Breton autonomy.

In the south, on both sides of the Franco-Spanish border, live the people in Europe who have the least in common with their fellow Europeans, the Basques. The origins of the Basques are buried in the mists of pre-history and are a matter of controversy among modern scholars. "Euskara," the name the Basques have for their language, is not an Indo-European tongue. Constituting another minority in the south are those who inhabit the large Mediterranean island of Corsica, north of Sardinia. The Corsicans, like the people of Provence, the Bretons, and the Alsatians, speak their own language. A Corsican nationalist movement keeps up a fitful opposition to the island's position in France, carrying out occasional acts of terrorism and vandalism, targeting tourism facilities for their displays of outrage.

The French nation-state reached its fruition in the period of the French Revolution and the empire of Napoleon I. In that age of the rise of the middle classes, the overthrow of the ancien regime, and the burgeoning of the idea of the nation and the related idea of national self-determination, the France of regions with its roots in the distant past was overlaid with a highly centralized political structure and administrative system. France's modern system of departments dates from that age. A glance at a departmental map of France makes the country look reassuringly uniform. The reality is quite different. The regions of France have survived the age of national self-determination, and they are poised today, in Europe's most centralized major state, to take their place in the Europe of tomorrow.

ITALIAN CITY-STATES

If France gives the outward appearance of uniformity, which, in reality, masks enormous regional diversity, in Italy there is not even any pretence at uniformity. More than in any other country, all of the ages of European history live in Italy, jostling each other, as sustained, unresolvable contradictions. There is no Italy. There are many Italys — city-states existing side by side, as they have for a thousand years in a myriad of shifting relationships with one another. Often they embody a single era to perfection, appearing to freeze it and preserve it.

Florence is the city that captures Europe's transition from medievalism to the Renaissance.[6] The city marries the arrogance and venality of rulers and the transcendent genius of writers, painters, sculptors, and architects. Florence captures the moment in Western history when the assumptions of the Church were no longer enough, when a new society revived the teachings of the ancients and began, in their own works, to surpass them. Here was a brief flowering of an élite individualist revolt. Florence was the city of merchant capitalism at its dawn. It anticipated the future and then was doomed to watch it emerge elsewhere, as the centre of the European world shifted from the Mediterranean to the Atlantic, and to the emergent political form of the absolute monarchies that were knitting together what were to become nation-states.[7]

Rome is forever the city of the universal state. Its ruins proclaim both the ambition of an eternal human order and its frailty. The notion of a Western civilization is inseparable from its Roman origins. Two orders are embedded in Rome, like the hydra heads of a creature always at war with itself — impossible to conceive of separately and yet deadly foes none the less. One Rome is that of the Empire, the temporal state that aspired to universality, to the ideal of a single government that would bestow laws fairly and even-handedly on all people. The other Rome is that of the Church, accepting the universality of the Empire but disdaining its temporal character as less worthy than its own spiritual mission.

On Christmas Day in the year 800, Charlemagne had himself crowned emperor by the Pope in Rome, thus laying the foundations of the Holy Roman Empire. The coronation kept alive the two great institutions that gave Western civilization a centre for hundreds of years — the Church and the Empire.

Milan is Italy's great contemporary city, never appearing to live off its past as Florence, and even Rome, often do. It is a productive giant, by far the greatest producer of wealth in Italy. The industrial-design capital of the world, Milan is a heterogeneous manufacturing metropolis, its diverse industrial sectors each inhabiting its own space in the city. While Milan has the energy of a business city, like Frankfurt or Tokyo, it is not one-dimensional.

The large number of tall, fair-haired Milanese emphasizes the difference between this northern metropolis and southern Italy, from which many migrant workers in the north still come. That Milan is contemporary is revealed in the way disparate images are juxtaposed. Classical Italian restaurants are right next door to Japanese eating places. Elsewhere fortune tellers sit outside chic bars ready to deal a deck of Tarot cards, perhaps to help you play the stock markets, which are so popular in this part of Italy that even communist newspapers provide tips to their readers on how to approach them.

The great metropolis of Lombardy has a northern feel to it. Milan is a city on the perimeter of the inner Europe that is now taking shape. To the west is Turin, Fiat's city, the centre of the Italian automotive industry. East and southeast stretch the other cities in this remarkable Italian industrial region, which has been one of the world's most successful since the Second World War, in striking contrast to the American Midwest and the British Midlands. In Italy's bustling, wealth-producing north, however, there is only one giant, and it is Milan.

Italy's harshest contrast is that between Milan and the *mezzogiorno*, the region to the south of Rome, which is another Italian universe entirely. The Italian south is the product of a long and tragic history. Of critical importance for the south was its fate at that fundamental turning-point in European history, the age of the Reformation and Counter-Reformation in the sixteenth century. For northern Europe, the social forces unleashed by the Reformation opened the way for the eventual consolidation of nation-states. Italy, by contrast, was dominated by ultra-Catholic Spain and by the Counter-Reformation papacy, with the result that the humanist traditions of the Renaissance were suppressed. While the Italian city-states in general experienced long-term decline in this period, Rome entered a phase of parasitic growth. New palaces, villas, churches, and works of art were commissioned in Counter-Reformation Rome — all of which helped foster a vicious cycle of taxation, baronial reaction, famine, and banditry. In the south, the already underdeveloped economy suffered further deterioration during two centuries of Spanish rule.

Although healing the divisions wrought by history has been one of the primary goals of Italian government since the unification of the country in 1871, success has been partial at best. The south has remained like another country, with its own social norms and continuing economic problems. Everywhere in Italy, the discontinuities of the country's history are experienced in the present day. In the prosperous north, the south is regarded as an undue burden and the government in Rome is disdained as Byzantine. In the spring of 1990, the most significant development in the local politics of northern Italy was the rise of the Lega Lombarda (Lombardy League), a noisy populist political formation that advocated taking taxation and lawmaking out of the hands of the central government in Rome, so that an autonomous Lombardy could be established. For the Lega, which specialized in large public demonstrations in and around Milan, the government in Rome was dismissed as corrupt and inefficient, and both "lazy" southerners and North Africans were castigated as unworthy migrants to wealthy Lombardy. I encountered similar attitudes in neighbouring Turin, where the fact that life on the streets peters out soon after dark is explained as a sign that this is a hard-working city. People go to bed early here, I was told, so that they can get up early and produce wealth. One Fiat office employee told me disdainfully that, in Rome, the doors to government offices regularly display handwritten signs: "Out for an hour" or "Will be back soon." If the Roman bureaucrats eschew putting in lengthy hours, I was told, those farther south have an even more creative approach to work. In Naples, a new job has been invented: people go to sleep at night and toil their nocturnal hours away, dreaming the numbers they think will turn up in lotteries the next day, and then sell the results of their dreams to tip-seekers in the morning. A cartoon aptly captured the feeling of northern alienation: a cow is shown feeding in the north, being milked in Rome, and defecating in the south.

Within the north, there is little show of solidarity among the northern "city-states" in their common animosity to Rome and the south, however. In Turin, one encounters bitter resentment of larger Milan for enticing economic and cultural activity away from the auto-manufacturing city. When Turin's football team plays Milan, the scene is reminiscent more of warfare than of sport.

Much farther north, in the German speaking region of Trentino-Alto Adige, there is considerable resentment of the rest of Italy. I have been told that, if one enters a restaurant in the region and insists on speaking Italian, one can be sure of being served last, in remarkable contrast to the warm reception Italian speakers receive when they cross into German-speaking Austria.

In Italy, empires, secular and spiritual, city-states, and nation-state are all present. In such a country, it is clear that nothing is resolved neatly through the passage of time, that one historical stage does not abolish what came before. New layers are established. Europe is present in Italy today, as it always has been. Italy's entry into Europe promises to be, if anything, more natural to it than the developments during its somewhat artificial existence as a nation-state.

SPANISH REGIONS

Spain is so many physical and human realities placed jarringly side by side in one country that it can be understood only as the product of a tortuous and cataclysmic history. The Iberian peninsula could have acquired a very different political map than it has today. Portugal could have ended up as a part of Spain, as, indeed at times, it appeared that it would. The Galicians, the Basques, and the Catalans, all of whom speak languages separate from Castilian (the language we call Spanish), could have developed their own independent nation-states, in which case a cluster of small, independent states like the Benelux countries would have come into being between Spain and France. In part the product of a very long-term occupation of much of the country by Islamic invaders, and in part the outcome of dynastic struggles, Spain entered the modern era as the extreme case of regional and cultural diversity. What is striking in Spain is the absence of anything approaching national cohesion.

The Catalans, who live in northeastern Spain and who speak their own language, are the most European of the Spaniards. Barcelona, the great Catalan metropolis, is the most commercial and industrious of Spanish cities. A banking and manufacturing centre, Barcelona often feels like many other cities farther north in its architecture and its streetscapes, except, of course, when one comes upon the buildings, park, and unfinished cathedral of the brilliant Catalan architect Antonio Gaudi, whose work forms such a striking contrast to the much more conservative buildings characteristic of the city.

All public signs in Barcelona and throughout Catalonia are in both Catalan and Castilian. By and large, the working language throughout the region is Catalan, though that may be changing. Newcomers attracted by the bustling economy almost always speak Castilian. In marriages between Catalan and Castilian speakers, Castilian almost invariably ends up as the language spoken in the home and adopted by the children. While Catalan nationalism is ever present, the high degree of autonomy granted Spanish regions since the rise of a democratic Spain following the death of dictator Francisco Franco in 1975 has satisfied most of the people of Catalonia.

If the Catalans are more at home in Spain than they were in the days when Franco tried to suppress their language and culture, such cannot be said for many of the Basques, whose nationalism forms the most thorny ongoing problem for the Spanish state. The crusade for a separate Basque state, an independent Euskara, has constituted one of the most fateful facts of life in the history of Spain. It had an important impact on the transition from dictatorship to democracy in the 1970s, when Franco's chosen successor, Admiral Luis Carrero Blanco, was assassinated by Basque terrorists.

Although there are Basque communities in France, most of the Basques live in Spain, and their drive for national independence has been centred there. During the Spanish Civil War, the Basques, who hoped for a full measure of autonomy in return, remained loyal to the republic during the conflict. In crushing Basque resistance, Franco's military forces carried out their most singular act of barbarism when, in April 1936, they undertook the systematic terror bombing of Guernica, a town that had special historic and cultural significance for the Basques. Once he had achieved victory, Franco brought the Basques under the ruthless control of the central government, doing what he could to eradicate their culture. Repression worked in the short term, but it was to engender the later creation of one of Europe's most irreducible terrorist forces, the ETA (Euskadi Ta Askatasuna), in the early 1960s. Despite a disputatious and divisive history, the ETA terrorists have continued to haunt the Spanish state, specializing in killing Civil Guards and political figures to the present day, their most illustrious victim to date being Carrero.

It is clear that Basque nationalism in its extreme form does not represent anything like a majority of the people of the Basque provinces, many of whom are satisfied with the autonomy they now enjoy, and yet the conflict grinds on, much like that in Ireland, a signal example of the failure of the nation-state.

In northwestern Spain live the Galicians, whose three million people share in common with the Catalans and the Basques the fact that they speak a language distinct from Castilian. Inhabiting a rainy, poor region, the Galicians are a forgotten people in Spain, where discussions of poverty tend to centre on the impoverished regions of the south.

When the Catalans, Basques, and Galicians are considered together, the significant fact is that they make up about twelve million of Spain's thirty-eight million people. For close to a third of the country's population, in other words, Castilian is not the first language.

GERMANY

Germany, too, is a land of distinctive regions. Prior to the proclamation of the German Empire in 1871, political division was regarded as the natural order of things for Germans. In striking contrast to the later perception of the Germans as militaristic and united around an implacable nationalism, the perception of the Germans before the era of Bismarck was that of an artistic, impractical people, who were incapable of achieving political unity. The condition of Germany was attributable to the geographical position of the Germans, historical circumstance, and the impact of the Reformation and the Counter-Reformation on Germany and the Germans.

While even an island people like the British, with the most "natural" of frontiers, has had severe problems clarifying its appropriate territory in relation to minorities such as the Irish, Scots, and Welsh, the Germans have had more difficulty than any other major people in defining the territory on which their nation-state ought to be erected. They are truly the "people in the middle" in relation to their neighbours, so that dynastic struggles, the ebb and flow of the military power of the major European states, and the migration routes of invading peoples have inevitably involved the Germans. In the west, the extent of the territory occupied by Germans shifted over time during frontier struggles with the French and the peoples of the Low Countries. In the east, the situation was much more fluid still. German communities existed side by side with those of other peoples. Sometimes the German merchants and princes dominated; sometimes they were absorbed or overrun by their neighbours.

The most devastating European wars prior to those of the twentieth century were fought during the first half of the seventeenth century. During the Thirty Years War, from 1618 to 1648, German territory was the battleground for a general European power struggle that intersected with struggles between Protestantism and Catholicism. Large parts of Germany were decimated. As much as 30 per cent of the German population perished in the terrible conflicts of the period. Major German rulers fought for the title "Holy Roman Emperor," and other great powers fought their wars on German soil. The consequence was that the German people were left divided into a myriad of political units, ranging in size from very small to large, in a condition of political disintegration that was to persist until the era of Bismarck.

In the nineteenth-century world of German states, characterized by their own peculiar institutions, their social solidarity, and their fear and suspicion of the outside world and of challenges to authority, two major powers, Austria and Prussia, struggled for hegemony. In victorious wars against Denmark, Austria, and France, Bismarck's Prussia realized the elusive goal of unifying the Germans, and simultaneously succeeded in overturning the existing European order. Although Prussian military power assembled the Germans into a national state, it did not manage to homogenize the regional identities of Germans, nor did it work through the contradictions borne of the impact of industrial revolution and modern thought on traditional communities in which deference to authority was deeply ingrained. While the German national project subsumed the many diverse parts of what was German, the parts remained half-digested, a dangerous concoction when the German Empire suffered military defeat in November 1918. When Nazi Germany was overwhelmed by its adversaries in 1945, the two Germanys that emerged as successor states in the post-war era in part reflected earlier traditional regional realities and in part exhibited a synthetic character as a consequence of the arbitrary manner of their creation.

Unification in 1990 was to produce a new form of regional identity, in which western Germans were sharply differentiated from eastern Germans, whom they resented not so much for their poor material circumstances as for the way they revived unhappy memories of the early post-war days of life in the Federal Republic.

THE PEOPLES OF THE BRITISH ISLES

If late 19th century German unification and the problems that arose as a consequence of German expansion were to prove so cataclysmic that they cast the value of the nation-state paradigm in doubt for all thinking people, Britain constituted a quite different kind of example, one in which gradualism and respect for the concept of limited government underlay the development of the nation-state. Reference has already been made to the consciousness of the British, peculiar to island peoples. Two other enormously important facts have set the British apart from all other Europeans. The first is the lasting effects of their experience of global power. The second is their position in the wider Anglo-American world. Both of these will be explored in a later chapter. Here, our purpose is to note that, while the national paradigm has been as successfully developed in the British case as anywhere, the presence of national minorities has prevented it from approaching the ideal. The trauma of English conquest of the other peoples of the British Isles has never been transcended and has prevented the emergence of a single people.

Wales, dominated for centuries by England before it was finally incorporated into the kingdom in 1536, has been more thoroughly absorbed than Scotland, not to mention Ireland, a bleeding sore for Britain, even in the period of its greatest global power.

In the 1960s, in response to the plight of the Welsh language (which decreased in common usage from 90 per cent in 1850 to 21 per cent in 1971)[8] and to economic problems, a Welsh nationalist movement became increasingly active. Its main objective was cultural preservation, centred on the revival of the Welsh language. One Welshman in his fifties, who had been educated at Oxford and spoke fluent French, German, and Italian, told me that he felt cheated because he had not been taught Welsh by his parents when he was a child, despite the fact that they both spoke it. During his childhood, the Welsh language had become a symbol of economic backwardness. His parents saw integration into the wider society as a way to avoid the hard life of their forebears, an attitude much like that of the educated Galicians in Spain vis-à-vis their language. While the Welsh nationalist movement received the active support of only a minority of the population, it included a small and noisy terrorist wing, whose specialty was burning down the "secondary homes" of English middle-class people in Wales.

Scottish nationalism has waxed and waned since the union of Scotland with England in 1707, but it has never disappeared. Scottish union with England took place under much more favourable terms than had Welsh union. Scotland remained an important administrative unit within the kingdom, with distinctive legal, educational, and religious systems. In 1885, the Scottish Office was established under the Scottish secretary, a Westminster government minister. In

1926, the position was upgraded to that of a secretary of state, giving it cabinet rank. By 1981, the Scottish Office was situated in Edinburgh, from which it administered health, education, agriculture, penal institutions, and important economic functions. Separate Scottish cultural, media, and sporting institutions helped maintain the distinctiveness of Scottish life from that south of the border. [9]

The Scottish National Party (SNP), with antecedents going back to the late nineteenth century, was founded in 1934, but did not become an important political force until the 1960s. The SNP has been the voice of Scottish nationalism, contending that the country's union with England has led to long-term economic decline and cultural subservience. In March 1979, a referendum was held in Scotland on the issue of establishing a Scottish Assembly with devolved powers to deal with local matters. Under the rules of the referendum, devolution would go into effect only if at least 40 per cent of the total Scottish electorate voted for it. While 52 per cent of those voting favoured the measure, since they constituted only 33 per cent of the Scottish electorate, devolution did not go ahead. Following the failure of devolution, the morale of the Scottish nationalists declined, and the SNP fell on hard times. By the end of the 1980s, however, the party enjoyed a significant revival. This time the nationalists drew strength from the almost complete alienation of the Scottish people from the government of Margaret Thatcher, which, in the 1987 elections, won only ten of seventy Scottish parliamentary seats. By the spring of 1990, public-opinion polls showed that 80 per cent of the Scots favoured either devolution or independence. [10] It is by no means fanciful to imagine a day when Scotland will itself be a member of the European Community, not as part of the United Kingdom, but on its own.

If Welsh and Scottish national movements have challenged the unity of the United Kingdom, it was in Ireland that the British national state came up against its irreducible adversary. The political rule of England was never accepted in Ireland from the time of the conquest of the country during Oliver Cromwell's regime in the seventeenth century. In the latter decades of the nineteenth century, the "Irish Question" became a perennial feature of British politics, to the point where the demand for "Irish home rule" threatened the orderly functioning of British parliamentary government and the two-party system. After decades of rancour, culminating in the bloody Easter 1916 revolt of Irish nationalists in Dublin, the Irish Free State was established in 1921, comprising sixteen of Ireland's counties, but not including the six counties of Ulster, in the predominantly Protestant north of the island.

In recent decades, terrorism has been an everyday fact of life in Northern Ireland, making life there a bloody test between IRA and Protestant militants and the British security forces.

Over the course of its development, the British nation-state proved incapable of absorbing Ireland, incapable of broadening its self-definition and its structure so that the Irish could feel at home in a federated kingdom. Not surprisingly, no one feels happier to be in Brussels than the Irish who work for the EC, the emerging great state of which their country is a full member, but is emphatically not Britain or the British Empire. For the Irish, the British nation-state was for centuries the cause of their own historical negation. Naturally, for them, Europe has been a welcome antidote, to which they have turned with marked enthusiasm.

REGIONS, NATIONS, EUROPE

The remarkable fact is that, though the nation-state system has been the dominant form of political organization for the past two centuries, the majority of Europeans do not live in the heartlands of the great nation-states. Rather, the European majority is constituted of people who live in regions within a nation-state in which the regional identity forms a strong counterpull to the nation-state; or in minority national communities where a regional language is spoken in addition to the language of the nation-state; or, finally, in small nation-states that, while independent, are none the less so vitally affected by the actions of their larger neighbours that they are in a position to enjoy little actual national sovereignty. It is the people who occupy the heartlands of the major nations who constitute the European minority — a favoured and enormously powerful minority, but a minority none the less. That the European majority should be constituted of odds and ends rather than of fully formed large nations becomes less remarkable when we consider the processes out of which Europe's nation-states have been formed.

The widespread existence of distinctive regions and national minorities does not provide positive evidence of the existence of Europeans. Far from it. What it does provide is evidence that the nation-states of Europe are multifold entities, the consequences of history, and of the working of historical processes that continue today. And when we encounter the diverse regions and the national minorities, the simple divisions of national stereotypes are obscured in a web of other reference points that create a pattern of astonishing variety and complexity. As we consider this complex pattern, we are making the journey from the national icons, from the shorthand, to the reality.

The more complex a civilization is, the more the people within it are capable of developing and displaying multiple identities. Moreover, these identities are shifting all the time, with some gaining in importance and others losing. What has distinguished the era since the French Revolution is that supreme loyalty has been demanded by the nation-state and, by and large, has been paid to it. In no earlier historical period was that true. What distinguishes the present period in Europe is that the nation and the nation-state are declining in importance.

Across Europe today there is an increased emphasis on the regions. Challenges against the centralized authority of nation-states are being mounted with ever-greater frequency and intensity. These movements are evidence of a transformation that is changing the position of the nation-state in fundamental respects. The historical process that is unfolding is driven by complex interacting causes. As with all such processes, it is uneven in nature, more pronounced and advanced in some places than in others. As the sovereignty of the nation-state declines, its former majesty is lost and, with this loss, a related shift in identity among the people who live in the nation-state is encouraged. Fundamental to the loss of sovereignty of the nation-state is the internationalization of the economy, the consequence of technological revolution, and the rise of multinational corporations. This process will be examined in detail in a later chapter, but one of its primary consequences can be noted here: the shifting of significant economic decision making beyond the realm of the nation-state. Indeed, the very processes of technological change and the extension of economic activity from local production and consumption to a much more extended system of production and consumption, processes that helped launch the nation-state in earlier times, are now undermining it. The nation-state does not disappear as a consequence of its loss of power. Rather, it loses its clarity, its character as majestic icon, and becomes integrated into a broader web of institutional arrangements, with important levels of decision making emerging below it, at the regional level, and above it, at the supranational level. As national sovereignty declines, as national governments become incapable of making the basic decisions that determine the well-being of their societies, identities also shift — and in two directions at the same time — to the European level, but also to the regional level.

The existence of disparate regions and unassimilated, and sometimes disaffected, minorities does not mean that there is a simple correlation between such minority status and disproportionately high support for European integration, although, in fact, this is often the case. Still less does it mean that political leaders from such minorities will play the critical role in charting the course for European integration. What is crucial about the existence of the unassimilated minorities and regions is the testimony their existence provides of how far the paradigm of the self-determining nation has been from being fully realized.

Are there Europeans? Yes. Do they identify themselves as such? Not normally. But, more and more, they comport themselves as Europeans. What we see everywhere in Europe are people who, while still dressed in their national garb, are behaving in convergent ways as Europeans. If we take notice of the national garb alone, and the undeniable and continuing power of nationalism, we will have failed to see how profound the present transformation is. Here it is worth examining what the nation-state system has wrought, because it is out of that system that Europe and Europeans are emerging.

THE RISE OF THE NATION-STATE

The nation-state was the seminal political invention of early modern Europe. It emerged in the centuries following 1500, and spread slowly across the continent. [11] While it never became the sole form of statehood in Europe, with enormous multinational states such as Austria-Hungary, the Russian Empire, and later the Soviet Union continuing to survive, the nation-state became not simply the dominant form of political organization, but the ideal form as well. For centuries, the nation-state was associated with progress. As recently as the end of the First World War, it seemed to intelligent analysts that the nation-state represented the inevitable and optimal future for humanity.

The origins of nationalism are buried deep in the early history of civilization. The idea of the nation — a community of people with a common geography and history, and usually with a common language, religion, and way of life — developed over millennia, only achieving its modern character in the eighteenth century, in the era of the French Revolution. Its ancient origins, as far as Western civilization is concerned, date back to the ideas and traditions of the Greeks and the Jews, who initially developed concepts that accentuated their own separateness from other peoples, from barbarians or gentiles. From this particularism, however, their philosophy and religion evolved into universal creeds, available to the whole of humanity, and not merely a part. The universalist thought of the Greeks and the Jews became, in the age of the Roman Empire, the ideological cement in a state that was itself conceived in universal terms. Transformed into Christianity and eventually embraced as the official doctrine of the empire, Judaeo-Christian thought survived the late Roman Empire and the subsequent age in which the universal state fell to pieces to be succeeded, after centuries had passed, by medievalism. Out of the ruins of the universal, secular state emerged the new order whose centre was the universal religion. The Church and the Pope became the new Rome, taking the place of the Rome that had fallen. Although this new Rome did not extend its sway to the territories that had made up the eastern Roman Empire, it did bring the Germanic tribes within its religious orbit. Out of this creation of Western Christendom was to come the notion of "Europe."

In his seminal work on the emergence of nationalism, Hans Kohn analysed this transformation:

> In Western Europe the universal claim of the Pope and the Empire of Charlemagne succeeded in forming out of the chaos produced by the Germanic tribes, a new civilization, "Europe" or "Occidental Christendom." . . . It dominated Western Europe for many centuries, until new forces, themselves a renaissance, prepared the ground for the later rise of nationalism. State and Church, Empire and Christianity were indissolubly linked. There was an all-dominating recognition of the necessity of a universal Empire, and this Empire was by necessity Christian and Roman at the same time. [12]

During the medieval period, the earlier secularism and rationalism that had been features of ancient thought were submerged in the "other-worldly" preoccupation of Catholicism. In principle, during the medieval period, the Church was superior to the State, and the universal ideal remained intact. Only with the Renaissance of the fifteenth century was the "other-worldly" preoccupation of medievalism challenged in a brilliant, although relatively brief explosion of rediscovery that recaptured the achievements of ancient civilization and hinted at the line of advance for the future.

The transition from feudalism to capitalism involved a shift in preoccupation to the concerns of this world. Technological and scientific developments were fundamental to this transition. Gunpowder gave monarchies the means to quash the rebellions of barons who had traditionally maintained their own armed forces. The printing press made possible the dispersion of intellectual and scientific materials on a wholly new scale. At the same time, the explosion of information about geography and nature associated with voyages of discovery confronted Europeans with new knowledge that challenged the wisdom of the past.

The quickening pace of economic development provided a material basis for the consolidation of royal power in the major European countries.[13] The phase of royal absolutism was not itself one of nationalism, but it did help to prepare the way for the modern nation-state. Royal power, which significantly replaced the authority of locally based aristocracy, opened the way for yet further economic advance. The notion that loyalty to the prince came ahead of any other loyalty, a seminal idea in the period of royal absolutism, was in striking contrast to the values of the universal state whose memory had lingered as an ideal in Europe since Rome. Rising royal power was crucial to challenges to the religious authority of Rome, and thus to the development of Protestantism in the sixteenth century. While Protestantism expressed its rejection of Rome in universal religious terms, its very nature helped further the creation of the nation-state and, in this way, of rival European nationalisms.[14] The Reformation promoted individualism through the Protestant insistence on the right of every person to approach God directly. It promoted individual accomplishment in the temporal realm, thereby adding an ideological underpinning to the gathering strength of capitalism and the drive for economic success. Of great importance, it promoted the use of vernacular languages as the medium of worship, helping forge the national languages that were so important to the emerging nation-states.

The transition from universalist to nationalist assumptions proceeded very slowly, only being fully completed in the late eighteenth century. The Renaissance initially opened the way for a more critical and individualist spirit within the relatively restricted ranks of the aristocracy and the new merchant élites, while leaving the mass of the population still living within the assumptions of Catholic medievalism. Moreover, the short burst of critical energy and secularism that was the hallmark of the Renaissance was soon followed by the renewed emphasis on religion characteristic of the Reformation and the Counter-Reformation. The Reformation shattered the universality of the Church, and, with its introduction of pluralism into the religious order, it helped open the way for the consolidation of the power and legitimacy of the nation-state, which was also being fostered by the new technology of gunpowder and the printing press.

Although the Renaissance, the Reformation, and the Counter-Reformation prepared the way for the emergence of the nation-state, it was only with the Enlightenment of the eighteenth century that the political assumptions of the modern state system appeared in a recognizable form. During the eighteenth century, the foundations of the old world of religion and social inequality were subjected to withering critique. [15] Replacing the notions of original sin and the rights of monarchs was a new appreciation of the world, based on the concept of natural law, which radically altered the understanding of human psychology. The traditional notion of human psychology had been that man was a fallen creature whose redemption was not possible in this world. In place of this dark and pessimistic doctrine came the idea that man was a "tabula rasa," a blank slate, capable of good if educated to be good, indeed inclined to goodness as a consequence of his natural desire to do well for himself. Working from the seventeenth-century ideas of Hobbes and Locke, which concluded that men were, in essence, equal, eighteenth-century thinkers, Rousseau the most important among them, developed the concept of popular control of government.

The understanding of the proper relation of the governed to the governors was being turned on its head. The Physiocrats in France and Adam Smith in Britain developed the idea of an unfettered market system and rejected the prevailing concept of mercantilism. With the Enlightenment and the French Revolution, the social relations of the modern world were established. [16] The assumption that the world was naturally divided into competing nation-states, each with its own exclusive nationalism and drive for national self-expression, came about as a result of this remaking of the world in the eighteenth century. Once that remaking was complete, the nation became, for the first time in history, the entity to which the supreme loyalty of those who made it up was expected. The exclusiveness of the national claim is captured in this statement by the eighteenth-century Swedish count Carl August Ehrensvärd: "Each nation has a beauty that belongs to it; each nation should be satisfied with the beauty peculiar to it; none deviate from its nature nor the temperament peculiar to it." [17] From this idea of the nation derives our contemporary notion of political legitimacy, the idea that nations ought to be self-governing, that, in the normal course of events, they should have their own sovereign governments, an idea that remains the "common sense" of our own age.

As we have observed, the nations of Europe have taken on the appearance of being wholly "natural" phenomena, as much so as the flora and fauna. When one is surrounded by the characteristic features of these nations, with all their traditions, their languages, their styles of architecture and of food, it is easy to believe that they are permanent, unchanging entities. One forgets that the nationalities and the nationalisms of Europe are political inventions of the past several centuries. Each of them was a difficult and an artificial creation whose realization involved immense struggles against those with a vested interest in earlier conceptions of the social and political order, conceptions displaced only through immense upheaval.

THE CRISIS OF THE NATION-STATE SYSTEM

Once we understand that nations are not natural phenomena, but the products of history, it becomes easier to see that history does not end with the creation of nations. The same processes that produced nations in one historical period helped create the supreme crisis of the nation-state system during the twentieth century, and, then, beyond that, created the conditions for the transcending of the nation-state system in the genesis of the post-national state.

The idea of national self-determination achieved its greatest ascendancy from the time of the French Revolution until the outbreak of the First World War in 1914. In their earliest manifestations, nationalism and the idea of the nation-state were closely associated with liberalism, with the notion of the self-determination of the individual, and with the concept of democracy. The nation-state provided the arena within which these broader notions could be realized. There was thus an apparently ideal marriage in which the particularism of the nation-state created the concrete conditions for the flowering of the universal notions of human liberty. Indeed, one appeared inconceivable without the other. In both Britain and France, the connection between the idea of the nation-state and the drive towards political liberty was very powerful. The achievements of these two countries were to serve as examples for the élites of other nations, who were all too eager to follow their lead and to establish nation-states of their own. Such nationalist movements were to arise in virtually every national group in Europe, all infused with the same vision of the uniqueness of their particular people, and their aspiration for national self-determination through the establishment of their own nation-state.

In the early 1870s, the nationalist aspirations of both the Italians and the Germans were realized with the establishment of Italian and German nation-states. During the epoch that opened with the creation of Bismarck's Germany, the European nation-state system reached its zenith, from which it approached the abyss towards which its underlying logic propelled it.

Each state was based in principle on the unique genius, and unique aspirations, of a particular nation. Here was a concept that fostered the idea that the members of each national community shared an inner fellowship among themselves, a fellow feeling that they could not enjoy with outsiders, with foreigners. While this notion could be a positive invocation of the values that tied members of a national community together, at least implicit in it was the idea that foreigners should be seen differently. Each nation-state was seen as an "individual" in its own right, an immortal individual it is true, but none the less an individual with its own selfish interests. In such a system of thought, the egotistical interests of the nation-state became the highest truth — *raison d'état*. While there could be practical reasons for not provoking the wrath of other nation-states, this came down to a mere matter of calculation. When the interests of the nation-state shifted, one's behaviour towards others would also shift.

Such a concept cut asunder notions of an underlying set of interests that tied nations together. Earlier concepts of a broader European community, whether based on religion, on solidarity among monarchs and rulers, or on humanism and toleration, were overridden by the idea of the righteousness of national egotism. Although it had been easy for those in the early nation-states, Britain and France, to believe that they would be content, and that it would serve their interests, if all Europe moved to a system of nation-states, overcoming archaic empires such as the Turkish, the Austro-Hungarian, and the Russian in the process, the later nationalisms proved to be less benevolent, arising, as they did, in an already more crowded landscape. The later nation-states had had to fight their way into a world in which their competitors were already well established.

For the Germans, the most important case, it was the military-industrial strategy of Bismarck, the man of "blood and iron," that bore fruit and succeeded in defeating the enemies of Prussia and in achieving German unification. With unification, the dark side of nationalism was already becoming apparent. Nationalism meant much more than the completion of democracy and of the ideals of the Enlightenment in the concrete environment of a particular people who shared common points of cultural reference, a common language and literature, and the memory of a shared history. It meant, according to the social-Darwinist norms so prevalent in the late nineteenth century, that some nations would flourish by overcoming other nations, that just as, in nature, the struggle for survival brought the fittest to the fore, so it would be with nations. With German unification, military power came to be seen as the supreme characteristic of the foremost nation-states. Nationalism, once the apparent twin of democracy, was becoming, by the late nineteenth century, the force that could threaten democracy on behalf of a new and authoritarian concept of the nation in pursuit of political and spiritual unity.

In the closing decades of the nineteenth century, European nations became involved in a frenetic, global, inter-imperialist rivalry. In Europe itself, a deadly system of military alliances grew up. By the first decade of this century, Europe was sitting on a powder-keg with the Triple Alliance — Germany, Austria-Hungary, and Italy — lined up against the Triple Entente — France, Russia, and Great Britain.

When the crisis came, nationalism was again the force that undermined the existing European balance of power. The First World War destroyed Austria-Hungary, the Habsburg Empire, which was an anomaly on a continent of rising nationalism and nation-states. By 1914, the Danubian Empire already existed on the sufferance of its powerful sponsor and ally, Germany. In the years before the outbreak of the war, a plethora of nationalisms, Czech, Romanian, and Polish, among others, had worked like acid on the fraying fabric of the Habsburg Empire. Hungarian pretensions and desire for aggrandizement had also made life difficult in the Dual Monarchy in which Hungary had achieved the status of a partner in 1867. But it was south Slav nationalism, centred on the little kingdom of Serbia, that was to prove the undoing of the empire, and indeed of all Europe. (Ironically the south Slav state, Yugoslavia, which was created after the First World War, is now itself wracked with internal nationalist dissension, and is, along with the Soviet Union, the state in contemporary Europe that is most likely to break apart.)

The First World War ushered in the acute crisis of the nation-state system in Europe. The defeat of Germany in the war opened the way for the radical transformation of nationalism, although this was not immediately apparent when the Allies were victorious over the

German Empire in November 1918. In many ways, it had been logical that Germany should win the war. The Allies, the British, French, and Russians, managed in the opening years of the war to hold the Germans off, but just barely. What was to decide the outcome, although Russia was to be knocked out of the war and to succumb to revolution, was the intervention of the United States. Europe's leading nation-state, Germany, was robbed of its victory by the entry into the war of a non-European power.

The importance of the United States in winning the war gave immense influence to Woodrow Wilson, the American president, in determining the shape of the peace. For Wilson, nationalism and national self-determination were still benevolent, liberal concepts, in his mind the natural allies of democracy. The post-war settlement rested on a simple and lethal contradiction. The basic principle on which Europe was reconstructed was that of national self-determination, the creation of nation-states to match the national communities of the continent. Into the post-war world, a lengthy list of new nation-states emerged: Finland; Latvia; Lithuania; Estonia; Poland, reconstituted after its long division among Russia, Germany, and Austria-Hungary; Czechoslovakia; and Yugoslavia, much enlarged on the base of pre-war Serbia. With the Austro-Hungarian Empire dissolved, Austria and Hungary began new lives as small, land-locked states in the heart of Central Europe, shorn of their former glory.

Never had the theory of national self-determination been so powerfully embodied in political practice. For a nineteenth-century liberal, steeped in the ideas of popular democracy and nationalism, the creation of these new nation-states would have seemed a triumph against the old Europe of dynasties and empires, and therefore a sound basis for harmony among peoples. In due course, the new nation-states revealed themselves as anything but sturdy purveyors of liberalism and democracy. The fundamental flaw in the post-war system, however, was the unresolved position Germany occupied in it.

If the new nation-states represented a vast experiment in national self-determination, the Treaty of Versailles imposed limitations on Germany that were precisely the opposite of that principle. Germany lost large blocs of territory and, with them, important natural resources, and it was saddled with making reparations for the wartime damage it had caused. It was required to limit its military force to 100,000 men, with no airforce. As damaging as these tangible penalties for defeat was the inclusion by the Allies of the notorious "war guilt" clause in the treaty, the clause by which the Germans

acknowledged that their country had been responsible for the outbreak of the war in 1914.

For the fledgling Weimar democracy, the Treaty of Versailles was
a catastrophe. Tragically, for the new German Republic, the old
regime had collapsed by the time the armistice of November 11,
1918, had come into effect. Kaiser Wilhelm II had fled with his
family on board his personal train to neutral Holland. The following
spring, with Germany in no position to object to the peace terms of
the Allies, it was the representatives of the new German democracy
who had been forced to make the humiliating journey to the magnificent Palace of Mirrors at Versailles to sign the treaty. The circumstances helped foster a crucial myth that was to haunt the German
democratic regime — the myth that Germany had not been fairly
defeated on the field of battle, but had been "stabbed in the back"
by defeatists behind the lines. From its birth, the Weimar Republic
was detested by the scores of militarists who had not accepted German
defeat, by right-wing patriotic political groups, and by those who
longed for the restoration of the former German Empire. If the
Republic could restore prosperity in Germany and win equal status
for the defeated country with its former adversaries, it could hope to
marginalize these opponents. If not, they could become an unstanch-
able cancer that would one day destroy the Republic.

American isolationism and Soviet impotence left the initiative
in the hands of the Europeans. For a time, it appeared that they were
using it well. With the Locarno agreement of 1925 and German
adhesion to the League of Nations, it seemed that Geneva, the headquarters of the league, could become the capital of a prosperous and
pacific Europe. Until 1929, Europe's economy flourished, and the
major powers moved away from the hatred and inequity that had
been the legacy of the Treaty of Versailles.

By the time the stock market crashed on Wall Street in
October 1929, the inter-war period was more than half over. As the
1930s began, it quickly became apparent that the prosperity and
good feeling of the past half-decade had been based on a very thin
foundation. The fundamental questions had remained unanswered,
and, as soon as the Depression hit, those questions resurfaced with
a vengeance. When it came to dealing with the underlying issues
at play, the Geneva system revealed itself to be little better than a
game of smoke and mirrors. It was the circumstances created by the
Depression that made acute the underlying malaise that had existed
through the life of the Weimar Republic and opened the door to

the appointment of Adolf Hitler as chancellor on January 30, 1933.

The Nazi regime pushed the idea of the nation-state to its extreme limits. While all varieties of nationalism create a "we–they" relationship between those who belong to the nation and foreigners, Nazi nationalism, in its very principles, was dedicated to the maximum aggrandizement of Germany. To the extent that the Nazi regime did not aggress against all foreigners, this was a matter of the tactical appreciation of Germany's position, not a recognition that other nations had rights that ought to be respected. Germany, still Europe's most important nation-state as a consequence of its population and potential economic and military power, had produced a regime in which nationalism was united with totalitarianism, with nihilism, with the rejection of the values that had underlain the evolution of European civilization for centuries. Such a development could only mean that, once the Nazi regime had been shattered in war, the nation-state system itself would be called into question as the ultimate cause of Europe's tragedy.

For Europeans, as the twentieth century ends, it is evident that, among the great currents of the century — fascism, communism, liberal capitalism, and the adaptation to revolutionary technology — has been the crisis of the nation-state system. The apogee of the nation-state system was reached in the heady days of early August 1914, when people in their tens of thousands mobbed the great gathering points in Berlin, Paris, Petrograd, and London to lend their raucous cheers to the move towards war. Enflamed by their mutually antagonistic nationalisms, Europeans were literally rejoicing at the start of an odyssey of slaughter that would go on through two world wars.

The nadir of the nation-state system came on May 8, 1945, a few days after Adolf Hitler committed suicide in his bunker, when Nazi Germany surrendered unconditionally. In the three decades between the two dates, tens of millions had been killed. Cities, towns, whole regions, and whole countries had been devastated. In the systematic genocide of the Holocaust, Nazi Germany had pushed the national principle to the extreme limit of the absolute denial of the rights of others. Europe, no longer the centre of the world, was divided in two, into the respective spheres of the superpowers. Europe's invention, the nation-state system, had led it to the depths of tragedy.

The European tragedy itself became the most eloquent possible testimony against allowing the nation-state system to continue to exist as the form of organization to which ultimate loyalty was due. Only its negation could turn Europeans away from their murderous past and their resultant impotence. That negation, however, would require an invention as arduous as that of the nation-states in the first instance, the invention of Europe and Europeans.

Everywhere one looks in Europe, there are signs of that invention in progress. I learned that the Berlin Wall had been opened on the morning of November 10, 1989, as I read the newspaper headlines in the Brussels Midi railway station. On that rainy, blustery morning, I was taking the train to Paris. A short time after we left Brussels, the train crossed the border into France, without stopping, without even slowing down. While French customs officials walked through the train, there was no systematic questioning of passengers. The officials simply got off at the next stop with no interruption of the journey. At the Parisian railway station the Gare de Lyon, where I was waiting for my next train later in the day, a military band marched into the cavernous building. Elderly French veterans, decorated with their ribbons and medals, had arrived to place a memorial wreath at the cenotaph located in a corner of the station. With the tricolour unfurled, the military band struck up the stirring chords of the "Marseillaise." I was sitting at a café table beside the cenotaph, in a crowd of about one hundred onlookers. Getting ready to climb to my feet for the national anthem, I waited to see what the others would do. One old man got up, the others remained seated. They did not seem unhappy to watch the military band or hear their national anthem, but they failed to stand to attention, something no earlier generation would have done. In my eyes, those Parisians sitting in the café on the day the news from Berlin broke of the most important development in Europe since 1945 were Europeans.

Chapter Five

DOING BUSINESS
IN THE NEW EUROPE

★ ★ ★ ★ ★ ★ ★ ★ ★ ★ ★ ★

ULTILINGUAL YUPPIES, ATTIRED IN THE FASHIONABLE
clothing of half a dozen European countries, with life
experience in a number of major cities, at home with
the cuisine and product preferences of the whole
continent — is this the profile of the new executives who will pilot
Euro-corporations to global success? Some corporate planners and
consultants think so and have been advising their clients to seek and
train such exemplars to run the Europe-wide companies that will
emerge from the single-market process.

Saxton Bampfylde International, a London-based company that
specializes in "head-hunting" for corporate executives, has produced
a report entitled *The Search for the Euro-Executive*. The report was
based on a survey of chief executives and other managers of 130
major U.K. companies; interviews with 25 commercial managers in
France, Italy, and Germany; and in-depth interviews with 20 executives who were involved in the drive towards Europeanization of
particular companies. Saxton Bampfylde concluded that "the ideal
Euro-manager, so the research suggests: comes from a smaller country
(Holland, Denmark); has a 'hybrid' background, with early experience of another culture and another language; has some multinational
experience (but not too much); has worked in financial services (particularly banking) and/or multinational consultancy/marketing; has a
flexible cast of mind, with social skills to match." [1]

In its study, Saxton Bampfylde unearthed a number of executive types it concluded were "on offer" to European companies that
have been recruiting so that they can become more effective in the

Single European Market. The first such type, the "Senior States-man," is depicted as an executive, typically based in a multinational corporation, who has had working experience in several European countries. He or she is over age forty-five, usually over fifty, and has spent much of his or her career within an expatriate community, closely tied to the company for which he or she works. While the "Senior Statesman" has the strength of familiarity with a number of European settings, his or her chief defect is a tendency towards a strong attachment to the womb-like environment of the large firm for which he or she has worked. This executive may be difficult to lure into a new job, and will certainly expect plenty of expensive support if he or she is lured.

The "Ex-patriate" is an executive type usually encountered in national companies that have the need to post people abroad. The trouble with the "Ex-patriate" is that, while he or she has been in a foreign environment, his or her experience is usually firm or sector specific, and once he or she returns to home office, his or her knowl-edge of foreign ways declines sharply.

"The Journeyman" is, on the surface, a more promising type. He or she has travelled very widely throughout Europe, with job experience in a number of settings. The problem with the "Journey-man" is that he or she tends to be "something of a specialist, scien-tist or researcher." With such narrow qualifications, this person is unlikely to be much good at the lateral thinking that will be impor-tant to operating in the new context of Europeanization.

The final type, the "Euro-yuppie," seems more promising to the authors of the report. This young potential executive is a professional who is sometimes single, sometimes married, and if the latter, is often part of a "professional 'team' marriage." He or she has travelled a good deal in Europe and is committed to overcoming shortcomings in foreign-language skills. The "Euro-yuppie" finds Europe fun, tends to think in terms of the "big picture," and is instinctively able to con-ceive of things in European terms. The downside to the "Euro-yuppie" is his or her lack of corporate experience.[2]

None of these types is ideal, the report concludes. Furthermore, because the onset of the single market involves such a major trans-formation, the demand for suitable "Euro-executives" will be intense, while the supply will be strictly limited. Although companies all over Europe will be feeling the pressure, companies in the United Kingdom will feel it most intensely, because the mind-set of British executives and their relative lack of foreign-language skills make their adjustment to the new environment particularly difficult. The report concludes that the British are not likely to be winners in the "Euro-executive" sweepstakes, because of the cultural baggage they carry.

Out of the crucible of the single market, a new executive type is thought by some, the authors of the report among them, to be emerging. The new Euro-manager can now be spotted at airports or in the kinds of hotels frequented by executives in major European cities. At the extreme end, he (it is usually a he) is something of a "man from duty-free," clad, as he is, in the internationally acceptable clothing one encounters in this "airport culture." Typically, such a man may be wearing a Saint Laurent blazer, Gucci shoes, Hermès tie, and Burberry trenchcoat.[3]

While this picture of "Euro-man unchained" is a stereotype, there is no doubt that the single market is transforming the way business is being done in Europe and, to a lesser extent, all over the world. If the Euro-executive is already appearing on drawing-boards, and to a degree in real life, what about the Euro-consumer? Euro-corporate planning will not get far without a continent-wide market in which consumers, while far from homogeneous, share many tastes in common.

How will spaghetti, Camembert, and sauerkraut fare in the single market? Will the French mind importing their *gigot d'agneau* (leg of lamb) from England, and their *foie gras* from Poland? No one has given more anxious thought to the question of taste in the single market than the French, whose bread, cheese, and wine is so central to their way of life. While some look forward to the homogeniza-tion of tastes that will help launch the single market, others fear it. Guy Jullien is an uncompromising practitioner of the art of traditional French cuisine. His restaurant, the Beaugravière, is located on the east bank of the Rhône, on the edge of the Rhône Valley with its vast and famous vineyards.

After one wonderful evening of *foie gras*, fish, lamb, fine regional cheeses, and nougat — each course served with an appropriate Côtes du Rhône wine — Jullien came into the dining room, as he always does, to converse with the diners.

Jullien is a pessimist about the future of French food and wine. He says that, increasingly, produce comes from the outside, from anywhere in Europe — the lamb from Belgium and Ireland because it is cheaper than the excellent product that comes from the Massif Centrale in France. And 90 per cent of French wines are already chemically produced.

For Jullien, "1992" is another long step towards homogenization, towards the destruction of standards, towards the creation of an undifferentiated consumer. It will all benefit the bankers and the big companies, he believes. As far as quality goes, however, the future is bleak in his view. The French love of quality is to be subjected to an assault that it will not withstand.

What makes Jullien despair — the homogenization of tastes in France and other European countries — is what makes others cheer, because, while homogenization strikes at the unique and the traditional, it creates the conditions for mass marketing. Antoine Riboud, chairman of the French manufacturing concern B.S.N., has described the evolution of European tastes and the need to adapt to the changes: "My grandfather was local, my father was national, and I have to become European. . . . It is no longer true that you can remain local and survive."[4]

At the bottom end of the food scale, the rise of fast-food chains is happening everywhere. McDonald's has made its appearance in Aix en Provence and Avignon, not to mention Barcelona, Budapest, Vienna, and Rome. It is everywhere in Europe, but so, too, are the lesser-known chains, and the local imitators that have brought hamburgers, hotdogs, soft drinks, and the tell-tale bags of litter in the streets to every corner of Europe.

Further up-market, the situation is much more quirky. For example, while other Europeans often find the cheeses the French most cherish — Camembert, Brie, Roquefort, and diverse varieties of Chèvre — too much for their palates, they love to import large quantities of Cheddar from France, although the French themselves consider it a lesser offering.[5] Similarly, on a continent where people love to eat pigs in a baffling variety of ways, tastes remain highly localized in character: the British prefer their bacon and eggs; the French have their own *charcuterie*; the Italians their special hams; the Germans their notorious sausages; and the Spaniards their mountain hams.[6] And while the French consume 33 kilograms per person of beef annually, the Portuguese eat just 10 kilograms. Spaniards, on average, eat 22 kilograms of poultry annually, while the Germans consume 9.5 kilograms.[7] Even where local and national traditions would be less expected than in the case of food, odd local patterns sometimes persist. The French insist on top-loading washing machines, while for the British only front-loaders will do.[8]

The quirks aside, the broad trend is towards European marketing and production. Europe's immense potential economic assets have, in the past, been substantially negated by the division of the European market into uncompetitive national units. Overcoming those divisions and allowing a single market to take shape is the equivalent of unchaining a giant.

Perceptions of how the forging of a single European economy will change the world have been evident, sometimes in the foreboding of non-European business leaders. "Only strong American companies will survive after the formation of a unified European market in 1992," said Steven Ross, chairman of Warner Communications Inc., after his company's merger in 1989 with Time Inc. American and Japanese companies have watched the development of the Single European Market with a combination of both anticipation and anxiety. Anticipation has come from the prospect of major growth in Europe as a consequence of "1992," growth that non-European companies hope will be profitable for them. Anxiety has been provoked by the prospect that the rules governing the EC market may be slanted to favour European over non-European firms. To use the word invariably associated with the risk facing the non-Europeans, the process is being watched to ensure that Europe does not become a "fortress."

Anthony Lloyd is well positioned to consider both the opportunities and the potential problems for non-European multinationals in the New Europe. He has been responsible for handling IBM's reponse in the United Kingdom to the transition to the single market. IBM is not a company that trembles at the prospect of change. Throughout the tempests and upheavals of the twentieth century, it has thrived, making its name a synonym for "multinational corporation." IBM located its first European operation in Germany seventy years ago. The company is not likely to underestimate Europe's importance to it, since, in 1988, 37 per cent of its revenues and 42 per cent of its profits were realized there.

The circumstances of my meeting with Lloyd made it easy for me to forget that IBM is, indeed, an American company. Lloyd is in manner the archetypical British executive. We met at the Royal Air Force Club on Piccadilly in a grand sweeping bar that overlooks Green Park. Nothing could be more British than this, and that is the way IBM has always played it, presenting itself in each country as a feature of the national business landscape. With some people this works, with others less so, as Lloyd recognized in his blunt assessment of Europe's leaders (we met in 1990 before Thatcher's resignation): "If you ask Maggie Thatcher, she'll tell you IBM is a British company.

If you ask Chancellor Kohl, he'll tell you it's German. But, if you ask Jacques Delors, he'll tell you it's American."

Lloyd told me that IBM has taken "1992" very much into account in making its plans. Without wanting to sound complacent, he said he believed the company would be fully prepared for the changes by the time the single market was completed. IBM has already structured its European operations so that, in each of its production locations, it produces for the whole of Europe, while marketing continues to be carried out on a national basis. Lloyd said it was not so different from the strategy of leading Japanese companies like Nissan.

Within IBM, intellectual property circulates globally. Ideas conceived in one part of the world within the company are freely used elsewhere. The chief executive officers of the IBM European divisions have been holding European board meetings, a sign of the importance they see in the single market.

John F. Magee, an American professional consultant, has had frequent assignments in Europe. He perceives a cycle through which American corporate attitudes towards Europe have passed. In an article in the *Harvard Business Review*, he discussed the reaction of many American corporations to the initial creation of the European Common Market in the late 1950s:

> Many American businesses rather naively assumed that Europe would become a relatively integrated marketplace like the United States. They tried to choose manufacturing locations and set up distribution networks much as they might have done in the United States — to serve a common market. They were disappointed to discover that Europe was not one market but many, with subtle and not-so-subtle barriers to multinational trade: regulations, transport barriers, national tastes, and cultural prejudices, to mention just a few. [9]

The consequence of this experience, according to Magee, was that as U.S. corporate holdings in Europe grew in size, each subsidiary tended to develop its own local market, so that coordination among the holdings of a particular U.S. company was often "limited or non-existent. This drift away from the notion of an integrated market was partly a reaction to European realities and partly a result of the kinds of acquisitions many U.S. companies made as a means of expanding. Local pressures called for local strategies. There was

simply no incentive to struggle for a unified European structure."
Having gotten over the idea of a European market once before,
Magee surmises, they have been slow to take it up again and to
develop a European strategy, with a structure capable of operating on
a European basis.[10] He points to the very recent efforts of major
American companies to catch up by establishing integrated corporate
strategies for Europe: only in the fall of 1988 did Coca-Cola reorganize its European, African, and Middle Eastern management to establish a new executive structure with specific responsibility for the EC;
only recently did Colgate-Palmolive, with production facilities in
nine EC countries, set up a pan-European management board; and in
its 1988 annual report, Heinz declared that the "potential for an integrated European market engages the Heinz imagination."[11]

As for IBM, the company feels at home in Europe, not simply
because of its long experience there, but from its strong position as
a producer in Europe. At present, IBM is the only manufacturer of
computer mainframes in Europe, all other mainframes there being
purchased from Japanese companies. Indeed, IBM is much better
placed than its European competitors, which produce computers and
related micro-electronic products, to face up to the rigours of the
single market. While the strong position of companies like IBM and
other American and Japanese firms in a number of key industrial
sectors means that they will likely fare well in making adjustments in
comparison with their domestic European competitors, they have
more than private competition to worry about. As corporations based
outside Europe, they have to worry as well about the public policies
of the New Europe, and how those policies will alter the investment
climate for non-European multinationals. The central focus for their
attention is the EC Commission in Brussels, the body that is critical
to EC innovations in trade, industrial, and investment policies. If
there is one cloud in the sky for IBM in Europe, it is the suspicion
that the EC Commission is biased in favour of European-based electronics giants like Siemens and that EC money for the support of high-
technology research is much more likely to go to such firms than to
an American-owned company, however distinguished its pedigree on
the continent.

What non-European multinationals perceive as bias is seen very
differently in Europe. Since much of the motivation to move to the
single market, despite all the pain it entails in adjustments by firms,
communities, workers, and governments, is to combat the competition encountered from the United States and Japan, there is a natural

and powerful desire to make sure that "1992" serves Europeans first. The critical question for Europeans and non-Europeans alike is how the European interest is best realized, and how that will end up affecting the global economic system.

COMPETITION AND INDUSTRIAL POLICIES

Europeans are far from united on how to approach the question of economic policy making. At one end of the European spectrum has been the position of the "classic liberals," whose most renowned European leader was Margaret Thatcher. In most respects, Thatcherism was synonymous with classic liberalism, whose leading tenet is that the state should be small; that it should provide security, infrastructure, and essential services; and that decisions about economic priorities should be determined in the marketplace by investors and consumers. The Thatcherite stance was that no distinction should be made between European firms and those based in the United States and Japan: let the market determine the outcome, was the position. For those of like mind, the fundamental imperative facing the EC was to develop its "competition policy," not its "industrial policy." For them, the single market, particularly in financial services, was a key goal precisely so that barriers to true competition could be eliminated. These "classic liberals" — "hyper liberals," as they have sometimes been called — have opposed the very idea of an industrial strategy in which the state forms a partnership with industry, and sometimes with labour, to target a line of economic advance, especially in high-technology sectors.

Within the EC Commission, the key personality with a classic liberal perspective is Sir Leon Brittan, appointed by Margaret Thatcher to succeed Lord Cockfield. Within the commission, Brittan took over two of the areas of policy that had come under Lord Cockfield's sweeping purview: competition policy and financial institutions. Brittan made it clear very early in his term of office that it was his intention to take a hard line against state aids to industry within the community.[12] He took aim at such aids and vowed to seek their reduction. Basing his information on a survey of state aids to industry within the community, Brittan concluded that, during the 1980s, the United Kingdom had sharply reduced such aids, and France had kept them at the same level, while West Germany had increased them somewhat, and Italy had vastly augmented them, making Britain and Italy the polar extremes on the question. Brittan made it clear that he wanted to reduce the most common types of state aids whose rationales were: to maintain so-called national champions — leading firms in key sectors; to shore up industries facing strong external competition; to promote exports to countries outside the EC; or to underwrite technological development. Of particular concern to Brittan was the status of nationalized industries, which were especially important in Italy and France: "feather-bedding of nationalized industries must be stopped. There can be no room for policies which have the effect, even if not always the intention, of discriminating against the private sector, which must be allowed to compete on equal terms."[13]

If the EC, the world's largest trading power, expected a fair deal from others, Brittan believed its own interest would be maximized by being non-protectionist itself: "Reduced aid levels are a visible sign that the completion of the internal market does not mean a retreat into Fortress Europe but shows our willingness to create an open free market economy," he declared in the speech where he set out his goals as an EC commissioner.[14]

Even though Brittan was appointed to the commission by Margaret Thatcher in large measure because his views so reliably mirrored hers, he, too, went "native" once in office and distanced his position from that of Thatcher on key issues. In his support for the idea of a social charter for the EC and for monetary union within the community, he took the side of the rest of the EC in its battle against the solitary opposition of the prime minister who had appointed him. Despite his differences with Thatcher, however, Brittan represents the classic liberal position on the commission more clearly than any other member, a position that can fairly be characterized as "European Thatcherism."

The 1980s was a decade of classic liberal renewal, particularly throughout the English-speaking world, but in continental Europe as well. Under the leadership of Margaret Thatcher and Ronald Reagan, this ideology of the marketplace was extolled with born-again fervour. Outside Britain, the renewed lure of the marketplace was echoed in powerful currents within West German Christian Democracy, in the U-turn in the economic policies of the French Socialists, in the entrepreneur-centred thrust of the Spanish Socialist government, and in steps towards privatization in Italy. However, what was like a powerful religious movement in the Anglo-American world was more like a pragmatic corrective in continental Europe. Despite the market emphasis of the 1980s, "corporatism" remained strongly entrenched in Europe, with a perspective on society and the economy at odds with classic liberalism in important respects. To understand where Europe's economic policies are likely to go as the single market takes shape, one must take account of corporatism.

While they certainly operate within a market concept of the economy, corporatists believe that, in an age of expensive and very sophisticated technology and of large corporations, classical theory is far from being a sufficient guide to success. They postulate that forward planning and *concertation* among government, business, and labour are essential to achieving optimum results. Furthermore, they believe that at least a degree of industrial policy is justified to counter similar efforts on the part of leading global competitors. [15]

In Europe, the corporatist critique of the hyper-liberal position is that the approach of Sir Leon Brittan would leave Europe wide open to Japanese and American industrial strategies, and therefore would undermine rather than strengthen domestic European firms.

The Japanese, it is contended, have not left things to the play of market forces in forging their strategic economic breakthroughs. Many Europeans believe that competing with the Japanese has about it an element of economic warfare that only the naïve would be unprepared to acknowledge. This point of view was strongly reinforced in May 1991 when Edith Cresson replaced Michel Rocard as prime minister of France. Cresson was an outspoken proponent of the idea of a European industrial policy to counter the techniques deployed by the Japanese. Notorious examples of the use of such techniques concern the Japanese successes in the field of computers and micro-chips, and in the field of industrial robots. In both cases, the Japanese Ministry of International Trade and Industry (MITI) planned strategy with leading firms. Temporary cartels were permitted so that competing firms could pool their efforts to achieve breakthroughs in basic product research. In targeted sectors, imports were restricted and small firms were assisted through subsidized loans to purchase or lease domestic products. Once an effective scale of operations had been achieved domestically, Japanese industry was ready to undertake its export offensive. The results were dramatic. In the half-decade from 1978 to 1983, the Japanese share of the computer export market for all OECD (Organization for Economic Cooperation and Development) countries increased from 5.2 per cent to 18 per cent — largely at the expense of Britain and West Germany, whose share of exports was falling.

The striking success of the Japanese has provoked alarm among

European electronics-industry executives. In a pamphlet used to lobby governments and the EC, the industry declared that it opposed "unfair competitive practices and . . . using a protected home market as a launching platform to attack world markets."[16]

Whereas the Japanese, through *concertation* between MITI and the private sector, have practised a direct industrial strategy, the Americans have adopted a strategy that has been the indirect by-product of defence spending. In the mid-1980s, defence spending in the United States constituted more than 6 per cent of the country's Gross National Product. Over 8 per cent of the American defence budget was directed to Research and Development (R&D). In 1985, defence-funded R&D amounted to $24.6 billion. This very large capital pool underwrote the research efforts of a vast array of private-sector companies, particularly those involved in high technology. While much of this research has undoubtedly been arcane, with only limited spin-offs for non-military product development, the effect has been to provide American companies with a massive subsidy.

A key sector where defence spending has been critical has been the aircraft industry. In 1984, for example, the U.S. government spent $12.6 billion on complete military aircraft and $4.3 billion on aircraft engines. Such huge amounts pump up the cash flow of the industry, pay for its overhead, and virtually guarantee the major American aircraft companies against failure in the marketplace. For Boeing and McDonnell Douglas, the two major producers of civilian aircraft in the United States, this public-sector support can hardly be overstated. Because of it, in part, Europeans assert, Boeing still accounts for 50 per cent of all production of civilian aircraft in the world.

A strong current of opinion in Europe holds that the aim of the Japanese and the Americans has been to use direct and indirect government supports for industry to put their own corporations in a position of overwhelming superiority in vital sectors. Having achieved supremacy, they then seek to pull the ladders to their own success up after them by loudly complaining if anyone else seeks to play an analogous game.

PHILIPS AND AIRBUS — COPING WITH THE JAPANESE AND THE AMERICANS

Nowhere is the issue of the industrial competition of Europeans with the Japanese and the Americans more dramatically illustrated than in Eindhoven, Holland. Eindhoven, population 200,000, is the city that

Philips built. Philips and Eindhoven have grown together since the company was founded in 1891. Over that century, the city has been the fiefdom of the largest electronics firm in Europe. Eindhoven feels like a company town, and never more so than on the day I arrived there in July 1990, when Philips was about to hold an extraordinary meeting of its board of directors to pick a new top man to lead the company out of the quagmire into which it had sunk. The company's bottom-line performance had been extremely anaemic, with some of its operating divisions turning in losses. It had been forced to sell assets and to undertake a major trimming and restructuring effort.

While Philips has 300,000 employees in sixty countries, this far-flung empire is run from Eindhoven, where 30,000 people work for it. The Philips name and logo look down from structures everywhere in this astonishingly quiet city, where more people ride their bicycles — every street has a bicycle lane — than drive cars. Eindhoven has its Philips Theatre, Philips Museum, and Philips Library, and the company sponsors the local football team, PSV Eindhoven. In the past, Philips used to build houses, which it rented to workers, although it no longer does this. Now there are many cooperatively owned houses, row after row of neat, identical dwellings, in the city. A trade-union leader I spoke to that day told me that, although the city government is "formally independent" of the company, behind the scenes, Philips wields immense power.

Over its century in existence, Philips has spread out in so many directions that the company is not exactly sure how many products it makes. Of one thing it is sure, however: Philips needs to rationalize, to shed losing lines, to concentrate on what it does best if it is to hold its own in the fierce competitive war with Japanese electronics firms. Despite its virtuosity as an innovator, Philips has been less than brilliant at marketing. A major error in perceiving the trend in the European computer market away from minicomputers to personal computers has undermined the company's position against European rivals like Siemens and Olivetti, not to mention Japanese firms.[17]

To turn the fortunes of the company around, Philips has sought salvation from Jan Timmer, a tough, strikingly bald, heavy-set manager. Timmer demonstrated his effectiveness when he ran the company's consumer-products division. Previously he had managed PolyGram, the company's music subsidiary, switching its emphasis from technical advances to marketing. Running head to head in successful competition with CBS Records, owned by Sony after 1987,

Timmer's PolyGram broadened its repertoire so that it stretched from rock stars to Luciano Pavarotti.

The consequence of the emergency session of the company's board on July 2, 1990, was that Timmer was moved up to the position of chief executive officer. As soon as he was in office, he announced that Philips would lay off 10,000 workers in Europe. The lay-off was no real surprise, but was grim news none the less for Eindhoven and Holland, where many of the cuts would take place.

Philips has been an archetypal European employer, with its paternalism, its large bureaucracy, and, until now, its slow adjustment to external competitive pressures. As Europe's largest electronics firm, with two-thirds of its work-force in Europe, the company has had plenty of clout in Brussels, clout it has used to give strong support to "1992." Philips wants a "domestic" market larger than those in the United States and Japan, but it wants something else — protection against Japanese competitors. Philips and other European electronics firms have used very strong language to depict the state of competition with Japanese firms, language usually reserved for military adversaries. Here is one example in a brochure aimed at Brussels: "The attack from the Japanese on Europe's Electronics industries is in the first place concentrated on new and high technology Consumer Electronics and Components. They wish to achieve the same global industrial domination as they have already achieved with products such as cameras, calculators, watches, printers, copiers and facsimile machines."[18] It was in this spirit that Philips and other European electronics firms lobbied the EC Commission on what it saw as the predatory pricing policies of Asian firms. In July 1988, this lobbying paid off when the commission decided to impose anti-dumping duties (duties to offset alleged predatory pricing policies) on fifteen Asian producers of compact-disc players.[19]

Philips has not been alone in its battle to salvage the European electronics industry in the face of Japanese competition. The Thomson Group, owned by the French government, is a major player in the European and global consumer-electronics business. On a global scale, Thomson, with its 100,000 employees, is the fourth-largest consumer-electronics company, after Matsushita Electrical Industry Co., Philips, and Sony. Chairman of the group is Alain Gomez, a political and corporate maverick; the grandson of a Spanish anarchist, he was once the founder of a far-left faction of the French Socialist party. When he was appointed chairman of Thomson, he decided that, to make the company competitive, he had to diversify its operations on a global basis, prepare it for the Single European Market, and play tough against the Japanese. Under his leadership, Thomson extended itself throughout Europe and the world, so that, today, 72 per cent of its sales come from outside France. What has made Gomez noteworthy among European chief executives has been his utterly frank depiction of the relationship between European and Japanese corporations. "The Japanese are waging a type of industrial war," he asserts. "There comes a time when you have to draw the line, when you have to say we just won't accept the loss of one per cent more of the market."[20] Having acquired the consumer-electronics business of General Electric and its RCA subsidiary in the United States in 1987, Gomez has manoeuvred his company to the position of being the largest supplier of colour televisions and video recorders in the United States.

Companies like Philips and Thomson have exercised a potent influence on the EC Commission. Moreover, today it is the commission, not individual European countries, that makes the key decisions on trade for Europe. This is a dramatic shift from past practice. Most members of the EC Commission, not including Sir Leon Brittan, are favourable to an approach in which Europeans map out critical economic sectors where they intend to build strength and to seek protection from outside competitors. Since the commission will never admit to being protectionist, it has chosen instead to make use of policies that protect European industry while avoiding the highly charged protectionist label. In this context, the use of anti-dumping measures has become the crucial weapon in the commission's arsenal of "functional protectionism." It has been deployed and could be deployed even more in the future, depending on economic circumstances, to limit access to Europe by overseas producers in sensitive industrial sectors.

Secretive top-level meetings between the heads of major electronics firms and Jacques Delors have been a part of the process. On a weekend in April 1991, Jan Timmer of Philips and Alain Gomez of Thomson, along with Carlo De Benedetti of Olivetti, Francis Lorenz of Bull, and Karlheinz Kaske of Siemens, met with Delors at a small hotel in Burgundy. The meeting came in the wake of large losses or reductions in profits for all five of the companies concerned. The top questions on the agenda were how to stave off Japanese competition and how to speed the opening of Europe's own internal market, particularly in the state-dominated telecommunications sector. While the majority of those present eschewed a frankly protectionist approach towards the Japanese, they did consider relaxing

EC anti-trust regulations to allow European electronics firms more lat-
itude in pooling research geared towards product innovation.[21]

While European electronics firms see Japanese industry and
Japanese industrial practices as the key threat confronting them in the
consumer-electronics sector, American economic practices have similarly produced a powerful European corporatist response, most
notably in the aerospace sector.

Airbus Industrie, a consortium of French, German, British, and
Spanish aircraft manufacturers, which produces civilian aircraft, is a
potent European response, not only to American aerospace companies, but to the U.S. government's support for these companies
through defence spending. Despite its teething problems, the consortium has managed technological and organizational triumphs that
have made Airbus the second-largest producer of civilian aircraft in
the world, next to Boeing.

The launching of Airbus, an impossibility without the backing
of European governments, was inspired by a range of motives. At
the most practical level, European aircraft manufacturers recognized
that, on their own, they had no hope of taking on Boeing and
McDonnell Douglas. There was a political motivation as well.
Airbus was essentially a Franco-German undertaking, much in the
same way as European union itself was. Indeed, Airbus was a concrete industrial venture in which the French and the Germans
would prove that they could work together in a single enterprise,
at the same time as they ensured themselves a degree of technological independence from the United States.

Airbus Industrie was established in December 1970. Its four full
partners are France's Aérospatiale (state-owned), which has a 37.9 per
cent share; Germany's Deutsche Airbus, also with a 37.9 per cent
share; Britain's British Aerospace, with a 20 per cent share; and
Spain's CASA, with a 4.2 per cent share. The Airbus structure is significant because it was one of the first ventures to make use of a new
legal form, known as the European Economic Interest Grouping
(EEIG). An EEIG functions according to a contractual agreement
among its founding members, operating under the laws of a desig-
nated home country. As an EEIG, Airbus coordinates the efforts of
the founding partners, so that they are able to design, manufacture,
and market aircraft together.

By the time Airbus Industrie itself was fully established, the first
venture among the partners, the A300 aircraft, a twin-aisle, two-
engine jet with a seating capacity of 267, was already in the planning

stages. It had its first test flight in October 1972 and entered into commercial service with Air France in May 1974. Between then and the beginning of 1990, Airbus sold 248 A300 jets, making its first offering a solid commercial success.

With the A300, European aircraft manufacturers were moving away from a past record of brilliant technological achievement allied with commercial disaster, the most outstanding example of which had been the supersonic Concorde, created in a joint Franco-British partnership, out of which only sixteen aircraft were built, eight for Air France and eight for British Airways. With the A300, technological prowess was linked to finding a major market niche. Even that could have proved a brilliant dead-end, however, had the consortium not gone ahead to plan the launching of other models so that, by the mid-1990s, a full "Airbus family" of jet aircraft will exist to provide the world with its only major non-American choice of civilian jets.

As it assembled its family, Airbus was also in the process of establishing a unique industrial enterprise that drew on the skills of companies and workers in a number of European countries. At the centre of this widespread undertaking is Airbus Industrie itself, with its coordinating role. The centre of this far-flung enterprise is Toulouse, on the arid plain in the south of France, not far from the Pyrenees and the Spanish border. A city of 200,000, Toulouse has been targeted as a potential technological and educational centre by the French government since the end of the Second World War. Airbus Industrie is located in an industrial area close to Toulouse airport. Within its office complex, where potential customers are received from around the world, virtually daily, English is the working language, making Airbus an English-language enclave in a major French-speaking metropolitan area. Not far from the Airbus offices are the lines where final assembly of the aircraft is carried out by Aérospatiale. The day I visited the line, which is the same one where the Concorde was assembled, Airbus jets, with markings for Middle Eastern, European, and North American airlines, were parked just outside the assembly area at the edge of Toulouse airport, ready to be flown to their destinations to go into service.

Final assembly constitutes only 4 per cent of the work that goes into the production of the aircraft. The other 96 per cent of the work is undertaken by the partners or by their associated companies or subcontractors. Airbus operates a unique "Skylink" fleet of four "Super Guppy" aircraft — giant transport aircraft with the appearance of fat, pregnant fish — whose job is to fly aircraft sections from partner factories to Toulouse. The Guppies fly out to Bremen, Hamburg, Chester, Nantes, Madrid, and other centres to pick up already manufactured sections of the aircraft needed in Toulouse for assembly. The successor to the A300, the A300–600, is built all over Europe, and gets its Pratt and Whitney engines from the United States. The nose section of the aircraft is provided by Aérospatiale in France, much of the body by Messerschmitt-Bölkow-Blohm in Germany, large parts of the wings by British Aerospace, and the tail wings by CASA in Spain.

Following the A300 and its replacement, the A300–600 (which entered service in 1984), have been the other members of the Airbus family. The boldest and most far-reaching move to date for Airbus was its launching in June 1987 of two new planned models, this time with larger seating capacities. The A330, a two-engine jet with a range of 4,750 nautical miles and a seating capacity of 335, will come into service in 1993. The A340, a four-engine jet with a range of between 6,750 and 7,550 nautical miles and a seating capacity of 262 to 295, will come into service in 1992. The two aircraft have been planned as a package and will have 80 per cent of their components — including cockpit, fuse-lage, wings (with differences limited to engine installation), and landing gear — a design achievement that will substantially reduce the cost of both. Once the A330 and A340 come into service, Airbus will offer a range of choices for airlines for short-, middle-, and long-distance flights, carrying passenger loads ranging from 150 to 335. Airbus believes that it has chosen its slots on the aviation ladder with care. It projects, for example, that a relatively small, long-range aircraft like its planned A340 will have a solid future moving passengers from one secondary location to another — say, from Nice to New Orleans — instead of having to fly everyone to a larger centre like Paris or New York first before moving them in a Boeing 747 to another larger centre, whence they can fly to their final destination. In December 1990, Airbus revealed just how bold its planning could be when it announced that it was considering the development of an aircraft larger than the Boeing 747, presently the largest passenger jet. The new plane, currently dubbed the A350, would carry up to 700 passengers and would have a range of at least 7,000 miles. Airbus projects that its share of the global market for the period 1988 to 2006 for new civilian aircraft will be over one-third, or 3,160 aircraft out of 9,200. Should this projection prove true, Airbus will reap sales of $179 billion — no mean sum.

What Airbus has already achieved and expects to complete is no less than a revolution in the civilian-aviation industry, a realm in which American dominance was almost total before the European challenge was mounted, a challenge that even the Japanese have shied away from attempting to date. Naturally, the giant American aircraft manufacturers could not be expected to welcome this massive assault on their turf. Cry foul they did, so loudly that, at times, the issue of Airbus has led to very sharp diplomatic exchanges across the Atlantic. What made the Americans cry foul was that, from the time the consortium was founded, the governments of the Federal Republic of Germany, France, Britain, and Spain have sunk nearly $9 billion into Airbus. While the Europeans say that these funds have taken the form of long-term, interest-bearing loans, the Americans insist that little, if any, of the money has actually been repaid. The result, the Americans charge, is that Airbus can profitably market a jet for $35 million to $40 million, whereas its true cost is $10 million to $20 million higher.

Airbus spokesmen are not much impressed by the complaints of their American competitors. When I put their case to an Airbus spokesman over lunch at the consortium's guest dining-room in Toulouse, he replied that, over a ten-year period, Boeing and McDonnell Douglas between them had received $23 billion in business from the U.S. Defense Department.

The war of words between the United States and the European governments that have backed Airbus continued in the summer of 1990 with the completion of a study written by Gellman Research Associates for the Department of Commerce in Washington. The study stated that subsidies from France, West Germany, Britain, and Spain made possible 74 per cent of the development spending undertaken by Airbus. Describing the attack as "ill-founded," Henri Martre, president of Aérospatiale, said it was evidence that "the United States has decided to follow an aggressive sales policy to correct its trade balance, and is turning to Europe after Japan." Mr. Martre repeated the often-stated European case that 70 per cent of American aircraft-company sales are made under government contracts, and that a very large part of the funding for the development of aircraft by these manufacturers comes from the Defense Department and NASA.[22]

By the beginning of the 1990s, Airbus was well on its way to capturing the 30 per cent of the global market for its products that had been the goal of the consortium. The road was not always smooth: there have been several highly publicized accidents involving Airbus aircraft, accidents the company claimed had nothing to do with defects in design or manufacture. Still, despite start-up problems and the five-year-old diplomatic battle between the United States and

European countries over Airbus, it was clear that the Europeans had no intention of backing down and that they saw the stakes as much higher than the success of a particular company. They conceived of Airbus as a strategy for ensuring their viability in a strategic high-technology industry whose spin-offs into related sectors were critical if Europe was to compete effectively with the United States and Japan at the high end of the economic ladder.

Philips has been on the defensive, while Airbus has been on the offensive. Both, however, are European giants whose common experience illustrates aspects of European industrial policy in the making, policy that defines the ways in which European governments and the EC itself are prepared to intervene to ensure European prowess in critical fields against the Japanese and the Americans. The use of EC anti-dumping measures to protect European electronics firms and the backing provided by European governments for Airbus are examples of the limits on Europe's willingness to rely on the market to determine results.

NOT MARKETS ALONE

The "1992" program has been driven by the logic of the market, the logic of globalization. However, powerful forces and traditions in Europe have resisted the idea of an unrestrained market economy and society. Corporatism has motivated the approach of the EC towards Philips and of European governments towards Airbus. If we are to understand the social model that is emerging in the EC, we need to see that, while the impetus of the market has been dominant, it is offset by powerful non-market tendencies, of which corporatism is but one. Non-market approaches are also evident in statism, and social democracy or socialism, tendencies that have an important influence in Europe. To be understood, corporatism and these other tendencies must be seen for what they are. So far, we have stressed the reactive character of corporatism, its use as the basis for industrial policies to protect key sectors in Europe from Japanese and American competition. Corporatism, however, amounts to more than a set of tools for dealing with economic problems. As the word implies, corporatism is anchored in the notion that society forms a unity of social groups, a corpus, that it is much more than an aggregate of individuals.

Corporatism has become important in countries where there has been a strong sense of social solidarity, where group rights are emphasized alongside individual rights. The quintessential corporatist country has been Austria, although Swedish social democracy has been strongly corporatist, and there have been important strains of corporatism in the Federal Republic of Germany (FRG). Corporatism also owes much to the evolution of Catholic social thought since the late nineteenth century. At its heart is the rejection of both the Marxist notion of class war and the overriding emphasis on individualism encountered in classical liberalism. Corporatism involves the idea that the different elements of society should work together, should share decision making so that the general interest can be advanced. In countries that attempt to put corporatism into practice, the emphasis is on the forming of a common set of social priorities through participation and consultation among government and the major social actors — business, trade unionists, and other groups. Corporatists often use the phrase "social partners" to depict the relationships that exist among business, labour, and government. The FRG and Austria have been models of the corporatist approach through worker participation in the management of companies and through close consultation and cooperation involving government with both business and labour.

Statism, while it overlaps in practice with corporatism, has a different philosophical origin. It derives from the idea that the state has an organic existence that transcends all of the particular interests in society and has a permanent and historical character that fuses the long-term purposes of the whole of society. France is the country with the longest and deepest statist tradition, a tradition that spans the whole of the political spectrum from right to left. French statism predates the French Revolution and is embodied in the works of Louis XIV and other monarchs; in its modern form, it goes back to the Napoleonic era. Since the Second World War, both the right and the left in France have drawn on the statist tradition in developing the country's economic policy. The first role performed in France in the post-war period by Jean Monnet was as commissioner general of the Secretariat of the "Plan," the touted national agency whose job it was to work out an economic strategy for the country in conjunction with business and labour. Far from relying on the ungoverned market, the Plan was based on the assumption that the leading actors in French society, including the state, needed to establish a common agenda and to work for it. Particularly in the early post-war years, when resources were scarce, the Plan was brilliantly successful in its efforts at *concertation*, at bringing key economic players together and keeping them together until they agreed on what the national agenda should be. Results attest to the effectiveness of the system. While French economic growth in the 1950s was not as spectacular as that achieved in the economic "miracle" of the FRG, it far exceeded that in Britain, and, indeed, in the 1960s, French growth surpassed that in the Federal Republic.

If corporatism and statism overlap in their consequences, so do both with social democracy. Western European social democracy or democratic socialism has diverse origins in particular movements, each with its own doctrinal emphases. It is clear, however, that social democrats across Europe share a wide range of assumptions and policy approaches. If French socialism is more statist and less corporatist than is social democracy in Germany, Austria, and Sweden, there is, none the less, a common commitment to government intervention both to ensure fairness in the economic system and to promote long-term development, which the market, with its short-term bias, is inclined to overlook. While the details of European socialist ideas do not concern us here, what is important is the adherence of socialist parties to gradualism, the transformation of society through parliamentary means, and to the partnership of the state with business and labour to promote economic development.

Meshing with and adding to the force of these non-market approaches has been the rise in Europe of the world's most powerful environmental movement. On April 26, 1986, the nuclear reactor at Chernobyl in the Ukraine exploded and then caught fire. Though much of the world received radioactive particles from the catastrophe, the greatest impact was on the immediate region and on adjacent countries. Chernobyl confirmed the worst fears of the ecology movement whose political strength had been growing rapidly in Europe over the preceding decade. No single event in the recent European past has made national frontiers appear so irrelevant. In Scandinavia and the Federal Republic of Germany, the effect was especially great. Fearing contamination, millions of people changed their consumption habits, giving up fresh milk and fresh vegetables in the aftermath of the catastrophe. They showed themselves unwilling to believe the soothing messages from government authorities, which were aimed at assuaging public concern.

By the time the Chernobyl accident occurred, the West German Greens, the most influential of Europe's environmental movements, were already represented in the Bundestag (lower house of parliament) of the Federal Republic.[23] Green parties and movements throughout Western Europe were dedicated to the proposition that the old economics and politics geared to the single-minded pursuit of growth were leading the world to catastrophe. For such movements, growth-centred policies, whether of the Right or of the Left, had to be rejected in favour of a new vision of humanity's place in the ecosystem. (Of course, within the ranks of Europe's Greens, there were very wide variations, with some elements of the movement ready to enter into coalitions with other parties, and others rejecting such compromises.)

So broad was the impact of the movement that virtually all political parties took up parts of its message, each attempting to assure people that they, too, were green. In terms of measurable political strength, the high point for the Greens came in January 1987 when the West German party won 8.3 per cent of the vote in a federal election. But, in December 1990, the Greens in western Germany were eliminated from the Bundestag in the first all-German election when they failed to win 5 per cent of the vote, the minimum needed for parliamentary representation. In eastern Germany, the Greens won eight seats under the heading of Alliance 90, a front that grouped them with other popular movements. Political observers attributed this electoral setback not to any waning of environmentalism, but to the inability of the movement to deal successfully with the overriding issue of German unification.

Whatever the electoral ups and downs of the Greens, the influence of the movement has been profound, with evident consequences for the conduct of business in Europe. Both the EC and national governments have been according a very high profile to environmental questions. Enforcing water-quality standards, raising auto-emission standards (which still remained less stringent than those in North America), setting targets to limit the production of greenhouse-enhancing agents, policing the disposal of toxic chemicals, emphasizing product recycling — these were some of the main points on the public agenda. Virtually the whole of this agenda involves increased costs for business, imposing a set of non-market goals on the functioning of the economy. And while green consciousness varied considerably from country to country and region to region, it was seen as a European issue, one in which national sovereignty had to give way to the imposition of common standards throughout the EC. Of particular significance has been the role of the European Court of Justice in rendering decisions that have begun to impose uniformity of environmental standards across the community.

Despite their conflicts and contradictions, the ideas and approaches of corporatists, statists, and social democrats, heavily influenced by the ecology movement, have fostered a de facto alliance among these forces in Brussels in the formulation of EC policies. There is no doubt that this range of ideas carries considerable weight with the commission under the presidency of Jacques Delors. Indeed, members of the European Parliament have told me that Delors has privately urged them to bring forward industrial-strategy proposals to offset the drive for a market-centred approach, which is, as we have seen, so much the thrust of "1992." Those who favour an industrial strategy often urge a number of principles on the EC to round out the market orientation of "1992." The principles include large-scale increases in regional-development funds to be spent by the EC to ensure that peripheral areas of Europe are not gutted economically by the single market with its tendency to promote a privileged "inner Europe"; the strengthening of Europe's anti-dumping code to ensure that the EC is not invaded by what are contemptuously described as "screwdriver" factories from outside, factories in which only final assembly occurs and in which there is no technological transfer to Europeans; and the elaboration of a social charter in the EC to ensure minimum wage and salary levels, worker benefits, and social programs across the community to guard against the risk of "social dumping," the movement of industries from high-wage regions where social programs are strongly entrenched to low-wage areas where social programs are much more minimal.

THE BATTLES OF BOURNEMOUTH AND BRUGES

Those who were concerned that the market approach alone would lead inexorably to unacceptable inequities favoured the adoption of a set of social principles by the EC to be accompanied by an action program, whose purpose was to offset the negative effects of the single market. The principles were to be enshrined in a social charter, which would enunciate the fundamental rights of workers and of communities throughout the EC. The political controversy engendered by the social charter was a revealing episode. It forced political groups across Europe to define their positions on the extent to which the market should be allowed, or not allowed, to determine economic results.

The battle over the social charter escalated from a political struggle to a personal brawl between Jacques Delors and Margaret

Thatcher. The question was inexorably personalized when the commission president accepted an invitation to address an audience hostile to everything the British prime minister stood for, the annual meeting of the British Trades Union Congress (TUC). Because of the subsequent significance of the speech, circumstances surrounding it have acquired elements of mythology. Several people, in conversation with me, have taken credit for having convinced Delors to make the speech at Bournemouth, including a member of the British Labour Group in the European Parliament, and one leading British trade unionist who claims he talked Delors into it while the two of them were out for a walk in Glasgow.

In the seaside city of Bournemouth, on September 8, 1988, Jacques Delors stood up in front of an audience of British trade unionists who had not yet decided what they thought of the bespectacled French intellectual who was their guest speaker. The wariness at the outset was understandable because the TUC had stood by the Labour party during the years when the party was opposed to British membership in the EC. Although by 1988, both the Labour party and the TUC had moved a long way from their former hostility to the community, their new attitude was a matter of calculation, not of passion. No one knew, when Jacques Delors stood up, that the British trade-union audience was about to fall in love. Delors had been concerned about the speech because his English is somewhat rusty, but, as the speech went on, the audience warmed. Delors saluted the British labour movement for the pioneering contribution it had made to the fight for the rights and dignity of workers. He emphasized the social dimension of "1992," stressing the EC funding of initiatives to overcome underdevelopment in disadvantaged regions, to fight long-term unemployment, and to provide jobs for young people. He assured his audience that the EC would not neglect the north/south problems so evident in Britain. Then he reached his peroration:

> Europe must reassert itself. The world is looking at us. It is watching you, the British; it is watching the Germans, the French, the Italians and all the others. It is wondering how these nations, which have fought each other over the centuries, have managed to rise up again when so much was pointing to their decline.
>
> The answer is that Europe is reaffirming itself by managing its diversity. You, dear friends, will remain British. More precisely some . . . will remain Welsh; others will

remain Scottish, Irish or English, and I am not forgetting
the others. . . . We will all maintain our individual ways
of life, and our valued traditions.

. . . this world is harsh, and rapidly changing. Properly
managed, 1992 can help us to adapt, to meet the challenges
and reap the benefits.[24]

As the speech concluded, the British trade unionists were on
their feet, cheering. Through the words of Jacques Delors, Jean
Monnet's vision of Europe had touched the hearts of people who had
long been doubters. It was no small matter that Delors had made his
audience feel important in a country in which the government
regarded them with disdain and that he had invited them to join with
the EC Commission as a social partner. In the end, though, it was his
appeal to them as Europeans — as Welsh, Scottish, and English, to
be sure, but as Europeans — that had brought them to their feet.

Margaret Thatcher was incensed. She had been attacked in her
own backyard by a man she saw as a Socialist politician who was
promising her domestic political foes that, with his support, they
would win their objectives through the intervention of Brussels in
Britain's social policies.

Thatcher struck back in kind on Delors's home ground. Twelve
days after the speech at Bournemouth, the British prime minister
addressed the College of Europe at Bruges, Belgium, a hot-bed of
European federalist sentiment, to refute the message of the EC Commission president. Christopher Prout, the Conservative leader in the
European Parliament, explained to me that the speech at Bruges had
been provoked by two things Delors had done — one of them was
the speech at Bournemouth, which had shown no regard for the
views of the British government of the day, and the other had been
Delors's statement a few months earlier that within a decade, 80 per
cent of social and economic legislation in EC countries would have a
European component.

Thatcher's speech at Bruges became her most famous address
as British prime minister, serving as an anti-European manifesto,
and as a sweeping rejoinder to the social ideas of Delors and all the
others who wanted a social charter for the EC. Thatcher's nationalism, her rejection of the idea of more power for Brussels, and her
passionate belief in a non-interventionist market system were powerfully combined in her address. In one memorable phrase, Thatcher
warned her foes not to transgress further on her home ground: "We

have not successfully rolled back the frontiers of the state in Britain only to see them reimposed at a European level with a European super-state exercising a new dominance from Brussels." The phrase spawned a movement in Britain, the so-called Bruges movement, made up of right-wing nationalists who were appalled at the idea that the EC might impose social policies on Britain.

Among the other member countries of the EC, there was no doubt that Thatcher's social thinking set her apart. In the European Parliament, British Conservative opposition to a social charter won no support from the rest of mainstream Europe. In the EP, the Social-ists, the Christian Democrats, and the Liberals formed a massive phalanx in support of the concept of a social charter.

In some ways, though, the gulf between Thatcher and the rest of the EC was more apparent than real. The political line-up in support of the concept of a social charter was massive and impressive. Once one looked beyond the principles and platitudes to the details of an action program, however, the real support for the social charter was substantially thinner. In some cases, differences arose out of the diverse circumstances of EC countries, and in others they reflected tac-tical considerations that were the consequence of divergent political priorities. One reason German Christian Democrats were inclined to support a social charter was that they were concerned about the risk that corporations might be tempted to escape high-wage Germany with its tough environmental provisions, its expensive social pro-grams, and its stiff regulations about laying off employees in favour of the low-wage and relatively unregulated European south. For exactly the obverse reasons, Felipe Gonzalez, the Socialist prime min-ister of Spain, did not really want a social charter with teeth because he looked forward to many of those "runaway" plants from north-ern Europe relocating in his country. Similarly, the Socialist govern-ment of France, while supportive of the idea of the social charter, had what it regarded as higher priorities. In the autumn of 1989, when the debate about the social charter was reaching its climax, France held the European presidency and had the job of chairing the key summit in December 1989, which would determine whether Euro-pean union would move forward or falter. Mesmerized by the revo-lutions in Central and Eastern Europe in the fall of 1989 and by the spectre of speedy German unification, the Mitterrand government was deeply concerned about tying the new Germany into the struc-ture of the EC, economically and politically. If this meant that the social charter had to take a back seat, so be it.

The British Labour Group in the European Parliament had its own particular agenda as well in these turbulent months. Having defeated Thatcher's Tories in the European elections in June, their foremost aim was to further humiliate the British prime minister as part of their long battle to regain office at Westminster. What they most wanted was an eleven-to-one vote at the European summit on the issue of the social charter, a vote that would demonstrate that Thatcher was both a social reactionary and without allies in Europe. Leading members of the British Labour Group made pilgrimages to Paris to try to convince the French government not to countenance any watering-down of the social charter in the hope of gaining wider support for European economic and monetary union.

In the end, no one was particularly happy with the result. At the December 1989 meeting of the European Council at Strasbourg, the heads of EC governments adopted a "non-binding" charter, no longer aimed at the rights of all citizens as had been proposed from the time Jacques Delors had first advocated the charter in May 1988, but dealing with the rights of workers only. The "Community Charter of Basic Social Rights for Workers," as it was finally called, was supported at Strasbourg by eleven EC heads of government and opposed by Margaret Thatcher. The majority of members of the European Parliament were bitter. They complained that the charter had been watered down to court Thatcher's support, without, in the end, winning it. In the process, the charter had lost its sweeping character as a proclamation of fundamental social rights for all citizens. From the viewpoint of the EP majority, the charter was excessively vague, and therefore no guarantee that the problems created by the market forces unleashed as a consequence of "1992" would be reasonably addressed.

Issues addressed by the charter included: free movement of workers; fair remuneration of workers; freedom of association and collective bargaining; vocational training; equal treatment of men and women; consultation and participation of workers in their places of employment; and commitments to protection of health and safety in the workplace and of children and adolescents, the elderly, and the disabled in work situations.

If the charter was not as strong as some of its advocates had hoped, its principles had, at least, been adopted as policy by eleven of the twelve governments in the community. Whether the charter would end as a mere gesture or as a serious basis for addressing social inequities would depend, initially at least, on how vigorously the commission decided to follow through on it. Even by the time the charter was adopted, the real weight of the debate within the community had shifted to the content of the so-called action program to be mounted by the commission to give it force. At the end of November 1989, the commission drew up a social-action program, related to the charter, which was adopted a few days later. The proposals for action to be undertaken directly by the EC focused on the social security of migrant workers, freedom of movement within the EC, employment and working conditions, vocational training, and the amelioration of the work environment.

Even though the charter would not have much immediate effect on the obligations of business, the principles enshrined in it could have serious implications for the long term. For the future, the charter held out the prospect that it would be much more difficult for enterprises to shift their operations from one EC state to another to seek the advantages of a less regulated environment. The ability of multinational businesses to move from state to state and to play jurisdictions off, one against another, has been one of the great advantages of capital versus labour and government in the present global environment. The social charter established a basis for redressing that balance within the EC. As European union proceeds, both economically and politically, the likelihood is that the action programs associated with the social charter will become more ambitious. That will affect the way European and non-European enterprises operate within the EC.

EC competition and industrial policies have been a function of two key impulses. The stronger of the two, the impulse underlying the drive towards "1992," has been the quest for competitiveness and the willingness to rely on the primacy of the market to achieve it. The second impulse has been the inclination not to trust the market fully, particularly in key sectors where external competitors are strong, where industrial policies of foreign governments are a factor, and when it comes to concerns for social and regional equity. In some respects what was being tested in each of the cases described above was the strength of corporatism among European decision makers in the context of the move to the single market. Naturally, the relative strength of these two impulses is continually subject to change, depending on general economic circumstances — in a recession, the corporatist impulse can be expected to strengthen. Arguably, the most important sector in determining such outcomes has been and will be the automotive industry.

Europe's Car Industry

It is not simply that the automotive industry is the largest manufacturing employer in Europe, and the EC auto market the biggest in the world. Europeans care much more about the fate of auto companies, from which they buy their cars and trucks, than they care about other sectors where the products are more anonymous. The auto sector is therefore a highly politicized battleground in which calculations of rational economic behaviour must always contend with considerations of national and European prestige.

The movement to the single market in the auto sector is more complicated than in others because special rules and exemptions have applied in this field. In November 1984, the EC's so-called Block Exemption Regulation took effect, and it is due to remain in force until June 1995. Under the regulation, the marketing of automobiles is partially exempted from the competition rules of the Treaty of Rome. The exemption limits the right of individuals to buy autos from whomever they like in the EC. Under it, a system known as "selective distribution" is established, so that exclusive franchises between manufacturers and dealers are allowed. The rationale for the exemption is that autos are sophisticated products that require servicing after sales have been made. What the exemption has done has been to ensure that Europeans buy cars in their own countries, although, under the regulation, auto makers and dealers are required to sell cars to customers that meet the specifications of other EC countries, if such vehicles are desired. One consequence, as we have seen, has been the existence of price differentials for autos among EC countries, even when tax differences and exchange-rate difficulties are taken into account. But, as specifications for cars among EC countries are becoming more uniform, and as the date for the end of the marketing exemption approaches, the auto industry is moving towards a single market, though down a somewhat different pathway than are other industries.

As the barriers between EC countries come down, a fierce new competition has been unleashed among European and non-European auto-producers. The prize in the contest is the lion's share of the world's largest auto market. Six major auto corporations have dominated production within the EC, four of them European-owned, two of them American-owned. They are: Volkswagen, Fiat, Peugot-Citroën, Renault, Ford, and General Motors. In addition to the Big Six, many other famous European car-makers round out the total, among them Rover, Daimler-Benz, and Volvo. European auto-makers face the difficult task of breaking out of traditional market positions that have been secured, in part, through the maintenance of non-tariff trade barriers, to establish themselves across the whole of the community market. Moreover, they must do this at the same time as Japanese car-manufacturers, the most efficient in the world, are making a concerted push to establish themselves much more substantially in the community marketplace. While, for the companies, the high-stakes game is for market share and profits, for the people of Europe, the issue is jobs. Directly or indirectly, the auto sector employs ten million people in the EC and contributes 9 per cent of the community's manufacturing output.

As European auto-makers move out from under protection and increase their productivity so that they can reduce the number of man-hours of labour required to produce a vehicle from the European average of thirty-one hours towards the Japanese average of seventeen hours, tens of thousands of jobs will be lost. While European consumers will undoubtedly benefit from the transformation, with cars that are cheaper and better engineered, the burning issue is whose jobs will be lost and which of the auto companies will be the big losers. Indeed, the job losses have already begun, and on a massive scale. In 1982, 2.03 million people worked in the EC, assembling automobiles or producing auto parts. By 1988, this number had dropped to 1.81 million, a loss of 200,000 jobs.[25]

Europe's auto war with the Japanese is entering a new phase, but it is not a new war, and cannot be understood without reference to earlier battles. During the 1960s, the auto-producers in EC countries were by far the most important world-wide exporters of automobiles. During the 1970s, the Japanese auto "miracle" changed that. European auto-makers were driven out of their non-European markets, so that, by the early 1980s, future growth for the Europeans had to be concentrated on their own domestic turf. The ongoing battle there will determine their survival or seal their doom. Not surprisingly, they have shown a determination not to be defeated on their home ground, a determination that has been driving them to take political action to protect their market position.

In the northwest corner of Italy, in Turin, where the Alps can be seen on a clear day, one of the Big Six auto producers is putting every ounce of its creative energy into the transformation, which, for it, is no less than a struggle for survival. Fiat and Turin are almost synonymous — almost, because the history of the city stretches back centuries before Fiat. Indeed, for centuries it was unclear whether the city would end up under French or Italian rule, and the legacy of French rule in the past is evident in the city's architecture, its northern feel, and the fact that French is widely spoken and understood there. At the same time, the legacy of Count Cavour, the mastermind of Italian unification, and of Victor Emmanuel, the sovereign under which it was achieved, are strongly felt in Turin, which was Italy's first national capital. Now, however, the city's former political role is long in the past. A capital city no longer, but a duchy perhaps — although Turin is overshadowed by Milan, its great rival, it still feels like much more than an auto town. The Agnelli family rules the contemporary dukedom, and Gianni Agnelli, the chairman of Fiat, has been the uncrowned ruler for many years.

In the hills overlooking the city, Gianni Agnelli lives in palatial and secluded surroundings, protected by guards who ensure that the uninvited do not stray too close. The imperious head of Fiat likes to swoop down on the city at high speed in a car he prefers to drive himself. At Fiat headquarters, he is notorious for winging through the company parking garage, going the wrong way in one-way corridors. Because he suffers from a heart ailment, he has undergone an operation in the United States for the installation of a pacemaker designed by Fiat's biotechnology program, one of the company's non-automotive ventures.

Fiat and Volkswagen are the two first-ranked auto producers in Europe. While Fiat sells more cars, the total value of Volkswagen sales is slightly higher. In 1988, Fiat sold 2.2 million vehicles world-wide, just over 1.9 million of them in Europe. All but 300,000 of Fiat's European sales were in Italy. The strengths and weaknesses of the company are evident from these figures. With 14.9 per cent of European vehicle sales, Fiat was apparently well positioned to take advantage of the move to the single market. Its problem, however, a problem characteristic of the other major European auto-makers as well, was its marked dependence on one national market — Italy, where its market share was over 69 per cent in 1988 (including the figures for Lancia, which is owned by Fiat).[26]

In the Italian market, Fiat had been partially protected against other European auto-makers and very tightly protected against Japanese competition. The onset of the single market meant the certainty of much more vigorous competition within hitherto protected national markets. Indeed, the consequences of heightened competition were sharply felt in 1990, when Italian auto sales fell by 0.6 per cent. Much more important was that Fiat's share of that market fell to 52.9 per cent, and, by November and December, it fell farther, to under 50 per cent. The pressure was coming from Ford, whose small Fiesta was a hit with Italian consumers, and from Volkswagen, whose sales in Italy grew by more than 23 per cent in 1990.[27] If this shock of competition from other European producers could be endured, it was the prospect of a massive invasion of their market by Japanese producers that filled the planners at Fiat with dread. The problem was that Italy had maintained the most stringent controls of any country in the EC to block the importation of Japanese cars, limiting their entry to a paltry 3,300 per year. To maintain its market share in Europe, Fiat would have to offset a declining share in the Italian market with an increased share in the rest of Europe. The challenge was to come up with an aggressive strategy to design and market cars that other Europeans would embrace.

Fiat's first answer to the challenge was a new model, the Tipo, introduced in January 1988. The Tipo, which required an investment of nearly $2 billion to launch, was deliberately designed as a "Euro car" aimed at the wider continental market. Fiat's goal was to replace the VW Golf as Europe's most popular car. With more than 200,000 vehicles sold in its first eleven months on the market, the Tipo's quality was saluted when it was voted Car of the Year in 1989 — a roomy, quiet, powerful car for the middle-class European public. In 1990, however, the Tipo's share of the European market outside of Italy was not up to the level Fiat planners had anticipated. Only if the Tipo and other Fiat models could capture more of the European market could the prospect of conceding some of the Italian market be contemplated with greater equanimity.

The word "equanimity," however, does not describe the attitude of Fiat executives when it comes to thinking about the Japanese. When I talked to a financial planner in Fiat's head office in Turin, he conceded that the company was "damned worried" about the Japanese assault on the European auto market as a consequence of "1992." His fear, encountered everywhere among European automakers, was that the Japanese car-makers would use the "screwdriver factories" they have been establishing to invade the European market from within. The financial planner at Fiat — he spoke with me on the condition that his name not be used — was at pains to point out that such operations, where a pre-packaged technology, management approach, and much of the real manufacturing has been effected in Japan, leaves little more than final assembly for the Europeans. The

Japanese, he complained, have already covered their development costs at home, where their own base market is secure. For them the European market is gravy, while, for the Europeans, it is the ground on which their survival will be won or lost. Fiat wanted a lengthy transition period of five to seven years for European auto-makers to reorder their own market positions in Europe, before they faced the full brunt of unrestrained Japanese competition. During the transition period, Fiat wanted strict quotas in place to limit Japanese market penetration. Even when quotas were finally lifted upon the expiry of the transition period, Fiat insisted that Europe must put in place a regime that guaranteed a high degree of "local content" — i.e., production — as far as Japanese operations in Europe are concerned. For a vehicle to qualify as European-made, a minimum of 70 per cent of the value added in the vehicle must be of European origin, Fiat insisted.

From the share of the Italian market Fiat (including Lancia) has held, the company can afford to lose up to eight percentage points to the Japanese, the financial planner told me; a loss beyond that would cut very deeply. In that case, according to a study done for the EC Commission, Fiat has plenty to worry about. By 1995, if Japanese auto-producers were allowed completely unrestricted access to the EC market, their share of the Italian market would be 16 per cent, twice the level Fiat believes it can absorb.[28]

Furthermore, although Fiat sees its position in Western Europe as a well-established base on which to build, it has a very different attitude to Eastern Europe, which, as a consequence of the revolutionary transformations there, must now be seriously considered as a market and production location for Europe's auto-makers. The markets in Western and Eastern Europe are, of course, fundamentally different. In Western Europe, the battle among the companies is for an increased share of an already mature market. In Eastern Europe, particularly in countries that have favourable economic prospects, sales are expected to grow very rapidly. Here the auto companies will be competing for shares in an expanding market, in which consumers are developing preferences that may determine which cars they buy, not only today, but far into the future.

Motivated by the rapidly evolving situation there, Fiat has completely overhauled its approach to Eastern Europe. In the past, along with other European auto-makers, the company entered into partnerships and joint ventures with Eastern European state-owned companies. Through these arrangements, they handed off ageing technology and participated in the production of autos that would have been unacceptable in the West. This is decidedly no longer the case. Now the priority is to establish production facilities in Eastern Europe along with local partners to produce vehicles there, not only for sale in the regional market, but also for re-export to Western Europe. "There will be no more Yugos," I was told. The Yugo, a Fiat joint-venture offering in Yugoslavia, was an expression of the tendency of Western European auto-makers to unload yesterday's technology on Eastern Europeans. Another notorious transfer from the West was the Romanian Dacia, a car that was actually an ancient Renault.

Now, Fiat is planning to establish state-of-the-art facilities in Poland and the Soviet Union to produce automobiles and engines for local and wider European markets. In December 1990, Volkswagen won a protracted battle with Renault and Volvo to take a major share in Skoda, the Czechoslovakian state-owned auto company, which was regarded as one of the few major prizes to be had in the East in the auto sector.[29]

Fiat's very substantial investments in new models like the Tipo, and its plans to establish major facilities in Eastern Europe, are all part of a wide-ranging struggle for survival in the very tough European marketplace of the 1990s. Although success is far from certain, Fiat is likely to be among the winners in this struggle, but there are just as certainly going to be losers. Insiders in the European car industry often point their fingers at Renault, the state-owned French auto-producer.

Renault, a company with a long and distinguished history, has had more than its share of problems over the past decade. At the end of the Second World War, the company was nationalized by the French government, both as part of the state development strategy for industrial recovery and because the private management of the company had been implicated as collaborators with the Germans during the Occupation. By the end of the 1980s, although the company had recovered from the shocking losses in earlier years, indebtedness, overdependence on the French market, and reliance on outdated production facilities posed problems for it, just as it had to contend with the challenges of the single market and the virtual certainty of heightened Japanese competition in France.

Under pressure from the EC to end subsidies to state-owned companies like Renault, and as a consequence of the Mitterrand government's conversion to the view that such companies must rise or fall in the marketplace, Renault has been going through an exceptionally painful process of rationalization. Most dramatic has been the decision to close a legendary auto plant in France in 1992, Renault's historic facility at Billancourt in the suburbs of Paris. Billancourt has been much more than a car plant. Its name has been synonymous with working-class power in the famed "red belt" around Paris, a fortress of the largest trade-union organization in France, the Communist-led CGT. Closing Billancourt will cost about four thousand jobs. During the 1950s and 1960s, Renault and Billancourt were seen as the "shop window" of France's industrial relations. Now, a new model is emerging in which the emphasis is on competitiveness and productivity, and, of necessity, on the paring of industrial jobs. The demise of Billancourt is one large step in the process of trimming Renault's work-force from 70,000 to between 45,000 and 50,000 by the mid-1990s.

As we have seen, pressuring the Europeans to make these changes is the realization that Japanese car imports will swell in the next few years. Even more important in prodding the Europeans has been the setting up of Japanese plants in Europe, particularly in Britain and Spain. The contrast between the Japanese plants and those of their European competitors is a study in the new and the old. The old is embodied in such facilities as the Ford plant at Dagenham in the dreary east end of London. Some have compared Dagenham to a "pigsty," where many workers have to change into their work clothes right beside the assembly line, and where parts arrive in slipshod fashion and are piled up around the corners of the work floor. The new is found in facilities such as Nissan's new plant at Sunderland in the north of England. It is located in a long-established industrial region, once famous for its steel production, and now for decades a victim of decline and high unemployment. And despite the fact that it has set up shop where labour relations among the English are sour, Nissan has managed to establish those things for which Japanese automakers are renowned: high morale in the workplace; just-in-time delivery of parts needed in the production process; a much lower level of defects per vehicle than is typical in Europe; and high productivity. (Toyota and Honda have also located plants in the United Kingdom.)

The productivity gap between European and Japanese automanufacturers is so large that overcoming it will involve an immense effort at restructuring on the part of the Europeans. The problem is easily summarized in the following statistics. In 1988, EC automanufacturers achieved a total of 65.2 billion Ecu worth of production, compared with a total of 53.5 billion Ecu worth of production by Japan's auto industry. But in order to produce about 20 per cent more, European auto-makers employed more than twice as many workers as the Japanese did.[30]

The Japanese advantage is formidable as well when it comes to quality. A survey by the Massachusetts Institute of Technology revealed that in 1986–87, on average, there were more than twice as many defects in European as in Japanese automobiles. Moreover, the drive for quality and innovation in Japan has not been slackening. Japanese auto producers have been spending more money on research and development than have the producers in the whole of the EC. With their willingness to make vast up-front investments and their technological virtuosity, the Japanese have been able, on average, to develop new models in two-thirds the time it takes the Europeans, an important factor in a market hungry for novelty.[31]

The Japanese challenge to European auto-producers not only tests the European auto-makers themselves, but has been forcing the EC to define itself more clearly as an economic bloc vis-à-vis the rest of the world. The five major auto-producing countries within the EC have been divided between a protectionist south — Italy, France, and Spain — and an anti-protectionist north — the United Kingdom and Germany. Italy has held Japanese sales to the tiny sum of 3,300 vehicles per year. France, through an informal arrangement with Japan, has limited the sales of Japanese auto-producers to 3 per cent of the market. Spain has deployed high tariffs to keep out Japanese vehicles (these tariffs have been coming down slowly).

In comparison with these highly restrictive arrangements, the British regime is anti-protectionist, although the British, too, have limited Japanese access to their automobile market. On the basis of a voluntary industry agreement, the Japanese share of the British auto market has been held down to 11 per cent. In Germany, Japanese auto sales have grown to 15 per cent of the market. The Germans, motivated by their own success in the Japanese auto market — in 1988, 68.6 per cent of the autos imported into Japan came from Germany — talk publicly about the need to open up Europe's auto market. They have been accused by EC Commission officials, however, of playing a double game, talking publicly against restrictive arrangements for Japanese auto-manufacturers, while allegedly supporting them in private.[32]

In general, the Italians, French, and Spaniards wanted a long adjustment period during which very strict limits on Japanese access to the European market would apply. In addition, they wanted a very tough definition of what constituted "European" production on the part of Japanese branch plants. The British and the Germans wanted a much more openly competitive regime with the Japanese right from the start.

Despite the restrictive practices of EC countries, the Japanese share of the overall EC auto market has grown to about 10 per cent. In EC countries without their own auto production to protect, the percentages are much higher, peaking in Ireland at 43 per cent.[33] (These figures are for 1988.) According to an EC Commission internal study, without restraints the Japanese share of the overall EC market would rise to 18 per cent by 1995.[34] The stark problem with such a projection is that it would mean that the Japanese would be selling one million cars more per year in the community in 1995 than in the late 1980s — the equivalent of the production of one of the European Big Six. Could Europe absorb the steeply increased Japanese penetration without one of the Big Six going under, or at the very least, without drastic rationalization and mergers?

Such rationalization and mergers have been proceeding at a rapid pace as Europe readies itself for the single market. To better position itself in the European market and to broaden the technological and product-development base it can draw on, Renault has formed an alliance with Sweden's Volvo. Public-sector Renault and private-sector Volvo have purchased shares in each other. While the companies have remained distinct and have retained their own product lines, they will work in tandem in marketing and in joint ventures involving other auto-makers. Volkswagen has purchased SEAT, the Spanish government-owned and chronic money-losing auto-maker. As mentioned above, VW beat out Renault/Volvo to acquire a share in Czechoslovakia's Skoda. VW's intention in this acquisition — ultimately it will have a controlling interest in the company — is to help upgrade Skoda's facilities so that the company can market more vehicles in both Western and Eastern Europe.[35] Ford has taken over the British luxury car–maker Rover, a company that despite a distinguished history has been a money loser in recent years.

The fierce battle within the EC on how much protectionism should be retained vis-à-vis the Japanese reached an apparent resolution in July 1991 when the EC Commission and the government of Japan reached an agreement on how much Japanese access to the Community automotive market will be allowed during a transitional period from the onset of the Single European Market on January 1,

1993 until the end of 1999. After that date, the Japanese industry is to have completely free access to the EC market. Under the arrangement, Japan agreed to monitor its exports to the EC, keeping them to 1.23 million automobiles per year, virtually the current level. For 1999, the last year of the transitional period, Japan has agreed that its exports to countries which have restricted Japanese exports will be: Britain 190,000 vehicles; France 150,000; Italy 138,000; Spain 79,000; and Portugal 23,000. In the agreement no mention was made about the level of production of Japanese auto plants in Europe. However, according to an EC Commission estimate, those plants are expected to increase their annual production to about 1.2 million vehicles during the transitional period, about a five-fold increase over the current level. This would give the Japanese auto makers a total market in the EC of just over 2.4 million vehicles annually by the year 2000.

The EC-Japan arrangement leaves open the considerable possibility that the assumptions regarding Japanese auto production inside the Community, principally in Britain and Spain, may turn out to be wrong. The vagueness of the agreement is almost certain to promote future wrangles within the EC between those countries with an interest in the increased production of Japanese automotive plants within their territory and those countries which fear a sharp rise in imports from those plants. The agreement, therefore, should be seen as changing the *terms* of the debate over the Japanese position in Europe's auto industry and market. It has not ended the debate.

A SINGLE MARKET IN FINANCIAL SERVICES

If the single market has promoted a wave of mergers and take-overs, managerial changes, and the rationalization of facilities and work-forces in the industrial sectors of the economy, it is promoting a revolution in another critical sector in the contemporary economy — financial services. Whether Europe can truly make of itself one market and, more than that, a united economic force, capable of competing head to head with the United States and Japan, depends to a considerable extent on whether a single market in financial services is established.

Unprecedented corporate and technological revolutions, which have been under way since the early 1980s, constitute the very centre of the process of globalization, the transition to a world-wide marketplace for capital movements and financial services. [36] The micro-electronic revolution has transformed communications so that, in a computer-linked world, capital can be shifted at the flick of a cursor from Tokyo to New York, to London and to Frankfurt. The technological potential has been a necessary condition in making possible a revolution in financial services, a revolution in which the distinctions between banks and other financial institutions are being eliminated and in which regulations restraining the flow of capital from one global centre to another are being jettisoned. A new world bound together by young men and women, their faces pale in the reflected light of their computer screens, playing the markets from time zone to time zone on behalf of their corporate masters, emerged in the 1980s. For the first time in history, the volume of capital movements dwarfed merchandise trade.

For Europeans, this transformation meant that their old, divided world of national currencies and financial institutions had reduced them to Lilliputian proportions next to the Americans and the Japanese. In order to stand up to their competitors, the Europeans had to remake their financial institutions and the rules that regulated them.

"Obviously, a single market calls for a single currency." These were the words of West Germany's most important private-sector banker, Dr. Alfred Herrhausen, speaker of the board of directors of Deutsche Bank. The statement was authorized for inclusion in remarks Dr. Herrhausen was to make when he delivered the Arthur Burns Memorial Lecture in New York on December 4, 1989. The speech was never delivered because, on November 30, Dr. Herrhausen was assassinated by gunmen in the streets of Frankfurt. And while Dr. Herrhausen, in the lecture he never gave, was thinking about "1992" and the issue of economic and monetary union in the EC, what was uppermost in his mind, not surprisingly, was the transformation of Eastern Europe, and particularly the revolution in East Germany. Dr. Herrhausen died three weeks to the day after the opening of the Berlin Wall.

If Western Europeans had expected an orderly progression towards Economic and Monetary Union (EMU) within the EC, it was not to be. The revolutionary transformations in Eastern Europe, and particularly in East Germany, meant that EMU would have to take shape in a tumultuous environment. West Germany, the financial powerhouse of the EC, could not help but be deeply distracted from EMU by the events in the East. For private-sector German bankers, as well as for the powerful Bundesbank, the West German central bank, ruled by the imperious Karl Otto Pöhl, EMU could not be separated from that of German Economic and Monetary Union (GEMU). This became starkly clear once the euphoria over the opening of the Wall was followed by the rapid collapse of the East German regime and the movement towards economic and political union with West Germany. EMU and GEMU were twins, whether anyone liked it or not. The critical question was whether they would become quarrelsome and even fratricidal.

During the early months of 1990, GEMU became an overriding concern in West Germany. Despite all the appeals for calm from both sides of the divided country, the torrent of people pouring into the Federal Republic did not subside. East Germany was haemorrhaging, losing an intolerably high proportion of its young, its enterprising, and its professional people. So perilous was the situation that the GDR's first democratic elections had to be held earlier than originally planned, on March 18. In the campaign, West German chancellor Helmut Kohl assured himself of victory by making East Germans an offer they could not refuse: the conversion of their Ostmarks for Deutschmarks on extremely favourable terms. Once he had won the election, in which he and his East German allies had pledged themselves to the rapid achievement of the monetary union of the two Germanys, to be swiftly followed by political union, Kohl handed the monetary details of the problem over to the Bundesbank and the private sector.

For German bankers in the private sector, the inevitable consequence of GEMU was that their attention was drawn east. On July 3, 1990, when I arrived in Frankfurt for meetings with German bankers, GEMU had been consummated two days before, on Sunday, July 1. The last frenetic hours of the Ostmark had been played out. The shelves of East German shops had been emptied of whatever bargains had been left over from forty years of communism. On Saturday night, the shelves were restocked with produce from West Germany. Deutsche Bank, the flagship of private-sector banking in West Germany, was ready in East Berlin to usher in the new era. In a publicity coup whose echoes were felt around the world, Deutsche Bank opened a branch in the Alexanderplatz at the stroke of midnight on Saturday night. By dawn, as I was told by one of the officials of the bank who had masterminded the midnight opening, Deutsche Bank had pumped ten million Deutschmarks into the hands of East Berliners from this one outlet.

The opening at the Alexanderplatz had much more to do with global publicity than with a quest for customers. The midnight launch had been handled with all the precision and secrecy of a military operation, so that Deutsche Bank could steal a march on its competitors, whose own openings the next morning were bland affairs by comparison. The coup was splashed all over the front pages of the world's most important newspapers. The other German banks were furious at Deutsche Bank for its midnight raid on the citizens of the GDR, who were deciding where to open their first accounts in an all-German banking system.

Still, it was an optimistic week in Frankfurt, a moment when German bankers felt that the world was their oyster. Deutsche Bank had prepared well for GEMU. By the time its branch at the Alexanderplatz opened, the bank had already set up 140 branches in East Germany, 122 of them in partnership with the retail arm of the East German Staatsbank. Deutsche Bank did not intend to let the formal partnership last long. While, for a time, the Deutsche Bank logo would share a billing with that of its partner at branches in East Germany, soon its logo would shine alone.

Along with the other major German banks, Deutsche Bank seized the opportunity to undertake very large investments in eastern Germany, both prior to and following formal unification. Due to the immense start-up costs involved, in acquiring property, assembling and training staff, purchasing and installing equipment, including a vast amount of computer and communications hardware, the bank does not expect to make a profit on these investments for at least three years. But Deutsche Bank does not see its major commitment to the former GDR in terms of the market there alone. It is counting on recruiting Germans from the East who have had experience in dealing with other countries in Eastern Europe. Many people in what was the GDR speak Russian, Czech, Magyar, and other languages of Eastern Europe and have had years of experience in business dealings throughout the region. These dealings can now be put to use by capitalist Germany, the planners at Deutsche Bank believe. The bank's major foray into the East, though much larger in scale than what came before, follows on previous experience in the communist world. Deutsche Bank has had a "representative office" in the Soviet Union for many years. The office was not set up to make deals directly; rather, it made contacts. When deals became possible, they were made at long distance between the Moscow principals and the bank's HQ in Frankfurt, no difficult feat in an age of modern communications technology.

German bankers no longer live in a world in which to the east of them is a communist monolith with which comparatively little business can be done. For them, as for Germany as a whole, this means that they now find themselves in the centre of a new Europe rather than on the eastern margins of Western Europe. This transformation has changed their perspective and has provoked anxieties in the rest of Western Europe.

The new perspective is clearly evident in Frankfurt, which, prior to German unification, was the unchallenged money capital of West Germany. The financial towers that dominate the city, visible everywhere, are the cathedrals of German banking, their functional, prosaic structures reaching upward towards a heaven of "financial services."

The immense global expansion of the financial-services industry during the 1980s has its German example here. Deutsche Bank's new tower, now the highest structure in the financial district, is crowned with the starkest of banker's logos, a single diagonal slash, mounted on a background square. So rapid has been the growth of the industry that even the new HQ may need to be replaced in the not-so-distant future, I was informed by an ebullient manager.

German bankers are steeped in the assurance that goes with being in the inner circle of an industry that has enjoyed an unprecedented increase in its global power. Moreover, bankers in capital-rich Germany occupy a powerful ring within that inner circle. In global terms, it is only Japanese bankers who inspire awe among the Germans, a consequence of the enormous capital pools on which Japanese banks can draw. To the Germans, the Americans appear debt-ridden and ill-disciplined; the British are thought of as experienced, but lacking in depth. When I asked one Frankfurt banker whether he thought Frankfurt would one day replace London as the financial capital of Europe, his reply showed that he was thinking in a different direction. He said he believed the long-run challenge to Frankfurt came not from across the Channel, but from Berlin. He put it as diplomatically as he could: "We might not like to think of it, but in the 1870s and 1880s, Berlin was the centre of Europe. It is becoming that again." His bank, he told me, is ready for this possibility. It has plenty of land on which to construct its new HQ in Berlin, if that is where the future leads. All this, he said, would take at least a decade. Then, he added, beyond that, no one could say what would happen. Perhaps Frankfurt would retain its pre-eminence for a long while yet.

Whatever Frankfurt's future is, there is no question that German financial institutions are the most important on the continent, and that they will play a great role in the EC's single market. As we saw in an earlier chapter, the Cecchini Report reckoned that the consequence of separate national markets in financial services has meant that individual and corporate consumers of such services have ended up paying, in many cases, prices much higher than should have been possible at a hypothetical "world price." The EC's establishment of a single market in financial serves rests on three propositions: that financial-services institutions based anywhere in the EC should have the freedom to establish their activities and to start up branches anywhere they choose within the community; that such financial-services institutions should have the freedom to offer their particular services anywhere they like within the community without having to be established in member states, apart from the one where they originate; and that capital should be free to move anywhere in the community without restriction.

To achieve a single market for financial services on the basis of these propositions, the EC has taken a multitude of steps, some of them in the area of liberalization of direct and portfolio investments across borders within the community, dating back to the early 1960s. It has been since the mid-1980s, however, under the impetus of the Single European Act, the White Paper, and the timetable set out by the commission for the completion of the "1992" program, that the most rapid advances have been made.

Steps taken towards the accomplishment of the single market in financial services have paralleled global technological and business developments. They have served to remove obstacles from the path that business has wanted to follow. In this sense, business has played the critical active role, while the EC has played an enabling role. As the barriers to the establishment of the single market in the financial sector have been dismantled, therefore, it has been up to the financial institutions to take advantage of the opportunities, to undertake mergers, acquisitions, to open new operations, in some cases to specialize to meet new competition. For Deutsche Bank, drawn to the East as we have seen, the transformation of the EC has remained a compelling, if more prosaic, taskmaster. The scale of business in the EC is much more important for German financial institutions. In its 1989 annual review, Deutsche Bank signalled the importance it attached to the EC single market: "We continue . . . to view the development of the internal market as the key economic influence affecting the Deutsche Bank Group."[37] To take advantage of the opportunities presented by the single market, Deutsche Bank has been aggressive in making acquisitions and in establishing branches in many parts of Europe, which now include: Banca d'America e d'Italia, based in Milan; Banco Comercial Transatlantico, with head-quarters in Barcelona; H. Albert de Bary and Co., in Amsterdam; Deutsche Bank Luxembourg; DB (Belgium) Finance, in Brussels; DB U.K. Finance, in London; and Deutsche Bank (Austria) in Vienna. Key recent moves specifically linked to the emerging single market have been: the acquisition of Morgan Grenfell, one of the U.K.'s leading merchant banks; and the establishment of Europäische Hypothekenbank der Deutschen Bank in Luxembourg, a subsidiary whose task is to take advantage of developments in the EC that allow for the issuing of mortgage-backed securities across Europe.[38]

EC moves to establish a single market for financial services have paralleled liberalization of the rules governing financial institutions within EC member countries. Such liberalization has broken down the distinctions dividing financial institutions into specialized categories, so that what is emerging is not merely a Single European Market, but an institutionally unified market as well. The consequence is that very large companies, generalists like Deutsche Bank, will have to pit their abilities against the "niche players," companies that provide a very particular service and are highly adept at doing it. The result of the mergers, the acquisitions, the offensive and defensive moves being made by European financial institutions is that the cost of such services to the consumer, either individual or corporate, should fall.

A CENTRAL BANK AND SINGLE CURRENCY

One immense barrier to a single financial market in Europe has been the existence, side by side, in the member countries of national currencies. National currencies, like national armies and navies, are not mere matters of practicality, but very much matters of the heart as well. Creating a single European currency to go with the single market is therefore a deeply emotional and political question, at the same time as it is a subject for economic controversy. The argument for a single currency in the EC is based on simple logic: the cost of exchanging currencies within the EC for businesses and for individual consumers is highly expensive, and is a major impediment to the very notion of a single market. In 1990, a European consumer organization estimated that, if an individual started out with £100 and simply exchanged that sum of money through each of the EC currencies, at the end of the process he or she would have only £50 left, having lost fully half the money in charges for exchanging the money.[39]

Architects of "1992," like Lord Cockfield, have understood

from the outset that the single market cannot be fully realized without the establishment of a central bank and, ultimately, a common currency for the EC. Only with such a transformed monetary system, they believe, can Europe expect to compete at the highest level with the United States and Japan. Economic and Monetary Union (EMU) has therefore been regarded as the highest pinnacle in the economic remaking of Europe. To be completed, EMU will take the EC much beyond "1992." When Lord Cockfield was planning the details of the single market, his model, as we have seen, was the great single market of the United States. EMU is similarly based on the working model of the United States, where an investor in New York can make an investment in Texas in a single currency, without the problems and costs created by exchanging currencies and by fluctuating currency-exchange rates.

Consider the case of the Deutschmark and the pound sterling to illustrate this point. Over the past two decades, the value of the Deutschmark has appreciated from about 10 DM to the pound to about 3 DM to the pound. Such dramatic shifts have had an enormous impact on the behaviour of investors. Since the early 1970s, shifts in exchange rates have been extremely volatile. Even a moderate change in exchange rates can wipe out a projected profit or change the terms of trade among countries so that a planned facility can become uneconomic. Such realities have forced investors to insure themselves against the risks of currency fluctuation in advance, and their behaviour has distorted investment and trade and has had a serious influence on interest rates. Investors have become players in a highly volatile exchange-rate lottery, a game that greatly complicates their other activities.

Debate about the merits of monetary union has gone on within the community for decades. Since 1979, however, with the establishment of the European Monetary System (EMS), significant progress has been made. And while monetary union is taking the EC well beyond the specifics of the "1992" process, the success of "1992" has been indispensable. As Lord Cockfield told me: "The single market has had the pole position." Steps towards monetary union, he asserts, proceed from the assumption that the single market is irreversible, and from the necessity of completing it.

The EMS was inspired by the efforts of EC Commission president Roy Jenkins, and was implemented when it was taken up by West German chancellor Helmut Schmidt and French president Valéry Giscard d'Estaing, whose collaboration, as we have seen, did much to revive the fortunes of the EC in the late 1970s. The EMS established an Exchange Rate Mechanism (ERM) whose purpose was to achieve currency stability among the member countries. The system was based on the European Currency Unit (Ecu), a unit that is a "weighted" basket of European currencies. Under the ERM, each currency in the system is allotted a position against the Ecu central rate and is allowed to fluctuate within a narrow range against that rate. For most currencies, the range is plus or minus 2.25 per cent. For currencies less integrated into the system — the Spanish peseta, the Italian lira, and the British pound (which joined the ERM in the autumn of 1990) — the range is plus or minus 6.0 per cent. The ERM has been fairly successful in reducing currency fluctuations within the community. While periodic revaluations of currencies within the system were necessitated, particularly in the early years, by the end of the 1980s most of the currencies operating within the ERM were being kept within their allotted bands by central bank interest-rate adjustments. Giving further weight to the Ecu was the requirement that EMS member states place 20 per cent of their gold reserves and 20 per cent of their dollar reserves in a very substantial reserve fund, the European Monetary Co-operation Fund (EMCF). By the late 1980s, the Ecu, the currency that had been issued in notes as legal tender only in Belgium, for limited commemorative purposes, had inspired such a degree of confidence that it had become the fifth most popular currency used for international bond issues. Particularly in the early 1980s, there was a rapid growth in international banking business in Ecus. The currency was attractive to investors interested in portfolio diversification and in securing a hedge against currency fluctuations. [40]

At bottom, what made the EMS a success was that, during the 1980s, European governments and their central banks came to accept the leadership and discipline of the Bundesbank, West Germany's central bank. The Bundesbank is unique, with powers that make it highly independent of the German government. The Federal Republic of Germany, mindful of the ruinous inflation of the 1920s that had done so much to destroy the German middle classes, set out to establish a central bank that would serve as a bulwark of monetary probity, that would be beyond the reach of politicians trying to solve their short-term problems. Until 1957, this was the Bank deutscher Länder, and from then on the Deutsche Bundesbank. Maintaining the value of the Deutschmark and thus avoiding inflation was the holy grail of the Bundesbank. During the 1980s, the German financial institution managed to make itself not only the guardian of the Deutschmark but the monetary pace-setter of Europe.

Critical to this expanding importance of the Bundesbank and therefore to the success of the EMS was the acceptance of German monetary leadership by France. This happened when the French Socialists had been through the devastating experience of their first two years in power in the early 1980s and had concluded that France, on its own, could not achieve economic reflation in defiance of wider European and global trends; the stage was set for a French recognition of the need to coordinate economic policies with Germany.

With France committed to economic convergence with West Germany, the EMS received political backing that helped to make it a success. In general, there were clear signs of convergence among the economies of countries that were members of the EMS, a tendency that was, in part, the consequence of the benefits of the monetary arrangement and, in part, the acceptance of German financial leadership. Between 1980 and 1985, inflation dropped in EMS member countries from an average of 12 per cent to an average of 5 per cent,[41] and currency fluctuation among member countries of the EMS was much reduced, as compared with the fluctuations of currencies outside the system.

The relative success of the EMS and the enormous momentum towards European integration as a consequence of "1992" opened the way for much more ambitious steps towards complete economic and monetary union. Designing the strategy for what was understood as a "quantum jump" beyond the single-market program[42] was a committee chaired by Jacques Delors. The committee was set up by the European Council at its meeting at Hanover in June 1988, and was asked to report a year later. That report was considered by the heads of government meeting in the European Council at Madrid in June 1989.

The Delors Report, as it came to be called, advocated a staged movement towards Economic and Monetary Union. The legal basis for the steps to date towards economic union, including "1992," had been the Treaty of Rome and the Single European Act. As the Delors Report concluded, however, these would not suffice for the completion of EMU, which would therefore require "treaty change and consequent changes in national legislation."[43] Treaty changes would be needed because the achievement of monetary union would require the vesting of responsibility in this policy area in one decision-making body. In the broader realm of economic union, the consequences of the single market and of monetary union would necessitate the establishment of "an agreed macroeconomic framework" that would be subject to "binding procedures and rules" aimed at avoiding "unsustainable differences between individual member countries in public-sector borrowing requirements" and at creating "binding constraints on the size and the financing of budget deficits."[44]

The ultimate goal to which the report was dedicated was the achievement of full monetary union throughout the EC and a very high degree of economic integration, the latter desired both as an end in itself and as a necessary means to make the monetary union effective. If monetary union, with a single currency as a final goal, was to be achieved, the report concluded, it would be necessary to deal with the strains and tensions that would be unleashed in the community on the way to it. Those tensions would be fully felt once exchange-rate parities among EC currencies had been "irrevocably fixed," a critical stage on the way to a single currency. At that stage, governments of EC countries would have lost the ability to make use of currency revaluation as an instrument of economic policy in times of duress. Countries concerned with mounting trade deficits, serious unemployment, and uncompetitive industrial sectors would not be in a position, as in the past, to use currency devaluation as a way to respond. Instead, such difficulties would manifest themselves as "regional disequilibria," as is the case for specific regions within a country, like the United States, where a single currency operates over an immense and diverse economic landscape.

To guard against the exacerbation of severe regional disparities within the community, the Delors Report favoured allowing market adjustment to do a part of the job. "Wage flexibility" and "labour mobility" would be an essential part of the solution, since they would allow the market itself to provide the adjustments needed. An effective competition policy whose goal was to remove barriers to competition within the community would also help. However, these market-based approaches would not be sufficient, the report concluded. To ensure that EMU did not lead to an even stronger tendency for economic development to be focused on the favoured central regions of the EC at the expense of its periphery, the report pointed to the need for a strong community regional policy:

> The economic and monetary union would have to encourage and guide structural adjustment which would help poorer regions to catch up with the wealthier ones.
> . . . in February 1988 . . . the European Council decided

to strengthen and reorganize the Community's regional and structural policies in several respects: the size of structural funds [funds for basic economic restructuring] will be doubled over the period up to 1993. . . . Depending on the speed of progress, such policies might have to be strengthened further after 1993 in the process of creating economic and monetary union. [45]

The advocacy of more EC spending to deal with regional disparities was intended to offset the concerns of EC countries with weaker economies, particularly those in the Mediterranean, where policy makers feared the emergence of a metropolis–hinterland dichotomy within the EC. Even with its inclusion, however, the overwhelming emphasis was on market adjustment, since community spending as a proportion of public spending within EC countries was very low and was expected to remain low for the foreseeable future (not to exceed 5 per cent of total public spending).

The Delors Report set out a three-stage process by which the EC could reach the goal of EMU. In each stage, parallel economic and monetary steps would be taken that would allow for a balanced advance. The idea was that, by the time each stage was completed, concrete gains would have been made, thus opening the door to the next stage. The report strongly emphasized the need at the outset for a political commitment to complete the entire process, and not simply to enter each stage on a piecemeal basis as an end in itself. [46]

The key elements of the three stages were as follows:

- Stage One: During this stage, to begin on July 1, 1990, all EC countries would come into the Exchange Rate Mechanism of the EMS. As well, the steps towards the creation of a "single financial area" within the EC (central to "1992") would be completed so that "all monetary and financial instruments" could circulate freely and "banking, securities and insurance services" would be "offered uniformly" throughout the EC. On the economic side, these monetary steps would be paralleled by increased budgetary policy coordination among EC member countries. [47]

- Stage Two: This stage, during which the EC would be breaking qualitatively new ground, would begin only when a new treaty had come into force among member states, a treaty that would allow for the exercise of substantial new powers at the centre. In the area of macro-economic policy, the experience gained during the first stage would allow for the setting of a "medium-term framework for key economic objectives" with a procedure for intervening "when significant deviations occurred." At the same time "precise, although not yet binding, rules" would be set with respect to the "size of annual budget deficits and their financing." As these steps, which struck at the very heart of economic decision making, were being made, the monetary union was to be consolidated. A European System of Central Banks (ESCB) was to be established. The ESCB was to provide the EC with a federally structured central bank. The ESCB Council was to be made up of the governors of the national central banks and it was to have a board, whose members would be appointed by the European Council. During this critical phase, a transition would occur during which authority for monetary policy would shift from national authorities to this new EC authority, obviously modelled on the U.S. Federal Reserve Board. As this stage proceeded, "the margins of fluctuation with the exchange rate mechanism would be narrowed as a move towards the final stage of the monetary union, in which they would be reduced to zero." [48]

- Stage Three: Again, as in the earlier stages, it might be necessary to enhance the regional and structural policies of the EC, to deal with problems emerging as a consequence of the reduction of national authority in monetary and macro-economic matters. During this stage, "the rules and procedures of the Community in the macroeconomic and budgetary field would become binding." This would mean that the Council of Ministers in conjunction with the European Parliament could take steps to "impose constraints on national budgets to the extent to which this was necessary to prevent imbalances that might threaten monetary stability." In the monetary field, exchange rates among EC currencies would be irrevocably locked. With this step the ESCB would find itself fully in charge of a single monetary policy, and "the change-over to the single currency would take place." [49]

In its dry and technical language, what was being proposed in the Delors Report was the completion of an economic revolution, a

revolution that had been begun long before with the creation of the
ECSC. The revolution had proceeded further with the launching of
the EEC in 1958, and much further as a consequence of "1992." At
the end of the long road, the final symbolic act would be the creation
of a new currency for Europe. By the time Europeans were spending Ecus in place of Deutschmarks, francs, and pesetas, they would
be living in a community in which their economy was no longer
organized on a nation-state basis but on a European basis.

The revolution was not to proceed unopposed. Indeed, its
most illustrious opponent, Margaret Thatcher, was to lose office in
her passionate effort to block it. Thatcher's failure to stop the historic advance beyond "1992" to EMU and to steps towards political
union were enshrined in a historic agreement reached in Rome in
December 1990.

To understand the road to Rome and beyond, we need to turn
our attention to the countries and regions that are coming together
to form the New Europe — and the most important of these is
Germany.

Chapter Six

GERMANY:
THE LAND IN
THE MIDDLE

★ ★ ★ ★ ★ ★ ★ ★ ★ ★ ★

W HEN THE LEADERS OF THE EC COUNTRIES GATHERED for their European Council meeting at Rome in December 1990, no one could doubt the importance of the event. At the summit were launched two inter-governmental conferences, one on Economic and Monetary Union and one on political union. The way was opened towards the completion of the economic union of the EC, a process that was to include the establishment of a central bank and common currency. And once a European monetary authority presided over a single currency, the necessity for a much greater degree of political union would follow. It had to follow. Critical prerogatives of the sovereign state were being transferred to the community. The goal of a "United States of Europe" had never seemed more possible.

These decisions, despite their significance, were overshadowed by the most important fact about the summit — that it was the first meeting of the European Council to be held after the unification of Germany just over two months earlier. When the meeting convened in Rome, there was indeed a New Europe. There could no doubt that the most influential power at the summit was the Federal Republic of Germany, representing seventy-seven million Germans. All residual authority exercised over the two Germanys by the four powers that had occupied the shattered country in 1945 had been signed away. The regime of the Western powers and the Soviets in Berlin, the very hallmark of the post-war epoch, had terminated, in a ceremony in which Checkpoint Charlie had been hoisted into the air and removed to a museum.

Indeed, what made the Rome summit such an important mile-
post was that European leaders were holding their first European
Council unencumbered by the superpowers, the United States and the
Soviet Union. The last time Germany, France, Italy, and Britain had
been the key players in a European summit of this importance had
been in September 1938 at Munich, when Adolf Hitler had received
the green light from the others to dismember Czechoslovakia.

If the mention of the Munich and Rome summits in the same
breath is jarring, it has the merit of sharply posing the question of
what role Germany is to play in Europe. The "German question" has
dominated Europe throughout the whole of this century. If the New
Europe has been constructed to resolve the German question,
Germany has now emerged at the very centre of the New Europe.
Are we witnessing the construction of a "German Europe, or a European Germany," to use the phrase that has haunted Germany since
the Berlin Wall was opened?

Since the creation of Bismarck's German Empire in 1871, proclaimed in Versailles in the splendid Hall of Mirrors, European history
has turned on the German question. For Germans, the issue was how
their late-industrializing country could take its place in the sun along
with the established powers, Britain and France. For the rest of
Europe, the question was how the rising industrial and military power
of Germany could be contained so that German hegemony could be
averted. While the German Empire was being brazenly proclaimed
in the heart of France, the French people were licking their wounds.
Tens of thousands had died in the orgy of civil strife that followed
Prussia's military defeat of France.

The German Empire, born in conflict, died in Europe's next
great conflagration. In November 1918, in the last days of the war,
the German Empire crumbled, to be replaced by a republic that was
unloved at home and despised abroad, at the moment of its birth.
Weimar, like the Empire, never overcame the circumstances of its
creation. And like the Empire, Weimar, too, had its moment at Versailles, not in splendour but in shame, when the miserable representatives of the Republic were forced to appear before their conquerors
to sign the Treaty of Versailles, accepting the burden of war guilt,
reparations, military restrictions, and a substantial loss of territory.

For a time, after the victors came to see the futility of continued harshness towards the defeated enemy, a democratic and apparently stable Germany made its appearance under the leadership of
Gustav Stresemann. With the Treaty of Locarno in 1925, Germany

recognized its western frontiers and promised not to seek changes to its eastern frontiers through the use of force. A new European order, with France, Britain, and Italy welcoming Germany into the fold, was apparently being consolidated. Far off-stage, in the age of Locarno, were the United States and the revolutionary Soviet Union. But even at Locarno, there was a shadow across this New Europe of the democracies. Mussolini's presence there, as the strongman of a Fascist Italy, was a warning for the future. It was the stock-market crash of 1929 and the subsequent onset of economic catastrophe that revealed the era of Locarno as one of illusion, in which the German question had been repackaged but not resolved.

Three years and three months after the crash, Hitler took power in Germany. Economic catastrophe opened the door to the Nazis, who not only spoke for the shattered middle classes who feared prole- tarianization at the hand of left revolutionaries, but had backing from powerful segments of business who hoped to "hire Hitler" to deal with the Bolsheviks. In the end, Hitler took power through perfectly con- stitutional means, acceding to the position of chancellor for the not inconsequential reason that he led the largest party in the Reichstag.

When Europe was confronted with the consolidated Hitler dic- tatorship that emerged out of the fabric of the democratic republic, it was torn politically between resistance and appeasement. Having begun in the 1920s to appease the Germans, it was not so easy to stand up to a much tougher Germany during a time of deep eco- nomic depression, especially when the leader of the New Germany had restored order in his country, was a welcome bulwark against Soviet Communism, and was employing the rhetoric of national self- determination, the very mother's milk of Western liberalism. Looking back from our vantage point, it is easy to ask why the British signed the Anglo-German naval treaty with Hitler, why the French did not send their forces into Germany when Hitler remilitarized the Rhineland, why the Western powers allowed the Nazis to march into Austria, and, finally, why the French and British sold out Czechoslovakia at Munich in September 1938. No doubt part of the answer lay in the social divisions within the Western powers them- selves, and part of it in the hope that Hitler might rid Europe of com- munism. Much of it, though, lay in the fact that the Western powers felt they had no choice but to try to live with Germany and to accept the word of its leader when he said that all the country wanted was national self-determination for the Germans and equality of status for his country with that of the other powers. The logic of appeasement ran out precisely when Hitler's targets for expansion exceeded any possible definition of national self-determination for the Germans. The military reoccupation of the Rhineland, the *Anschluss* with Austria (overwhelmingly upheld in an Austrian referendum), and even the occupation of the German-speaking Sudetenland, could all be seen as steps towards the realization of German national objectives.

But, in the winter of 1939, when Hitler occupied the rump of Czechoslovakia, he crossed a line that even British prime minister Neville Chamberlain, the leading architect of appeasement, could not fail to understand. From that point on, the slide to war was a matter of strategic manoeuvring and the calculation of great-power advantage. After Munich, Hitler abandoned the ruse that he was seeking reconciliation for Germany within the European order, and made it plain that his goal was a German hegemony, to be imposed by force. The road lay open to the destruction of Germany and Europe and to the control of the fate of the continent by the United States and the Soviet Union.

If the German question had dominated Europe from the time of Bismarck, the terms of the question were transformed by the Second World War and the Holocaust. The reformulated question cannot be avoided in an assessment of the contemporary New Europe, since it involves problems that lie at the centre of our understanding of the history of the twentieth century, and even our understanding of the nature of humanity. Was it tragic circumstances that caused the Germans to descend into a totalitarianism without equal, to negate the rights of others in the Holocaust on such a scale that their collective behaviour constituted the darkest moment in modern history? Or was that descent rooted in the flawed character of the German society and nation? The case for circumstance is readily made. The foregoing brief historical discussion has already touched on its basic elements; one needs to add consideration of the spawning ground for Fascism that Germany became in the 1930s. In Germany, as in other parts of Europe between the wars, impoverished and socially uprooted middle-class elements became a mass base prepared to carry out an assault on aspects of the bourgeois order, while resisting the threat of proletarian revolution. In all such cases, the defence of the fatherland was a central rallying cry against the perceived threat of Bolshevik internationalism. In the Nazi case, this exaltation of the fatherland was embodied in a formalized theory of Aryan racial supremacy. Nazism was infected with a virulent strain of the anti-Semitism, that was commonplace in much of Europe, particularly Central Europe. In a longer historical time frame, to all of this can be added the exceptionally traumatic transformation of Germany from pre-industrialism to its position as the most industrialized society in Europe, a transformation that provoked severe alienation in a once paternalistic and traditional society that had not passed fully through the Western bourgeois-democratic revolution of the eighteenth century. If historical experience, both long term and more immediate, had made the Germans different from their neighbours to the west, there is the additional issue of the leadership of the Nazi movement. There has been a vast emphasis on the personality and career of Adolf Hitler, in the search for an explanation. And yet faced with the crimes committed, faced with the decision taken at the very top to carry out the systematic murder of an entire people, faced with concentration camps in every corner of Germany and the occupied territories, the explanations pale and acquire an obscene quality, even if there is merit in them. The explanations have always tended to relativize that which is irreducible.

No foreigner who is honest with himself or herself has ever gone to Germany without considering these questions, which cry out for answers as much today as they did in the immediate post-war period. The more humdrum and normal the surroundings, the more the Germans one encounters appear perfectly civilized, the more the questions well up inside. It cannot be otherwise; it will not be otherwise for a very long time. Paradoxically, the more economically successful and democratic today's Germany is, the more the questions become unendurable, the more they seem to unearth deeply disturbing answers, not about Germans, but about the human race.

The ghostly absence of the Jews in today's prosperous Germany always brings the question to the fore. In 1933, Berlin was the fifth-largest Jewish city in the world. Then its Jewish population was 160,000; today about 6,000 Jews live there,[1] although this population is now growing as a consequence of migration from Eastern Europe, where Jews are experiencing a renewal of anti-Semitism. That Jews today see Berlin as a haven attests both to the continuing problem of racism in Central Europe and to the relative success of the Federal Republic of Germany in dealing with the burden of its past.

If Germany's history can never be forgotten by non-Germans, it continually roils the life of the Germans as well. It is not that German television, which has broadcast an estimated 30,000 hours on the subject of the Third Reich in the past three decades, has avoided the subject.[2] At times, such as when the U.S. television production *Holocaust* was broadcast in the late 1970s, the response in Germany was an overwhelming public airing of the treatment of the Jews in Nazi Germany.

Well known also have been the efforts to sweep the past under the rug. To some extent, this was begun at the highest levels in the post-war years, when the Allied occupation forces showed themselves willing to work with administrators who had a Nazi past. And while the FRG's first chancellor, Konrad Adenauer, was completely free of any personal Nazi taint, his government was notorious for appointing former members of the Nazi party to high government posts.

And yet many Germans do seem to want to expiate the sins of the Nazis. At Ludwigsburg, north of Stuttgart, the government of the FRG has operated its central office dedicated to the pursuit of Nazi criminals since 1958. At one time, the operation was a large one, employing 120 people. Now, as the criminals actively pursued have become a tiny and aged remnant, the centre has been focusing on its function as a museum, maintaining a vast file of documents on individuals, military units, police, and installations involved in Nazi crimes. Particularly in the early days of its operation, the presence of the centre was seen as a blemish on the community, whose members were known to forbid their children to play with those of the prosecutors. Now more accepted in the community, the centre often deals with requests from individuals who want to know about the behaviour of their own relatives during the war. These inquiries often come in the form of requests for information from the relatives of men who have recently died. Haunted by what fathers and husbands might have done, those who remain have turned to the centre.[3]

If the individual and collective record of the Germans in the Nazi era is still a burning question in contemporary Germany, it was the wartime Allies, in the closing stages of the Second World War, who first had to make decisions about the fate of a people with such a history. They began with the assumption that Germany should not be allowed complete control over its future destiny and certainly should be allowed no say over the destiny of others. The initial post-war superpower division of Europe rested, therefore, not merely on their superior force, but on the overwhelming ethical case that Germany must be controlled. At first, indeed, the view that Germany must never again be in a position as an industrial power to threaten its neighbours was the official policy of the Allied powers.

The initial policy of enclosing the Germans did not survive, could not survive, and the arguments, instead, for containing the Germans by embracing them and then in the long term, by trusting them, became overwhelming. At first, those reasons were extrinsic. The Germans, even in defeat, held the key to Europe. In the Europe that was taking shape in the early post-war years, the pieces of occupied Germany formed the strategic high ground in the contest between the United States and the Soviet Union, which was transforming the wartime allies into Cold War adversaries. Defeated Germany was divided into four zones. In 1947, the American and British occupation zones were united for economic and administrative purposes, and a year later the French zone was joined with them. In 1949, the Federal Republic of Germany was established, and, in the Soviet zone, the German Democratic Republic.

By former German standards, the Federal Republic was a modest affair, and deliberately so. In 1949, when the FRG was established, the rules of political life and organization were embodied in a Basic Law, so called in preference to the word "constitution," to make clear its temporary character prior to the establishment of a constitution for a future united Germany. This provisional constitution was drafted in Bonn by a parliamentary council with representatives drawn from the states in the American, British, and French occupation zones. Bonn, the prosaic university city on the Rhine, most noteworthy for being the birthplace of Beethoven, was selected as the capital of the new state — on a temporary basis. Everything in the FRG was interim. "Interim" formed a pleasing and deliberate contrast with vast conceits of the "thousand-year Reich" that had gone before. In 1949, war-weary Germans preferred it that way, and so, too, did the wary authorities of the occupying powers, who still had the final say in the fledgling Federal Republic's affairs. In choosing Bonn, the founders of the FRG were stressing the modesty of the new state, but were also making the point that, some time in the future, a united Germany would return to Berlin as the country's historic capital. When I first visited the Bundestag (the lower house of the federal parliament), Bonn had been the capital of the FRG for over three decades, longer than the combined life-spans of the Weimar Republic and the Third Reich. Still, the point was made that this was only a temporary seat of government. The building that housed the Bundestag underscored the point. A post-war functionalist office building, it could have been an administrative building for a suburban college somewhere. From the time Bonn was selected as the "temporary" capital of the FRG until Germany was unified in October 1990, the world was reassured by the image projected from this quiet city on the Rhine. Bonn was in the western reaches of the

FRG, in the Rhineland, with its historic pro-French sympathies, far
from war-like Prussia.

As capital, Bonn gave foreigners and Germans alike the pleas-
ant sensation that there was no connection between the FRG and the
pre-1945 past. That this notion of a Germany that is wholly a post-
war creation is illusory is quickly seen in the countryside around
antiseptic little Bonn. The dark hills along the Rhine, dotted with
towers and the ruins of castles of a great age, are a reminder that this
is the heartland of immemorial Germany. And there are also jarring
reminders of a more recent past. In Bad Godesberg, in September
1938, just up the river from Bonn, Hitler held his second meeting
with Chamberlain on the subject of the Sudetenland, en route to
the final meeting a few days later at Munich. I discovered that the
Hotel Dreesen in Bad Godesberg where I was staying had been
Hitler's headquarters during the conference with the British prime
minister. The manager of the hotel, over coffee in the manicured
café-garden of the hotel, told me of his memories of the Dreesen
during the war when it had served as a place of internment for
important foreigners, including Léon Blum, who had been France's
prime minister in the days of the left-wing Popular Front government of the mid-1930s. My first guest at the hotel, an adviser to
Chancellor Helmut Schmidt, could not help referring to the sinis-
ter history of the place as we sat out on a balcony overlooking the
gloomy Rhine. "Which one of us shall play Hitler and which one
Chamberlain?" he quipped.

If the surface impression of a new Germany with no connections to the past is ruptured at frequent points, the constitutional
framework established by the founders of the FRG definitely was an
acknowledgement of the past, since it so clearly attempted to avoid
its pitfalls. Throughout its troubled history, the Weimar Republic was
politically assaulted from both the far right and the far left, at the same
time as it was rendered politically ineffectual by the splintering effect
of an electoral system based on a wide-open variety of proportional
representation. The Basic Law aimed to strengthen the political
coherence of the government of the FRG. The Federal Republic's
novel system of so-called personalized proportional representation has
the following features:

- Half the seats in the Bundestag are allocated to local constituencies, the other half to lists of candidates from the political parties. Every citizen is to cast two votes, one for a local

constituency member — chosen through the first-past-the-post method — and one for a political party. Distribution of both votes cast is made according to a formula that ensures that the Bundestag is constituted in proportion to the votes cast — in other words, a party underrepresented in the election of constituency members is compensated through extra seats from its list. Those who voted for losing candidates in local constituencies do not end up unrepresented. Their votes contribute to seating members from party lists. The chancellor — generally the leader of the largest party in the governing coalition — is chosen by members of the Bundestag after each election.

- To prevent the kind of political splintering that was so disastrous in the Weimar period, the FRG imposes a floor level of support, so that only those parties receiving at least 5 per cent of the national vote are represented in the Bundestag. The result is that significant political tendencies are represented, while the number of parties is still kept manageable.

- To promote governmental stability in the Bundestag, the FRG has adopted a system known as the "constructive vote of no confidence" to handle challenges to the sitting chancellor and administration. What this means is that, for a vote of no confidence to pass, with the result that the chancellor and the administration must resign, the motion must include in it the name of the proposed chancellor who is to replace the present one. (Chancellors are seated in the first place through a vote in the Bundestag.) This system prevents parties from forming purely negative majorities to bring down governments and means that only when an alternative administration has the support of the majority of members will the present government fall.

The enshrining of individual rights in the Basic Law was also clearly conditioned by the experience of Nazi rule. While those who drafted the Basic Law were determined to entrench individual rights for the first time in German history, they were also determined that the democratic order should not be open to wholesale challenge and, to that end, were prepared to place some limits on individual expression. Political movements that advocate the overthrow of democracy can be banned. In addition, freedom of speech is limited in order to prevent its abuse against individuals or groups of people. Legal action can thus be taken against those promulgating doctrines such as anti-Semitism, [4] or the attempt to deny the Holocaust as an historical event.

Both the constitutional provision allowing for the banning of anti-democratic political formations and the 5 per cent floor level needed for parties to elect members to the Bundestag have ended up playing a role in constraining the far right and far left in the FRG. During the 1950s, two political parties were banned as undemocratic by the Federal Republic's Constitutional Court — the neo-Nazi Socialist Reich Party, in 1952, and the Communist Party, in 1956. In both of these cases, the government of Chancellor Konrad Adenauer initiated the legal action before the court. The court ruled on the basis of Article 21 of the Basic Law, part of which provides: "Parties which, by reason of their aims or the behaviour of their adherents, seek to impair or abolish the free democratic basic order or to endanger the existence of the Federal Republic of Germany, shall be unconstitutional." [5] The inclusion and use of such a sweeping provision in the Basic Law testifies to the defensive stance of German democracy, particularly in the first decade of the FRG. The Weimar Constitution of 1919 took the more expansive view that political parties were simply an outgrowth of the rights of individuals and that, therefore, to restrict them meant placing undue limits on individual freedom. The FRG Basic Law took the more confining view, the result of tragic experience, that political parties did not merely express the views of people, but helped shape them as well, and that therefore they must be free to play their critical role, but only if they respect the fundamental principles of democracy. [6]

In 1968, a new Communist Party was established. By then, a new far-right party, the National Democratic Party (NPD), was also on the scene, winning some support in state elections and attracting widespread notoriety. The NPD, while avoiding an outright endorsement of Nazi philosophy, espoused an extreme nationalist political line, focused on the growing resentment in the FRG against the rising number of foreign, mainly Turkish, guest workers. Neither the Communist Party nor the NPD was banned as their predecessors had been. Instead, they were kept out of the Bundestag in the crucial 1969 elections when neither of them managed to win the support of the required 5 per cent of the electorate. [7] That the re-emergence in the late 1960s of such political parties was dealt with through electoral marginalization rather than through an effort to have them banned was a sign that the political order was more relaxed than previously about potential threats to democracy.

Since the founding of the FRG, German democracy, while highly effective, has also been carefully controlled, watched over by a political class whose members have shared a high degree of consensus about fundamental goals. The political leadership of the FRG has been wary of excessive populism, and highly defensive about any risk of chaos or unrest. While there have been many political crises in the history of the FRG — scandals, spy sensations, terrorism and the responses to terrorism, anti-immigrant agitation, vituperation among politicians — the leadership of the very wide political centre has kept a firm hand on affairs and, for the most part, has operated within a consensual framework.

Proportional representation and the intertwining of federal and state institutions in the FRG reinforce the consensual tendencies within the system. Proportional representation, as practised in the FRG, fosters two results. First, it is very difficult to elect a government comprised entirely of members of one party. Second, the number of parties in the Bundestag is kept to a relatively small number as a consequence of the 5 per cent rule. These two consequences taken together tend to favour politicians who are consensus-seekers. The German system would never produce a Margaret Thatcher or a Ronald Reagan, and while, in the case of Konrad Adenauer, it produced a leader with Gaullist trappings, it is not tailor-made for a Charles de Gaulle either. German political leaders, whatever their special personality traits and credentials, must nurture coalition partners and make deals with them on an ongoing basis. In only one federal election since 1949, that of 1957, has a single political party, the CDU/CSU (the Christian Democratic Union, together with its Bavarian sister organization, the Christian Social Union), won an absolute majority of seats in the Bundestag. In all other cases, the party from which the chancellor has come has won a minority of seats and has been compelled to form a coalition with one or more other parties. Indeed, even in 1957, the CDU/CSU chose not to govern alone, but formed a coalition with the small German party.[8]

This political environment is notably different from that of the United States, Britain, and the France of the Fifth Republic. In the American system, a popular candidate, such as Ronald Reagan, who has major financial backing and a very clear ideological position, is capable of capturing the presidential nomination and then winning office. After his victory, Ronald Reagan could project his ideological vision from the White House, sometimes winning in Congress and sometimes losing, but he never had to engage in the muck-slogging and deal-making with coalition partners that is the lot of the German chancellor.

While the British prime minister, like the German chancellor, has to operate with friends and foes in Parliament and not in the special sanctuary of a presidential mansion, he or she can normally count on heading up a political party that has a majority of seats in the House of Commons. Margaret Thatcher's three electoral majorities in the United Kingdom were all achieved with the Conservative Party winning under 45 per cent of the vote. Had she been a politician with similar results in the FRG, Mrs. Thatcher could well have ended up in opposition, and had she formed a government, she would have been required to do it by negotiating a coalition with one of the other political parties, in the process conceding a significant amount of power and necessarily compromising her principles. With her well-known aversion to compromise, she would have been lamentably ill equipped to play the political game that all leaders of the FRG have had to play. It is consequently extremely difficult in the consensual German system to undertake a sustained effort to transform the political and social system in the way Thatcherism transformed Britain. The system in the FRG gives an edge to politicians who move towards the centre. Similarly, the German system is no habitat for the paternalism and haughtiness of a Charles de Gaulle, who disdained daily contact with politicians, and who created the Fifth French Republic, with its powerful seven-year presidency, in his own image.

In some ways the powerful figures who dominated the early period of the FRG were less characteristic of its consensualism than those who came later. Konrad Adenauer, the first chancellor, and Kurt Schumacher, the Social Democratic Party (SPD) leader who was his great opponent, although he never won office, were men who shaped the FRG more than they were shaped by it. Adenauer, who was over sixty when Hitler came to power, had long played a role in the Catholic Centre Party. Post-war Christian Democracy, of which Adenauer was a key architect, emerged out of the tradition of Catholic political action. Ousted as mayor of Cologne by the Nazis, he had sat out the years of the Hitler dictatorship at his country home. In 1945, the British occupying forces had called on him to resume his position as mayor of Cologne and then, within a few months, had removed him for insubordination. The dismissal was a key to the making of the septuagenarian as an important political figure in occupied western Germany. He was able to devote his energy to the formation of the CDU. A long political career predating the Nazis, a clean record during the Hitler years and evidence of being willing to stand up to the occupiers — these were useful personal assets to bring to the political scene in shattered post-war Germany.

Adenauer presided over the Parliamentary Council that drafted the Basic Law. As a result of the 1949 elections, in which his CDU/CSU narrowly edged out the SPD as the largest party in the Bundestag, he was installed as chancellor. The old man, "Der Alte" as he became known, remained in office for fourteen years, longer than the span of the Third Reich; he was eighty-seven years old when he stepped down. Adenauer was a low-key, moralistic leader with a very clear perception of the overriding need to align the FRG with the West, not only in terms of security policy, but in remaking the fabric of shattered Germany so that it would grow naturally into the West economically and socially. His paternalism was ideally suited to the launching of the FRG, but, not surprisingly, it grew ever more tiresome as the "economic miracle" ran its course and as the German society of the 1960s developed a desire for rewards as well as sacrifices, turning its attention towards issues of social equality and away from an all-consuming work ethic.

Schumacher, Adenauer's major opponent, was a figure whose personal and political formation had also occurred before the creation of the FRG. He had been a stalwart foe of the Nazis and had not been freed from a German concentration camp until 1945, suffering serious physical disabilities. He clung to a social democracy with roots in a more distant past, a social democracy in which the ideas and traditions of Marx and Eduard Bernstein (founder of Marxist revisionism in Germany) still had currency. And while Adenauer was from the Rhineland, Schumacher came from the Prussian East, which ended up in the GDR. He was deeply opposed to Adenauer's plan to graft the FRG onto the West. The Social Democratic Party leader did not trust the capitalist West and did not want Germany to end up under the control of the United States. His first priority was the unification of Germany, which he believed could never occur if the FRG became an outpost of a Western military alliance.[9]

In the early post-war period, it had appeared that the SPD would emerge as the most powerful political formation. It had been the only party to vote against Hitler's Enabling Act of 1933, a fact which gave it immense legitimacy. The SPD was well placed to take advantage of the radical revulsion among Germans against top industrialists who had been close to the Nazis. However, at a time when western Germany had come under the occupation of the Western powers and the economic and ideological influence of the United States, the anti-capitalism of the SPD proved to be a crippling disadvantage. Under the circumstances, it was Adenauer and the Christian Democrats, with their unshakable Western orientation, who became the keystone in the arch of German politics. Economist Ludwig Erhard's concept of the "social market" economy, combining market capitalism with the notion of a social partnership, perfectly fitted the aspirations of the largest number of people in western Germany. The CDU/CSU was to form a part of every government in the FRG until 1969. By that date, the Social Democrats had long since remade themselves to fit in with the basic elements of the Erhard economic model. At Bad Godesberg in 1959, the SPD convoked an extraordinary convention whose purpose was the remaking not only of the party's program, but of its long-cherished philosophy.

In the so-called Godesberg Program, the SPD abandoned the theoretical framework the party had clung to since the late nineteenth century. Marxist gradualism had been the special property of the SPD — the combination of the Marxist theory that capitalism made class war inevitable, with Bernstein's reformist notion that the socialist struggle should be carried out piecemeal, step by step, through parliamentary, non-revolutionary means. In the Godesberg Program, the Marxist past was swept into the dustbin, to be replaced by the idea that European democratic socialism was an outgrowth of Christian ethics, humanism, and classical philosophy. It even accepted the notion of private ownership. The SPD was no longer to be a "working-class party," but was to seek support from all parts of the population. Also at Bad Godesberg, the Social Democrats abandoned the neutralism and anti-militarism of Schumacher, and accepted the position of the FRG in the Western Alliance.

Once the Godesberg Program had been adopted, the consensual nature of federal politics in the FRG was fully inaugurated. From then on, political contests in the Federal Republic did not turn on questions of fundamentals, such as whether West Germany was to be capitalist and a member of the Western Alliance. Instead, they turned on the balance between economic competitiveness and social justice to be pursued within an accepted larger framework.

In adopting the Bad Godesberg program, the SPD was reforming itself so that it could become an alternative party to which the German people would entrust power. Their opportunity was to come in the 1960s, when the economic miracle slowed appreciably. Throughout their tenure in office, the Christian Democrats had stuck to their emphasis on capital accumulation and investment at the expense of wages and salaries, and had not made any effort to pursue a counter-cyclical (Keynesian) fiscal policy. By the mid-1960s, German workers were becoming highly critical of a policy that appeared to be at their expense. They had played a major part in rebuilding the economy and they wanted their reward. In 1965, the CDU lost considerable support in federal elections, while the SPD gained ground.

Conflict within the coalition between the CDU/CSU and the Free Democratic Party (FDP) gave the Social Democrats their golden opportunity. Even though they were only the second party in the Bundestag, they could choose a coalition with the FDP that would give them a razor-thin majority of three votes, or a coalition with their arch opponents, the Christian Democrats. After a period of intense political negotiation, the upshot was the formation of a so-called Grand Coalition government in which the Christian Democrats and Social Democrats formed a cabinet made up of members from each party, leaving the FDP in opposition. The SPD conceded the chancellorship to the Christian Democrats, the larger of the two parties in the Bundestag. The new chancellor was Kurt Georg Kiesinger, a controversial figure who, despite his apparently sincere conversion to democracy, had been a member of the Nazi party during the years of the Third Reich. At Kiesinger's side in this odd cabinet was Willy Brandt, who had been the SPD candidate for chancellor in the election, the anti-Nazi who had chosen exile during the years of the Hitler dictatorship. Brandt served as vice-chancellor and foreign minister.

Brandt, who had doubted the wisdom of entering the Grand Coalition, ended by being the real winner as a consequence of it. In the 1969 federal election, the SPD gained seats, while both the Christian Democrats and the FDP lost seats. Following the election, Brandt became chancellor in a government in which the SPD formed a coalition with the FDP. The so-called social-liberal era that was thus begun was to last until 1982.

The most original and lasting departure of the "social-liberal" regime was not its economic approach, but its *Ostpolitik*, its opening to the East. The *Ostpolitik* began a long-term reorientation towards the East that would bear its ultimate fruit when the Gorbachev regime in the Soviet Union opened the door to German unification. The *Ostpolitik* and unification will be considered later in this chapter.

Brandt's tenure as chancellor lasted four and a half years, and included the successful re-election campaign in the fall of 1972, which resulted in a comfortable majority for the social-liberal coalition in the Bundestag and left the SPD, for the first time, with a larger number of seats than the CDU/CSU. With this success behind him, Brandt's sudden announcement in May 1974 that he was resigning as chancellor came as a shock to West Germans. His fall was precipitated by the public revelation a few days before his resignation that one of his closest advisers, Günter Guillaume, had been a long-term spy for the GDR. Though Brandt stepped down as chancellor, he continued as leader of the SPD. His replacement at the head of the government was Helmut Schmidt, who was strikingly different from Brandt. While Brandt exuded warmth and inspired trust, and even love, in his followers, Schmidt was a reasoning machine. With his middle-class background, his record of service in the military during the war, his skill as a pianist and yachtsman, and his personal polish and intellectual precision, Schmidt was far from typical of German social democrats. [10] In his followers, he inspired respect, not affection.

One consequence of the replacement of Brandt by Schmidt was further disillusionment within the left and youth wings of the SPD about the course being followed by the party leadership. That disillusionment took shape around two key issues: economic policy, where the SPD's more radical instincts were held in check by the economic liberalism of their coalition partners in the FDP; and defence policy, where the powerful German disarmament movement, strongly represented in the left wing of the SPD, was alienated from what they saw as the militarist posture of Helmut Schmidt. When I visited Bonn in the spring of 1980, minds were focused on the second oil-price crunch that followed the Iranian revolution, on the Soviet invasion of Afghanistan the preceding winter, and, above all, on the steady build-up of Soviet SS 20 missiles in Eastern Europe. A gloomy political mood prevailed in the West German capital, created in large measure by Helmut Schmidt's open disdain for U.S. president Jimmy Carter, whom the German chancellor believed was completely incapable of dealing in a coherent fashion with the rising Soviet threat. Despite the strong disarmament movement in the FRG, Schmidt's government held to the view that, unless the West matched the Soviet nuclear build-up, the Soviet Union might succeed in driving a wedge between the American and European wings of NATO.

The late 1970s and early 1980s constituted a "little ice age" in the relations between East and West, which followed the earlier detente of the 1970s and preceded the great transformation that came after Gorbachev's arrival in power in 1985. During this gloomy period, the theory was widely held in the West that the Soviet Union was an unstable state whose excessive military establishment, resting on an inadequate economic base, forced it to be expansionist. The Soviet invasion of Afghanistan, the first assault on a foreign country by the Soviet military since 1945 outside of Eastern Europe, and the relentless build-up of Soviet missiles in Eastern Europe, gave considerable weight to this hypothesis. In Schmidt's Bonn, such concerns were felt much more deeply than elsewhere, as they always were in Germany, because the FRG was the West's front-line state. Any war in Europe, between the two global blocs, would begin with divided Germany as the killing ground, with Germans killing Germans, while Soviets, Americans, and others also killed Germans as they fought each other.

Although it was an immense economic success, therefore, the Federal Republic remained a unique hostage to fortune. The very survival of the Germans would ultimately be determined by others. Living in such a cauldron, the Germans could not help thinking more deeply than others about the limits of sovereignty and the utter interdependence of peoples, which was dictated by late-twentieth-century technology. For the Germans, therefore, a solution to their specific problems could be realized only through the achievement of general solutions to European, even global problems. In that sense, it was not surprising that the dichotomy in Germany was not so much between political parties as it was between those who sought a radical redefinition of the conundrum through disarmament and environmentalism, on the one side, and those who clung to the traditional exercise of state power, including reliance on military alliances, on the other. These were years in which the German state and German industrialists were besieged by a wide array of extraparliamentary forces, ranging from large and peaceful movements to tiny and clandestine terrorist organizations, whose stock in trade was the kidnapping and murder of personalities associated with the establishment.

Despite his high intelligence and rationality, Helmut Schmidt could do little under circumstances of economic duress and renewed Cold War to ease the mood of his countrymen. Indeed, the very qualities that made him the most respected Western leader of his day may have contributed to the sense that the state was remote from the

German people. His successor could not have been more different.

Helmut Kohl had the appearance of a caretaker leader for years after he became chancellor. Indeed, following the unification of Germany and his emergence as the most powerful political leader in Europe, it became his proudest boast that he had always been under-estimated and that that had proved the undoing of his foes. Unlike his predecessor, who had the sure physical air of a sportsman and the sleek intelligence of a master strategist, Kohl had twin trademarks — his great weight and his bumbling speech. Even his manner of achiev-ing office did him no credit. Kohl was the only chancellor in the history of the FRG to come to power through the use of the "posi-tive vote of no confidence." His opportunity came as a consequence of the disintegration of the social-liberal coalition. The end for Schmidt came when the FDP joined forces with the Christian Democrats to defeat Schmidt over social-policy issues and install Helmut Kohl as chancellor.

Helmut Kohl was born in a suburb of Ludwigshafen, a Rhine port whose name is synonymous with the chemical industry, which has been its mainstay and was where the future German chancellor got his start in life. It is a pedestrian industrial town, not the sort of place one associates with the launching of a statesman of global importance. And yet the place of his birth taught Kohl something crucial to his later political success, that large and lofty goals are only achieved by paying attention to grimy details. Throughout his polit-ical career, Kohl has always known how to play to the basest motives of his followers, and then to reach beyond them. The resulting "Kohl shuffle," an ungainly progression across the dance-floor of German politics, has confounded analysts as to the true purposes of the chan-cellor. The shuffle can be seen at the critical moments in Kohl's stewardship of his country's fate. On November 10, 1989, the day after the Berlin Wall was opened, Kohl rushed to the city, breaking off his visit to Poland to join in the celebrations, as 100,000 East Berliners streamed into West Berlin. What the world saw was a German leader standing in the heart of Berlin, incanting words that could only send a chill through those with any memory of history: "Long live a free German fatherland," he shouted to the crowd, adding, as if by way of reassurance, "a free united Europe." "We are and will remain one nation," the chancellor continued. [11] Germany is a country where history has placed a great burden on vocabulary. Because of the Nazi past, words that are innocent elsewhere carry sin-ister baggage. Kohl has made people uneasy with his constant use of the word "fatherland" (*Vaterland*), a notorious Nazi favourite. And yet his commitment to Europe appears deep and sincere. Twelve days after the chancellor's appearance in Berlin, the members of the European Parliament were treated to the historic and moving spectacle of Helmut Kohl and François Mitterrand walking together onto the floor of the Assembly, symbolizing the unity of their two countries at a critical hour for Europe. Here Kohl delivered the same message he had delivered in Berlin, but with a very different emphasis. "Now is the hour of European solidarity," he said, and proclaimed that "German problems should be solved under the European roof." On the need to increase the unity of the EC: "There is no alternative to strengthening integration."[12]

A curious incident in the chancellor's youth gave weight to his contention that he had always been a convinced European and was not simply posturing to open the way for German unification. When he was nineteen years old, Helmut Kohl had journeyed with some friends from Ludwigshafen to the French border. There, they hoisted banners advocating Franco-German friendship and a united, free Europe. To underline their point, they tried to burn down the barriers dividing Germany from France, and for their labours were rewarded with overnight detention and a lecture from the French border police.[13] Fittingly, the mature Helmut Kohl was to be the leader of his country when the borders with France, the object of his childish prank, were finally thrown open.

But although Helmut Kohl could be reassuring to Europeans in the aftermath of the opening of the Berlin Wall, he could chill them again in the early months of 1990 on the issue of the Polish frontier. Kohl's political problem in the winter of 1990 was to react speedily to the disintegration of the GDR. With German unification looming and with Kohl determined to make use of his West German political machine to build an electoral organization in the GDR, the chancellor wanted to hold on to all the elements of his political support. Among his most fervent supporters were the several million Germans who came from the territory east of the Oder-Neisse boundary between the GDR and Poland, territory that had been German in 1937. In the years before unification had become a live issue, politically influential organizations in West Germany had kept alive the dream that one day the Germans might return to the lost territories. On many occasions, as these Germans had stood misty-eyed to sing of their lost Silesia, on his feet in their midst was the ample figure of Helmut Kohl. Now that the Soviet Empire was collapsing and

Germany was unifying, these Germans from east of the Oder-Neisse wanted Helmut Kohl to stand by them once again. Caught between a part of his constituency and the historic need to establish a settled place for a newly unified Germany in Europe, Kohl tried to weasel out by asserting that, as chancellor of West Germany, he could not guarantee the border between the GDR and Poland. Only the government of a unified Germany could do that, he claimed.

But the facts of life in the governmental system of the FRG, with its perennial reliance on coalition government, were already forcing Kohl to climb down from the fence on which he had been sitting. Kohl's foreign minister, Hans-Dietrich Genscher, appeared on national television and split publicly from the chancellor on the issue of the Oder-Neisse Line. Twenty-four hours later, Kohl backed down, announcing that he would request from the Bundestag a declaration that a united Germany would sign a treaty with Poland confirming the border, thereby giving up even the shadow of a claim Germany might have on its lost pre-war territories. [14]

For his less-than-statesman-like performance, Kohl earned public rebukes from around the world. In the end, however, both his mean and his noble aspirations were realized. Kohl had never seriously intended to make an issue of the Polish border; his commitment to securing a stable place for a united Germany in Europe was far too strong for that. By dragging his feet, however, he managed to demonstrate to his most nationalistic followers, the dispossessed Germans from the lost territories, that he cared more about them than had any other political leader. Kohl the statesman and Kohl the ward-heeler, Jekyll and Hyde — the two were inseparable.

Of crucial importance in keeping the Kohl government on an even keel, with long-term goals kept clearly in view, has been the FDP and foreign minister Hans-Dietrich Genscher. The FDP has played a part in almost every cabinet since the founding of the FRG, in partnership with both the Christian Democrats and the Social Democrats. The relatively small liberal party, with its predominantly professional and middle-class following, is quite unlike the mass populist North American liberal parties. The FDP is an élite formation whose political commitment is to democracy and civil liberties, and to defending a market economy and, therefore, limiting the size of government and the welfare state.

It is indicative of the success of the party through the Schmidt and Kohl years that Genscher, foreign minister for both chancellors, has regularly been singled out as the most popular politician in the country by public-opinion polls. Historically, the party has seen itself as a rudder in German politics, steering the FRG away from the dangers of Christian Democratic hegemony in the 1950s and 1960s, moderating the welfare-state aspirations of the SPD during the Brandt and Schmidt years, and countering the periodic partisan blundering of Helmut Kohl during the critical period of German unification.

Within the consensual system of the FRG, it was not coalition partners alone who helped steer a sometimes aberrant chancellor like Helmut Kohl. Of considerable importance in keeping the German state on course throughout the history of the FRG has been the Bundesbank, in recent times through the influence of its president, Karl Otto Pöhl.

As we saw in an earlier chapter, the Bundesbank was established with a very large measure of autonomy so that it could devote its attention to maintaining the soundness of the Deutschmark. The founders of the FRG felt that such autonomy was needed to ensure that the central bank could not be easily swayed by a government looking out for its short-term interests. Karl Otto Pöhl, whose original political links were to the SPD, began his career as a financial journalist. He was appointed to head the Bundesbank by Helmut Schmidt. Throughout the debates on German Economic and Monetary Union (GEMU) and Economic and Monetary Union (EMU) in Europe, Pöhl maintained a high profile, and remarkable candour about what should be done and not done, even when this contradicted the solemn proclamations of the chancellor. With the German government broadly committed to the stages towards EMU outlined in the Delors Report, Pöhl, who was chairman of the Committee of EC Central Bank Governors, did not hesitate to throw cold water on the path to EMU envisaged by the EC Commission president. "As long as such divergences as we have today exist — differences in inflation rates between 1 and 7 per cent amongst ERM [Exchange Rate Mechanism] countries, for instance — it is hard to conceive how the exchange rate can be given up as an instrument of adjustment."[15]

Pöhl's tough-minded assessment led him to conclude that EMU would occur only when much greater economic convergence had been achieved among EC countries. Indeed, he leaned to the view that a two-speed Europe was likely on the issue of EMU, just as the removal of frontier controls had actually begun with the Schengen agreement among five EC countries.

Pöhl's divergence from the position of Helmut Kohl shocked other Europeans, not used to the structure of decision making in

Germany, where well-established power centres existed quite independently of the leadership of the central government. From Pöhl's point of view, however, he was simply doing his job as the head of the state within a state that is the Bundesbank. While he ultimately supported the goal of a single European currency, for him a still higher priority was the soundness of the currency and that, he believed, could be achieved only if Europe's central bank was set up along the lines of the Bundesbank: "independent of the instructions and pressures of national governments and European institutions." [16] Pöhl knew perfectly well that such public utterances made life more difficult for the chancellor and would not be tolerated in any other EC country. In the FRG, it was a normal part of the governing system.

If chancellors of the FRG have to share power with coalition partners and the president of the Bundesbank, they also share power with state governments, the *Länder*, which not only have their own areas of jurisdiction but also control the federal upper house, the Bundesrat. The division of responsibility between the federal government and the *Länder* resulted directly from the circumstances facing Germany after 1945. Both the occupying powers and the emergent post-war German political leadership were determined to avoid overcentralization of power in the FRG, and so they set up new state governments.

Indeed, it was the *Länder* that preceded the federal state in the FRG. The state governments established by the occupying powers chose the delegates who came together to draft the Basic Law. Despite a gradual shift of power, particularly financial power from the *Länder* to the federal government, the states have remained important political players. In significant fields of jurisdiction, the federal government and the *Länder* share authority, which reinforces the FRG as a multipolar system of power holding. Under the Basic Law, a number of important areas of legislative competence are assigned to the federal government, the most important being monetary policy, foreign affairs, defence, citizenship, immigration, copyright and patent, and the overseeing of the postal, rail, telegraph, and telephone systems. Beyond these fields are other important areas in which the federal government can assert authority if it believes that uniformity throughout the whole of the FRG is important. These include: health and welfare; competition policy; highways; and civil, criminal, and labour law. Residual powers within the system, that is, all powers not specifically assigned to the federal government, fall within the jurisdiction of the states. Education, including higher education, is within state jurisdiction, although federal authority can be asserted in such a field if a policy affects the country as a whole.[17]

For those used to thinking of federalism along the lines of the eighteenth- and nineteenth-century federalist projects of the United States and Canada, the German system appears anomalous. German federalism involves a "horizontal" rather than a "vertical" distribution of power. This emphasis is strengthened by the fact that in a number of areas the federal government and the *Länder* share responsibility and are thus required to negotiate and cooperate so that both levels of government can carry out their responsibilities. Significant joint policy-making entities, the Science and Educational councils, the Financial Planning Council, and the Economic Planning Council, reinforce the need to achieve cooperation in key fields.[18]

What gives the *Länder* additional influence at the federal level, particularly during periods when the division of political forces in the country is closely balanced, is their control over the Bundesrat. The FRG's federal upper house is analogous to the American and Canadian senates and the British House of Lords. In the case of the FRG, however, the governments of the *Länder* appoint the members of the Bundesrat, and the members from each state (three to five, depending on population) are required to vote as a bloc, following instructions from the state government. In areas of jurisdiction that touch on the powers of the *Länder* — more than half of all federal laws do — the approval of the Bundesrat is necessary for legislation to pass. In areas of purely federal competence, the upper house has the right of objection but can ultimately be overruled by the Bundestag. In situations of disagreement between the two houses, mediation committees, including members from both the Bundesrat and Bundestag, must be convened to achieve a compromise, an effort that is usually successful. Because one coalition can control the Bundestag while another dominates the Bundesrat, the system again serves to check the power of the chancellor.

Taken as a whole, the FRG has proven to be a masterful political creation. Power has not been centralized in the hands of one group of decision makers. Reinforcing this governmental system of multiple, though interconnected power centres, has been the structure of the economy in the FRG. The post-war transformation of German society involved an important shift in the organization of the economy. In the pre-war German economy, cartels were prevalent in key sectors. What was changed in the part of Germany that became the FRG in the post-war period was not private ownership — often, industries remained in the same hands as before — but a shift in the system from closed cartels to competition. The key power nexus in designing the new German economy was the link between the American occupying authorities and the younger, more entrepreneurial elements of German business who were prepared to do away with the closed system of parcelling out market shares within cartels. The new German corporate structure ended by looking much more like the structure of American industry than it had in the past.

Once the economic miracle of the 1950s had been launched, that fact led many Americans to believe that the FRG was a carbon copy of their own economy. When it came to the structure of industry, there were elements of truth in this, but it was not the whole story. The economy of the FRG, like the structure of the state, was based not only on private capital operating in a competitive system, but on a corporatist foundation as well. The beginnings of the economic miracle preceded the founding of the FRG. The first step in the process was the currency reform undertaken in the Western zones of occupation in June 1948 under the direction of the hitherto little-known economist Ludwig Erhard, who was the architect of the "social market" economy. The social market economy combined two opposites, adherence to a competitive market economy, allied to a commitment to general social well-being and to the view that labour as well as management ought to have a say in how enterprise was run. Codetermination of industry differentiated the German from the American model of a market economy. In the chaotic atmosphere of the immediate post-war period, with German industry threatened with deconcentration by the occupying powers and by trade-union agitation for working-class power, important industrialists, hoping to head off the threat, compromised and negotiated agreements for the introduction of an equal number of worker representatives on their supervisory boards. Although trade-union power waned in the early years of the FRG, because of both the renewed confidence of industrialists and the hostility of the Americans to "socialist experiments," in 1951 the Bonn government, under the threat of strikes, enacted a codetermination law. Under the law, enterprises in the coal and steel industries with a thousand or more employees were to have workers' representatives on their supervisory boards; each of these firms was to have a worker director on its board of directors. The following year, the Works Constitution Act extended the concept of decision-making input to workers in almost all firms in matters of social welfare and personnel. Codetermination significantly altered industrial relations in the FRG, contributing to a non-adversarial style in labour-management relations, and was one reason why West Germany was to have so few strikes compared with other Western countries. In the social-liberal era, further extensions were made to the codetermination system.

The parallels between codetermination in industry and a system of multiple power centres and consensus in the state are obvious. Indeed, the two systems were linked at many points. While German industry operated in the context of a private, market economy, state intervention to assist particular sectors, and even some state participation in the ownership of industry, tied the private sector and the state, both at the federal and the *Land* level, closely together. The consequence was a corporatist approach in economy and society that made the German model substantially different from that prevailing in the United States and Britain.

THE UNIFICATION CHALLENGE

The intermeshed political, economic, and social systems of the FRG have to be considered a very substantial success story over the four decades from the founding of the West German state to the crisis of German unification. That crisis, which emerged with extraordinary swiftness in 1989, was to test the architecture not only of the Federal Republic, but of all Europe as well. The FRG was born at the heart of a system of double containment that shaped its existence for forty years. In that system, the Federal Republic was the keystone front-line state in the global containment of the Soviet Union and its satellite states. West Germany, as densely populated per square kilometre as India, was occupied by hundreds of thousands of NATO military personnel, most of them American. Through its limited airspace, jet fighters constantly shrieked, and, all too often, Germans opened their newspapers to find that another aircraft had crashed, sometimes destroying property and sometimes killing civilians. Running through the heart of countryside that had been German from time immemorial was the ugly, unnatural scar of the frontier with East Germany, beyond which was the death strip, a vast Soviet conventional army and, as time went by, an ever-more-lethal array of Soviet nuclear missiles whose targets would be the conurbations of West Germany. The essence of double containment was that the Americans held back the Soviets in the heart of Germany, and, in doing so, also held the West Germans, though certainly not against their will, within the ambit of American global power.

The Germans recognized from the very beginning that their ability to alter this unenviable position was largely in the hands of others, that only a historic change in the fortunes of the superpowers would allow them to transcend it. Within these confines, however, a German–German relationship existed between the FRG and the GDR, and it evolved over time.

In one crucial respect, there was a consistency of view within the Federal Republic concerning the GDR that never changed. The Bonn government refused to recognize the GDR as a foreign state.[19] And if the GDR was not a state foreign to the FRG, the Adenauer government reasoned, then third states should not accord diplomatic recognition to it. Under this so-called Hallstein Doctrine, the FRG itself refused diplomatic recognition to any state that recognized the GDR, with the exception of the Soviet Union. While Adenauer and his CDU successors clung rigidly to the Hallstein Doctrine, when he became chancellor, Willy Brandt, while holding fast to the view that East Germans were not foreigners, was prepared for changes. Brandt's *Ostpolitik* was based on the notion that, while full diplomatic recognition of the GDR should not be accorded, an approach should be made to the regime in East Berlin to seek a normalization of relations that could result in improved conditions of life for Germans living east of the Wall. A period of dramatic and delicate negotiations with the leadership of the GDR, the Soviet Union, Poland, and Czechoslovakia ensued.

At first discussions with the GDR were far from promising, but negotiations with the Soviet Union were more productive. The result was the signing of the Treaty of Moscow in August 1970 between Bonn and Moscow. In the treaty, a mutual non-aggression pact, the two sides agreed that they had no territorial claims to each other, and none to any other state. They proclaimed the inviolability of all existing frontiers, including that between the FRG and the GDR and that between the GDR and Poland (the Oder-Neisse Line).[20] There was something in the deal for both sides. The Soviets had won Bonn's acquiescence to the settlement of frontiers in the East, which were the consequence of the Second World War. For their part, the West Germans had been able to achieve a settling of accounts with Moscow that did not require them to accord the GDR full diplomatic recognition, despite the Soviet Union's long-held insistence that this ought to happen.

The Treaty of Moscow was followed by a treaty with Poland four months later. In the Treaty of Warsaw, the FRG recognized the Oder-Neisse Line and established diplomatic relations with the Polish government, thus abandoning the Hallstein Doctrine.

To reach an understanding with the GDR, the fundamental goal of the *Ostpolitik*, the Brandt government placed great pressure on the Western allies to reach an accord with the Soviet Union to normalize the status of Berlin. In September 1971, a deal was reached between the allied powers and the Soviets. The West acknowledged that West Berlin was not a part of the FRG and could not serve as the site for plenary meetings of the Bundestag and Bundesrat; in return, Moscow abandoned its former position that West Berlin was within the territory of the GDR and, therefore, subject to its authority. The Soviets also recognized the right of the FRG to represent West Berliners internationally and the right of the Bonn government to locate government agencies in West Berlin (which it had already done on a large scale).

Willy Brandt won the Nobel Peace Prize for his work, but the Christian Democrats charged that the government was consigning East Germans to perpetual exile behind the Iron Curtain and hopelessly compromising the goal of reunification. The resulting CDU/CSU positive motion of no confidence failed to gain an absolute majority in the full Bundestag by a mere two votes. In the months that followed, growing dissension among the Christian Democrats about their opposition to the *Ostpolitik* doomed the campaign against the Brandt government, and after more political manoeuvring, the treaties of Moscow and Warsaw were finally ratified in May 1972.

The *Ostpolitik*, popular with the people of West Germany, was to result in a permanent change of posture towards the East on the part of the FRG. The high point of the process, from the viewpoint of the Bonn government, was the achievement of a working relationship with the government of the GDR, embodied in the Basic Treaty negotiated by the governments of the two Germanys in late 1972. The FRG and GDR recognized the frontier between them as inviolable, renounced the use of force in their mutual relations, and acknowledged each other's independence and authority. The Federal Republic thus gave up its claim to be the sole legitimate representative of the German people, and the GDR agreed to increase the extent of visits by citizens between the two Germanys. While the FRG continued to refuse to extend full diplomatic recognition to the GDR, Bonn and East Berlin agreed to establish permanent missions in each other's capitals. For the Federal Republic, the Basic Treaty meant that East Germany was accorded recognition, not as a foreign country, but as another sovereign state in the bosom of the German nation.[21]

The *Ostpolitik* was a German achievement, but critically, it occurred during a time of East–West detente. When a renewed chill in Soviet-American relations occurred in the late 1970s and early 1980s around the nuclear-arms build-up and the Soviet invasion of Afghanistan, the gains that had been made in the German–German relationship remained intact, for the most part. In the first phase of its history, under the leadership of Konrad Adenauer, the FRG had become indissolubly a part of the West. In the second phase, under the leadership of Willy Brandt, the FRG, while remaining a part of the West, achieved normalized relations with the other German state, and with the rest of Eastern Europe. Both fundamental principles, the *Westpolitik* of Adenauer and the *Ostpolitik* of Brandt, were essential to the role the FRG was to play when the mighty drama of the East European revolutions unfolded in 1989.

REVOLUTION IN THE GDR

Of all the revolutions in Eastern Europe in 1989, Europe's great year of change, the most astonishing was that in East Germany. The country had been different from other East bloc states from the start. From the Soviet point of view, it had always been by far the most strategically significant of the satellite regimes. The Soviets had paid in blood for their piece of Berlin. In East Berlin an enormous Soviet military cemetery provides mute testimony to the vast cost of the final assault on Hitler's bunker.

The East German regime was always the most politically dependable handmaiden of Moscow's wishes, less nationally idiosyncratic than those in the other Eastern European countries. Over the course of the post-war decades, it was to become something of a role model for the entire Soviet sphere in a socio-economic sense. Despite the wholesale transfer of industrial assets from what was to become the German Democratic Republic to the Soviet Union in the immediate post-war period, East Germany developed a substantial industrial base. Before the Wall was opened, and the world discovered firsthand the nightmare of pollution and technological backwardness that characterized East German industry, it was common for GDR officials to brag about their country as one of the world's leading industrial powers. As a consequence of the deals made with the FRG in the era of the *Ostpolitik*, the political leaders of the GDR believed they had achieved respectability, a rough equality of status with their rivals in Bonn.

Despite the empty boasting, however, the East German regime was a hot-house phenomenon from the beginning. It was ruled by the Socialist Unity Party (SED), a shot-gun marriage among the major political forces — Communists, Social Democrats, Christian Democrats, and others — in which all these parties theoretically merged their interests to pursue a common line. The shabby truth was that this amounted to no more than the ruthless suppression of all groups on behalf of the Communist leadership, which ignored the formal democracy guaranteed in the GDR Constitution. A critical instrument of repression was the Stasi, the East German secret police, whose ubiquitous presence was to cast a long shadow over Germany after the opening of the Wall, as rumours and revelations were aimed at one political figure after another, destroying careers among both Christian Democrats and Social Democrats. In the new era of democracy, the first leader of the East German Social Democrats, and the first (and last) democratically elected prime minister in the GDR, were both accused of involvement with the Stasi.

Two historic events revealed the truth about the GDR. The first was the workers' uprising of June 17, 1953, provoked by the East German government's decision to increase work quotas by 10 per cent with no increase in pay. Beginning with a spontaneous downing of tools on June 16, the movement grew quickly into a massive protest at two hundred locations throughout the GDR, centred in East Berlin, by the next day. With no clear leadership, the upheaval was already subsiding when Soviet tanks and troops arrived to repress it. According to official figures, twenty-nine people died in the revolt, although the evidence is that the death toll was much higher, and that hundreds of others were injured. The revolt was followed by harsh repression, the execution of ringleaders, and jail and work camps for many others.

The second telling event was the building of the Berlin Wall, which was begun on August 13, 1961. Both the uprising and the Wall were stark indications that the regime was utterly artificial, that it was a pestilence imposed on the East Germans through overwhelming external force. At the time the Wall was built, there had been some who had believed that East Germany would succeed in snuffing out West Berlin, that people would gradually leave the western enclave, that business would find it a costly and unprofitable location. Despite its aggressive appearance, however, from the very beginning the Wall testified to the grave weakness of the East German regime. It had been built to keep East Germans inside, to stop the tide of human flight to the West that was undermining the productive base of the GDR.

As soon as the threat of Soviet force was withdrawn by Mikhail Gorbachev in the fall of 1989, it became instantly apparent that the flame of resistance had never been quenched in the hearts of East Germans. Over many years it had been kept alive, in part by the virtually complete access of West German television and radio to all parts of the GDR.

In the end, the East German regime, impregnably defended along its front with the West, succumbed to a collapse in the rear. The GDR had constructed massive ramparts between itself and West Germany to prevent the flight of its people. While that system proved impervious to all but the most ingenious attempts at escape, a door was suddenly opened through which East Germans could flee. When the Hungarian government announced that it would no longer stop East Germans — who were allowed to travel to Warsaw Pact countries — from crossing into Austria, the GDR was plunged into a crisis that the ruthless regime of Erich Honecker could not manage. Complaints from East Berlin that the government in Budapest was sabotaging the Warsaw Pact were to no avail. Past the drab, concrete border point on the Hungarian side of the Austro-Hungarian frontier came the first endless procession of crowded Trabants into Austria. The first and last letters on their DDR decals had often been crossed out, leaving only the "D" of the Federal Republic in place. Soon a new route of escape was found through Czechoslovakia, where East Germans crowded into the West German embassy compound in Prague. Acting in response to direct appeals for humane treatment of these refugees from Mikhail Gorbachev in Moscow, the faltering Communist governments in East Berlin and Prague coordinated the movement of the East Germans from Prague to West Germany. In one of the great dramas of 1989, the East Germans crossed their former homeland in sealed trains, passing through railway stations guarded by the military of the GDR. Later some of those who had made the trip told of their fear of being locked in the trains. These comments touched a sensitive historical nerve.

By the early autumn of 1989, the human flight was no longer the main problem for the Honecker regime, which now faced gigantic and crippling demonstrations against its authority, centred in Leipzig and East Berlin. For two years, weekly peace vigils at the Nikolai Church in Leipzig had been drawing ever larger turn-outs. Now the throng filled the outside courtyard, doubling in size and then doubling again, until it numbered hundreds of thousands. It was impossible to point to an immediate cause. The shortages of vegetables, meat, and fruit, the work in pollution-belching factories, the tedium of organizing everyday life, the resentment at the finely graded system of privileges for the friends of the regime — these had all been present for years. The swelling movement, whose political expression came in the New Forum, was in response to all these provocations. The final explosion was born of hope, of the calculation that the oppressors no longer had the means of overwhelming coercive force at their disposal. Mikhail Gorbachev had made it clear that the 400,000 Soviet troops stationed in East Germany, without doubt the ultimate arbiters of force in the country, would not intervene to support the government against the people in the streets. From the Nikolai Church in Leipzig and from the Gethsemane Church in East Berlin, the people went forth without microphones, without well-established leaders, and toppled the regime. In doing so, they placed a straw on the back of the post-war global geopolitical order that caused it to disintegrate as well.

Without a reliable instrument of repression in its hands, the GDR leadership had no choice but to give in to the popular movement. From that moment, the supreme authority of the Communist Party in East Germany was doomed. Erich Honecker was forced to resign and soon was placed under house arrest, the subject of charges of massive corruption. His smiling replacement as Communist Party chief was Egan Krenz, notorious as a former hard-liner who had publicly backed the use of force against the pro-democracy movement in Beijing the previous spring. Once in power, Krenz became the embodiment of "Gorbachevism in a hurry." A dizzying sequence of democratic reforms and assurances of the right to travel abroad was capped on November 9 by the historic decision to open the Berlin Wall.

The question of who gave the order to open the Wall is shrouded in controversy and in self-serving retrospective claims. In the final days, the regime lurched uncertainly between thoughts of repression and gestures of appeasement. Finally, an order to speed up the issuing of visas to East Germans wanting to visit West Berlin and the FRG was garbled and then announced as a decision to open the Wall immediately to completely free travel to the West, with visas to be issued at border crossings to anyone wishing to cross. From this point, there was no turning back. Crowds of East Berliners descended on the crossing points at the Wall, and, after momentary hesitation, the uniformed figures in grey were transformed from armed guards to traffic cops and functionaries issuing instant visas. The champagne bottles popped, women danced with East German guards, and hats, buttons, and uniforms changed hands for Deutschmarks.

All the revolutionary acts in Eastern Europe in 1989 were over-shadowed by the great event of November 9. What had been decisive in the opening of the Wall had not been the crisis management of Egan Krenz, a transitional figure, who was out of office within a few weeks. Of critical importance had been the historic gamble taken by Mikhail Gorbachev to allow events in East Germany to unfold without the threat of Soviet intervention. Whatever second thoughts leaders might later have, that decision had unilaterally ended the position of Germany as a defeated power. It opened the door to a new Germany, a reordered Europe, a potentially eclipsed Soviet Union, and a less influential United States. While Berliners and other Germans joyously celebrated the end of their long journey through the valley of national humiliation, the rest of the world had to absorb the shocking implications of what had occurred.

After all great wars, a moment comes when the post-war order established by the victors disintegrates to be replaced by a new order. In Europe, the order established by the victors in the Second World War came undone on November 9, 1989, and began to be replaced by a new one.

First, Soviet hegemony in Central Europe was over; Gorbachev had believed that the only way to rebuild the U.S.S.R. was to dramatically cut back on military spending, and that meant giving up the authoritarian, military-based control that tied Central Europe to the Soviets.

For France, the opening of the Berlin Wall was a moment of truth. Invaded by German armies in 1870, 1914 and 1940, the French have developed a veritable national psychosis about Germany. Despite the possession of nuclear weapons, always seen as an equalizer for France vis-à-vis Germany, many in France feared that the balance between the two countries would be irretrievably tipped if seventeen million East Germans joined the West Germans. As we have seen, for forty years, France's policy had been to cement a special relationship with the West German government in Bonn, so that a new Europe could be constructed around a Franco-German axis. Now the critical question was whether France possessed the weight to sustain this policy. While the Mitterrand government ended up on the side of German unification, once it became obvious that it was unstoppable, for a time there was an uncertainty in the French position that could not help but cloud Franco-German relations. Briefly, Mitterrand explored the possibility with the Soviet Union of acting to slow the movement towards German unification, dropping this idea when it became clear that Gorbachev was not interested. But the aftershocks of November 9 rumbled through France for months afterwards.

Less dramatically, but no less substantially, November 9 altered the positions of the Americans and the British as well. Like that of the Soviet Union, the American global position had also rested on a German pillar. Because American policy in Europe has been habitually understood in terms of the containment of the Soviet Union, its other aspect was often obscured. American policy rested on double containment, keeping the Soviets at arm's length while embracing, and thus also containing, the Germans. The opening of the Wall meant that in the future Germany would no longer be a client of the United States, and that Europe's position as a whole would be transformed vis-à-vis the United States.

The British risked being more marginalized than they already were. Because of its historic tendency to avoid continental entanglements and to draw strength from the broader English-speaking world, Britain once won General de Gaulle's epithet that it was America's "Trojan horse" in Europe. Increased German power and a weaker role for the United States in Europe could not help but affect the British. In the year following the opening of the Wall, British leaders would wrestle with their need to come to terms with the New Europe that would centre on Germany. A consequence of that anguished appraisal was the fall of Margaret Thatcher.

No less anxious were the West Germans. The opening of the Wall threatened the FRG with the loss of much that it had gained in its forty-year history. West Germany had made itself the model capitalist state. The world's largest exporter of commodities, the FRG had become one of the three economic powerhouses of the world, along with the United States and Japan, and was the engine of the EC as it moved to the single market. The collapse of the GDR opened a vacuum that the leadership of the Federal Republic felt compelled to fill from the first instant. While Kohl and other leaders of the FRG understood the historic opportunity that had presented itself, they were initially motivated as much to prevent severe dislocation in West Germany as they were to achieve unification. In its early days in the summer of 1989, the flood of East Germans into the FRG had been joyously welcomed. When the Wall was opened, East Berliners were the toast of West Berlin, enjoying discounts at stores, free admission to the zoo, and a warm greeting from the local populace. A backlash was not long in coming, however. Reception facilities for East Germans were overwhelmed, in poorer neighbourhoods competition was building for jobs between the newcomers and those already there, and in some parts of the country friction and outright hostility towards the incoming East Germans soon reached dangerous levels. During the first two months of 1990, the tide of migrants to the FRG from the GDR reached two thousand a day, placing great pressure on Kohl to complete the economic and political unification of Germany quickly. "We had to move fast or the people in the GDR would have fled," said Kohl.[22]

Since its inception, the FRG, a careful and defensive democracy, has abhorred any hint of anarchy above all else, in this way forming a notable contrast with other democracies like the United States, Canada, France, or Britain. The Kohl government's response to the collapse of the GDR was the supreme illustration of this tendency. The leadership of the government in Bonn had no intention of pausing at all to find out which way the populace in East Germany wanted to go. Fear of where an unguided populace could go is simply too deeply ingrained a feature of the politics of the FRG.

Instinctively sure of his response to the crisis, in a way that much more sophisticated political leaders were not, was Helmut Kohl, placed by good fortune in a position to become the second unifier of his country. If Bismarck, Germany's first architect of unification, had been a Prussian *Junker* who was the foremost geopolitical strategist of his time and whose weapons were blood and iron, its second architect was a Rhineland Catholic burgher whose weapons were the wealth and security of the West and the Deutschmark. From his first appearance at the Wall, the day after it had been opened, Helmut Kohl seized the issue of unification and pushed it while others hesitated, in the end catching not only his Social Democratic opposition, but the European powers and the United States completely off guard.

The first in the process to lose its valiantly forged political clout was the popular movement that had grown up in Leipzig and East Berlin and had given the leadership of the GDR its final push to oblivion. For a few weeks after the Wall was opened, East German political idealists dreamed of a special future for the GDR. It would be a part of neither the East nor the West. It would be neither communist nor capitalist. A "third way" would be forged in which a market system would be created, but one in which social justice and social security would not be forgotten. The East Germans in their new and democratic free state might form a loose confederal arrangement with the FRG. Under this arrangement, the wealthy West would not simply overrun and annex the East, but, instead, the special truths and identity, the hard lessons of their imprisonment, would inspire a new East Germany. Comparisons were made with the relationship of German-speaking Austria to the FRG, or with the relations among the cantons of Switzerland, to suggest how the GDR might position itself next to West Germany.

This idealistic and intellectual conception of the future represented a strain of radical democracy in East Germany, which at first appeared potent, but was soon buried beneath the waves of fear, anger, revenge, authoritarianism, and renewed racism that were also authentic voices of the new East Germany. Paranoia and revenge had gripped East Berlin by the time I visited the city in early December 1989. Even low-level party functionaries told me they were living in fear of physical attacks being made against them. For Vietnamese and other visible minorities in the GDR, as law and order broke down, there was rising fear of the skinhead extremists who were haunting the streets of the larger cities. Although the number of skinheads was small, not larger than in parts of northern France, Belgium, and England, their appearance, together with their overt racism and anti-Semitism, contributed to the growing public unease. Although the opening of the Wall staunched the flood of East Germans to the West for a few weeks, the westward-flowing human tide soon resumed its full force. East Germany was losing its young and its well-educated — and its rootless. A sharp increase in the number of abandoned babies and small children was reported in the GDR as some adults decided to leave for a new life in the West, entirely unencumbered. The idealistic amateurs from East Germany who had toppled the Communist regime were soon replaced by political professionals directed from Bonn.

As East Germany teetered on the brink of political and economic collapse in the weeks following the opening of the Wall, the caretaker Communist regime, robbed of its fangs, was forced to move up the date of the East German election to March 18. Opinion polls in the first weeks of 1990 suggested that the Social Democrats could win 50 per cent of the East German vote. But experienced social-democratic campaigners I met in those days before the election could see problems. They soon learned that, as elsewhere in Eastern Europe, people freshly liberated from formerly Stalinist regimes now wanted to put as much distance as they could between their future and anything that reminded them of the past. The word "socialism" itself was such a reminder. When she was campaigning in the GDR on behalf of the Social Democrats, German-speaking Carole Tongue, deputy leader of the British Labour Group in the European Parliament, was cautioned by SPD friends not to use the words "socialism" or "comrade" (the British Labour Party's traditional greeting) when addressing an election rally in Leipzig. The word "Europe" was fine, she told me, and so too were references to social programs. Christa Randzio-Plath, the SPD member of the European Parliament for Hamburg, a long-time and experienced campaigner, discovered that distributing red West German SPD buttons did not meet with favour when she was electioneering in the GDR. Indeed, on the eve of the election, she was candid with me in predicting that the Social Democrats would be defeated in the GDR and would then go on to lose the first all-German elections.

In the FRG, SPD politicians allowed themselves to be pushed by the onrush of events, not only out of political contention in the immediate GDR elections, but in Germany as a whole. Following his own convincing re-election as minister-president of the working-class Saarland in January 1990, Oskar Lafontaine was picked as the SPD's candidate for chancellor for the elections that were to be held in the FRG in December 1990. When he was chosen, it was not yet clear whether those elections would be for a newly united Germany or for West Germany alone. A diminutive, eloquent pepperpot who could talk rings around the ungainly Kohl, Lafontaine was known as the "Napoleon of the Saar." In his controversial and ultimately disastrous performance as SPD standard-bearer, Lafontaine was to form a highly illuminating contrast with Kohl throughout the year of unification. Within a few weeks of the opening of the Wall, Lafontaine was stressing the costs to West Germans of the flood of East Germans into the FRG and was predicting that the ultimate economic cost of unification with the GDR would be ruinously high, leading inevitably to the imposition of higher taxes on West Germans. Instead of stressing that the two Germanys constituted one people and that they belonged together in one state, Lafontaine appeared to hope that if the flood of migrants could be staunched, by according them a less generous financial welcome if necessary, then the GDR could be stabilized and the Germans could ponder their future in a more temperate fashion. It was a position that counted on a backlash developing among working-class West Germans against the new migrants and against the high costs of monetary and political union.

Instead of the backlash he hoped for, the one that developed was against him, and came from within his own party. From the very beginning, there was grumbling within the leadership of the SPD against Lafontaine's posture on the unification issue, although there was certainly sympathy for him throughout the country when he was slashed in the throat by a deranged woman at a political rally in a suburb of Cologne in April 1990. Following his recovery from the attack, Lafontaine stuck to his position on unification. By the middle of the year, SPD politicians were telling me, off the record, that Lafontaine had no political judgement and that he had never learned how to listen to other people. When he threatened to try to hold up the ratification of the terms of union with the GDR, dissatisfaction among leading Social Democrats was there for everyone to see. The most celebrated remark within his own party was Helmut Schmidt's contemptuous comment that the SPD did not deserve to win. Schmidt's open dismissal of his party candidate for chancellor did not win him plaudits from other Social Democrats, many of whom already felt estranged from the former chancellor who had become wealthy on the world lecture stage, but Schmidt's comment, none the less, expressed the opinion of most of the German political élite.

If 1990 was to be a dismal year for the SPD and Oskar Lafontaine, it was a year of triumph for Helmut Kohl and the Christian Democrats. In some ways this was no surprise, since Kohl held all the high cards in the German political game as the year opened. Furthermore, Kohl was wise to savour 1990, since it was sure to be followed by times of difficult reckoning once unification had been achieved. Helmut Kohl was in a position to make East Germans an offer they could not refuse, and he had no qualms about making them that offer. What was not understood in the first weeks following the opening of the Wall was the depth of anxiety and insecurity about the future that gripped the East German population. While among intellectuals there was much talk about a "third way" for the GDR and about a slow and careful consideration of what the relationship between the two German states ought to be, the mass of East Germans felt quite differently. They saw a rapid way out — immediate economic and political union with the FRG.

As chancellor of the FRG, Helmut Kohl could address that anxiety as no one else could. He personified the simplest option for the East Germans, annexation by the FRG under Article 23 of the Basic Law, which provided for the right of German territories to join the Federal Republic when they so chose. In contrast, the SPD's talk of a slower pace, with a lengthy negotiation leading to a new all-German constitution, appeared too vague and faint-hearted to the East Germans. The heart of Kohl's offer, however, was much more enticing still. He promised the East German electorate that he would exchange their Ostmarks for Deutschmarks, hinting that this would be at the extraordinarily generous rate of one to one, making this plank in his platform one of the most fabulous bribes ever placed before any electorate anywhere. When monetary union came at the beginning of July 1990, the rate of exchange was not quite so generous, but still very favourable to those holding Ostmarks.[23] The unrealistically high rate for the Ostmark was to contribute within a few months to the onset of economic disaster in eastern Germany, by pricing its producers out of the market. The high price of monetary union was not fully evident until the winter of 1991, months after political union had been completed.

Despite their early organizational weaknesses in the campaign, the allies of Helmut Kohl in the GDR were cobbled together into an electoral organization whose efforts were directed by the professionals from Bonn. On election day, March 18, the conservative Alliance for Germany, made up of three political groupings, the largest of which was the East German CDU, won a stunning 51 per cent of the vote, leaving the Social Democrats a weak second and consigning those who had directed the struggle against the old regime before November 9 to political oblivion, in the very weak showing of the New Forum.

A striking feature of the vote was the pronounced tendency of working-class East Germans to attach themselves to the allies of Helmut Kohl. In the dirty, polluted factory towns of the GDR, the unambiguous desire of the populace was to place its future in the hands of the FRG and its chancellor. In more middle-class areas and in East Berlin, the GDR capital, with its large number of government functionaries, the electoral showing of the SPD and the Party of Democratic Socialism — the reconstituted Communists — was much better. The East German election made it resoundingly clear that unification would be quick and would involve the annexation of the GDR by the FRG and not a more complex union of two states.

In the only free election in their history, the East Germans determined the course of unification for all of Germany. By the time Germans voted again on December 2, 1990, this time in the first all-German democratic election since 1932, first monetary and then political unification had been accomplished. Indeed, by the time voters went to the polls to pick their post-unification government, the sense of anti-climax was overwhelming. For months, the polls had pointed to an easy victory for the CDU/CSU-FDP coalition. Germans were content to put their future in the hands of the ebullient "King Kohl" and the calculating "Genschman," as the German tabloids described the two dominant figures in the government.[24]

The real drama in Germany after March 1990 was not electoral, but economic and social. The opening of the Berlin Wall forced a social and economic merger between the two Germanys because it made possible the mass flight of the East German population to the FRG, thus creating a crisis on both sides of the intra-German border. To stop that flight, the FRG was forced to offer the East Germans both monetary and political union. But the task is far from complete. The unequal collision between the two Germanys is illustrated in the fact that, during 1990, West Germany's economy expanded by 4.5 per cent and 800,000 new jobs were created, while, in East Germany, the economy contracted by a staggering 33 per cent and 1.1 million jobs were lost.

For producers in the GDR, economic union was for the most part an instant economic catastrophe. On the night of June 30, when merchants' shelves in East Germany were restocked with goods from the West, East German products were driven from the marketplace. While East German industry was extensive, the quality of its products and its level of productivity were far below those of the West. To make matters worse, at the same time as East German industry was devastated in the German marketplace, it was losing its place in other Eastern Europe markets as well, because those countries, too, were turning to the West for industrial products.

As the old factories shut down by the score, there was the promise of new investment from the FRG and from other parts of the EC. But there were serious doubts about how extensive that new investment would be. One reason was that property-holding itself had become an extremely vexing matter in the former GDR. Land and assets that had been taken over from private owners by the Communist GDR were now being reclaimed. Thousands of claims involving hundreds of thousands of items of property were being made and, while the principles for resolving the issue had been set down in the unification treaty between the two Germanys, those principles were being challenged in court cases that would not be resolved for some time. Meanwhile, such controversies added an additional barrier to productive investments in eastern Germany. For many energetic, younger people the option of migration to richer western Germany was still being taken. For many others, who lived close to Berlin or to the former intra-German boundary, working by day in rich

Germany and sleeping by night in poor Germany was an option. While Volkswagen and Mercedes-Benz have decided to build new plants in eastern Germany, and banks like Deutsche Bank, as we have seen, have been making major investments there, many companies have seen little advantage in locating there. After all, they have concluded, adding a new shift at an existing facility in western Germany can produce enough additional product to supply the new market of seventeen million people in the East. Even the new state governments in the East have been sustained on life-support systems from the West. Each morning, top bureaucrats, from Bonn and elsewhere in western Germany, board flights for the East, spend the day there, and return home on the evening flight. [25]

Dislocation on the scale that has been experienced in eastern Germany can have extremely grave social consequences. The crucial question is whether the life-support systems established by the FRG to promote the East's transition to a market economy are up to the task. The risk that the former GDR will constitute a backward region from which people will continue to flee is a very great one. The further risk of social disintegration and of the growth of authoritarian ideology among those who remain in eastern Germany cannot be ignored. In this sense, eastern Germany shares much in common with its neighbours in Central and Eastern Europe. (The risks and prospects facing the region are the topic of a later chapter.) The wealth and energy of the FRG, with its solid foundation in Western Europe, is the best hope that eastern Germany can be integrated effectively. It should be noted here, as it will be in the later discussion of Central Europe, that freedom is not the only road that can lead from the revolutions of 1989 and that the risks of xenophobia, authoritarianism, and the politics of ethnic exclusion form an ominous alternative course, which is also possible.

Despite the risks, the Federal Republic of Germany is not merely the economic engine of the New Europe, it is the state that in many ways most ideally fits within it and points the way towards its future. The Federal Republic was not sovereign when it made its modest appearance in 1949. The occupation statute remained in effect until May 1955. Even after that date, the victorious powers had certain rights in Germany that subjected the two German states to constraints not felt by other states. Only on October 3, 1990, when the GDR joined the FRG, did those constraints disappear, and even then there were the left-overs of history, the most noteworthy being the dismal Soviet army in eastern Germany, whose dispirited legions were staying on until they could be resettled at home at the expense of the Germans. The reason sovereignty was not gained on October 3, 1990, was that, throughout Germany's post-war history, two processes had been at work simultaneously. All the while the FRG was overcoming the constraints imposed as a consequence of Germany's unconditional surrender on May 8, 1945, it was also voluntarily pooling its sovereignty with its neighbours in the creation of the European Community. By the time Germany was the first among equals within the EC in the fall of 1990, all the members of the community had ceded significant sovereignty to the body they had created in common.

Gordon Smith, professor of government at the London School of Economics, has made the critical point that the FRG, as established in 1949, was a state "without a centre."[26] With West Berlin an island surrounded by the GDR and the Soviet military, the isolated city could never be the true metropolis of the FRG. (Formally, of course, it was not even a full part of the FRG.) West Germany became a state with no metropolis, and, over the long term, this proved to be a great advantage. European nation-states with powerful metropolitan centres have suffered the tensions of centre–periphery relationships — one need only think of Britain and France to see how true this is. The FRG was spared this. With no centre, it had no periphery. To be sure, there were more or less advantaged regions and, over the decades following 1949, there was a shift from older industrial areas such as the Ruhr, and shipbuilding centres such as Hamburg, towards newer industries and the south, favouring the rise of cities such as Munich. The classical, historically based relations between an overriding centre and "the provinces" was avoided, however.

With its provisional character; its modest as opposed to imperial character; its porous interdependency, involving federal, state, and EC institutions; and its lack of full sovereignty, the FRG was the large state most suited to the building of the New Europe. Essential to the construction has been a shift in the character of the nation-state from the organic, quasi-religious sovereign of the past to the provisional, interdependent, indeed transitional, entity of today. Circumstances have made the FRG the foremost of these transitional states. As such, the FRG has helped resolve one of the most difficult questions in Germany. Prior to the FRG, the state was regarded in German thinking, much more than in the West, as a kind of deity that stood above civil society. Historically, the functionaries of the state were accorded a deference that would have been seen as out of place, even absurd, in the West. Living for decades in a provisional state has helped to break this conception and has brought the state down to a more mundane level. That same process is now under way in all EC states.

The West Germans or "Bundies," as they were called by the East Germans, may not have presented a heroic face to the world, but that was surely their most singular virtue, the source of their enormous success. Exasperated critics in the United States and Britain have sometimes found in the German unwillingness to play a role in crises, such as that in the Persian Gulf following Iraq's invasion of Kuwait, evidence that the FRG seems to aspire to nothing more than to be a big Switzerland. If the old, martial Germany is far from view, many will find that a vastly positive change. They will wonder, however, what the consequences of unification will be for the modest FRG.

On the evening of October 2, 1990, Germans gathered in public places in the FRG and the GDR to await midnight, the moment when their post-war division would end. In Bonn, a city once described by John le Carré as "twice as big as the central cemetery in Chicago and twice as dead," people gathered for the celebration, even though at that very moment a united Berlin was becoming the capital of the FRG. (Berlin was named the seat of government as well in a decision taken by the Bundestag on June 20, 1991, following a lengthy and emotional debate. The move to Berlin was to begin in 1995 and was to take a decade to complete, with several major government departments remaining based in Bonn.) Thousands of residents of Bonn joined a 120-member choir from the European Community to sing the EC's anthem, Beethoven's "Ode to Joy." In Berlin, tens of thousands gathered where the Wall had been, to fête the end of division. All day long Berliners celebrated with sausages, beer, and champagne. Richard von Weizsäcker, president of the FRG, reminded Berliners of the historic meaning of division: "The division of Germany was the central expression of the division of Europe. We cannot talk our way out of it. None of us will forget that without the war begun by Germany under Hitler, it would never have come to partition."

Not all was light-hearted. In Berlin, thousands of anarchists skirmished with police. In Leipzig, Magdeburg, Schwerin, and Frankfurt an der Oder, small gangs of neo-Nazis fought with police. [27]

The mark of a truly epochal development that changes the course of history is that it leaves virtually all established authority in disarray. According to this exacting test, the unification of Germany was just such an event. The world's leading political personalities seemed less powerful, less sure as a consequence of it. Mikhail Gorbachev, who launched the process of official reform in the Soviet Empire and who made the critical decision against the use of force in East Germany, was a less important man. For better or worse, the Germans had been released from their historical imprisonment. There could be no surer harbinger of the waning of Soviet superpower status. For George Bush, a corner-stone of the American global edifice had been lost, leaving the United States to play an inevitably declining role in Europe's future. François Mitterrand looked older, smaller, and less the visionary of the New Europe.

It was not a question of what these more or less worthy leaders had done or not done. The simple fact was that Germany had become immeasurably more powerful. Even the Japanese no longer looked quite so much as though they were about to carry the future before them. It was a reflection of how true Lenin's dictum remained: "He who has Germany, has Europe."

As long as Berlin was on its margin, the centre of gravity of Western Europe could rest comfortably on the Rhine, the frontier between France and West Germany. With unification, that Europe, with its enclosed space, was transformed. The New Europe stretched eastward, defying easy definition, of necessity forcing rethinking among Western Europeans, not least of all the French.

Chapter Seven

FRANCE:
BELONGING AND NOT
BELONGING

★ ★ ★ ★ ★ ★ ★ ★ ★ ★ ★ ★

CARPENTRAS IS A QUIET, BOURGEOIS CITY OF 25,000 people. Throughout France, the very name of the city was, until the spring of 1990, a synonym for a place where nothing ever happened. If the Provençal city is a little dull, its physical location is splendid enough. Carpentras is located in the Rhône Valley, between Mont Ventoux, which is the highest mountain in Provence, and the Rhône River. The valley is a major wine-producing region, the celebrated vineyards of Châteauneuf-du-Pape situated only a short distance from the city. On Friday mornings, merchants from the surrounding countryside set up their stands in the narrow streets of old Carpentras, transforming the centre of town into one of the largest weekly markets in the area. Thousands of people are drawn to the Carpentras market, where herbs and spices, lamb and rabbit, olives and goat cheese, clothes and shoes are on sale. Since Carpentras enjoys three hundred sunny days a year, those who visit the market are almost sure to be able to sit outside at one of the cafés in the central square, unless the Mistral, the vicious northwest wind, which is the curse of the Rhône valley, happens to be blowing.

Some of the people drawn to Carpentras are there to visit the oldest synogogue in France. The city has had a Jewish community for centuries, originally because, in the Church-controlled region close to Avignon, Jews were allowed to locate, something not often permitted in neighbouring parts of France. A few years ago, a friend of mine explained to me that the Jewish cemetery, located in an out of the way valley on the northern edge of Carpentras, provides a key to the history of the Jews in France. He and his wife had visited it and had traced the headstones from the earliest days to the recent past. Noting the names, they could reconstruct the migrations of Jews to Carpentras from other parts of Europe, and could follow the waxing and waning of the fortunes of the local Jewish community, down to the tragic time when the government of Vichy France passed its own anti-Semitic laws and helped round up Jews for expulsion to Germany, where their final destination was the death camps. [1]

On May 10, 1990, news was spreading across France about the ghastly desecration of the Jewish cemetery in Carpentras the night before. Gravestones had been ripped up and broken. The body of an eighty-one-year-old man, who had died three weeks earlier, had been disinterred and left to lie amidst the broken headstones. The earliest reports said that the body had been impaled by a parasol.

Carpentras. For ten days, nothing else in France mattered. The terrible news galvanized the country into a powerful wave of revulsion against racism. Newscasts spoke of little else. Regular television schedules were jettisoned. A few nights later, all of the country's channels simultaneously broadcast a film on the Holocaust. Demonstrations were mounted on the streets of cities and towns in every part of France, the largest in Paris, drawing hundreds of thousands of people into the protest against racism. When François Mitterrand marched in Paris with the demonstrators, he was the first president of the Republic to join such a demonstration since the liberation of Paris in 1944. Jacques Chirac, former prime minister and leader of the Gaullist Rassemblement pour la République (RPR), entered the principal synogogue in Paris wearing a yarmulka, telling the press that, at such a time, "we are all Jews." In the wake of the desecration, a number of demonstrations and rallies against racism were held in Carpentras itself, the most moving of them a procession of 20,000 marchers who filed into the cemetery for a quiet ceremony.

Public wrath against the desecration helped overcome the fear and isolation that initially was so palpable among Jews and members of other minority groups. I experienced the feelings of despair and isolation firsthand when I visited an elderly Jewish friend at his home a few kilometres from Carpentras, the day after the news of the attack. He told me that there was a sense among Jews he knew that the extremists "won't even leave us alone when we are dead." The terrible trauma of the Holocaust was in the air. There were stories of long-time foreign residents of France saying that they would have to leave the country, and of Jews from abroad telling their friends that they could never return to their favourite places in the south of France.

As a result of the demonstrations and the public outcry, despair began to be superseded by solidarity, by the conviction that, if there were racists in France, there were more anti-racists. In Carpentras, some local residents who had never been active politically wore the Star of David on the streets and taught their children why they should do the same.

Tragically, desecretions of graveyards, particularly Jewish graveyards, have not been altogether infrequent occurrences in many parts of Europe and North America. What happened in Carpentras, while shocking and repellent, was not unique. The response to it was singular, however, because it exposed with crystal clarity the troubled state of French society in the spring of 1990. The desecration at Carpentras was not dismissed as the act of marginal or deranged people because, at the time it occurred, France was in the midst of an agitated debate about who did and did not belong in French society.

Just before the desecration, Jean-Marie Le Pen, leader of the Front National, had complained on national television that the Jews had too much influence in the French media. Telling the French that the political and media élites in France are servants of foreigners, and that they jointly conspire to keep the truth from the people, has always been a favourite message of the leader of the Front National. In 1990, a poster of Jean-Marie Le Pen, showing him wearing a large white gag across his mouth, was plastered across the country on hoardings and telephone poles — the message: the tribune of the people was being muzzled for telling the truth.

In mobilizing the French against foreign influences and the presence of foreigners, Le Pen's preferred target has always been the North Africans, particularly Algerians and Moroccans, of whom there are nearly three million in France. Just days after the opening of the Berlin Wall, when all Europeans were focused on the theme of reconciliation among peoples and the end of the Cold War, Le Pen was leading ten thousand of his followers to a cemetery in Avignon to honour the memory of a slain woman whose killer had been a North African. For Le Pen, the problem is simple, and so, too, is the solution. Europe is threatened by the power of the Brussels bureaucracy, which, under the influence of a Marxist intelligentsia, has opened the continent to "millions of immigrants whose cultural, sanitary and professional level has done more harm than good." The leader of the

Front National deplores European impotence in the face of AIDS, "the fall in our birth rate, [and] the rise of Islam."[2]

The efforts of the Front National and its demogogic leader have played relentlessly on the insecurity and vulnerability of significant sections of the French population. Insecurity that leads to a yearning for a simpler past, for a renewed sense of community, and for strong, even authoritarian leadership has a long history in France. The country that, more than any other, unleashed the notions of modernity on the world in the great philosophical and revolutionary movements of the eighteenth century has remained spiritually divided for the past two centuries. French thought and French society have formed two vast streams since the Revolution — one adhering to the ideals of equality, rationalism, and progress, the other to those of tradition, religion, and preservation. Often the bitterness of these two Frances, one against the other, has been more profound than the antagonism of France towards potential foreign enemies, even in times of national peril. The ferocity with which the Paris Commune was crushed in 1871 surpassed the intensity of the war against the Prussians. In the late 1930s, with social tensions running extremely high between left and right, the epithet "Better Hitler than [French prime minister] Léon Blum" became a watchword for sections of the right. From the supreme tragedy of modern French history, the German occupation from 1940 to 1944, what left the deepest wounds was not the occupiers themselves, but the internecine strife between collaborators and the Resistance. These wounds are only partly healed today. Everywhere in France, the memories, the suspicions persist. The vicious struggles of the Vichy period are handed down in families from one generation to the next, colouring the relationships among neighbours.

These divisions have their roots, of course, in the French Revolution, which, even two centuries later, engenders passions in France, as was so evident in 1989 during the bicentenary of the outbreak of the great revolution. The course of all subsequent modern history was prefigured in the phases of the French Revolution, giving it a contemporary significance far greater, for example, than that of the American revolution. While all Americans can look back with easy satisfaction on their revolution, its heroes and its outcomes, so that a hotdog at a July fourth celebration has no ideological connotations, such is not the case for the French with their revolution. A vast kaleidoscope, the French Revolution is full of moments treasured by some factions and detested by others. The night all feudal obligations were swept aside, the Declaration of the Rights of Man and Citizen, the flight and capture of the king, the executions of Louis XVI and Marie Antoinette, the radical terror, the civil war in the Vendée, the dictatorship and subsequent execution of Robespierre, the rise of the Directory, and the coming to power of Napoleon Bonaparte — every political faction in France celebrates the triumphs and nurses the wounds it feels in these events.

A secular France committed to human rights, material advance, and the opening of spiritual windows to the world is at war with a France that fears instability, rapid modernization, and the threat posed by outsiders. It is around the issue of North African immigration that this ever-present fault line has revealed itself in contemporary France. It runs right through the political forces of French conservatism. When the French went to the polls for the first round of the presidential election on April 24, 1988, Jean-Marie Le Pen won a stunning 14.4 per cent of the vote, in what he exultantly depicted as "a political earthquake."[3] His electoral strength struck a body blow at the mainstream French right. Its standard-bearer for the second round of the presidential contest would be Jacques Chirac, prime minister and leader of the Gaullist RPR. Chirac was left facing an insoluble dilemma. He had won only 19.9 per cent of the vote, against Socialist François Mitterrand's 34.1 per cent.[4] To defeat Mitterrand in the second round, he would have to appeal to centrist voters, many of whom had supported former prime minister Raymond Barre (16.5 per cent) in the first round, but he would also need the support of virtually all of Le Pen's adherents as well. If Chirac made an overt appeal to Front National supporters, by promising more restrictive policies to deal with immigrants, he ran the risk of alienating Barre supporters, and pushing them into the arms of Mitterrand. The extent of Chirac's inability to meet the challenge was evident when Mitterrand won a decisive 54 per cent of the vote in the run-off election two weeks later.[5]

Chirac's acute dilemma in the spring of 1988 illustrated the unfavourable strategic position occupied by the French right as a consequence of the rise of Le Pen. Despite the fact that the French right, when its votes were combined, enjoyed a slight edge over the combined forces of the left, its divisions deprived it of power, not only at the presidential level, but also in the National Assembly election two months later, which brought the Socialists, with Michel Rocard as prime minister, to office. (Presidential and National Assembly elections are held separately, and for terms of office that differ in

length.) The National Assembly elections ended the two-year experiment known as "co-habitation," during which Chirac had served as
prime minister, while François Mitterrand continued as president. (In
the French system, the president, who deals extensively with foreign
affairs, actually chooses the prime minister, who generally handles
domestic affairs, from the ranks of the National Assembly.)

For the mainstream right, the Gaullist RPR and the Giscardian
UDF (Union pour la démocratie française), the threat posed by Le Pen
provoked contradictory responses. Some wanted to seize the immigration issue for themselves and, through a judicious combination of
electoral alliances with the Front National, thereby depriving it of its
main issue, open the door for the right's return to power. Charles
Pasqua, who had served as minister of the Interior in Chirac's government, was a leading proponent of this viewpoint. Others, who
feared the danger to French society that would result from legit-
imizing Le Pen, wanted a policy of "no deals" with the Front
National, in the hope that such isolation would lead to the political
suffocation of Le Pen.

The sentiments swirling around Le Pen were encountered
everywhere. Conservative acquaintances of mine in Provence, the
region where the Front National's support is highest, have often told
me that, while they regard Le Pen as dangerous, they agree with his
position on immigration. Indeed, they argue that, unless serious steps
are taken to limit immigration and to expel illegal immigrants, Le
Pen's support will increase. Adopt his ideas to stop him, the frequently made argument goes.

In the south, to have an everyday conversation about the major
cities of France, especially Marseille, is to invite a discussion of North
African immigration. Farmers in Provence often informed me (falsely)
that the cities of Marseille, Lyon, and Bordeaux now all have North
African majorities. During trips to Marseille, acquaintances have complained to me, as we drove through North African districts, about the
unwillingness of these immigrants to dress like the French and to
adopt the French way of life.

In the fall of 1989, the suspicion in France that the North
Africans in their midst were an alien group that could never be assim-
ilated to the French way of life was further inflamed by the issue of
the *foulard*. In keeping with their religious views, which involve a
strict code of female modesty, a minority of Muslim parents in France
were sending their daughters to school with their faces veiled by a
foulard (scarf). Some school and municipal officials decided to ban the

foulard on the grounds that the offending garment was a religious symbol and that, since the French public-school system was secular, all religious practices were prohibited within its precincts. For some on the left, the *foulard* had to be opposed to defend the hard-won separation of school and church, and for some feminists the *foulard* was an outrageous symbol of female inferiority. Overwhelmingly, however, the outcry against the *foulard* came from the right and involved the visceral rejection of an alien group in the midst of French society. Immigrants to France should adopt the customs of their new country and should leave behind aspects of their way of life that were bound to offend the French, the argument went. For others, the Muslim assertiveness behind the wearing of the *foulard* was a sign that an ancient conflict, that between Christendom and Islam, was still under way, and that the two civilizations could simply not live together. While these passionate controversies proceeded, for a very large number of people the whole thing was a non-issue, an absurd distraction from more important questions. If young girls wanted to go to school with scarves wrapped around their heads, surely this was a matter for themselves and their parents, and France, as a tolerant country, had no business interfering.

What made the issue of the *foulard* so explosive was the way it enflamed the larger debate about belonging and not belonging in French society. Does being French involve ethnicity as well as culture? Is the definition of what it means to be French changing, losing much of the cohesiveness and certainty it had in the past? Are the French open to changing their self-definition, and, above all, are they open to having immigrants play a central role in altering that self-definition?

NOT A FRENCH DEBATE ALONE

While the debate about the role of outsiders in France has importance for the whole of Europe, the point needs to be underlined that the controversy in France is not unique.

For the British, the difficult question of who belongs came to the fore in the Salman Rushdie affair. Some Muslims in Bradford, the northern English city that has become a symbol of the Muslim presence in the country, publicly supported the call of the Iranian government for the offending author to be put to death. Is this a religious issue, a question of free speech, or a criminal provocation in which some people have been inciting others to violence? And what is England to do about the fact that its head of state, the Queen, is also the head of the Church of England, and that laws remain on the books prohibiting blasphemy against the Church? Should there also be laws to prohibit blasphemy against Islam and, if so, should Salman Rushdie be tried in court as the author of a blasphemous tract? Whereas France had completed the separation of Church and State as a consequence of the French Revolution, this process was incomplete in Britain, with implications for how the British would treat the debate about belonging and not belonging in their society.

In Italy, as well, the issue of who belongs has been a vexing one. In addition to numerous reports of assaults against Africans in major Italian cities, regional protest movements have emerged that make use of anti-immigrant feeling to boost their political impact. The Lega Lombarda, appealing for greater autonomy for wealthy Lombardy, has used attacks on southern Italians and North Africans to make its point.

Austria, too, where the ultra-nationalist Freedom Party has gained strength within the political right, has been fertile ground for the politics of race. Thanks to the Kurt Waldheim affair, which focused world attention on the wartime activities of the Austrian president and former United Nations secretary general, Austrian attitudes have been scrutinized much more than in the past. On the basis of a study she undertook in the mid-1980s of Austrian attitudes towards Jews, Professor Weiss at the University of Vienna concluded that almost a quarter of all Austrians were "virulently anti-Semitic."[6] Many of them continue to hold the attitudes towards Jews that helped form the world view of Adolf Hitler, whose own anti-Semitism was learned in Vienna. Anti-Slavic and anti-gypsy sentiments are also a fact of life in contemporary Austria.

Everywhere in Europe, the question of who belongs has become highly sensitive. How much immigration is the right amount, where should the immigrants come from, how should the newcomers be brought into the host society, and how much of their own culture should the newcomers retain? In part because of their relatively low birth rates and their ageing populations, it has been the practice for affluent European countries to admit foreigners who are prepared to work in agriculture and industry. The terms on which these outsiders are permitted to enter, to work, to raise families, and whether or not they should be granted citizenship have become troubled issues everywhere in Europe. Although immigration has existed throughout historical times, making the notion of the ethnic purity of particular European peoples mythological, it is, none the less, true that, in comparision to societies of immigrant-based countries like the United States and Canada, European societies have been highly homogeneous. For such societies, the arrival of large numbers of immigrants in recent decades, and, particularly, the arrival of large numbers of non-white immigrants, has produced a social and political shock.

In this respect, the French debate has been typical rather than exceptional. What has given the issue special significance in France has been the way in which it has contributed to the fracturing of the French right wing, and has therefore affected the general course of French politics. In light of the historic divide in French ideological life, and the seminal role of France in the remaking of Europe, the progress of the debate there is important for all Europeans.

The Front National is the most potent voice of the extreme right in European politics. Its roots lie deep in the history of France, especially among elements of the population that have felt themselves vulnerable to the transformation of French life as a consequence of technological change and the disruptive effects of market forces. Before the Front National, there was the extreme right-wing Poujadist Movement, which won more than 2.5 million votes in the 1956 national election. Where the Poujadists railed against the state, big business, the power of Paris, French withdrawal from Algeria, and high taxes, the Front National has singled out North Africans and other immigrants, homosexuals, intellectuals, liberal Catholics, trade unionists, and Communists as special targets of abuse.[7] While Jean-Marie Le Pen has been guarded about attacks on the Jews, his notorious remark in September 1987 about the gas chambers of the Second World War as a "detail of history" made clear his underlying attitude towards them.

The Front National presents itself as the voice of outraged traditional, national virtues that have been trampled by alien forces. According to it, criminals should be more harshly dealt with and capital punishment restored, North African immigrants should be sent back to their homelands, AIDS patients should be isolated from the rest of society, and the power of the state should be curtailed.

Le Pen has succeeded in drawing together the traditional strands within the French extreme right. These elements include those who favoured the cause of Algérie française, which in their eyes was betrayed by Charles de Gaulle when his government conceded the independence of Algeria in 1962. Among the approximately one million French who returned to France from Algeria following the North African country's independence, the so-called *pieds noirs* (black feet), are a large proportion who are supporters of Le Pen, himself a paratrooper in the war. In addition to those for whom the loss of French Algeria was the key to their adhesion to the extreme right are the wartime collaborators and one-time supporters of Marshall Pétain and their political heirs. Beyond them are monarchists, Catholic fundamentalists, believers in white-supremacist racial theories, and anti-Semites. There have been, as well, more moderate elements, which include drop-outs from the other parties of the right and local politicians who maintain a friendly relationship with the Front National. Well beyond these groupings, which make up the core of the extreme right, have come the key social cohorts that have been attracted to Le Pen, most important among them the marginalized, who feel themselves threatened by contemporary economic and social changes. Thirty-one per cent of shopkeepers and small businessmen voted for Le Pen in the first round of the presidential election in 1988, while Mitterrand drew only 15 per cent of the votes of these groups, and Chirac and Barre drew 23 per cent each.[8] Le Pen has also drawn particular support from males, the young unemployed, and non-practising Catholics. Groups especially unlikely to support Le Pen have included women, trade unionists, the well educated (especially teachers), the non-religious, and practising Catholics.[9] Le Pen has drawn votes from all parts of the country, though his support has been concentrated in Provence, in cities such as Nice, Toulon, Aix-en-Provence, Marseille, and Avignon, as well as in the Alsatian cities of Strasbourg and Mulhouse, and in the working-class suburbs of Paris.

Not all those who have supported Le Pen can be classified as being, in any consistent sense, right-wingers. The Front National has scored well among former voters for the Communist Party, in areas like the famed "red belt," urban districts on the outskirts of Paris, which were once strongholds of the Communist Party. Among those who voted for Le Pen in the first round in 1988, about one million supported François Mitterrand against Jacques Chirac in the second round. For such voters, outrage against the high unemployment that plagued France throughout the 1980s was a key issue. Significantly, the success of the Front National came in the years of economic turmoil that followed the election of the Mitterrand government in 1981. Le Pen has been very effective in combining the immigration and unemployment issues, since he constantly blames the newcomers for displacing French citizens from their jobs.

That logic, which has worked well for political movements in many parts of Europe, can easily be faulted as simplistic. The French are not unaware that West Germany grew prodigiously in the 1950s because of the migration into their country of ten million Germans from the East, making immigrants a backbone of the German economic "miracle." But when I have pointed this out to acquaintances who run small businesses in the south of France, they have usually dismissed it with the comment that it all depends who the immigrants are — ten million hard-working Germans would be one thing, North African immigration quite another. And since disputes about stereotypes are notoriously unrewarding, the fact that there is no evidence that North Africans are anything but hard-working people, doing jobs the French are usually happy to leave to others, also cuts little ice. Small-business operators and shopkeepers do have plenty to worry about as a consequence of the enormous economic upheaval taking place across Europe. Country-wide and continent-wide chains are already devastating many businesses that sell appliances, food, clothing, film, china, and hardware. But, for those whose real problem is with well-capitalized big businesses, it is often easier to vent emotions about young, dark-skinned men hanging around the centre of town.

As we have seen, the success of Le Pen and the Front National has placed the traditional forces of the right in a position of unaccustomed impotence. For the Gaullist political movement, whose illustrious founder established the Fifth Republic, and at times ran it with scant regard for parliamentarians and the constitution, it has been extremely difficult to adapt to a long journey in the political wilderness. Having lost the presidential election in 1974 to non-Gaullist Valéry Giscard d'Estaing, who in turn lost the 1981 election to François Mitterrand, the Gaullists hoped for a return to power in the next presidential election. Their hopes for an end to the era of Socialist power seemed to have arrived when the right regained control of the National Assembly in 1986 and RPR leader Jacques Chirac, the mayor of Paris, was sworn in as prime minister.

THE SOCIALIST EXPERIMENT AND THE U-TURN

When Chirac came to office, the Socialists had been in full retreat from the radical elements of their 1981 program for several years. For the two years during which Chirac served as prime minister, Mitterrand played a cat-and-mouse game with the Gaullist leader. The fact that the Socialists themselves were already pursuing a more conservative economic agenda was both advantageous and disadvantageous for the president. The Socialist electoral victories in 1981 had given them control both of the presidency and of the National Assembly, presenting the French left with its greatest opportunity since the days of the Popular Front government of the mid-1930s to implement a program of sweeping changes. The Socialists had come to office apparently determined to change the very shape of French society, to make France a beacon in the development of human liberation and socialism. During the electoral campaigns, Mitterrand had advanced the so-called 110 propositions — a program of transformation whose purpose was to make France the citadel for the "liberation of man and the construction of socialism." The Socialists aimed for political liberalization, decentralization, and workers' rights — no less than a "new style of citizenship."[10]

During their first year in power, the Socialists had steamed ahead with the most comprehensive program of nationalization of industry and financial institutions in French history. They also boldly embarked on a program of public spending that was designed to boost demand and, therefore, to create jobs. The strategy quickly led to a soaring balance-of-payments deficit. Instead of finding themselves on the road to socialism, the Socialists found themselves leading their country towards international insolvency. Beginning in 1982, and still more completely in the spring of 1983, the Socialists undertook what has been called the "U-turn." Under an austerity program, public spending was sharply curtailed and temporary wage-and-price controls were imposed. Before the U-turn was complete, the government was forced to give up its temptation to take France out of the Exchange Rate Mechanism of the European Monetary System, to stop throwing huge sums of money at the nationalized industries, and, instead, to make the fight against inflation and the pursuit of the health of the French private sector the leading economic goals. For Mitterrand himself, the U-turn involved a series of bitter lessons that ultimately opened the way for him to play a critical role, as we have seen, in the launching of the EC's single-market program and subsequent moves towards European economic, monetary, and political union.

Over the long term, the decision of the Socialists to jettison the notion of a fundamental transformation of French society in favour of steering the economy towards higher productivity, the Single European Market, and monetary convergence with Germany was to prove successful. Its execution, however, alienated many among the Socialist Party faithful and, because of the loss of jobs it entailed in exposed sectors such as steel, resulted in disillusionment among traditional working-class voters. The repositioning of the Socialist Party opened the door to the victory of the right in the National Assembly elections of 1986, and for a time placed François Mitterrand in a highly exposed political position.

During the era of "co-habitation," Mitterrand's tactic was to give Chirac room to implement his economic and social agenda. For his part, the president stressed his role in foreign policy and presented himself as a non-partisan leader of the whole of the French nation. Initially, Chirac and his supporters believed they would have the advantage in the contest, not only because they had control of the day-to-day affairs of the government, but because the Socialists had already legitimized the non-interventionist, market path that the right intended to follow.

In the end, however, the elusive Mitterrand, the master tactician of contemporary French politics, proved himself more than a match for the somewhat brittle Chirac and his frayed and divided right-wing coalition, which had to pay attention to Le Pen as well as to the president. The intra-mural division within the mainstream right between the RPR and the UDF meant that Chirac would have to fight it out with Raymond Barre to determine who would be the final standard-bearer for the presidency against Mitterrand. He won the battle but lost the war.

THE TROUBLED RIGHT

The problems of the French right have gone much deeper than a question of electoral arithmetic. The rise of neo-liberalism as a dominant perspective among French conservatives over the past decade and a half has widened the chasm that runs through the right. Neo-liberalism, the essence of Thatcherism and Reaganism, has at its heart the idea that the state should be reduced in size and power and that the marketplace should be freed from both social and public-policy constraints. Under the pressures of the 1970s — the collapse of the Bretton Woods monetary system, the stagflation worsened by the oil-price shocks, and the rise of industrial competition from Japan and the newly industrializing countries — much of business in the West was won over to the neo-liberal agenda, which necessitated the end of the compromise with the organized working class. In the 1980s, neo-liberal regimes such as Reagan's and Thatcher's set out to break the power of unions and roll back the size of the welfare state. Moreover, they were prepared to live with much higher unemployment than their predecessors had been. Permanently higher levels of unemployment further strained the welfare state and contributed to the disintegration of the working class — propelling its better-trained elements upward, while weakening the position of unionized workers in traditional industries. Their greatest social consequence was to feed the growth of the underclass, the segment of the population that became permanently unemployed and underemployed.

While these developments, common in varying degrees throughout the West, kept socialists, social democrats, and trade unionists on the defensive, they also provoked ever-larger divisions within the ranks of the conservatives themselves. The expanded underclass provided a part of the mass base for a more visceral conservatism whose program turned on the politics of exclusion and authoritarianism, along the lines of Jean-Marie Le Pen and the Front National. At the same time, fear of the underclass helped generate support among middle-class elements for a more authoritarian conservatism. The disruptive impact of neo-liberalism, therefore, had the effect of threatening the political unity of the right. While this meant that issues like controls on immigration would come to the fore, it also opened the door, in some cases, to power for the centre left.

In France, this is precisely what happened, though the left has itself been forced to alter its own basic goals. In this vexing political environment, François Mitterrand has been accused of deliberately playing on the tensions within the right. His master stroke in this regard was to rewrite the electoral rules for the 1986 National Assembly election, putting in place a system of proportional representation, the effect of which was highly advantageous to the Front National. When under the new rules, the Front National won thirty-five seats (the Socialists and their allies winning 234 seats and the traditional right 289 seats), Le Pen and his colleagues were presented with a platform for influencing the public debate in France far beyond anything they had previously enjoyed. Even though the same election brought Chirac to office in coalition with the UDF, Le Pen's higher profile helped set the stage for his shockingly strong performance in the 1988 presidential election.

Mitterrand has been accused of deliberately opening the way for the electoral rise of the Front National, because the divisions it would foster in the right would help establish the Socialist Party as the country's essential party of government. René Remond, an academic authority on the French right, who has made this case, commented on the way Mitterrand had set the stage for the first round of voting in the presidential election of 1988: "It's a dangerous game. And it's not a responsible game."[11]

The accusations against Mitterrand miss the fact that the right has created much of its own misfortune. Until the late 1960s, Gaullism drew together many elements of the right — but it was as much a personality cult as it was a political movement. When de Gaulle stepped down in 1969, his followers needed to redefine their movement into an effective conservative political party, even though, from the beginning, the Gaullists had always shunned the word "party," preferring to see themselves as being a movement for national regeneration above petty factionalism. To be effective against the left, the imperative for the Gaullists was to strike a deal with the non-Gaullist elements of the right, which had themselves come together in 1978 to form the Giscardian UDF.[12] While the Gaullist RPR and the non-Gaullist UDF have espoused the need for alliance against the left, and have succeeded in forming coalition governments, history and personalities have stood in the way of effective unity. Whereas the RPR comes from a tradition that has stressed national unity, the independence of France, the defence of a strong state, and the rejection of class war, the UDF descends from the liberal parliamentary tradition, with its emphasis on the marketplace and its greater willingness to embrace European union. From the mid-1970s to the end of the 1980s, three dominant personalities have locked horns in a contest over who is to lead the right: Jacques Chirac, Valéry Giscard d'Estaing, and Raymond Barre. If it has been a characteristic of French political leaders that they dominate their parties for decades — witness de Gaulle and Mitterrand — the internecine struggle of the three leading right-wing politicians for over a decade helped make the Socialists the key party of government.

MITTERRAND'S EUROPEAN PROJECT

While the French right has been struggling with its own disunity, the very goals of the French Socialists have been radically transformed, as we have seen. The present project of the Socialists is itself subject to an inherent fragility. When Mitterrand came to power in 1981, he brought with him the vision, and the baggage, of decades of left-wing ideas for the remaking of France. The Socialist Party (PS) was a volatile amalgam of more than half a dozen major factions and tendencies, each with its own leadership, program, and analysis. The PS carried with it not merely the history of the interaction among these factions, but also that of the struggles for dominance within the left between the Socialists and the Communists, who were initially coalition partners in the new government.

As we have seen, the opening years of the PS government was a time, first, of trying to achieve the historic goals of the left; then, of coming to terms with the implacable obstacles to their achievement; and, finally, of adopting new goals. If the old project involved large-scale public ownership and planning of the economy and of the creation of full employment, centred in traditional industries, the new project involved managing the country's adaptation to the twin forces of globalization and technological revolution. By 1984, the Socialists had accepted the necessity of France's full economic integration into Europe. Indeed, the achievement of the single market, and the further steps towards monetary and political union — in a word, Europe — replaced the idea of socialism in an autonomous France. Ever since then, the goal of François Mitterrand and his associates has been to make France economically competitive with Germany, and through European economic and monetary union, to force Germany to share its power over monetary policy with France and the rest of Europe.

This strategy, with its emphasis on technology, rationalization, and the rapid adaptation of France to competitive conditions in Europe and globally, has been born of experience, even necessity. It is subject, none the less, to serious risks and pitfalls. What makes the strategy particularly risky is the extent to which dualism still characterizes the French economy, so that high-tech competitive industry coexists side by side with fractured, localized, inefficient industry.

In France, dualism is highly visible. Ultra-modernity is seen in transportation, in high-speed trains and state-of-the-art jet aircraft. At the Gare de Lyon in Paris, the classic railway station, with its echoes of the *belle époque*, one encounters the juxtaposition of the space-age passenger train with the surroundings of a more sedate age. The sleek orange monster on the track, with the bullet-shaped twin engines, is about to leave for Avignon in the south. The TGV (*Train à grande vitesse*) is the pride of the SNCF, France's publicly owned railway company. After you purchase a ticket and board a first- or second-class car and take your reserved seat, you find yourself in a spotless, comfortable cabin that feels more like an aircraft than a traditional rail car. Usually, you can set your watch by the departure of the train. Through the heart of Paris and the suburbs, the TGV eases along the track, only a quiet hum audible inside the train. On the outskirts of the city, the hum becomes more high pitched as the TGV accelerates swiftly to its cruising speed of 270 kilometres an hour. On the flat lands south of Paris, the track runs for a time alongside the autoroute, where cars in the passing lane are often going 160 kilometres an hour. As the TGV overtakes them effortlessly and leaves them far behind, you sense how quickly this smooth, electric-propelled bullet is really moving. An hour out of Paris, the train curls through the rolling farms and vineyards of Burgundy, then through Beaujolais, bringing it to Lyon, just two hours from the Paris station. (TGV travel from Paris to Lyon is now so fast and frequent that gourmets regularly take the train south in the morning to lunch in Lyon, thought by many to be the food capital of France, and return to Paris in the afternoon.) After slowing to pass underneath the heart of Lyon, the TGV crosses the Rhône for the last leg of the journey to Avignon. South of Lyon, the TGV travels at only half its previous speed, on track not yet dedicated to its full potential. The TGV system is now reaching out to the corners of France and beyond, with the extension of the system beyond Lyon to Marseille and Nice, and from Paris to the Chunnel. Plans are being made to link the French system up with those of neighbouring countries, so that Brussels, Frankfurt, Geneva, Milan, and Rome will ultimately be linked by high-speed trains. Expansion of the TGV, and the setting of speed records by French trains, engender general enthusiasm in the country, while provoking intense opposition in many small towns through which the extended system is to pass.

The technologically advanced face of France is also seen in the science-based industries of Grenoble, in Toulouse, in the aerospace industry, as we have seen, and in the growth of micro-electronic industries in Provence in centres such as Aix-en-Provence, Antibes, and Nice. Much of this high-tech development has state support, a significant proportion of it occurring in state-owned industries. François Mitterrand and his parliamentary allies remain strongly committed to pushing forward these technologically advanced sectors of the economy, sometimes in France alone, sometimes in Europe-wide programs.

The other face of France, of vulnerable, localized economic activity and declining industries, is also highly visible. Across much of Lorraine, there is the pungent sting of heavy industry in the air. There is also the depressing spectacle of slag-heaps of coal and abandoned industrial sites. In the towns of the region, there is bitterness towards the Socialists who came to power with the faith that any industry, including theirs, could be successfully modernized, a faith that was abandoned after several years of costly failure.

The competitive and uncompetitive sides of France can be seen in rural areas as well. Since the founding of the Common Agricultural Policy (CAP) of the EC in 1958, there has been an enormous increase in the productivity of French agriculture. Indeed, for the quarter-century between 1960 and 1984, French growth in real value added per person (productivity) in agriculture increased by a very substantial 5.5 per cent per year, as compared with only 2.9 per cent per year in the United States and 3.7 per cent per year in Canada.[13] The fundamental story in French agriculture for the past three decades has been one of rapid productivity growth accompanied by a very large reduction in the number of farmers. Despite this general trend, however, marginal farms still exist in many regions of the country. They remain a legacy of what was one of the most enduring of the outcomes of the French Revolution, the expropriation of the estates of the nobility and the division of the land among the peasants. The Revolution led to the establishment of a vast class of small landholders, a force that, once created through revolution, became itself a backbone of social conservatism. By contrast, in Britain, which never went through such a revolution, ownership of land has been much more concentrated.

I lived among small farmers in Provence, where I watched them toil throughout the year, preparing their fields, harvesting their crops, repairing their machinery, working seven days a week from early in the morning until sundown. Shifting their attention from melons to olives, to wine grapes, driving their produce long distances in the middle of the night to wholesale markets to get the best price for their products, the farmers are tied to their land and their work to such an extent that the very idea of a holiday or an extended leave usually strikes them as an impossible frivolity. Farmers have explained to me how difficult it is to convince their sons to stick with this spare and demanding existence when it is so easy for the young to migrate to the cities.

When I think of small, marginal farms in France, one experience in the Dordogne stays with me, partly, no doubt, because the heat had been so oppressive there for several days in mid-July that even the effort to drive to the farm, with an old goatherd who wanted me to buy some chickens, seemed disproportionate. Accompanied by the old man, who had been telling me stories of the wartime resistance in the area, I drove half a dozen kilometres through the narrow but well-paved roads, up steep hills and around sharp bends, until we finally rolled into a dusty farmyard, past ancient stone outbuildings. The barnyard was alive with ducks racing about, a few scrawny chickens, sand and dust blowing around the car. A mangy dog of indeterminate origin strained at the end of a long rope, and the flies were everywhere.

As the car stopped, a robust woman in her fifties appeared at the door of the kitchen. There were no steps at the front of the dwelling. She walked straight out into the swirling chaos.

In a moment, we went into the kitchen. Sitting at the table was the woman's husband, whose age was not easy to judge. His face had an unwell, furry appearance, his cheeks red and sallow. When the wife sat down, we talked about the oppressive weather. I could understand the goatherd and the woman, but not the man of the house, whose speech sounded like a guttural growl.

Once seated, with greetings out of the way, I was struck by the kitchen itself. There was a large-screened colour TV in the corner and, beside it, a modern electric coffeemaker. On the other side of the room was a telephone. Overwhelming these touches of modernity, however, was the general state of disrepair of the place. Sand and dust blew in through the open kitchen door. A chicken clucked right at the entrance. The kitchen was actually an entension of the farmyard.

At last the chickens were brought in, freshly killed and cleaned, and labelled with their prices — 59 francs, 54 francs, and so on. We picked four and left. When cooked, they were delicious. As is so often the case, the small farmers of France raise poultry and lambs and make cheese that puts the large, factory-style operators to shame. But, like the industrial workers of Lorraine, the small farmers of France are in a highly vulnerable position, despite EC subsidies. In an economy whose strategy is rationalization and the pursuit of competitiveness, their position is anomalous. While the farmers defend their interests with tenacity, which sometimes includes ferocious demonstrations in Paris and Brussels, attacks on truckers importing foreign produce, and even the bombing of government buildings, the small producers are running against the tide. In France's constant puzzling over who belongs and who doesn't, these people are, in a way, becoming outsiders.

FRANCE AND THE NEW GERMANY

From marginal farming to France's relationship with Germany might seem a long step, but it is not. The strategy of the Socialist government for steering France successfully through a fundamental social transition is predicated on deepening and extending the relationship with Germany. The "old left" project of the Socialists in 1981 was based on a class coalition among blue- and white-collar workers, professionals and farmers, and on an autonomous France. The new strategy, adopted by 1984, was based on a class alliance to include the better-educated sections of the working class, the richer farmers, the competitive industrialists and financial institutions, and on European integration. In the first case, the Socialists wanted to turn their backs on Germany; in the second case, they intended to embrace the FRG to a greater extent than had any French government since the establishment of the Franco-German partnership in the early 1950s. As we have seen, following his government's U-turn, Mitterrand not only favoured linking the franc tightly to the Deutschmark, but wanted the most rapid possible movement of the EC to the creation of a European central bank and common currency. Since 1984, Mitterrand has constantly pushed the Germans on EMU and political union. Having accepted that France has no choice but to fuse its economy with that of the FRG, what Mitterrand wants is a major say over monetary policy and an end to the special power over Europe's fortunes now exercised by the Bundesbank.

For the French, as for all other Europeans, the revolutions in Eastern Europe in 1989, and above all German unification, came as an unexpected shock. In the case of France, these momentous developments threatened to throw the strategy of the French government for European union into disarray. Would France, long used to playing the leading political role in the movement for European integration, be able to remain a partner with a united Germany? Among the French people, the opinion polls showed a solid majority who welcomed the opening of the Berlin Wall and who favoured German unification. The Germans could see the foreboding within the French political class, however, and they felt bitterness that new freedom for the Germans provoked anxiety and not unalloyed joy from their partner.

Throughout the critical year of 1990, as unification took place by stages in Germany, the Franco-German relationship experienced stressful episodes, but remained intact. As we have seen, Mitterrand was openly critical of the government of the FRG on the issue of the Polish frontier during the election campaign in the GDR. Despite some anticipation that the Germans would lose interest in European union and that the French would step back from their close alliance with the FRG to pursue counterbalancing ties, the partnership between Paris and Bonn stood the test on all the key issues of the year. It was

Franco–German unity that cleared the way for the launching of the intergovernmental conferences on EMU and political union at Rome in December 1990.

Dominique Moisi, the associate director of the Institut Français des Relations Internationales in Paris, expressed the sentiments of much of the French political class when he cautiously welcomed German unification as the price that had to be paid for ending the division of Europe. He wrote:

> Nothing would be more dangerous than for France to say today to Germany, "We fear you." If we do that, we will help create the kind of Germany we would deserve.
>
> . . . Conversely, Germany has a special responsibility it must continue to shoulder. The Germans cannot forget their past. Unity for them should be seen as a means to ensure democracy and freedom for all Germans. Unity is a path towards normalization. It is not normalization yet.
> . . . Unity is the ultimate test for Germany. How deeply European and democratic are the Germans? This is the question. We in France must trust them and help them. In fact, we have no other choice.[14]

If the French had no choice but to live with a unified Germany, across the Channel the British were discovering that they had no choice but to live with a unified continent.

Chapter Eight

AMBIVALENT BRITAIN

★ ★ ★ ★ ★ ★ ★ ★ ★ ★ ★ ★

DENIS HEALEY, FORMER CHANCELLOR OF THE EXCHEQUER, whose savage wit was feared by Tories and colleagues in the Labour Party alike, once remarked that being attacked by Sir Geoffrey Howe was like "being savaged by a dead sheep." On November 13, 1990, it was the "dead sheep" whose attack on Margaret Thatcher in the House of Commons fatally wounded the Conservative leader who had led her party to three successive electoral victories. When Howe, who had served throughout the Thatcher revolution as chancellor of the exchequer, foreign secretary, and deputy prime minister, rose to make his speech a week after resigning from the cabinet, the prime minister was in her place in the front row of government benches. Howe had finally left the cabinet because he had become convinced that Thatcher's approach to the European Community, and particularly to the question of monetary union in the community, was leading Britain into a perilous position. Howe had long been uneasy about his leader's stance on Europe, and tension over the issue had led to his demotion in the summer of 1989 from foreign secretary to the less prestigious post of deputy prime minister.

Howe began his speech to the hushed House by praising the many accomplishments of Margaret Thatcher, but then he launched the assault that made it clear that he was intent on an epitaph and not a vote of confidence. He accused Thatcher of looking at the "European enterprise" as "some kind of zero-sum game," so that she was constantly on the look-out for the surrender of British sovereignty. Because of her suspicious and negative attitudes towards Britain's EC partners, Howe said, she "seems sometimes to look out upon a continent that is positively teeming with ill-intentioned people scheming, in her words, 'to extinguish democracy,' 'to dissolve our national identities,' to lead us 'through the back door into a federal Europe.'" His conclusion was a dire warning of the consequences of keeping Thatcher at the helm: "The tragedy is — and it is for me personally, for my party, and for our whole people and for the Prime Minister herself, a very real tragedy — that the Prime Minister's perceived attitude towards Europe is running increasingly serious risks for the future of our nation. . . . The time has come for others to consider their own response to the tragic conflict of loyalty with which I have myself wrestled for perhaps too long."[1] Howe's split with Thatcher brought to a head a conflict that had brewed within the British cabinet for years. The division was over the fundamental question of what Thatcherism itself had been about from the very beginning.

When Margaret Thatcher led the Conservatives to an electoral victory over the governing Labour Party in the spring of 1979, she was determined to resolve Britain's social and political impasse by overturning the "social democratic mode of economic and political regulation"[2] that had existed in the post-war decades and had become increasingly ineffectual during the crisis years of the 1970s. There has been much debate about the extent to which "Thatcherism" involved a project for the replacement of Britain's socio-economic order with a consistent and thought-out alternative.[3] The very term "Thatcherism," first an epithet coined by ideological opponents, later a badge of pride adopted by supporters, illustrated the very wide perception that what began in Britain in 1979, while perhaps not a "revolution," was much more than an ordinary change of government.

In 1975, the year Margaret Thatcher successfully challenged Edward Heath for the leadership of the Tory party, she proclaimed: "There are too few rich and too few profits."[4] Her most basic goal was to rid Britain of socialism, once and for all. By socialism, she had in mind the vast post-war expansion of the role of the state, both as an owner and as a manager of the economy and as a provider of expensive and pervasive welfare programs. She also had in mind the power of the British trade-union movement, and the assumption of post-war governments that trade unions had to be consulted on major socio-economic changes. If her strategy included the demolition of trade-union power and the removal of the state from the running of the economy, her goal was to establish, or perhaps to re-establish, an enterprise economy in which private decisions determined the direction of things and private rewards constituted the incentive. Thatcher wanted to restore the respectability of profit-making and to combat what she saw as the misdirected paternalism of the state.

To remake Britain as she intended, Thatcher had to set her course not only against the record of the former Labour government, but against the post-war consensus that had prevailed in Britain, a consensus in which her own party had played a key role. In fact, the very notion of "consensus" was anathema to Thatcher, as she made clear when she said: "To me, consensus seems to be the process of abandoning all beliefs, principles, values and policies. . . . It is the process of avoiding the very issues that have got to be solved merely to get people to come to an agreement on the way ahead."[5]

Although it is easy to exaggerate the extent of common ground that existed between the Labour Party and the Conservative Party in the post-war decades, common ground was none the less discernible. It did not take long for the Labour government, led by Clement Attlee, in 1945 to give up any radical vision of a completely socialized British economy in favour of the building of a welfare state and the investment of public capital to patch up ailing sectors of the economy. Despite the radical goals enshrined in the Labour Party platform, the Attlee government was less willing to establish a general system of economic planning than was the government of post-war France. The most noteworthy reform of the government, and the one that has been most enduring even through the era of Margaret Thatcher, was the National Health Service (NHS), which came into effect in July 1948 and provided uniform health care to all without any payment. When people think of the British "socialism" of the age before Margaret Thatcher, they think, above all, of the NHS, and they often do so with a combination of pride in what the system had meant to them and sadness at how the system was allowed to wither under Thatcher. "When Nye Bevin brought in the NHS, it was a great thing," I was told by a worker in a quarry not far from Bristol. "I had an operation and was in the hospital. I could never have gotten by without the NHS." This life-long Labour Party supporter, who was near retirement age, received regular pay of £140 weekly, which he was able to augment to just over £200 by working eleven hours overtime each week. While he resented the taxes he paid, making him work a day and a half a week for nothing, as he put it, he did not at all resent the £39 a week that he and his employer put into the NHS on his behalf.

Post-war Tory governments, in their turn, pledged themselves to denationalization and to holding the line on spending on welfare-state programs. What established the consensus was that political debate between the two parties was confined to the question of how much government intervention was the right amount and how large the welfare state should become. Neither party disputed that a degree of intervention and welfare state were necessary. Indeed, it was the Conservative government of Harold Macmillan, in 1961, that, inspired by the example of French planning, established the National Economic Development Council, known as NEDDY. National NEDDY and local NEDDIES were to bring business and labour together with government to consider goals for the economy. While the process was a pale imitation of the French original, the idea smacked of continental corporatism, and, not surprisingly, the NEDDIES were later reviled by Margaret Thatcher.

It was long-term economic failure that doomed the consensual system from a popular point of view and opened the way, in the 1970s, for radical assaults on the conventions that had prevailed during the era of compromise.

Those assaults were mounted from both the right and the left. In the early months of 1979, as Labour prime minister James Callaghan was preparing to meet the electorate, Britain was passing through the so-called winter of discontent, the collapse of the notion of a social contract between business and labour, and the return to naked confrontation marked by large-scale labour stoppages and social unrest. In the early months of 1979, lorry drivers and public-service workers went on strike. Violence on picket lines and the practice of secondary picketing, the support of workers in a strike by other workers, made trade-union power appear malevolent to a large part of the British electorate. The Labour government had now lost its ability to deliver labour peace, its great asset over the Tories during the preceding two decades. When the dissolution did come, through the defeat of the minority Labour government in the House of Commons by one vote on March 28, Labour was forced into an election with its policies of wage restraint and labour peace in tatters. During the subsequent election campaign, Margaret Thatcher promised an end to social strife through the curbing of trade-union power. She offered, as well, cuts in the income tax, and deftly targeting upwardly mobile sections of the working class for support, she promised the advantageous sale of public housing to tenants.

Once in office, it quickly became apparent that the Thatcher government was unlike any British government since the war in its determination to take the country in a fundamentally new direction. Much influenced by conservative intellectual Sir Keith Joseph, the new prime minister had been won over to the monetarist approach of American economist Milton Friedman, who believed in the abandonment of Keynesian notions of fiscal and monetary policies, and their replacement by monetarism, a policy that involved setting strict limits on the expansion of the money supply to squeeze inflation out of the economy. Thatcher was also drawn to the ideas of political economist Frederich von Hayek, who believed that the job of government was not redistribution of wealth, but the creation of conditions that would allow wealth to be produced by private-sector forces acting in the marketplace. Recognizing that the views of his admirer marked an ideological departure in British politics, Milton Friedman commented: "The thing that people do not recognize is that Margaret Thatcher is not in terms of belief a Tory. She is a nineteenth-century Liberal."[6]

Eventually, the Thatcher government shifted its focus from setting monetary targets to the goal of lessening the Public Sector Borrowing Requirement (PSBR). The initial policies of the Thatcher government, though they failed to implement anything like orthodox monetarism, did have the effect of causing interest rates to skyrocket and economic output to shrink. This result, while it plunged the country into a severe recession, did dramatically weaken the trade-union movement, since the bargaining power of organized labour was shattered as a consequence of sharply rising unemployment.

THATCHERISM

When analysing the record of Margaret Thatcher as prime minister, it is important to consider the day-to-day pressures of office and the tactical shifts of position adopted by the government, but it is necessary, as well, to analyse the record more broadly, to consider it as a totality. Only by distinguishing between momentary tactics and broader trends can we gain a picture of Thatcherism as distinct from the detailed performance of the Thatcher government. Thatcherism was much more than monetarism, much broader than a strategy for improving Britain's economic performance. It was a project for remaking the structure of society, the role of politics, and the obligations of the state. At its heart was both a negative or defensive aspect, and a positive or creative aspect. Its negative goal was the destruction of the social-democratic institutional framework and social relations that had developed since the war. Targets of the Thatcher government were the power of the unions and local governments, aspects of the health-care and educational systems, corporatist practices embodied in entities such as the NEDDIES, large-scale public housing, and the whole complex of nationalized industries. The positive objective was the creation of a mass social base for neo-liberal economic and social practices.

This wide-ranging project did not simply spring out of the air as a consequence of the personality and ideas of Margaret Thatcher and the intellectual leanings of her mentors. Rather, it was a response to the long-term decline of the British economy relative to that of its competitors, and, more immediately, to the acute economic crisis of the 1970s.

British economic performance in the post-war decades needs to be seen from two quite different perspectives — one internal to the country itself and one comparing Britain to the rest of the industrialized world. Judged from the first perspective, Britain's post-war economic performance was a considerable success; from the second, it was a deepening failure. During the 1950s and 1960s, the British economy grew more rapidly than at any time in its history. The result was a steady and appreciable growth in the incomes of the British people. For the twenty-year period from 1953 to 1973, growth of the British Gross Domestic Product, minus inflation, averaged 3 per cent a year. This figure compared very favourably with earlier periods in British history: 1856–73, 2.2 per cent; 1873–1913, 1.8 per cent; and 1924–37, 2.2 per cent. The satisfactory rate of post-war real growth provided the material basis for the age of political consensus, during which centrists in both major political parties, as we have seen, supported the development of the welfare state. If they disagreed on the extent of the welfare state and redistributive policies, they none the less subscribed to the notion that there should be some sharing of the spoils of British prosperity by all segments of the population. This situation was in marked contrast to the subsequent divisiveness of Thatcherism, which frankly assumed that there would be clear winners and losers as a consequence of government strategy.

When we compare the "satisfactory" British rates of growth during the post-war period with growth rates elsewhere, we can see how the British economy was headed, in the long run, for severe problems in terms of international competitiveness. During the period 1953–73, the real annual growth rate in other European countries averaged as follows: France, 5.3 per cent; West Germany, 5.5 per cent; Italy, 5.3 per cent; and Austria, 5.7 per cent.[7] The continental nations soared past Britain, achieving living standards well above those in the island nation.

Until 1973, more rapid economic and productivity growth in other countries posed only a potential threat to Britain. While it was true that British living standards were falling behind those in other countries, they were still improving, and unemployment remained within reasonable bounds. After 1973, however, all this changed. The chronic problems facing Britain became acute. The manufacturing sector of the British economy, a pillar of the country's very survival since the beginning of the industrial revolution, entered a period of absolute decline.[8] As the output of British manufacturing declined, there was a very steep decline in employment in the manufacturing sector. In 1974, 7.87 million people were employed in British manufacturing; by 1981, this figure had dropped to 6.04 million.[9] While some other countries experienced a decline in the number of workers employed in manufacturing, no other country replicated the severe drop in employment that occurred in Britain.

As the long-term decline of Britain's economy relative to that of other advanced countries developed into an acute crisis, and political support for the post-war consensus disintegrated, Thatcherism became the right-wing alternative. It was anchored by the critical elements of business in Britain. By the Thatcher era, business in Britain was more internationalized than in any other major country, with the exception of Canada. In addition to domestic British capital, whose leading component was located in the financial-services sector, there was large-scale American and Japanese investment as well, both in the financial sector and in manufacturing and petroleum. With the well-being of leading elements of business in Britain tied so strongly to external developments, the historic split between the financial sector, centred in the City of London, and the weaker manufacturing interests, located in the Midlands and the north, grew even stronger. Thatcherism was tied to the fortunes of the City, and its free-market ideology was very much a function of the global role of the City. If this meant that much of the manufacturing sector would be allowed to wither on the vine, then that was a trend that, in any event, was long established.

THE LEFT ALTERNATIVE

As steep economic decline appeared to be the consequence of the election of the radical right to power, many in the radical left believed that Thatcher was opening the door to their own potential success. Just as Thatcher's leadership of the Conservative party marked a new departure on the right, the late 1970s also saw the rise of a new challenge on the left to the system of consensual governing. The pre-Thatcher Labour government had been forced to deal with a particularly severe version of the high inflation and economic stagnation endemic to industrial countries during the years following the oil-price shock of 1973. Under these pressures, the government took the first steps away from Keynesianism and towards monetarism, away from the failing social compromise and in the direction of the Thatcherism to come. As the government moved to the right in its economic policy, carrying most of the parliamentary Labour Party with it, a left-wing ferment was developing among the party's activists. That left was by no means united, comprised, as it was, of constituency activists who clung to the historic Labour Party commitment to socialism; supporters of the far-left militant tendency, with its frothy radical and Marxist notions; and Trotskyites who had entered the party simply to lead its adherents to their own "correct line," as well as Cambridge economists and other intellectuals who gave the movement its analytical fire-power.

The leading personality within this wide and disparate left was a figure inconceivable as a radical standard-bearer anywhere but in England. Heir to the title of Lord Stansgate, Anthony Wedgewood Benn made history when he won the right to resign his peerage, quitting the House of Lords so he could stand for election to the House of Commons. Tony Benn, as he insisted on being called, was the leader of this variegated crusade for the soul of the Labour Party. While he served in various cabinet positions when Labour was in office, he never became party leader. When I first met Tony Benn, in the living-room of his comfortable home in fashionable central London, to drink tea and conduct a television interview, Margaret Thatcher had been prime minister for just over a year. At a time when Britain was sinking into recession, and trade-union resistance to the Thatcher government was increasing, many, including Benn, believed that Margaret Thatcher's abandonment of the former style of consensual governing could bring her to grief: "If you talk seriously among industrialists or bankers, you will find there is a widespread view that Mrs. Thatcher's policy will fail, because not only of the damage it is doing to British industry, but also the fact that she has pulled out all the links with labour, which have enabled, if you like, a modified form of capitalism to carry public consent."

If Benn thought that Margaret Thatcher was likely to fail, he did agree with her on one crucial point. He, too, believed that the post-war consensus could not be put back together again, and that, if the British were to reject the radical right, their only alternative would be the radical left. For him, that alternative meant reasserting British economic sovereignty, in practice, pulling the country out of the EC so that it could be reindustrialized through a massive program of public investment and an extension of trade-union power "beyond the narrow wage bargain, so that trade unions negotiate not just about wages and working conditions but about the investment program, about manpower planning, about what they do with profits."

For Thatcherism, the first priority was to destroy the power of trade unionism, while, for the supporters of Tony Benn, the goal was a vast extension of trade-union power. It was clear in the first years of the Thatcher government that the struggle over the role of trade unions would be decisive in determining the outcome. At the epi-centre of that struggle, although he was far from being at the centre of the mainstream British trade-union movement, was Arthur Scargill, president of the National Union of Mineworkers (NUM). In the first years of the Thatcher government, no one on either the left or the right had forgotten that the last Tory government, led by Edward Heath, had come to grief in its confrontation with the coal miners' union in the bitter crisis that extended from the fall of 1973 until the election of the Labour government in February 1974.

When I met Arthur Scargill to conduct a television interview in London just a few days after my conversation with Tony Benn, the militant leader of the NUM was in a feisty mood. If the Thatcher government wanted a confrontation with the trade unions, they would get one, he promised. And just as Edward Heath had discovered the power of the miners, so, too, would his successor. Scargill, however, had failed to take into account the impact unemployment would have on organized labour, the general public perception following the "winter of discontent" that trade-union power must be curbed, and the determination of the Thatcher government to bring labour to heel.

Although the early economic performance of the Thatcher government did not appear to bode well for its re-election to a second term, it found other assets — an unpopular opposition, which proceeded to split, much to Margaret Thatcher's electoral advantage — and victory in a short, highly popular war. The same left wing that had helped discredit Labour with voters was critical to driving an important segment of the moderate leadership out of Labour's ranks and into a new political undertaking, the launching of the Social Democratic Party (SDP).

In 1981 and early 1982, the so-called Gang of Four — Shirley Williams, David Owen, William Rodgers, and Roy Jenkins — who founded the SDP appeared to have created a political vehicle that might well succeed in winning Britons away from a government on the right, whose economic policies were unpopular, and from an opposition party on the left, whose policies and past record were not attractive to most voters. In a string of by-elections and public-opinion polls, the SDP, which formed an electoral alliance with the Liberals, sailed forward — until the crisis in the Falklands gave Margaret Thatcher the issue she needed to regain her lost support. Following her Falklands triumph, Thatcher remained in the lead in the public-opinion polls until the general election just over a year later, on June 9, 1983. The Thatcher government won a massive 144-seat majority in the House of Commons, even though she received less of the popular vote (42.4 per cent) than she had in the previous election (43.9 per cent), when she had a 43-seat majority. [10]

Having led her country to military victory in the Falklands, Margaret Thatcher was able to imbue her regime with the aura of nationalism, with the defence of historic British values, positioning herself as the heir to the traditions of empire, thus making herself much more than a neo-liberal economic reformer. By the time of the Falklands war, she had already taken legal steps to rein in the power of the trade unions. Psychological victory over the labour movement, Thatcher's "domestic Falklands," was to come, however, with the utter defeat of Arthur Scargill and the National Union of Mineworkers in the bitter and violent coal miners' strike of 1984–85. It was during this period of the second Thatcher government that replacing social democracy with an entrepreneurial society and popular capitalism emerged as the fully developed project of Thatcherism.

Critical to the realization of that project was the unprecedented program of privatization undertaken by the Thatcher government. Whereas in 1951, at the end of the reign of the post-war Labour government, six of the leading ten British companies, as measured by volume of sales, were publicly owned, by 1986, this number had dropped to just one. Part of the explanation for this change was the decline of basic industries — coal, steel, and railways — but the other factor was the selling off of public enterprises by the Thatcher government. [11] Among the major concerns to be privatized, wholly or in part, were British Aerospace, British Petroleum, British Telecom, Jaguar Cars, Sealink, and British Airways. By the end of Margaret Thatcher's reign as prime minister, fifty major companies, constituting more than two-thirds of the industrial holdings of the state in 1979, had been sold off or were scheduled for sell-off. [12]

Privatization on this scale was questioned even by some Conservatives, such as Edward Heath, whose own government had carried out no privatizations. Heath criticized the Thatcher government for using the revenues from the sale of companies to reduce taxes instead of providing revenues for reducing unemployment. Harold Macmillan, the Earl of Stockton, accused the government of selling off the "family silver." [13]

Despite the criticism from the left and from more traditional Tories, who conceived of their party as an instrument for social stability and therefore deplored radical neo-liberal reform, the Thatcher program was winning the support of key social groups who were sharing in the renewed prosperity that developed in the mid-1980s. As we have seen, the Thatcher government was closely tied to the financial sector of British business and to foreign-based business. However, its ability to retain political power depended on building a base of support that extended far beyond these key business groups. While traditional pursuits such as manufacturing, coal mining, and shipbuilding were in decline, the financial-services sector, real estate, defence and high-technology industries, and North Sea oil were areas of economic opportunity. Overwhelmingly, those benefiting were concentrated in the south of England, in particular, in the southeast, where there was large-scale expansion of employment, particularly in the service sector.

The period from 1985 through 1988 was to be the high point of the economic success of the Thatcher government, the era of the so-called Thatcher miracle, when Britain's growth in real GDP ranged from just under 4 per cent to just under 5 per cent annually for four consecutive years. In 1989, that growth slowed to 2 per cent and in 1990 to a mere 0.5 per cent, as the British economy slid into recession, at the same time as Britain's inflation rate was the highest among the major countries. As Britain resumed the position of being the "economic sick man of Europe," doubts existed about the long-term achievements of Thatcherism, which had been so confidently discussed only a short time earlier.

During the period of Thatcher's economic success, jobs were

created, particularly in the southeast, the City of London was a highly successful participant in the globalizing financial-services industry, and a land and housing boom underlined the success of a newly prosperous class of Britons. Some of the indicators of the economic and social transformation were: membership of the Trades Union Congress (TUC) fell from over twelve million in 1979 to just over eight million in 1989; shareholders in Britain soared from about three million in 1979 to over ten million in 1990; between 1979 and 1989, owner-occupied dwellings increased as a proportion of total housing stock from under 60 per cent to over 66 per cent, while the proportion accounted for through town-council rentals shrank from nearly 30 per cent to 20 per cent; and public spending as a proportion of total GDP shrank from 44 per cent in 1979, after a number of years of higher rates attributable to recession, to 39.5 per cent in 1990.[14] During those years, it appeared that a major social transformation had been achieved, that a new and self-assured capitalism had sprung into being, leaving the post-war era of social democracy an increasingly distant memory.

One mark of Thatcher's success could be seen in the breaking and marginalizing of her left opponents. When I met Arthur Scargill again in the summer of 1985, this time in Sheffield, in the offices of the NUM, the union leader had himself become a metaphor for the defeat of the trade unions, just as dilapidated Sheffield was a metaphor for the decline of what were once world-renowned manufacturing centres. By the mid-1980s, the "two nations" strategy of Thatcherism had further widened the gap between the enterprising south and the defeated north. Scargill was a part of the defeated north. In place of the pugnacity I had noted in Scargill in 1980, there was resignation. The tell-tale sign of the changed mood was that, in Sheffield, Scargill was no longer looking towards the future, but, instead, was justifying himself in ideological terms and reminiscing about the past. Even though the NUM leader had never been a part of the mainstream of the trade-union movement, and had been tainted with charges of corruption and discredited as a consequence of ties with Libya and the Soviet Union, the defeat of the coal miners none the less was symbolic of the loss of power of all organized labour.

Tony Benn, although he had lost none of his serenity, was no longer a threat to the Tories and to the leadership of his own party when I had tea with him again in December 1989 in his London home, three weeks after the opening of the Berlin Wall. Having failed in trying to reshape the Labour Party and the country, Benn found comfort in taking the long view of things. Considering himself very much an exile in British politics, not unlike the position that Alexander Dubček had occupied for many years in Czechoslovakia, for Benn the fact that many anti-socialists regarded the revolutions in Eastern Europe as the end of socialism was cause for rejoicing: "I am cheered by the blinkers of people who think we are dead." For the snowy-haired man, who remained as articulate as in his glory days, the revolutions in East Germany, Poland, Hungary, and Czechoslovakia were putting democracy "back on the agenda" and, since "socialism is about democracy," it, too, could only benefit from the transformation.

Benn, who remained a member of Parliament, representing the riding of Chesterfield, and who acknowledged the change in his own role with the quip that he had "now moved above the management level to the educational level," saw hope in Western Europe, as well, as a consequence of the revolutions in Eastern Europe. He believed that the federalist project in the EC would go "down the chute" now that the position of Germany had been transformed. For him, the dreams of Jacques Delors and François Mitterrand had nothing to do with socialism and were, instead, aimed at imposing a capitalist uniformity on Western Europe. Through all the political disappointments of the past decade, Benn had retained his belief that economic sovereignty should be exercised at the level of the nation-state. The idea that the fate of the unemployed in Britain should be determined by market forces in Europe was completely unacceptable to him. If he were once again minister of Industry, he would feel the need to violate the Treaty of Rome, to which Britain was subject. In the spring of 1989, Benn had introduced a bill in the House of Commons whose purpose was to restore full self-government to EC countries and to strike down any supranational authority exercised by community institutions. In a speech to Parliament, advancing this position, Benn said: "Some people favour a fully federal Europe. I can understand why. We would all have a vote and elect a president and two Houses. It would be fully an American system. But I favour a commonwealth of Europe — an association of fully self-governing states that would harmonise as quickly as it could, where it mattered, but in which no majority would have the power to push legislation through against the wishes of others." [15]

Benn's "commonwealth of Europe" was, of course, essentially the same as Margaret Thatcher's vision of a Europe of independent nation-states. Despite Benn's stout rejection of any suggestion that there was common ground between his views and those of Thatcher, denying that he was a "little Englander," by the end of the 1980s, both Benn and Thatcher were sovereigntists, fighting a rear-guard action against the integration of the United Kingdom ever further into Europe. By that time, the Labour Party had become moderately pro-European. [16] As I was told by a key adviser of Labour leader Neil Kinnock at the party's headquarters on Walworth Road in dreary south London, Labour made a decisive shift towards a pro-EC position at its annual conference in October 1988. Although the party had not yet adopted a position on the latter stages of Economic and Monetary Union, it favoured steps towards monetary integration, provided that the pound sterling could be pegged low enough against the Deutschmark for British manufacturing to have a chance for survival. All this smacked of pragmatism. As the Kinnock adviser told me: "We're not starry-eyed about Europe." Indeed, he went on to illustrate that by telling me what a low opinion he had of EC institutions and of members of the European Parliament, not excluding Labour's own members. To underline his feelings, he concluded the interview by saying, "When you go to Strasbourg, ask yourself this, would you trust these people to govern 320 million people? The place is a circus." Tepid though this posture towards Europe remained, it none the less marked a dramatic shift from Labour's position as recently as the 1983 election, when the party had campaigned to withdraw Britain from the EC.

Even though Thatcherism had defeated Bennism in the 1980s, Margaret Thatcher was facing a much sterner opponent from across the Channel in the movement for European union. In portraying Thatcher as an opponent of European union, it needs to be pointed out that by no means all aspects of integration were repugnant to her. As we saw in an earlier chapter, the British government, with reluctance, went along with the Single European Act (SEA). There is evidence that Thatcher was prepared to accede to the act's extension of qualified majority voting in the EC because she so disdained the thought of small countries like Greece being able to hold up the making of decisions. Important elements of the "1992" program were also to Thatcher's liking, particularly the promise of a single market in financial services. But she was staunchly opposed to the adoption by the EC of the Social Charter. The debate within the EC concerning the Social Charter forced political groups across Europe to define their positions on the extent to which the market should be allowed to determine economic outcomes. As such, it was a part of the larger debate about the social philosophy of the New Europe, a debate that, as we have seen, came to a head when Jacques Delors and Margaret Thatcher waged the battles of Bournemouth and Bruges.

Indeed, so incensed by the Bruges speech was former Tory leader and prime minister Edward Heath that he took the trouble himself to appear at the College of Europe in Bruges, on the first anniversary of the Iron Lady's appearance there, to refute what she had said: "I have come here today to wipe away the stain on the principles and beliefs of the College left behind by the Bruges speech of the British prime minister." Heath was an embittered, long-term foe of Thatcher's, and his strong language was no indicator of Thatcher's standing in her party in the autumn of 1988. For the moment, Heath was a lonely voice, espousing a point of view that, two years later, would become a rallying cry against Thatcher.

In fact, Thatcher's ideas about Europe provoked controversy and opposition within the Conservative Party for years before they became the ground on which her opponents rose to drive her out of 10 Downing Street. Within the Conservative Party, concern about the social divisiveness of Thatcher's policies — her so-called two-nations approach — tended to coincide with a perspective contrary to hers on Europe. For years, Thatcher battled with leading members of her cabinet on Europe. Maintaining British sovereignty against Brussels, vowing never to give up the pound sterling for a European currency, became political watchwords for her. They provided a populist, nationalist counterpoint to her severe marketplace ideology, helping to rally her "Falklands constituency," this time against the enemy across the Channel. In place of the struggle against the "Argies," the call to arms in this battle was "Up yours, Delors."

A fundamental aspect of Margaret Thatcher's world-view was her vast preference for things American, as against things European, her instinct for maintaining the "special relationship" with the United States through her genuine rapport with Ronald Reagan, and, at the very end, her staunch support for the position of George Bush in the early months of the crisis in the Persian Gulf. For Thatcher, the United States provided a social model through which the British could find the way to their own greatest past — the mid-Victorian era. Her own nationalism came straight out of the celebration of the British values associated with the zenith of her country's power. Inescapably, this meant the values of Victorian England, the celebration of individualism and enterprise in an imperial setting that were the very essence of Britain's being in its days of maximum global sway. Margaret Thatcher, herself a product of much that was Victorian, said in a 1983 television interview: "Victorian values were the values when our country became great." [17] For her, as for her predecessors at the helm of British affairs, to lead the British simply into Europe meant the betrayal of her nation's classic strategy for greatness, playing some Europeans off against others so that glory could be pursued in the wider world.

Although Michael Heseltine was by no means her only opponent on Europe within the party — Nigel Lawson quit as chancellor of the exchequer in October 1989 on the question of monetary integration and Sir Geoffrey Howe fought her on Europe within the cabinet — this former Defence minister who left the cabinet in a stormy affair over defence procurement in 1986 was her most effective adversary. The good-looking, upper-class Heseltine, known as "Tarzan" in the tabloid press, had views similar to Thatcher's in important areas. Like her, he was a hawk when it came to defence policy, and he was, as well, a strong believer in privatization. The differences between them, however, were more crucial. Heseltine was an advocate of a form of industrial policy in which the state, along with the private sector, would work to pick "winners," not leaving success entirely up to the market. He was, in crucial respects, a "one nation" Tory, an advocate of an interventionist government role to rebuild decaying inner cities and to move jobs to disadvantaged areas. Most important, he was pro-European, seized of the view that Britain's standoffish attitude towards the rise of the EC had been a mistake from the very beginning, a mistake that meant that, by the time the British acceded to each further step in European integration, all the key decisions had already been made. [18] He believed that Britain's future was inexorably linked to the process of European union; that the British should accept this imperative, and, in doing so, win for themselves an important place in designing the EC to suit themselves, rather than leaving key decisions up to the Franco-German partnership. In his 1989 book on Europe, Heseltine presented a perspective that was a complete rejection of Thatcher's approach:

> The British people and government are left with two choices. The first is to play a leading role, seeking to influence the changing institutions and laws of Europe on lines which further British interest, or which at least do us no

harm. The second choice is to settle for a two speed
Europe, with Britain bringing up the rear, more sure of
what we are against than of what we are for. . . .
. . . Every negative speech by a senior politician on
European affairs, delivered in ringing nationalist tones to
a domestic audience, is heard abroad and can have damaging consequences. Every hostile speech provokes at best
despair, at worst contempt. The French and Germans, at
every sign of British aloofness, draw closer together.[19]

The problem for Thatcher was that Heseltine's perspective on
Europe represented the views of critical élite elements of British
opinion, as well as of the opinions of an increasing proportion of the
wider public. For the City of London, whose financial-services sector
had benefited so handsomely from Thatcher's policies, the prospect of
being left out of European monetary union was virtually unthinkable.
In the summer of 1989, at a garden party attended by members of the
London law firm Slaughter and May, I was given the clear impression
that to be left out of the process of European integration was simply
not to be considered. The solicitors at this gathering were careful men,
attired in dark suits, stiffer than their North American counterparts,
weighing their comments carefully. They ranged in their political attitudes from high Tory to liberal Green, but mostly Tory. There was no
enthusiasm for Europe in the gathering, only a sense of inevitability,
the recognition that something irreversible was under way and that the
City of London could not afford to be left out.

Among the population at large, as well, a long-term shift of
opinion towards a greater acceptance of European union was observable. A comprehensive survey of British opinion undertaken by ICM
(International Communications and Marketing Research) for the
Guardian in September 1989 revealed the trends. Forty-four per cent
of those surveyed agreed that "Britain should have a closer relationship with the EC even if it means some loss of sovereignty"; 41 per
cent disagreed. Even raising the threat of sovereignty, as this question did, led to a plurality favouring closer ties, with 50 per cent of
Labour voters agreeing, while 36 per cent disagreed; among Conservatives, 38 per cent agreed; 49 per cent disagreed.[20]

Significantly, this poll showed that Labour supporters, in the past
the most anti-EC bloc of opinion in the country, had become more
pro-EC than Conservative supporters. And, even among Conservative
voters, while more supported than opposed Thatcher's defence of

British sovereignty, there was very substantial dissent. Just as significant, the poll revealed that, after her decade in power, Margaret
Thatcher's free-market philosophy was far from commanding general
support. Sixty-two per cent of those surveyed said they opposed privatization of profitable state industries, while only 20 per cent were
in favour. Only 16 per cent agreed that the National Health Service
was "safe in Mrs. Thatcher's hands," while a stunning 70 per cent disagreed, a result that showed that Thatcher was highly vulnerable to
the charge of posing a threat to the most vital of social services for
ordinary people. Remarkably, 38 per cent said they believed "more
socialist planning would be the best way to solve Britain's economic
problems," while only 29 per cent rejected this proposition, making
it clear that the most basic tenets of Thatcherism had failed to win
the adherence of the majority.[21]

By the autumn of 1990, Margaret Thatcher was highly vulnerable, both on domestic issues and on Europe. The Poll Tax was both
the substance and the symbol of her domestic woes, a regressive levy
that required each adult to pay an identical sum, regardless of income.
"Why should I pay the same amount, one hundred and thirty pounds
a year, as Lord Oxford, the Lord of the Manor?" an elderly worker
outside Bath asked me as he clipped a hedge, earning extra money
for himself as a gardener in the evenings. It was that sentiment,
expressed countless times across the country, that made the Poll Tax
a political millstone for Thatcher and her party.

The issue of Europe was not so visceral as that of the Poll Tax,
yet it was the critical question on which the revolt within the Conservative Party smouldered and finally burst into flame in November 1990. When Sir Geoffrey Howe delivered his devastating resignation speech in the House of Commons, the uprising that toppled
Thatcher was precipitated. Analysing the event four months later, at
a time when Margaret Thatcher herself was raising questions at social
gatherings — including one with the Soviet ambassador — about
whether she had been the victim of a conspiracy, the *Economist*
reconstructed the events and concluded that the Conservative leader
had been the victim not of a tightly knit cabal, but of a "barons'
revolt," whose chief actors were Michael Heseltine, Nigel Lawson,
and Sir Geoffrey Howe.[22] While Heseltine's strategy had long been
to fight a battle of attrition against Thatcher, Howe's speech had
forced matters to a head, precipitating the leadership bid, which
left Thatcher fifteen votes short of the total she needed to defeat
Heseltine on the first ballot.

Once she had announced her resignation, Thatcher used her very great influence with large numbers of back-bench Tory MPs to direct them towards chancellor of the exchequer John Major, who emerged ahead of foreign secretary Douglas Hurd as the candidate to stop Heseltine. For the right wing of the party, the Thatcher loyalists, for those who resented Heseltine's attack on the leader and who were suspicious of his corporatist tendencies, John Major became the alternative.

Likable, if somewhat phlegmatic, Major had enjoyed a meteoric rise in the government over the previous year and a half. His good fortune had been intimately linked to the demotion and fall of Sir Geoffrey Howe from the foreign ministry and Nigel Lawson from the office of chancellor. As these ministers fell, Thatcher promoted Major into their vacated positions. A self-made man, a school drop-out at age sixteen, Major shared Thatcher's distaste for the more aristocratic wing of the Tory party, with its old-boy network and its paternalistic conception of its place in the nation. Unlike Thatcher, however, Major was not an emotional opponent of European union, and he had a softer attitude than she on key issues such as tax fairness and the welfare state.

When the second ballot placed Major very close to outright victory, Heseltine, who was in second place, immediately announced that he was withdrawing from the race and placing his support behind the youthful chancellor, a move that was to assure him a place in the new cabinet, where he was to preside over the demise of the Poll Tax in March 1991. In one of the most élitist systems for selecting a leader in the democratic world, Britain had jettisoned a prime minister who had won three successive majority governments in favour of a new head of government who was, at best, untested.

The succession kept the issue of Britain's place in Europe uncertain, as it had been for four decades. But despite this element of continuity, there had been significant change as well. The Labour Party and the Trades Union Congress had become moderate supporters of European union, eschewing any trace of the Bennite preference for building socialism at Westminster in favour of a pragmatic social democracy that took for granted a market economy and a place for Britain in the New Europe. The Tories had changed too. No business community in Europe was more committed to the single market than British business, in particular, its upper levels in the major corporations and the financial sector. While Heseltine, the pro-European, had been rejected, the new prime minister soon showed how different he was from his predecessor at the Rome EC summit in December 1990. At the European Council, the familiar pattern of Thatcher against the others gave way to a new pattern in which Britain gave its wary assent to participation in the intergovernmental conferences on Economic and Monetary Union and on political union.

As the vast enthusiasm of the British for the Persian Gulf War and for the American connection was to show only a few weeks after the Rome summit, however, the British identity remained divided, part Anglo-American, part European.

Chapter Nine

CENTRAL EUROPE:
BEGINNING AGAIN

★ ★ ★ ★ ★ ★ ★ ★ ★ ★ ★ ★

O NE CONSEQUENCE OF THE FIRST WORLD WAR WAS
the creation in Central Europe of a bloc of new states, the
successors to the empires consumed in the conflict; a consequence of the Second World War was the reduction of
these successor states to the position of satellites in the Soviet sphere
of Europe, a function of the bipolar division of the continent between
the United States and the Soviet Union. In both cases, the outcomes
were, for the most part, collateral, the result of the waxing and
waning of the fortunes of others.

Austria opens the door to historic Central Europe and to the
Central Europe that is being reborn as a consequence of the collapse
of the Soviet Empire. When approaching Austria from the west, one
is reminded that the life of Europe has been shaped around three great
rivers, all of them spawned in a remarkably small knot of territory in
Switzerland and southern Germany: the Rhine, flowing north and
west from this mountainous heartland to the North Sea; the Rhône,
flowing west and south to the Mediterranean; and the Danube,
flowing southeast to the Black Sea. Each river opens its own world.
The Rhône makes me think of vineyards and Provence, far to the
south. The Rhine brings to mind the passage of coal-laden barges in
the cool mists that envelop the hills across the river from Bonn and
Cologne. The Danube opens the way to another Europe. The
Austro-Hungarian Empire tied the lands of the Danube together,
until the ethnic tensions within the empire helped precipitate the First
World War and doomed the Habsburg Empire, once the Central
Powers had lost the war.

Otto Habsburg, who was born in 1912 in its sunset years, provides a living link to the vanished empire. Had the empire survived, this slight, elderly man, with the ramrod bearing and the near perfect command of French and English in addition to his native German, would be the emperor. He is, instead, a member of the European Parliament, a member of the Christian Social Union (csu), the Bavarian allies of the Christian Democratic Union (cdu). The legacy of the Habsburgs is frequently encountered in the lands of the former empire, in triumphal arches and statues left over from the past, and in the ornate public architecture that is the hallmark of the vanished realm whose symbol was the double eagle. The centre-piece, of course, is Vienna, whose dark imperial edifices dominate the core of the city. The rooms in the Hofburg Imperial Palace are kept as they were when they were occupied by the Habsburgs, as though the ruling family had left temporarily and was about to return at any moment to the baroque splendour of the furnishing and decoration. Imperial Vienna is Europe's leading reminder of the fleeting character of arrangements of political power. Otto Habsburg, who began life in the last days when Vienna presided over an empire of fifty-five million people, has lived long enough to see the countries that once made it up in a position to determine their own fate. For him, it is a delicious irony that the unity the empire once brought to a large part of Europe is now considered a model for the construction of a possible economic union among many of its component parts. The most concrete attempt to revive the unity of the former Habsburg territories is the Pentagon Initiative, so called because it groups together five states: Italy, Austria, Czechoslovakia, Hungary, and crisis-ridden Yugoslavia. The five-country grouping, under Italian leadership — the association's president is Italian foreign minister Gianni De Michelis — has been considering development on a regional basis, with an emphasis on improving rail and highway links, as well as establishing integrated communications networks.[1]

The territory of the Habsburg Empire was the pathway of tribes and peoples who invaded Europe from the east, one such invading people being the Magyars, from whom are descended the modern Hungarians, whose language, related to neither the Germanic nor the Slavic tongues, is a signpost of that chaotic past. Entering Austria, the gateway to the whole region, one feels the cultural, intellectual, and political forces that have been exported from this region to the world. If Mozart, Schubert, and Freud were nurtured in Austria, Adolf Hitler, too, was a native son, born in the Danube city of Linz. Indeed, critical chapters in Hitler's life unfolded in the relatively small area around the city of his birth. It was to Vienna that the young Hitler journeyed to make his way in life as a student of art, and, while unsuccessful in his chosen vocation, in the flop houses of the city he did pick up the racist theory and the anti-Semitism that prepared him for another career. Much later, after the First World War, when he set out on his pursuit of political power, Hitler located in Munich, in the chaotic world of demobilized soldiers, of Bavarian separatism and red scares. Munich is just over an hour's drive on the autoroute from Salzburg, which is a stone's throw across the Austrian border from Bavaria.

From Salzburg, across the Alpine peaks, it is only a short distance to Berchtesgaden, the location of Hitler's famed "Eagle's Nest," where he hatched many of his schemes for the aggrandizement of Germany once he had consolidated his power within the Reich. Indeed, it was from the Eagle's Nest that Hitler did much of the planning for the take-over of his own native homeland early in 1938. When I arrived in Salzburg, I asked the proprietor of the small hotel where I was staying if you could see Hitler's mountain top from the Austrian city. She informed me that a number of other peaks blocked the view of the Eagle's Nest, and I suspect that she put me down in her mind as something of a touristic oddball, less interested in Mozart or the filming of *The Sound of Music*, two of Salzburg's premier attractions, than of the life of the Austrian native son everyone would rather forget.

The price Austria paid for the career of its native son was very considerable, although, in the end, it paled in comparison to the long-term price paid by the countries of what became the Soviet sphere of Europe after the Second World War. Austria, like Germany, was subject to a four-power occupation in the post-war years, an ordeal that came to an end in 1955 with the signing of an agreement under which Austria became permanently neutralized and forswore any future *Anschluss* with Germany.

Under the leadership of Austria's great chancellor, Socialist Bruno Kreisky, himself a product of the Jewish bourgeoisie that had been so important in the past in Vienna, the country became the very model of a corporatist welfare state. Neutral Austria, with Kreisky at the helm, was able to make Vienna an important international centre, the European headquarters of the Organization of Petroleum Exporting Countries (OPEC), the base for the International Atomic Energy Agency, and a site for superpower arms talks, to name a few key activities. Austrian society involved a myriad of interlocking relationships linking the state with business, and business with labour, some of these links above the table, some of them below. By the late 1980s, it was evident to the leadership of both major parties in Austria's governing coalition of ruling Socialists and the conservative People's party that the country's somewhat cosy arrangements would no longer do. To overcome productivity problems and declining market shares in important industries, Austria needed economic rationalization and restructuring. In July 1989, the Austrian foreign minister, Alois Mock, presented the president of the EC Council with the request of the Austrian Parliament, passed by a large majority, for the accession of the country to the EC. Austria's bid for membership in the EC was predicated on a number of conditions: the safeguarding of the country's social-security system; the maintenance of programs to sustain the rural, agricultural, and forestry-based sectors of the economy; and, most important for the EC, the safeguarding of Austria's "internationally recognized status of neutrality." In its "Letter to Brussels," the Austrian government stated that, as a member of the EC, the country would be committed to fulfilling "the legal obligations emanating from its status as a permanently neutral state and to [continuing] its neutrality policy as a specific contribution to the maintenance of peace and security in Europe."[2]

Because, with the exception of Ireland (always regarded as a special case), all the member countries of the EC are members of NATO, the question of Austria's neutral status was regarded as the key problem to be resolved in bringing the country into the community. Austria's official bid for membership came just months before the revolutions in East-Central and Eastern Europe, one consequence of which was a complete transformation of the security regimes in the former Soviet satellite countries and the official demise of the Warsaw Pact (by 1991). The unification of Germany and the collapse of the Warsaw Pact inspired a comprehensive reconsideration of European security policy and raised fundamental questions about whether the EC itself would play a security role in the future. Since Austria was a democratic country with a socio-economic system essentially like that of Western Europe, its admission to EC membership raised few serious questions, apart from the issue of neutrality. From the perspective of Brussels, the fact that Austria would be the next country to be admitted did not provoke serious concerns. It was seen as raising the security issue and opening the door to the rest of Central Europe, where revolutions had brought to power regimes that also aspired to EC membership, an aspiration whose realization would be much more daunting than the accession of Austria.

HUNGARY

It is only a one-hour drive from Vienna to the border of the country that formed the key partnership with Austria in the Dual Monarchy, the final form taken by the Habsburg Empire, enduring from 1867 to 1918. Hungary is not only linguistically remote from Austria. Its socio-economic and political experience since the Second World War have been entirely different. The journey from Vienna to Budapest is a lesson in the discontinuities of life in Central Europe. Not far east of the Austrian capital, on the flat plain that reaches out towards the Hungarian border, the prosperous towns, so numerous west of Vienna, are nowhere to be found. As elsewhere, the territory on the western side of a Communist border in Europe has been plagued with the economic shadow that has fallen on it as a consequence of its position at the edge of one of the continent's socio-economic spheres. In such a space, it is easy to imagine that the earth is flat and that you are about to fall off the edge. Just before the border is reached, one passes the Austrian towns specializing in selling electronic gadgetry and blue jeans to Hungarians who have accumulated hard currency.

I made the trip from Vienna to Budapest in the winter of 1990 in the middle of the first free election campaign to be fought in Hungary since 1945. Like those of other countries to have been submerged in the Soviet system, their true signature is not to be found in the heart of their capital cities with their large pre-Stalinist legacies, but in the secondary cities and towns where what meets the eye has mostly been built since 1945. Györ is such a town, the first large one to be encountered inside Hungary on the Vienna-Budapest highway. This town is wearyingly grey in every aspect. The apartment buildings, in the cinder-block Stalinesque style that is *de rigueur* in this part of Europe, have been dropped down onto the unkempt plain with minimal thought for aesthetic impression. On the main street, the heavy, dull buildings merge in their coat of soot with the sidewalk. The fleet of vehicles is the usual collection of Trabants, Wartburgs, Dacias, and, if you are lucky, the odd Skoda. When combined with those of smoke-belching commercial vehicles, their emissions create a stinging, pungent flavour in the nostrils that never goes away, even when you close the door and windows in your hotel room.

Budapest, too, is proof of the proposition that here the elegant tends to be old and the new, shabby. Once past the sprawling, depressing outskirts, the passage from the heights of Buda down across the Danube, much mightier here than in Austria, to the Pest side, is truly majestic. Budapest is a gritty survivor. In 1956 Soviet tanks rolled in to suppress the anti-Stalinist revolution of the Hungarian people. The rise of the Hungarians against the Soviet-installed regime was the most cataclysmic event in European history between 1945 and the revolutions of 1989. During the tragic weeks in autumn, when Hungarians came out into the streets to face Soviet tanks, often only with their bare hands, the world saw what, for a time, appeared to be the liberation of Hungary. In the end, three thousand Soviet tanks decided the issue. Thousands died both during the suppression of the revolution itself and in the reign of terror that followed. Among their number was Hungarian prime minister Imre Nagy, himself a reform Communist who had brought non-Communist elements into his government in the last desperate days and had announced the withdrawal of his country from the Warsaw Pact. Nagy was executed by the Soviets following a secret trial, and was buried in a pauper's grave. In June 1989, with the Communist regime tottering, tens of thousands of people attended a public funeral for Nagy on the grounds in front of the Parliament in the heart of Budapest. A massive statue of Lenin had been removed from the scene in time for the occasion.

"The last time I ate here," said Charlie Coutts, the ageing Scottish expatriate, as he looked up at the high ceiling of the dining-room in the once fashionable Astoria Hotel, "there was a Russian tank outside the door." Having spent his life working for Hungarian radio, combatting the "Voice of America," this formerly idealistic Communist acknowledged the complete collapse of the social experiment it had been his life's dream to build. When I asked him to what he attributed the utter failure of the system, he admitted readily to its complete lack of freedom. For him the failure to build socialism was not so mysterious — the system could not motivate people. Without motivation, the Eastern European adage — "we pretended to work for them and they pretended to pay us" — held sway. While Coutts still thought that, in principle at least, socialism was a good idea, he believed that Hungary would go through a long period of capitalism before anyone there would again consider socialism as an attractive option. Ironically, Charlie Coutts, who had devoted decades to battling the "Voice of America," faced the prospect of ending his career working with it. The radio station that employed him was about to be sold to a media company that planned an affiliation with the "Voice of America."

The system, whose failure even its one-time adherents acknowledged, had rested on common foundations in all the countries where it had been established. At the centre of the system was a special kind of state, the party-state, in which the Communist Party was formally held to be the only legitimate political voice for the guidance of society. The ubiquitous presence of the party-state led to the absence of what is the essence of Western societies, the existence of a civil society whose calling-card is a myriad of intersecting, self-generating, and self-renewing relationships — in business, culture, education, intellectual life — in all areas of life. In the Soviet-style system, all major industries and financial institutions were owned by the state and were managed by the planning mechanisms of the state, under the direction of the top leadership of the Communist Party. The emphasis was on industrialization, on large-scale capital investment in sectors such as steel, chemicals, and energy, which were believed to hold the key to economic take-off. The idea was that the consolidation of heavy industry would someday usher in an age of human plenty.[3]

In the meantime, a simpler bargain, a form of rudimentary social contract, prevailed. According to it, everyone would have a job, and the prices of basic necessities, foodstuffs, and rent would be fixed at low levels, requiring a permanent state subsidy to make this possible. The whole system was underwritten during the post-war decades by the wide availability of Soviet resources, including petroleum, at lower-than-world prices. The big winners in the system were top state bureaucrats and leading party functionaries. In every country in East-Central and Eastern Europe, the consequence was the creation of a rich and powerful élite, a class of people whose privileges depended on their willingness to subordinate their individual predilections to the general line of the leadership.

For the general population, the costs and benefits of the social contract were obvious enough. While they had little power, little opportunity, and few incentives, they did have a stake in hanging on to the basic minimum the system guaranteed. This minimum they clung to with tenacity, which meant that any attempt on the part of the regime to increase the fixed prices for basic commodities was habitually met with political fury. The prices of bread, meat, and rent were much more politically sensitive than was the level of wages. In ways that were reminiscent of eighteenth-century France before the

Revolution, the bread riot was a more typical form of protest than was the strike for higher wages.

The long-term tendency of the system was towards stagnation, towards entropy. No Soviet-system country ever actually reached the plateau where a successful level of industrialization was achieved, so that the economy could be redirected to make the meeting of consumer wants the top priority. Indeed, over the long term, there was even a tendency to slip backwards, so that certain achievements of an earlier period — levels of production, medical care, and education, to name a few — were once again in doubt.

In the early 1960s, despite the ruthless repression of the 1956 revolution, the regime that had been imposed by force offered Hungarians a new deal, a deal that, while retaining the basic features of the system just outlined, proposed significant modifications. Under the leadership of Janos Kadar, who had been installed by the Soviets, the Hungarian experiment in what Khrushchev called "goulash communism" was initiated. Press liberalization, the allowing of a much wider degree of public discourse, and the issuing of exit visas so that, by the 1970s, more than one million Hungarians a year were visiting the West, were accompanied by economic reforms that allowed many private firms to operate, permitted foreign firms to invest in Hungary, and fostered production of consumer goods to a greater degree than in the past.[4]

A noteworthy feature of reform communism in Hungary was that it was initiated by the Communist leadership itself in a context in which popular resistance and popular institutional forms had been broken in the brutal repression of 1956–57. In some respects, reform communism became a remarkable success and helped foster a quarter of a century of social tranquillity from the early 1960s until the late 1980s, when a new set of socio-economic crises ruptured the uneasy consensus. During this period of reform or consolidation, the regime sought to provide the population with "guarantees of existential security."[5] The guarantees entailed: full employment, price stability, non-eroding pensions, the provision of necessities at subsidized prices, and affordable rent and utilities. In addition to these basics, the regime eased repressive controls, allowing for greater expression of opinions, and allowing the burgeoning of a so-called second economy in which consumer goods could be acquired in a semi-legal setting — the authorities tolerated developments to which they did not give official sanction.[6]

The Hungarian experiment stopped short of establishing pluralism in politics or a market economy.[7] Indeed, as the circumstances in which it had been launched altered, the system began to unravel, so that the gains it had made were threatened. Sustaining a commitment to costly and unproductive heavy industry, keeping people in non-productive jobs, subsidizing the price of basic necessities, and maintaining the material and social advantages of the top bureaucracy were inherently heavy burdens. What sank the system was that, once the whole labour force had been mobilized, there was no longer an unlimited supply of cheap labour to be tapped. In addition, after the early 1970s, Hungary could no longer count on a plentiful supply of resources priced far below world-market levels. To put off the day of disequilibrium and social reckoning, the regime turned to Western lenders, from whom vast loans were negotiated. On borrowed money and borrowed time, Hungarian reform communism was able to eke out another decade of existence. In the end, rising external debt charges, the unsustainable costs of the system, and the absence of productivity gains together spelled catastrophe. Hungary, along with the rest of the Comecon (East bloc trade group) countries, was dropping from the middle rungs of the global economic ladder to a position of stagnation that had much in common with parts of the third world. In the last days of the Communist regime, Hungarians were exposed to rapidly rising prices in the formerly protected sectors, a punishing rate of general inflation, the collapse of the heavy industrial sectors, and the shutting-off of cheap supplies of resources, all while they had to cope with the highest per-capita external debt in East-Central Europe, which totalled $20 billion in early 1990.

Limiting the Hungarian experiment throughout was the fact that the Soviet Union remained the ultimate source of power in the country. Hungary became a school for cynicism. As time went by, any real belief in the system dissolved, and this dissolution of belief extended to the very top of the Hungarian structure of authority. To hold high-level jobs, it was necessary to adopt a wearying official doubletalk, which acknowledged problems but recognized that power still lay in Moscow. [8]

The Hungarian system had rotted away from within by the time it was confronted with a fatal combination of challenges in 1989: the withdrawal of Soviet backing and the rise of a popular movement and opposition, which the Communist leadership did not have the stomach to resist.

A central question in this saga, relevant to Hungary, but also to other countries in the region, is why the social system proved such a failure, so that once brute force no longer held it in place, it proved incapable of being reformed. To explore this question, when I was in Budapest, I met with economist Andrea Nagy, who describes herself as a non-aligned social democrat. In Western Europe, she would certainly be a member of a socialist or social-democratic party. Given her ideological leanings, I was particularly struck by her forceful rejection of the idea that a so-called third way, between socialism and capitalism, might be possible for Hungary. As far as she was concerned, Hungary's future would be capitalist, and there was no viable alternative to that. She shared the view that the system was undermined when it could no longer count on cheap raw materials from the Soviet Union. Of critical importance, she believed, was its failure to negotiate the contemporary global technological revolution. "The *perestroika* solution," she said, "depended on providing higher salaries for white-collar professionals. But since not everyone could be bought, everyone was dissatisfied." Instead of solving the problem, *perestroika* simply opened Pandora's box and doomed the system. When she said this, Andrea Nagy did not have Hungary alone in mind. She believed that the Gorbachev approach was destined to failure everywhere, including the Soviet Union itself, and that the whole of the Soviet bloc was headed for capitalism. In a larger sense, she believed, the failure of the Soviet socialist experiment was a function of economic and technological globalization. It was her view that Eastern European communism would leave behind no positive legacy of achievement, that its only legacy would be the discrediting of socialism, even social democracy in its Keynesian form.

What Nagy and other observers were saying about the impossibility of a "third way" was borne out by the thrust of the Hungarian election campaign, which was in full swing at the time I spoke with her in February 1990. As the Hungarian Socialist Party, the renamed former Communist Party, plunged in the public-opinion polls, attention turned to the opposition parties from which the next government would be drawn. In what was becoming an increasingly mean-spirited campaign between the two front-running parties, the Hungarian Democratic Forum and the Free Democratic Party, the central issue was how the country would negotiate the transition to a private enterprise–centred market economy.

When the election campaign began, many people believed that it would prove to be a straightforward coronation of the Hungarian Democratic Forum, the most established of the opposition groups, and apparently the natural new governing party. The Democratic Forum was a broad political front, combining a wide range of elements in the new Hungary. At its centre was the old middle class, both in Budapest and in the rural areas. Its political model was German Christian Democracy. Members of the Democratic Forum openly depicted themselves as following in the footsteps of Ludwig Erhard, the father of West Germany's economic miracle of the 1950s, based as it was on the notion of a "social market economy." The Democratic Forum would privatize the key sectors of the economy, although gradually, so that most of it would end up in the hands of Hungarians, and not foreign investors. At the same time, they would emphasize social programs to protect those dislocated by the transition to a market economy.

The Democratic Forum proudly acknowledged its Hungarian nationalism, if at times somewhat defensively. As Dr. Istvan Forrai, secretary of the Foreign Affairs Committee of the Democratic Forum, asked me in the airy, high-ceilinged old building that housed his party's headquarters on the Buda side of the Danube: "Why should we have to apologize for speaking up for Hungarians?" The rhetorical question was intended to parry the attacks of the Free Democrats who charged that the Democratic Forum was much too cautious in its approach to privatizing the country's industry and moving Hungary into a European economic environment. Dr. Forrai rejected the rapid privatization advocated by the Free Democrats both because it could result in too high a proportion of Hungarian industry being owned by foreigners and because the rapid unloading of state-owned companies could lead to massive unemployment. Rather pointedly he said that his party's economic mentor was Ludwig Erhard, not Margaret Thatcher.

The Free Democrats diverged from the Democratic Forum not only in their approach to the economy but in the style of their politics as well. Whereas the Democratic Forum was located in the official quarter of Buda and was running a careful and deliberate campaign, their opponents had their headquarters in a crowded street in Pest and were mounting a high-energy campaign, marked by invective and panache. The Free Democratic Party was frank in its espousal of a quick move to capitalism. Miklos Haraszti, the distinguished author who was one of the leaders of the party, told me bluntly: "Beating inflation is our first priority. We know that will create some unemployment. We have to acknowledge this and then deal with its consequences."

He leaned forward, talking intensely in the crowded room, as fellow campaigners milled around us, marking lists on the walls, operating computers, answering telephones, in what looked much more like the last dash of a North American election campaign than the more stately effort being mounted by the Democratic Forum.

Putting inflation ahead of unemployment had prompted the accusation that the Free Democrats were Thatcherites, an epithet they did not relish. "We are not Thatcherites," Haraszti volunteered. "We are slightly to the left of centre." Terms like "Left" and "Right" have lost all sensible meaning in East-Central Europe. What was clear was that, despite their insistence that they would mount generous social programs, the Free Democrats would integrate Hungary more rapidly into the global capitalist economy, opening the country to foreign investment, combating the power of old-line Hungarian trade unions, and pursuing the goal of membership in the European Community with fewer qualms than would their opponents.

What gave the Free Democrats an odd ideological flavour as compared with parties in the West was their commitment to rigorous free-market economics in combination with a profound insistence on political freedom. The Free Democrats were civil-libertarian and pro-European, rejecting what they saw as the Hungarian-ethnic focus of the Democratic Forum.

A few days earlier, the Free Democrats had thrown the Democratic Forum off balance by accusing them of being nationalist, not clearly pro-European, and of having reached "under-the-table deals" with the former Communists. Dr. Forrai of the Democratic Forum hotly rejected the charges of deal-making with the Communists and issued his own charges: first, that the leading Free Democrats or, in some cases their fathers, were themselves former Communists; and, second, that, in the hour of their conversion, they had become adherents of a mean-spirited capitalism in the image of U.S. economist Milton Friedman. In Hungary, as everywhere else in the new democracies of the region, the starting-point for all political invective is the Communist regime of the past and the relationship that people had to it. And since for over four decades the Communist Party was the only legal political entity, by definition anyone who was involved in any political activity, or even in any relationship with the state, was involved with the Communist Party. In Hungarian politics, everyone accuses everyone of having been involved with the Communists, making such accusations a ubiquitous stain on the newly minted democratic political order.

Also disturbing was the emergence of anti-Semitism in the campaign. Anti-Semitism has deep historical roots in Hungary. Along with liberal and democratic sentiments, the new openness provided the opportunity for expressions of hostility towards Hungary's small Jewish community. During the election campaign, statements were made by public figures close to the Democratic Forum suggesting that the media was dominated by elements "not truly Hungarian." For the Free Democrats and others, these were transparent code-words that added up to anti-Semitism. Harasziti, while far from charging the whole of the Democratic Forum with being anti-Semitic, castigated its leadership for failing to disavow those who made the statements. Off the record, leading figures among the Free Democrats were much more critical than this, telling me that many key figures in the Democratic Forum had been describing the Free Democrats as "the Jewish Party." When I put these charges to a spokesman for the Democratic Forum, I was told that, indeed, some of the statements that had been made were insensitive. The spokesman told me as well that all this endless searching for anti-Semitism was likely to have the effect itself of sponsoring anti-Semitism.

On March 25, 1990, a week after the historic election in East Germany, 65 per cent of Hungary's seven million eligible voters went to the polls to participate in a voting process that combined proportional representation with first-past-the-post selection of representatives.

After two rounds of voting, Hungarians, having rejected the Left in the first round, made a clear choice between the two front-running parties, giving the Democratic Forum 43 per cent of the vote, and the Free Democrats only 24 per cent. [9] With that result it was not difficult for Jozsef Antall, the leader of the Democratic Forum, to form a government in coalition with other smaller parties, leaving the Free Democrats in opposition.

While the country now had a freely chosen government, its problems remained. Sandos Nagy, who headed up management training for the Hungarian Chamber of Commerce, told me he believed that having escaped from communism, Hungary now needed to avoid ending up being ruled by the International Monetary Fund (IMF). Without some reduction of its crushing burden of foreign debt, Hungary would have little surplus to begin a rebuilding process, he said. He believed that, unless the West sponsored a moratorium on Hungary's debt for from three to five years, the country would experience a shaky economic performance and would fall victim to a series of weak governments, characterized by shifting coalitions among the parties. With such a moratorium, Nagy felt that Hungary could achieve economic growth, inspire investor confidence, and create the conditions for stable government. His blunt assessment was that, although Hungarians aspired to live like the Viennese, their present living standards were close to those of the Portuguese.

Although Hungarians wanted to find their place in the new European "home" that was under construction, many of them feared that they could end up occupying rather unenviable quarters in that home. Their ultimate goal was full membership in the EC. Membership would secure their access to the rich market to the west and allow them to work anywhere they liked in the community. It would also provide them with political security against the rising tide of ethnic quarrels that was engulfing Central and Eastern Europe. With the meagre economic security they had known during the Communist era gone, many Hungarians were holding two, or even three, jobs to make ends meet. For the time being very hard labour would be their lot, as they worked for the day they hoped would bring them a prosperous European future.

CZECHOSLOVAKIA

While Hungary had gone through a long process of reform communism prior to the collapse of the regime in 1989, Czechoslovakia had experienced a much more orthodox communism following the crushing of the regime of Alexander Dubček by Soviet invasion in 1968. Czechoslovakia's hour of reform communism had burned brightly during the "Prague Spring" when artistic and personal freedoms had been expanded before being extinguished as a consequence of the installation of a new regime totally dependent on Moscow for its survival. While the Prague Spring and the more distant historical legacy of Czechoslovakia as the home of an impeccable democracy in the period between the two world wars meant that there were reasons to believe that democracy could flourish there, few people expected the collapse of the country's stolid Brezhnevite regime even as late as mid-1989. Certainly Vaclav Havel himself, who had been released from prison only months before the so-called Velvet Revolution, had had no inkling that the transformation he had worked for was so close at hand. Czechoslovakia's astonishing revolution began with a student demonstration on November 17, 1989, eight days after the opening of the Berlin Wall. It built through a crescendo of demonstrations in which hundreds of thousands of people filled Wenceslas Square until November 24, when the government and party leadership resigned en masse.

The secret of this rapid transformation is unearthed in Vaclav Havel's depiction of Communist ideology as a "conventionalized system of ritual communications"[10] in which slogans were mouthed by people so that they could gain personal advantage, and not because anyone actually subscribed to the content of the slogans. And that state of affairs prevailed right to the top, in a society where people were encouraged to concern themselves with improving their cottages, with the purchase of a car, with the private details of life, rather than with politics.

Until very close to the end of the Communist regime, the Czechoslovaks followed the advice of their leaders, avoiding politics and devoting their energies to their private concerns. Czechs were famous for the care they bestowed on their cottages, those personal retreats, with their garden plots, which, however modest they might be, were their own kingdoms, oases to which they could escape from the limitations of their larger social condition. Because the country had been so quiescent and because people had devoted themselves so completely to the private and the personal, no one knew, until the very moment of the explosion, how they would respond to the opportunity to be rid of the regime. As in Hungary, however, when it became clear that the regime had lost its Soviet backing, the Czechoslovaks took to the streets and drove the leaders of the despised party-state from power.

I was in Prague on July 5, 1990, the day the freely elected Czechoslovak Parliament elected Vaclav Havel as president.

The centre of Prague is the urban masterpiece of Central Europe.[11] Its narrow streets, lined with baroque and medieval buildings in muted colours, are focused around the vast space of Wenceslas Square, which opens up a gradual incline to the top of the hill. This was the stage on which the revolution of November 1989 was played out. At the lower end of the square is located an oddly shaped five-storey white building, the headquarters of the Civic Forum, the organizational heart of the revolution, and now, confirmed in the elections, the political organization that held power in the new government. On that cool summer morning, Czechoslovakia was to see the installation of a democratically chosen government following the four decades of Soviet domination that came after the Communist Party's seizure of power in 1948 and, before that, the era of Nazi occupation, which was initiated by the Munich agreement of September 1938. By very good fortune, I was able to spend the historic morning with leaders of the Civic Forum in their upstairs office as they watched the installation of Vaclav Havel on television. Before the ceremony, I talked with two key figures in the movement (on condition that I not quote them by name), one a mathematician, the other a sociologist-anthropologist. Though the new regime may be short of practical experience, it is certainly long on intellectuals, some of whom once served as the fabled janitors of Prague buildings when their political views made it impossible for them to do any other sort of work.

While we were waiting for the proceedings to begin at the Czechoslovak Parliament, we discussed the problems facing the country. At the top of the list was the need to establish a new legal and constitutional regime that would decentralize power to lower levels of government and create the framework for privatization of most of the economy. The process of legal redefinition had already begun. Indeed, one of the first priorities of the new provisional government following the revolution the previous fall had been to start unravelling the regulations and laws that had underlain Communist rule. One of the very first to be repealed was a notorious regulation that gave members of the *Nomenklatura* the right of way in their vehicles, their easily recognizable black limos, over all other traffic, including police and fire engines.

To undo the regime of central planning, a complete overhaul was needed, an overhaul that would have to spring first from new thinking and then from the translation of that new approach into the creation of a legal basis for finance and business, for schools, health care, police, and local enterprise. The problem was that, while such notions existed largely at the abstract level, there were few people in the country outside of the Communist bureaucracy with any practical experience at implementation. Everywhere one turned, one confronted the problem of the Communist bureaucracy, the spider's web at the heart of all official and economic life, an interwoven network of influence, expertise, and access to scarce goods and capital without which it was hard to make anything work. The new government had won control at the very top of the state, and it had the support of the majority of the population, but it had not yet taken control of the web of influence at the centre of the state.

When the officials at the Civic Forum talked about this spider's web, they described it as the "Communist Mafia," which they said still had immense control, varying in its extent from region to region, over the security apparatus, other aspects of state administration and in a myriad of economic enterprises. Everyone above a certain executive level in economic enterprises had been a member of the Communist Party. "The core of the mafia," I was told, was a communications web linking these key groups of people together. Now that the regime had changed, it was not that the people in this mafia continued to proclaim any loyalty to the fallen ideology — this they had shed with alacrity — what they retained was what had actually linked them in the first place, their drive for power.

The implications of the Communist Mafia for privatization were very real. As a consequence of their standing in the former system, those who were well positioned were typically the first to accumulate capital, which meant that they were certain to buy into state-owned companies when they were privatized. "The first generation of businessmen in my country will be members of the Communist Mafia," a Civic Forum official told me. It was a lament heard throughout East-Central Europe.

One example of how the mafia both blocked privatization and benefited from it could be seen in the restaurants of Prague, which were doing a very brisk business in the summer of 1990 because of the flood of foreigners who were taking a look at the new Czechoslovakia. Most of the restaurants were still state-owned, and it was no secret that the food they were serving was pretty bad. In principle, there was nothing to stop newcomers from opening their own private restaurants. In practice, it was not so simple. The mafia, it seemed, could block you from getting all the basic electrical gear, cooking equipment, china, etc., that you would need to start up. As the state restaurants privatized, it would likely be the present purveyors of unappetizing food who would be at the head of the line because they had the connections.

The problem of what to do about the Communist Mafia was being considered and debated by the new political leadership. It was one of the consequences of a revolution that had been so "velvet" that almost no one had been jailed or charged with crimes, and where those who had run the old system were almost embarrassingly anxious to recant. The Czechoslovaks, unlike the people in some other former Communist countries, exhibited remarkably little appetite for revenge towards the old regime and those who had benefited from it.

What occupied the minds of the country's new leaders was the paramount question of what kind of economic regime to install, how quickly to privatize, and what kind of welfare-state system to establish. Though the country had a long history of industry and successful entrepreneurship, all of that was now long in the past. Teaching people how to run businesses was seen as a top priority. When I pointed out to a Civic Forum official that pre-war Czechslovakia had had a standard of living on a par with that of Western Europe, he replied ruefully, "In this country, we forgot." Trying to encourage people to become entrepreneurs would be no easy matter, even in a cultural sense, I was told. Many Czechs were happy with their lives, and wanted to go on focusing their attention on their homes and cottages. Many people appeared to want dependable salaries and benefits and not the riskiness of business. In this enjoyment of personal life, one new element was certainly welcome, the opportunity for foreign travel. Despite their right to take only very limited quantities of hard currency abroad, large numbers of Czechs were on the road in the summer of 1990, filling their Skodas to capacity or taking bus tours, to visit the rest of Europe. Their favourite destination was Venice, the closest point on the Mediterranean, where they spent their time taking in the sights at the Piazza San Marco, and returned with plastic gondolas in tow.

Even though Czechoslovakia did not have the immense foreign-debt burden that plagued both Hungary and Poland, it needed to create conditions that would be attractive to both domestic and foreign business, and that included the fostering of a culture of entrepreneurship.

The Civic Forum was itself a very broad alliance of quite disparate forces. Its adherents were firm democrats, but once they had achieved the overturning of the Communist regime and the establishment of a democratic system, they were bound to divide among themselves along philosophical lines. By the time Havel was elected president, the divisions within the Civic Forum were already quite clear. Right-wing, social-democratic, and environmentalist tendencies had emerged. A debate was already looming within the ranks of the Civic Forum, between those who advocated major investments at once to protect the health of the environment and those who believed the country must put economic restructuring first.

The key personality around whom this debate was taking shape was Finance Minister Vaclav Klaus. When told by some in the Civic Forum that environmental measures could not be put off because they would be much more expensive later, Klaus was quick to retort that his overriding problem was "the health of money." Around him, a right-wing tendency, whose first priority was to wrestle down inflation and to launch a privatized economy, had already developed. Those who wished to place a higher priority on the establishment of a welfare state and on the protection of the environment were describing Klaus as a monetarist, a Friedmanite. It was already apparent along what lines the future party structure of the country would take shape once the Civic Forum had completed its job and more traditional parties had emerged.

Vaclav Havel hoped that it would be some time before the present governing alliance was divided into competing political parties. He believed that all good people should serve the country and work things out among themselves, a system that Civic Forum insiders told me left most key decisions in the hands of an inner group of about fifty people. Given the enormous challenges that faced the country, Havel's preference for keeping the Civic Forum together was understandable, however difficult it might prove in the longer term.

One reason the president did not want a system of divisive political parties to emerge quickly was that Czechoslovaks were divided not only along ideological lines, but along ethnic lines as well. When Czechoslovakia was established at the end of the First World War as one of the successors to the Habsburg Empire, it was a state that grouped together two peoples, the Czechs and the Slovaks, each speaking its own language. Tension between them was rife in the inter-war decades and became particularly pronounced as Nazi Germany began to threaten the country's integrity. Germany occupied the Sudetenland in October 1938 and seized the rest of Bohemia and Moravia early in 1939, leaving a rump Slovak state, which became a satellite of Berlin. Once the revolution of 1989 had ended the Communist regime, it was inevitable that the internal national question would emerge again. For some Slovak nationalists, the solution lay in a completely independent Slovakia. For others, the answer was a highly decentralized confederation of peoples in which most powers would be exercised by constituent republics and not by the central government. In the sensitive political atmosphere with respect to national rights inside the country, government jobs were being handed out very carefully to reflect its ethnic make-up.

Given their daunting problems, it was understandable that the officials at the Civic Forum wanted to spend the morning of the president's election enjoying themselves and thinking about what they had accomplished. When the time came for the vote in Parliament to be taken, there were about ten of us sitting around the table, watching the event on television. The election of Havel as president by a comfortable margin was itself an event without much drama, an interlude between the first act in the real drama that had begun the previous fall and the beginning of the next act, as those now in power struggled to complete the dismantling of what had been one of the most thorough-going of the Stalinist regimes.

Czechoslovakia, like Hungary, faced west in its hopes and aspirations, also seeking full membership in the EC as an ultimate goal. In some ways, the Czechoslovak odyssey appeared more likely to be successful than that of any other former Communist country. Historically, democracy and a Western market economy were not unknown to the country, and Czechoslovakia was not burdened with a crushing foreign debt. Unlike the Hungarians, however, the Czechoslovaks had lived with a hard-line Brezhnevite regime for two decades prior to the revolution of 1989. Goulash communism had done much to prepare Hungarians for the transition to a market economy. In Czechoslovakia, that transition had barely begun.

POLAND

Unlike Hungary and Czechoslovakia, Poland endured its greatest misery at the hands of the Soviet Union before the Second World War was finished and before a Communist regime had been established in the country. The moment of national tragedy came in the summer and early autumn of 1944, when the resistance in Warsaw rose up against the Nazis and held the centre of the city for two months, until the Nazis succeeded in systematically wiping out the whole of the opposition in the city, killing 200,000 people in the process. What made this a Soviet as well as a Nazi crime was that for much of the duration of the Warsaw uprising, the Soviet army sat on the far shore of the River Vistula, watching the Nazis go about their work. Stalin, who had agreed to divide Poland with Hitler in 1939, now received a final gift, the destruction of much of the legitimate leadership of Poland, from his one-time ally. For two centuries Poland had suffered at the hands of the Russians and the Germans, two nations that, whatever they thought of each other, could always agree on their contempt for the people who had the misfortune to occupy the space between them. Stalin's aim at the end of the Second World War was to establish the Soviet military firmly in eastern Germany and to keep it there. To do that, he needed to hold onto Poland to secure the supply route for the Soviet army.

During the war, the Allies accepted the Soviet proposition that post-war Poland should be moved bodily westward, and at Potsdam in July 1945 they provisionally agreed that the Oder-Neisse Line should constitute Poland's western border with Germany.[12] These decisions handed over a very large swath of eastern Poland to the Soviet Union and, as compensation, Poland was given Silesia and Pomerania from Germany. Thus was the new Polish state physically constructed to serve as the Soviet Union's European antechamber. Significantly, it was given a huge vested interest in the post-war settlement with Germany.

Communism in Poland managed a higher degree of autonomy from Moscow than communism in East Germany, Czechoslovakia, and Hungary. All three of the other countries had had their moments of autonomy, and, in the cases of Hungary and Czechoslovakia, outright moments of defiance. Poland, although it was perilously close to a Soviet invasion in 1956, managed to avoid that catastrophe. The Polish Communist leadership portrayed itself to the Polish people as the lesser of evils, standing between them and direct rule from Moscow. But despite its show of autonomy, the Polish leadership faithfully followed the disastrous Soviet path to economic development. That path combined immense capital investment in heavy industry, steel mills, and shipbuilding, with low fixed prices for basic foodstuffs. The combination led over time to unbearable burdens for the Polish state and to a depressed and backward farm sector that was incapable of feeding the nation.

By the late 1970s, the Polish regime was caught in the bind from which it could never escape. While paying mounting interest on its foreign debt, it had to support a bloated, unproductive heavy-industry sector, at the same time as it subsidized food prices and held down the income of farmers. Having worked itself into this trap, the regime had to endure the rise of popular forces with which it had no chance of competing for the affection of the Polish people. Of great importance was the election of Karol Wojtyla, the Cardinal Archbishop of Kraków, as Pope in October 1978.[13] Throughout the years of subjugation, the church was always the critical national institution in Poland. That this remained true was apparent to everyone when Pope John Paul II returned on a pilgrimage to his homeland in 1979, where he was received by millions of his compatriots. The Pope was soon followed as the real leader of the nation by a grass-roots movement of workers and intellectuals, which won its position through strikes and political agitation in the industries on the Baltic, centred on the Lenin shipyard at Gdansk. Following victory in the historic strike-occupation at the shipyard in August 1980, the Solidarity movement for the establishment of "free-trade unions" spread across the country. These "free-trade unions," unique in the Communist world, were distinct from unions in the West as well. Located not in single plants or trades, but throughout the country, Solidarity was not only a union movement, but a political organization, indeed a critical "national" organization.

Once Solidarity had formed, the people of Poland had an alternative national leadership that continued to be recognized in preference to the government throughout the period of open conflict, state of emergency, and subsequent struggles, until the final crisis in 1988–89 brought down the Communist regime. To save the regime, General Wojciech Jaruzelski masterminded the coup of December 1981, which brought the military to power. The military government banned Solidarity and undertook thousands of arrests, but although repression led to a period of sullen resignation, it did not allow the regime to consolidate its position and did not destroy the legitimacy of the opposition. Towards the end of the 1980s, as the country hovered on the brink of bankruptcy, with falling living standards and soaring inflation, it became necessary for a new social deal to be worked out so that the burdens of economic adjustment would be accepted by the population. To work out that deal, the government eventually was forced to recognize Solidarity, something it had refused to do in the period after Jaruzelski's coup. Solidarity's recognition was followed with the concession that free elections would be held to fill all the positions in the Senate and 35 per cent of the seats in the Sejm (the Polish parliament). In those elections in the spring of 1989, Solidarity won virtually all the contested seats, completely unmasking the Communist leadership.

In August 1989, when the Communists were unable to win enough votes to install a new prime minister, Solidarity's moment had arrived. Although the Communists were to hold key posts in the subsequent Solidarity government, the installation of Tadeusz Mazowiecki as prime minister marked the effective end of the Communist regime, although the dismantling of the state bureaucracy and economic apparatus would take much longer. For the first time in over forty years, an Eastern European country had a non-Communist government.

For Poland, the road to a political democracy and a market economy has been more painful than has been the case in either Hungary or Czechoslovakia. The reasons have had to do with the depth of the economic crisis in the country and the nature of the political system and leadership that replaced the Communist regime.

In the first year after the fall of the Communist government, living standards fell dramatically as the first steps towards a market economy were taken. Simultaneously, Poland entered a period of political crisis. Just as a variety of political tendencies were observable within the Civic Forum in Czechoslovakia, and to a lesser extent within the Democratic Forum in Hungary, there was a wide ideological spectrum within Solidarity. Furthermore, the most important Solidarity leader, Lech Walesa, had chosen to stay out of office during the first period of non-Communist government. By the spring of 1990, Walesa was highly critical of his erstwhile allies in the new government, particularly of the performance of the prime minister, Tadeusz Mazowiecki.

These tensions were released in the politically damaging Polish presidential election held following the resignation of General Jaruzelski from the presidency. The election campaign in the autumn of 1990 revealed the extreme dangers confronting Poland. As Lech Walesa took on Tadeusz Mazowiecki in the contest for president, many of his former supporters feared that he had become power-mad, erratic, egotistical, and even undemocratic. [14] This was a far cry from the legendary Walesa, the electrician who had constructed a workers' movement that had gained the adherence of intellectuals, a movement that he had led with patience, skill, and courage against persecution, confronting a system against whom no one had ever won. Now in the presidential campaign, he exhibited personal vitriol against the man he had endorsed as Poland's prime minister just over a year before (as in France, the Polish president chooses the prime minister). The campaign took place against a backdrop of strikes by coal miners and transport workers who wanted a big pay increase to reverse a steep drop in their standard of living. Earlier in the year, Walesa had persuaded striking railway workers to return to their jobs. Now, the supporters of the prime minister believed that some of the present strikes were politically motivated and were being used to Walesa's advantage.

Anti-Semitism also appeared to be influencing some voters who saw Mazowiecki as having "Jewish connections" and expressed their desire for a "true Pole as President." [15] In the bitter campaign, Walesa accused the Mazowiecki government of not having moved quickly enough to rid the country of the Communist *Nomenklatura*, much of which was still in place throughout the state and economic bureaucracies. He wanted a much quicker pace in the process of privatization, as well.

The first round of voting in the presidential election on November 25, 1990, produced a shocking result. While Walesa came first, Mazowiecki did not finish second, but ran behind a quixotic millionaire candidate, Stanislaw Tyminski, who had made his fortune in Peru and Canada. On the surface, it was laughable that Tyminski should be taken seriously as a candidate for the presidency of the country against two figures who had carved out heroic reputations for themselves in the struggle against tyranny. Having been out of the country for twenty years, Tyminski offered the apparent qualifications of an ice-cool television manner, a record of personal fortune building, and a supply of very well tailored suits. After pushing the prime minister out of the contest, Tyminski proceeded to wage a campaign of innuendo against Walesa, alleging that he had a suitcase full of "serious personal material" about the Nobel Prize–winning Solidarity leader. The second round of the contest was noteworthy as well for a smear campaign against Tyminski, which suggested that he was the agent of a Communist counterrevolution and that he had a Libyan connection.[16]

In the end, although Walesa won the presidency with a convincing majority, his own reputation was besmirched in the process. Tyminski's popular appeal revealed the extent to which demogoguery unconnected to any serious political reality could win a large hearing in the extremely unsettled conditions of Poland a year after the revolution.

WHICH FUTURE?

In the autumn of 1989, the people in the Soviet satellite countries, in a series of political explosions, had risen in affirmation. They had affirmed their right to run their own societies, and had affirmed their profound desire to be a part of the Europe that was rising to the West. These affirmations had made 1989 a great year in the history of democracy, arousing a new confidence in many parts of the world that the future did, indeed, belong to true popular government. By early 1991, it all seemed much less certain. The transition to market economies would be very difficult, and would demand very unequal sacrifices from the people of the region. Much could be done by the West to lessen the painful transition. Would foreign loans be forgiven in time? Would the EC look eastward and establish favourable trading relationships with countries that aspired in every case to join the community? Would businesses in the capitalist world invest so that new industries would rise to replace those that had to be shed? How long could the new democracies endure the sacrifices before the quality of their democratic practice was itself threatened?

Beyond Hungary, Czechoslovakia, and Poland, the newly liberated countries of Central Europe, were the much more problematic cases of Romania and Bulgaria, whose journeys to democracy and market economies promised to be even longer and less certain. Considering the prospects for the whole region, social analyst Ralf Dahrendorf concluded that freedom was one possible outcome for the countries that had shed the yoke of Soviet-style communism, but that it was not the only possible outcome. Although he was not predicting it, Dahrendorf could not avoid considering what he saw as the greatest risk:

> Certain social processes are going on in at least some of East Central Europe. . . . which bear an uncanny resemblance to the syndrome which gave birth to fascism in the 1920s.
>
> Fascism above all thrives on the sudden impact of the forces of the modern industrial world on a society which is unprepared because it has retained many of the characteristics of an older, status-ridden, authoritarian age. The two simply do not match. Important groups find themselves dislocated and disoriented. They are stuck halfway between old and new. They hate capitalism as much as socialism, the newly rich as much as the newly poor. . . .
>
> . . . the extent to which outdated social structures have been preserved in the communist countries is striking. [17]

The risk of fascism is mentioned here not because it is a more likely outcome than democracy and modernization, but because the risk is serious enough to deserve consideration. Nor need the outcomes be the same throughout the enormously varied universe of Central and Eastern Europe. Here Western Europe, and principally the EC, are fated to play an exceptionally important role, either through action or inaction, in influencing those outcomes.

The countries in East-Central Europe do not form a genuine bloc, although they were tied together in the Soviet bloc for forty years. Each of them looks westward, seeking its own place in a united Europe. On the present evidence, that place will not be fully secured for many years. In practice, Hungarians, Czechoslovaks, and Poles look to the West for two things: large-scale investment from private corporations, and full membership in the EC. There is a chicken-and-egg problem with both objectives. Private investment will flow east on a large scale only when the region appears stable, and the region will be stable only when the investment flows East. Full membership in the EC is desired as a stepladder to economic success and political maturity, but the EC will not let these countries mount the top step on the ladder until they are well on their way to achieving both these goals.

In the summer of 1991, the violent struggles in Yugoslavia and, particularly, the failed coup in the Soviet Union revealed just how much the new democracies of Central Europe could be affected by the death throes of the old Communist order. The coup — launched in Moscow on August 19, 1991 and quashed sixty hours later — was a desperate bid to bolster the authority of the Soviet military, the KGB, the police, the privileged echelons of the Community party, and the old-style economic managers. As the short-lived coup unfolded, the nightmare of a return to a Brezhnevite past cast shadows not only over the peoples of the Soviet Union, but also over the newly-won liberty of the states of Central and Eastern Europe. With the suppression of the coup, a crippling blow was dealt to the Soviet party-state which had coexisted with the new democratic institutions of the Soviet republics. While in 1989 Gorbachev reformism had stayed the hand of the Soviet military against the revolutions in Central and Western Europe, it was not until August 1991 that the Soviet Union itself underwent a parallel revolution. As Europe moved toward unification, with the new democracies of Central Europe knocking at the door of the EC, the Soviet Union, a multi-national state left over from the past, careened toward dissolution.

Chapter Ten

THE NEW EUROPE:
TOWARDS THE
TWENTY-FIRST
CENTURY

★ ★ ★ ★ ★ ★ ★ ★ ★ ★ ★

THE EARLY MONTHS OF 1991 WERE A PAINFUL TIME OF testing for Europe. Instead of confidence, a bout of "Euro-pessimism" followed the launching of the two EC inter-governmental conferences in Rome, on Economic and Monetary Union (EMU) and on political union. The new and negative mood was the product of two crises: the Persian Gulf War and the deterioration of conditions in the new democracies of East-Central and Eastern Europe, including eastern Germany. Germany, the heart of the New Europe, endured the two crises simultaneously. The problems revealed just how far the dream of a United States of Europe remained from completion. For those who had thought that the EC could comport itself on the world stage as a coherent entity, the Gulf War demonstrated the opposite: the British were keen supporters of the American position in the Gulf throughout the crisis; the French pursued their own line until hostilities broke out, then fought along-side the Americans and the British, to great popular acclaim at home; the Germans stayed out of the war, and were subjected to harsh criticism from the United States and Britain. They ended up making a huge financial contribution to the fighting of a war that cost less, in the end, than the Pentagon had expected.

European disarray in the Persian Gulf crisis revealed the extent to which the EC remained, to borrow a phrase often used to describe the Federal Republic of Germany, an "economic giant and political dwarf." For some, particularly in Britain, the disarray of the EC during the Gulf War was welcome proof that matters of defence and security were beyond its capacities and that the nation-state remained the essential framework for addressing such problems. For others, disarray pointed to the need for further steps towards union so that the EC could take major responsibility for defence and security in the future.

From a European standpoint, the crisis in East-Central and Eastern Europe had more serious long-term implications than the Gulf War. As ethnic tensions increased in the former Soviet satellite countries and, as economic conditions worsened, the optimism that had accompanied the revolutions of 1989 became a distant memory. Whether the member countries of the EC liked it or not, their Europe, the cosseted, wealthy, western enclave of the continent, had disappeared along with the Soviet Empire as a consequence of the revolutions. For the first time since the Second World War, there was one Europe, and the EC could no longer afford to take its time about "deepening" its own institutional union while it reached out to the East. The community would have to deepen and widen simultaneously, with all the disruptive prospects that could entail. The launching of the European Bank for Reconstruction and Development (EBRD) in the spring of 1991 with Jacques Attali — Mitterrand's former chief adviser at the Elysée — as its president was a step in discharging the EC's responsibility towards the former Communist countries. The EBRD, to which European and non-European countries belonged, was setting out with an initial capitalization of ten billion Ecu and a mission to help former Communist countries succeed in the transition to market economies. [1]

Euro-pessimism needed to be seen for what it was, a natural reaction to crises and even, to some extent, a corrective to the Europhoria that had existed for the several years preceding the shift in mood. Shifts in mood concerning the prospects for the construction of a federal Europe have occurred many times since the signing of the Treaty of Paris in 1951 launched the supranational experiment. Shifts in mood have been endemic to the New Europe because of the extent to which its creation has been a function of political will, requiring sustained adherence to common goals on the part of diverse political élites. As we have seen, it is much easier to disrupt such exercises of will than to sustain them, and key national leaders, such as de Gaulle and Thatcher, have been able to impede progress towards European union for lengthy periods.

There is another reason for the periodic bouts of Euro-pessimism. The EC is located somewhere between two paradigms of political organization. It has already transcended the nation-state system of the past in a pooling of sovereignty unprecedented in history, but it is not yet a federal union. Europeans are in the process of inventing a new kind of state, the post-national state, about which I will have more to say in this chapter. Because that invention is not complete, and because it is not even certain that it can be completed, there is a powerful tendency to reassert the primacy of the nation-state system whenever the European project runs into difficulties. And yet, the project has endured many crises in its forty-year history, and is today far closer than ever to realization.

The immediate future of the movement for European union depends on the outcome of the two intergovernmental conferences launched at Rome in December 1990.

As we have seen, the Delors Report proposed a three-stage process for the establishment of a European central bank and single currency. Stage one in the process, whose principal objective was to bring EC currencies into the Exchange Rate Mechanism (ERM) of the European Monetary System (EMS), was near completion in the autumn of 1990 when Britain joined the system, leaving only Portugal and Greece outside it. Stages two and three will be more difficult since there are serious disagreements about what the goals should be and how to reach them. The most serious disagreement about goals comes from Britain, as it always has. The government of John Major, though it did not stand in the way of the launching of the intergovernmental conference on EMU, and though it has adopted a much less combative tone than the Thatcher government before it, has so far not agreed that the final goal of the process should be a single currency for Europe.

For the eleven countries that agree that a single currency should be the ultimate goal, the question is how quickly, and what criteria should be used to judge readiness to take the remaining steps in the process. Of greatest importance is the fact that France and Germany have disagreed about the process. France has stuck very closely to the propositions set forth in the Delors Report. The French government, having linked the franc to the Deutschmark and its economy to the German economy, wants a single currency as soon as possible so that France will have some say in monetary policy, which is now a monopoly of the Bundesbank. The Germans, however, coping with the immense economic problem of German unification, have become wary of a rapid move to create a European central bank, and beyond that a single currency. Under the influence of Bundesbank president Karl Otto Pöhl, they preferred a process that emphasized a high degree of economic convergence in inflation rates and government deficits as key steps in the process towards EMU. Although both the French and the Germans have supporters for their respective positions in the EC, an agreement can come only when a compromise has been reached and a single Franco-German position adopted. When that happens, it is virtually certain that the rest of the community, with the exception of Britain, will fall into line. At that point, the British will have to take the fateful decision whether to enter a community monetary union or to allow a two-speed Europe to develop on this critical issue. Indeed, a two-speed progression towards monetary union is not unlikely. A core group of countries may well adopt the Ecu as their currency before others do. In the spring of 1991, this position, favoured, as we have noted, by Pöhl, appeared to be gaining powerful adherents. (When Pöhl announced, in May 1991, that he was leaving his post at the Bundesbank, it was not expected that the policies of the German central bank would change dramatically as a consequence.)

Although obstacles stand in the path of EMU and though the full goal of a single currency may be a decade off, the subject of the second intergovernmental conference, the question of where political union will end, is more problematic still. Here the critical problems include the reform of EC institutions to respond to the so-called democratic deficit and the widening of community jurisdiction through the adoption of new treaties to give the EC new areas of authority — most controversial among these areas being security and defence.

Problems both of intent and form have stood in the way of agreement on the reform of EC institutions. Although there has been a wide range of attitudes across the community about how much power should be shifted to EC institutions, with Britain, as usual, being the least enthusiastic major country when it came to such a shift, there was a considerable disagreement, again between the French and the Germans, about the form that institutional change should take.

The French government, while prepared to shift more key areas of policy making to the community, wanted to reserve power within the community largely to the institutions directly controlled by the member states. This meant that the French government wanted more power for the European Council (the summits of EC leaders) and for the EC Council, the legislative body comprised of representatives of state governments. To some degree, this was a function of the French desire to maintain a strong "national" presence in the EC, a position with overtones of Gaullism.

The Germans, by contrast, favoured more power for the European Parliament, which fitted with their own parliamentary and federalist institutional experience. Again, the resolution of these differences would depend on finding the political will to fashion a common position.

Much more difficult than the balance of authority between the council and the parliament was the very thorny problem of the role of the EC in defence and security. Control over defence and the military comprise the very centre of the sovereignty of the state. The Western European Union (WEU), a security scheme proposed by the British government in the mid-1950s, was supposed to provide some coordination among the European members of NATO. But the WEU, which now includes nine member states of the EC, has always been a marginal institution. Historically, what gave it some importance was that France was a member of the WEU, while, after 1966, it was not a member of NATO's integrated military structure, so the WEU became a convenient forum for coordination among the allies in cases involving France. Thus the WEU coordinated European naval operations in the Persian Gulf, beginning in August 1990.[2]

In the early 1980s, there was briefly a heightened interest in the WEU; it lapsed when the EC failed in 1984 to extend its concept of political cooperation to include security.[3] The critical defence organization has, of course, been NATO, which has tethered all the EC states, with the exception of Ireland, in an alliance whose dominant player is the United States. With the end of the Cold War and the demise of the Warsaw Pact, there has been intense consideration of a new defence and security regime for Europe.

At one level, the discussion has centred on the institutional framework best suited to meeting the defence and security needs of Europe, focusing on the roles of NATO, the WEU, the EC itself, and the Conference on Security and Cooperation in Europe (CSCE), the latter being an umbrella organization that includes the United States, Canada, the Soviet Union, and both Western and Eastern European states. At another level, the debate is about more fundamental underlying issues. Should there be a supranational approach to defence and security in Europe or should European nation-states retain sovereignty in these sensitive fields? Should there be a fully developed "European" component of the Western alliance or should European states continue to operate as individual members of the NATO alliance, alongside the United States and Canada?

In the immediate aftermath of the Gulf War, the EC was divided. The French and the Germans were proposing closer coordination of the military policies of EC countries as an aspect of political union.

To achieve this goal, they favoured a gradual increase in the military role of the WEU, which would be closely coordinated with the EC. Eventually, according to the Franco-German position, the WEU would become an arm of the EC, just as the European Monetary System had.

For some time, the French and German governments have desired the creation of a European rapid deployment force that could be used in crisis situations. In 1988, the two countries set up a Franco-German brigade, a joint force, as a step in that direction. Helmut Kohl has made it clear that the Franco-German brigade is his model for a European force, and François Mitterrand has favoured the establishment of a "rapid reaction force."[4]

The logic of the Franco-German position is clear enough: in a more federal Europe, in which the political role of the EC is much more pronounced, it is logical for the community to have a developed military role as well. The collapse of the Soviet system in East-Central and Eastern Europe, the rising ethnic tensions in Yugoslavia, and the Persian Gulf War have combined to drive defence and security questions to a much higher level on the EC agenda. The 1980s notion that competition among states had moved primarily to the economic realm has been replaced by the grim realization that military power still counts. Those who favour the Franco-German idea of a unified European defence policy and military capability, under the WEU umbrella, and ultimately under the direction of the EC, recognize that this would constitute a basic shift in the nature of the Western Alliance. Karl Lamers, chief parliamentary foreign-policy spokesman for the German CDU, said bluntly: "The American position that everything should remain just as it is cannot be maintained." While he was committed to the preservation of NATO, he believed the "alliance cannot go on the way it is."[5] What he wanted, and here he was expressing the consensus position of the French and German governments, as well as of most other EC governments, was the creation of a European partnership with the United States, fashioned around two pillars.

Washington is deeply hostile to this potential development for the obvious reason that it would have the effect of reordering the American relationship to Europe, from one in which the United States stands head and shoulders above a number of smaller allies, to a one-on-one relationship between two more equal partners. Keeping NATO strong, with the EC very much in the background on defence and security, has been the Bush administration's preference since the collapse of the Warsaw Pact has made this a live issue. In this debate, to no one's surprise, the British have lined up on the side of Washington. British opponents of an EC role in defence have made the point that, in the Gulf crisis, their country might well have been hampered from intervening alongside the Americans had the decision been taken in Brussels.

The experience of the Gulf War has cut both ways, however. Though it has been cited as proof that an EC role in defence would be a bad idea, others, including Jacques Delors, have seen it as evidence that the community must speed up its political integration and enter the defence sphere so that Europe will never again be left in disarray when a crisis develops. In March 1991, in the immediate aftermath of the Gulf War, a proposal calling for the creation of a common defence policy for the EC was published with the backing of the commission and the governments of Germany, France, and Italy. The development prompted energetic American opposition. The U.S. ambassador to NATO, William Taft IV, made a series of speeches in Europe, and in Frankfurt he declared: "There is no other organization, now or in the future, which can perform the essential functions fulfilled by NATO. It will remain the principal organization to provide for European security."[6]

The controversy about the future of Europe's place in the Atlantic alliance was bound to be affected by a number of critical factors. If Paris and Bonn, with the support of most other EC countries, continued to back the idea of a common defence policy, coordinated by the WEU but increasingly run by the EC, they would likely get their way, as they had in the past on major community issues. The British and the Dutch could hold up the development, and the issue could be further embroiled by the problems posed by neutral Ireland, pacific Denmark, and prospective neutral EC members Austria and Sweden.

In June 1991, Britain and the United States were able to take advantage of France's absence from the NATO command structure when at a meeting of NATO defence ministers, it was decided to create a NATO Rapid Reaction Corps. The corps, under a British commander, although with a multinational staff, was to include American personnel and equipment. With support won from Germany, this diplomatic move succeeded in putting off the idea of a rapid force to be directed by Europeans alone. For the time being, the Anglo-American initiative parried the potential for an alternative Franco-German proposal for an all-European force. It was far from being the last word on the subject, however.

Ultimately the realizing of the Franco-German preference, for a European force, would depend on the solidity of the Franco-German relationship, which had been strained as a consequence of German unification. Though there had been much discussion about the sharply negative reaction in Paris to the process of German unification in the first months after the opening of the Berlin Wall, there was evidence by the spring of 1991 of a calmer attitude.[7] At the core of this revived confidence was the calculation that Germany was afflicted with so many problems that Bonn could simply not afford to dispense with the historic and special Franco-German relationship. While France had gained self-esteem as a result of its participation in the Gulf War, Germany had shown itself to be ineffectual. While France had successfully restructured its economy and economic policy to operate in tandem with Germany, the Germans were embroiled in a much more difficult struggle to launch a successful market economy in eastern Germany than anyone had expected. And while France had drawn closer to the United States and Britain in the Gulf War, Germany remained exposed in the East, fearing political instability in the Soviet Union, with some Soviet troops to remain on German soil until 1994, and with the prospect of several million Eastern Europeans and Soviets seeking refuge in the West in the next few years. But, although the factors that had prodded the Germans and the French into their historic relationship in the early 1950s had changed in very important respects, the fundamental need for the relationship remained.

The Franco-German relationship had survived major spats in the past and was likely to endure the vast upheavals begun in 1989. Furthermore, the outlines of a possible deal between Paris and Bonn to reinforce the relationship were evident in the spring of 1991: Germany would firm up its commitment to proceed to monetary union, so that the Deutschmark would lose its special position, while Germany would remain the economic centre of the New Europe; France would make concessions on the shape of the political union to be established in the EC; and the two partners, while determined to maintain their ties to the United States, would push forward their idea of a common defence policy, which would give France, with its nuclear-weapons force, a special position in European defence. The British, with the support of the Americans on the defence question, would chip away at Franco-German resolve and would try to lead the community into a less encompassing, less federal form of European union. To the east, the vast imponderable of how things would turn out in the Soviet Union was bound to affect the outcome. The

Germans, who had responded with compassion and calculated self-interest to the food crisis in the Soviet Union, knew better than their neighbours to the west just how dangerous a newly hard-line government in Moscow, or even civil war in the Soviet Union, would be for Europe.

OF MARKETS AND STATES

While the immediate European agenda is a daunting one, no analysis of the course of development of the New Europe can be complete without considering long-term forces that continue to draw Europe together. Although political will has been critical to the creation of the European Community, its evolution has rested on much more than that. The EC has emerged as a consequence of a shift in identities and in political, social, and economic structures. At its centre has been no less a phenomenon than a paradigm shift from the ideal of the sovereign nation-state to the onset of the post-national state. And essential to that paradigm shift has been the altered relationship between markets and states. The discussion that follows explores the transformed political economy of the era of globalization, not to proclaim the presence of anything so mechanistic as historical laws, but to point out how tendencies that once converged now diverge.

For two centuries, nationalism and the movement for the creation of nation-states were forces closely allied to the creation of viable capitalist economies. In today's international, even global economic order, driven by the latest technological revolution, the nation state is losing the seminal position it formerly held at the juncture of the political and economic systems. Where there was once convergence between the construction of the nation-state and economic development, there is now often divergence, and this has opened the door to a new historical epoch centred not on the nation-state, but on its successor, the post-national state.

In the early stages of capitalist development, markets were overwhelmingly local in character. The critical industries provided food, clothing, and housing, utilizing the overwhelming majority of the labour force and making use of the rudimentary technology that was then available. Given the primitive transportation system, only luxury goods, small in bulk in relation to their value, could be marketed on other than a local basis. Chief among the commodities marketed over great distances were spices, furs, jewellery, sugar, tea, spirits, tobacco, and books.

The dynamic engine enabling society to move beyond this relatively primitive state of affairs was, of course, new technology. Revolutions in agriculture, industry, and transportation were necessary for the development of markets over a much wider area. These revolutions, proceeding at different times in different places after the mid-eighteenth century, paralleled the rise of the nation-state system. While local markets prevailed for a very large number of commodities, large-scale regional, national, and international markets took shape. As transportation became cheaper, through the development of improved sailing vessels and canals, and later through railways and steamships, it became possible to move commodities to market over ever-greater distances. These improvements in transportation dovetailed with the development of specialized agriculture on a vast scale in regions such as the great plains of North America, where formerly such activity would have been impossible. Specialized and efficient agriculture, with foodstuffs marketed far from the point of production, opened the way for the channelling of labour into manufacturing industries, whose products could also be sold in distant markets.

By the late nineteenth century, in the most advanced countries, industrial mass production was firmly established. National and international markets by then existed in forest products, minerals, wheat, cheese, and a wide range of manufactured products. New technology and business organization, as well as mass marketing, were fashioned at the same time as the nature of the state was being altered. In the advanced countries, the state no longer primarily catered to the commercial and agriculture interests it had served before. Instead, it acted primarily on behalf of the newer industrial and financial businesses that had become dominant. The first countries to industrialize, and later those that achieved the highest levels of productivity, used their power to promote freer international trade, whereas the late industrializing countries sought to protect, subsidize, and nurture their domestic industries. Britain was the first great free trader, to be followed, in turn, by the countries that overtook it, such as the United States and Japan.

Depending on their stages of development, states employed offensive or defensive strategies. In the most advanced countries, which promoted free trade and the free international flow of capital, business was already moving beyond the national to the multinational stage of development. These countries sought to break down the protective barriers erected by weaker states so that they could gain access to foreign raw materials and markets for their producers. These first-rank industrial powers could make a virtue of their advocacy of laissez-faire, insisting that it served the general interest of the largest number of countries and not just their own selfish interest. In their turn, less advanced states defended their right to remain protectionist so that their local industries would have a chance to develop, so that they would not be crushed by the industrialists of the more advanced countries. These "late industrializing" countries used techniques of state intervention, which were denounced as unethical by those in the advanced countries, unethical because they violated the principles of the free market.

In this increasingly complex economic environment in which international interdependence was already pronounced, the nation-state did not operate in a situation of pristine independence, as indeed it never had. A hierarchy of states existed in which an international as well as a national division of labour was determined. Increasingly, this hierarchy of states deviated from the formal hierarchies that had existed in the imperial and colonial systems operated by the leading European powers. Although such systems continued to exist until after the Second World War, the hierarchy of power among the leading states was determined by how advanced their industrial and financial sectors had become. In the nineteenth century, Britain was the dominant power in the system. From 1914 to 1945, there was an interregnum. Following 1945, the United States was dominant. [8]

In the decades after 1945, while the United States and later Japan were economically the most successful nation-states and were home to the largest number of multinational corporations, there was an increasing tendency for economic activity to grow beyond the bounds of even the largest nation-state. In this age of globalization, within the advanced industrial countries, the state played an ever more critical role in relation to the market. Formerly, the state had performed limited functions, which had included the provision of military and police protection for property, the levying of tariffs and other measures to protect national industries, spending on educational and social services, and on the development of industrial and transportation infrastructure. Since the Second World War, this state role has expanded enormously, so that it has come to include a much higher proportion of the Gross Domestic Product of advanced countries. In this period, the state has vastly increased its outlays for subsidies to industry and agriculture, with particular emphasis on support for research in high-technology fields; the gearing of military spending to benefit critical industries; immense outlays for mass transportation and communications systems; enormous support for technical and university education; and the vast expansion of social spending in the fields of health care, old-age pensions, unemployment benefits, and welfare. In sum, advanced capitalism depends on its complex and myriad interconnections with the state for its functioning and its very survival in a way that dwarfs the state-market relationship of the past.

The point that the state is more involved than ever before in the evolution of capitalism seems to fly in the face of the experience of the advanced countries during the 1980s, when the notion of state intervention came under concerted attack and when, in some respects, the activities of the state were attenuated. To comprehend the true nature of the phenomenon, we need to understand it for what it is — a vast, even revolutionary reorganization of capitalism, and not a general diminution of the role of the state as is sometimes claimed. In some countries, the state's role has indeed been curtailed in two vital and interrelated ways — in the provision of social programs and in the elaboration of industrial policies. Both of these developments are indicative of the new imbalance in power between the multinational corporation and the nation-state, which is the very hallmark of capitalism in our age. Technological revolution on an unprecedented scale, wedded to corporate restructuring, is the driving force behind this transformation. The current technological revolution has, as in the past, vastly expanded both the scope and the necessity for the further internationalization of markets.

The move to even wider markets is being led by the strong, those capable of shedding labour through the introduction of new technology. In this process, multinational corporations have the advantage, and labour is everywhere placed on the defensive. As international trade becomes ever more important and as capital flows ever more readily from country to country, it is becoming increasingly difficult for nation-states to maintain their own "social contracts" (relationships between management and labour) in which labour fares more favourably than is the norm elsewhere. This reality gives capital a new-found advantage in its dealings with labour, even in countries, such as those in Scandinavia, where labour has been strongly organized and has traditionally won advantageous deals for itself. Managers of footloose capital and footloose corporations become ever more able to dictate their terms across the advanced capitalist world. Under these circumstances, the economic program advanced by the most powerful sector of capital, the multinationals, centres on two objectives: halting the further advance of the welfare state and blunting the operations of industrial policies by individual nation-states that interfere with the free operations of capital.

In this phase, in which multinational corporations have the edge and nation-states and labour are on the defensive, the nature of political democracy is being altered and the range of democratic decision making narrowed. In the advanced democracies in the era from the late 1940s to the end of the 1960s, political debate and the mobilization of social forces turned on the issue of how far the welfare state should be developed. Labour, socialist, and liberal parties mobilized their working-class and middle-class constituencies around the extension of the welfare state in opposition to conservative parties, which were supported by business and the affluent who wanted to limit the size of the welfare state and the public sector. As a consequence of these political struggles, carried on within individual nation-states, the development of the welfare state and the nature of its financing varied widely. Keynesian counter-cyclical economic policies, implemented through fiscal and monetary policies aimed at maintaining full employment, were workable on the assumption that nation-states were relatively self-contained economic units. If it were otherwise, stimulus applied through expansionary fiscal and monetary measures adopted in one country could easily lead to increased imports from other countries. This so-called leakage, if it became too great, could make such policies unworkable by saddling the countries that undertook them with serious balance-of-payments deficits.

Ultimately, globalization was to make such "national" economic policies unworkable, because the assumption no longer held that nation-states were relatively self-contained economic units. Even the United States was reaching the point where it was vulnerable to trade and investment policies adopted by foreign businesses and governments. For smaller nation-states, the change meant that the former assumption that social and economic policies could be made in a domestic setting was no longer sound. A crucial demonstration of this truth, as we have seen, came when the French Socialist government discovered that its program of national economic reflation was not viable and opted, instead, for European integration. An important lesson was being learned, and not only in France.

In our epoch, the contest for power within society has swung in favour of multinational corporations because of their freedom to operate substantially wherever they choose. The result is that the nation-state is becoming increasingly unable to pursue policies less favourable to multinationals than policies in competing jurisdictions. In principle sovereign, the nation-state has been reduced to an administrative unit in which global corporations have enormous freedom of action. Those who direct the affairs of the state have retained ample capacity to decide as they choose on matters of detail, but not on fundamentals.

The consequence of this process has been a very significant redefinition of the nature of politics in the advanced industrial countries. Since capital is free to move almost everywhere and international trade is much more important than in the past, the major advanced capitalist countries have been pressured into an economic game that can be described as "competitive deflation," to use the phrase of Cambridge economist Ajit Singh.[9] In this game, the over-riding objective is to run a lower-cost economy than is being run by competing countries. Maintaining a ceiling on labour costs and on government expenditures are the keys to the strategy. Success in the "game" of competitive deflation turns on minimizing labour costs and state outlays for social programs. Moreover, the pursuit of success by competing countries has the cumulative effect of reducing the power of labour and allied social forces to resist what becomes the pervasive new realism. There is an important ideological consequence here. A stripped-down market philosophy tends to emerge as the only conceivable functional response. Social democracy — any notion of redistribution of power and income in society — recedes into a utopian netherworld. As a consequence, an "entrepreneur-centred" social culture strengthens, and its advocates gain confidence in the singularity and truth of their vision. And while the sphere of decision making allocated to the private sector expands as a consequence of the strengthened hegemony of the leading element of capital, the multinational corporations, the sphere allocated to the public and to democratic decision making, erodes reciprocally.

What then does this analysis lead us to anticipate as globalization proceeds? Is the only possible course the further development of corporate culture into an indefinite future with notions of citizenship and the redistributive state bound to atrophy? To expect such a course is to ignore the further working of the dynamic elements that brought globalization into being in the first place. The very engines that have propelled capitalism to globalization themselves have the tendency to produce within it new internal strains that lay the basis for the next series of ideological challenges to the market-centred society, challenges that can mature only in the context of political developments transcending the nation-state. These contradictions arise because of two outcomes of globalization: the rise of the post-national state, and radically altered alignments of the class make-up of society. These two outcomes can be discussed separately, although ultimately they need to be understood as interrelated tendencies.

The European Community, by far the most important global example of the post-national state, is emerging as the consequence of complex historical forces. In the final analysis, it cannot come into being without the active sponsorship of critical political and economic élites in the nation-states that come together to pool sovereignty. As we have seen, there has been, throughout the history of capitalism, a critical interrelationship between the state and the market, the state and capital. Beyond the case of the European Community, we may speculate about the general tendencies that contribute to the emergence of the post-national state. The pooling of sovereignty into a new supranational or post-national state is one possible response to globalization and technological revolution. It contains two warring tendencies — its creation serves the purposes of the dominant corporations, at the same time as it brings into being an entity that may be capable of outflanking the corporate sector and reasserting a more equal balance of power between the state and the market. The post-national state thus has a contradictory relationship with capital. It is an essential springboard for the launching of corporations capable of competing globally. However, it is also a state with the potential to restrain and control capital on behalf of various types of projects, including that of social democracy.

The state, while representing and serving capital, has its own interests and nature that both parallel and contradict those of capital. It comprises an immense array of forces and interests, with political parties only the tip of a giant structure. In a fully developed state, this structure includes the government bureaucracy, judiciary, police and military, parts of the media, and elements of the educational system and intelligentsia. Because the state, by definition, is a monopolist in the exercise of its functions, its critical decision-making elements have a very strong tendency to guard their monopoly against any outside challenges. Since this is undeniably the case with respect to the nation-state, it is only under very particular circumstances that the decisive elements in a group of nation-states are willing to take steps down the long road towards the establishment of a post-national state to which they all concede important components of their sovereignty. The post-national state can be said to exist when sovereignty has been irretrievably transferred from a group of nation-states to a new confederation or federation established among them. Once it has come into being, a new domestic space is established, comprising the adhering nation-states so that the rules governing economic activity, individual mobility, and citizens' rights operate throughout the new confederation. No region of the world has yet established a post-national state in the full sense of the term, although the EC countries are much further down that road than is any other region.

It is helpful here for us to consider further the difference between the nation-state and the post-national state. The nation-state rests on a simple idea. Nation-states have political legitimacy because they exercise power over people who share a common adherence to a particular nation. Over the past five centuries it has come to be accepted that the people of a nation share common ties — history, language, religion — that make it their natural right, and usually their will, to govern themselves. Indeed, as we have seen, we take the nation-state for granted, as though it is a natural phenomenon, forgetting that, like any other political concept, it is an invention. Like other novel political notions, it took a very long time to work itself out. Today, the world's great states are nation-states, with the major exception of the Soviet Union. The United States, China, and Japan are all nation-states. Their immense power rests on the legitimacy their states derive from giving expression to the will of particular nations. The Soviet Union, by contrast, is a traditional empire, a legacy from the Czars, in which the Russian nation exercises domination over many other peoples. The fact that the Soviet Union is not a nation-state is its greatest political weakness.

The post-national state derives its legitimacy from factors other than the representation of people who make up a particular nation. If peoples with a sufficiently common economic interest, social system, and commitment to a particular form of political decision making decide to establish a common state, the result will be a post-national state. What makes the post-national state so potent is that adherence to it is not limited to people with a common culture, language, and history. When a nation-state attempts to annex non-nationals to its territory, it is seen as practising imperialism. A post-national state can expand precisely because the basis for membership in it is not exclusive to one particular national culture.

The post-national state is the political counterpart of the multinational corporation. Multinational corporations have discovered the secret of operating across state boundaries. The world has been their oyster. A multinational state can cope with multinational corporations on its own terms. It can set the rules instead of having the rules dictated to it. The post-national state reasserts the power of the state to control and direct the market. It is an invention whose potential will take decades to be fully realized. Much of the global history of the twenty-first century can be expected to turn on its burgeoning and the responses to it.

The forces that make possible the creation of the post-national state also underlie the social transformation taking place in the advanced capitalist world. Economic globalization sponsors vast dislocation, heightening the speed with which the class make-up of society alters. As technology has advanced and as markets have expanded, there has been a tendency for corporate size to become larger. Big companies push out and take over small ones. When this process is seen over the long term, it is evident how dramatically the social make-up of capitalist society has altered. A century ago, farmers, small businessmen, and independent artisans made up a very large proportion of society. Decade by decade, all of these groups have shrunk in size, first, vis-à-vis the traditional proletariat and, later, vis-à-vis the rising white-collar work-force. For the past half-century, the traditional proletariat has also shrunk in size in relation to the emerging white-collar sector, which now constitutes the majority of the labour force in every advanced capitalist society.

The extension of market size and market power has resulted in the drastic weakening of both the farm and small-business sectors, and the relative weakening of the working class. Its consequences for the nature of political alliances within society are enormous. In the late nineteenth and early twentieth centuries, the customary popular class alignment in opposition to the politics of big business consisted of farmers and elements of small business allied with the emerging working class. This alliance favoured the extension of trade-union rights and the mounting of state-supported social programs. It also upheld the interests of small capitalists against large ones, advocating restraints on the logic of the market to that end. Naturally, as the decades passed, the balance of power within the alliance shifted dramatically in favour of the working class, which became far more numerically important than its erstwhile allies.[10] The existence of the alliance, of course, had the effect of limiting the goals of its partners. Obviously anti-capitalism would not appeal to farmers and small business, however much it might appeal to some sections of the working class. As the class balance in advanced capitalist societies shifted with the rise to decisive prominence of the new white-collar sector, with its wide range from clerical workers to semi-professionals and professionals, the early variety of popular alliance between small capitalists and the working class was threatened. In some cases, this meant the undoing of traditional social democracy; in other cases, it meant a shift in alliances so that the working class became allied to the new white-collar groupings. Shifts in alliances of this kind were necessarily accompanied by shifts in the political programs of popular parties. The egalitarian emphasis in earlier social democracy tended to be downplayed in favour of a new emphasis on the striving for economic democracy.

These shifts in the nature of the class structure, and consequently of class alliances, in advanced capitalist society were occurring, of course, in the context of nation-states. The advent of globalization and of the dawn of the post-national state are speeding up these processes dramatically. Because these developments are so recent, we can only speculate about the effect they may have on the nature of political alliances in the future. The present era has been marked by disarray among popular movements. In some cases, such as Britain and Germany, they have lost power in favour of the right; in other cases, such as France, Spain, and even Sweden, they have held onto power but have been compelled to carry out many of the market-centred policies advocated by the right. Caught by the logic of globalization and the increasing impotence of the nation-state, popular movements have been unable to mount a convincing program linked to a viable political strategy, whether they have remained in government or not.

The consequence is that it has appeared that the industrialized world has entered a golden age of capitalism. But do the forces that at present dominate the political life of the advanced countries have an indefinitely rosy future ahead of them? Or will success in promoting globalization, with its characteristic uneven development, bring in its train new contradictions around which new popular forms of opposition will take shape?

SOCIAL EUROPE

The "1992" program has been driven by the logic of the market, the logic of globalization. However, as we have also observed, powerful forces and traditions in Europe have resisted the idea of an unrestrained market economy and society. In an earlier chapter, we saw how corporatist tendencies motivated the approach of the EC towards threatened sectors such as the electronics and automotive industries. If we are to understand the social model emerging in the EC, we need to remember that, while the impetus of the market has been dominant, it is offset by powerful non-market tendencies, of which corporatism is but one. Non-market approaches are also evident in statism and social democracy or socialism, tendencies that have an important influence in Europe.

Without the completion of political union in the EC, the community will remain a vast single market with an incomplete political structure. The Social Europe, advocated in one form or another by all those who reject the idea of the unfettered marketplace, can be achieved only through political union. It is the logic of the transition to the post-national state that Social Europe is now beyond the capacity of individual nation-states to achieve and must await Political Europe.

The shape of Social Europe will depend on the outcome of the political process within the EC. The completion of the single market and, beyond that, the completion of economic and monetary union are stimulating the creation of a genuinely "European" political process. Such is the case because, once the community has a central bank and common currency, member states will no longer be in a position to make use of monetary policy and will have a very restricted ability to make use of fiscal policy to address their economic problems. States that cannot devalue their currencies or freely decide on their tax rates and the size of their government deficits will be forced to seek redress for their regional problems from the EC itself. Problems that were formerly national are becoming regional. To address the regional disparities that may, in many cases, be exacerbated by the single market will force Europe-wide political action on an ever-greater scale, and will force the EC to increase its revenues so that it can be effective in mounting regional-development programs. As the EC's share of European taxes increases, so, too, will the demand for democratic accountability.

EUROPE IN THE WORLD

For outsiders, dealings with the New Europe will be strained because of the misunderstandings that are inevitable in dealings with a highly complex organism in the process of rapid transformation. Positioned, as it is, between the paradigm of the nation-state and that of the post-national state, Europe's locus of decision making is hard to locate precisely because it is undergoing change. International systems are always less prone to accident and conflict when the rules underlying them are clear. Where power is shifting, the risk of unintended tensions and disputes is markedly higher. In important instances, power rests both with the governments of EC member states and with EC institutions. Sometimes the EC acts as one, sometimes as twelve. In critical economic areas such as trade, investment, and competition, it acts increasingly as one, although, even here, national governments retain key powers. Over the course of the 1990s, the EC can be expected to act ever more as one in the economic sphere as the process of Economic and Monetary Union is completed. In social and environmental matters, EC authority is increasing and can be expected to become much more substantial as the impact is felt of community regional-development funds and of social and environmental standards set by community legislation and enforced by the Court of Justice. In defence and security matters, as we have seen, the future is much more difficult to fathom. Debates within the EC and pressures from the United States and the Soviet Union, and from those countries clambering to join the community, will affect the outcome. The Bush administration has already decided that European integration beyond a certain point does not serve the interests of the United States. But, while Washington tries to maintain its central role in European security, instability in the Soviet Union and in Central and Eastern Europe will prompt EC countries to fashion their own defence arrangements.

As Europe shifts ever more to the consolidation of its post-national state, non-Europeans will have to change their perceptions and expectations of Europe, and they will have to change the way they relate to Europe economically and politically. A very substantial reason for this change is that however porous, uneven, and incomplete Europe remains, it is none the less a giant, with a vast economy and enormous political and military potential. And because power accumulated becomes power used, non-Europeans need to prepare themselves for this reality. What follows is a brief listing of some important areas in which the New Europe can be expected to change the world.

TRADE

The New Europe will force a fundamental revision of the global trading system. That system, centred, as it has been, on the General

Agreement on Tariffs and Trade (GATT), established in 1948 as a part of the American-centred Bretton Woods international economic order, is already being subjected to intolerable stresses. The consolidation of the EC is certain to increase these strains because of the vast weight the EC will possess as a single trading entity. Already the world's largest market, with a population of 340 million people, that market will grow much larger still as more countries join the community. By the turn of the century it is not unreasonable to project an EC with Austria, Sweden, Finland, Norway, Iceland, possibly Switzerland, and almost certainly Hungary, Czechoslovakia, and Poland as members. (While these major additions to EC membership are occurring, it is probable that Malta and Cyprus, Europe's lost children in the Mediterranean, will join as well.) To this community of twenty-two or twenty-three members must be added other European states, Turkey and possibly the Soviet Union, with which free-trade arrangements will have been made. (Although Turkey has applied for EC membership, it is unlikely to advance beyond an improved form of associate membership by the turn of the century.) Beyond this sphere of EC members and countries with free-trade deals with the EC will be another tier of states in North Africa and the Middle East that can also be expected to make special trade arrangements with the community. In sum, the EC will be at the centre of a trade bloc with a population of close to a billion people.

Beyond the European bloc itself is a further grouping of countries, the so-called African, Caribbean, and Pacific (ACP) states, now sixty-six in number, countries that are former colonies of EC member states, which have developed a special trading relationship with the community. Based on conventions signed in Yaoundé, the capital of Cameroon, in 1963 and 1969, and in Lomé, the capital of Togo, in 1975, 1979 and 1984, the ACP countries have gained duty-free access to EC markets for most of their products and have become recipients of various forms of grants and aid from the EC.

By its very nature, the European bloc will not be able to trade with the rest of the world according to the present theory of GATT, which is based on the idea of an international system of sovereign states. Although the GATT system was based on the assumption that regional trading arrangements were not necessarily incompatible with a truly international trade regime, the degree of union achieved in the EC has basically nullified GATT. As the most powerful of the world's trading blocs, the EC and its associates will certainly expect to get their way on many key issues as the world trading system is redesigned.

Europe's social philosophy dictates a conception of trade and commerce in which markets are not the sole criteria, and that philosophy is bound to have an effect on the kind of trading system the EC will prefer. Though the EC will not want to build a wall around itself, it will be strongly inclined towards managed trade through bloc-to-bloc trade arrangements. And although the United States and Japan, as well as other countries and blocs, will have much to say about the trading system of the future, no voice will be stronger than that of the EC. For the rest of the world, that voice will dictate an adjustment of thinking and behaviour.

TOWARDS A GROUP OF THREE

The Group of Seven industrial nations is destined to become an anachronism. As the EC completes its economic and monetary union, so that the rest of the world will be dealing with the Ecu as the single currency of the community, with a monetary policy governed by a European central bank, it will make no sense for Europeans to conduct economic conclaves with other parts of the world with nation-state leaders as their representatives. At present, the Group of Seven includes the leaders of Germany, France, Italy, and Britain who meet with the leaders of the United States, Canada, and Japan. By the turn of the century, this structure will almost certainly have been replaced by a Group of Three: the EC, the United States, and Japan.

The emergence of a Group of Three among the leading industrialized countries can only further the long-term trend towards a global trading and financial system in which bloc-to-bloc deals become ever more important. For countries that are not a part of one of the major blocs, such a development will add to pressures to become associated with a bloc. For Canada, which stands to lose its membership in the steering committee of advanced industrial states, the effect may be to provoke a debate about whether even closer association with the United States is the answer, or whether special deals should be sought with each of the major blocs. Other smaller industrialized countries such as Australia and New Zealand will experience similar debates.

MULTINATIONAL CORPORATIONS

Multinational corporations are bound to be increasingly affected by the regulatory environment established by the EC. In the early years of the "1992" program, there was considerable anxiety in the United States and Japan about whether the single market would prove to be protectionist and would have a negative effect on corporations based outside Europe. Much of this controversy about whether the EC was constructing a "fortress" missed the point. While, as we have seen, there have been sectors where European industrial policies, anti-dumping regulations, and sectoral protectionism have played a role — in aircraft manufacturing, electronics, and the automotive industry — the major orientation of "1992" has been towards a widening of markets. There have been far more examples of the EC opening up its business environment, to both European and offshore firms, through a much tougher competition policy than examples of new restrictions to protect key sectors. In that sense, the much-touted fortress has not materialized.

However, the matter does not end there. As Europe's economic and political union is completed, the impact of EC regulations on the behaviour of corporations is bound to increase appreciably. Over the past decade, the old structure of national regulatory environments came under assault as a result of the move to European union. Over the next decade, the new European state, motivated by the multifold political currents in the community, will erect its own regulatory structure. By the year 2000, it is highly probable that corporations, wherever they are based, will be forced to adapt their behaviour to social and environmental legislation in the EC substantially different from the regimes in the United States and in Japan. In the United States, for instance, multinationals can move from states where labour is costly to states where labour is cheaper. However, if this option is restricted in Europe, multinationals operating there can be expected to increase their drive for technological advance as a way to shed labour, and thereby cut their costs.

If multinationals can expect to be required to adapt to the social models adopted by the great economic blocs, they can also be expected to thrive in the coming period. The rise of the blocs has been promoted by the power of multinationals and they will continue to be key actors on the world stage.

HEGEMONY

By the turn of the century, the United States is almost certain to lose its position as the central player in the defence and security arrangements of Europeans. The revolutions in Central and Eastern Europe, the collapse of the Warsaw Pact, and the socio-economic implosion of the Soviet Union have all combined to reduce any eastern military threat to Western Europe almost to the vanishing point. In the future, no conceivable ideological cement can be found to give the Atlantic alliance the cohesion it has had in the past. The position of American forces in Europe will become ever more anomalous, from both an American and a European standpoint. Americans will resent the outlay of funds to defend a wealthy competitor against a vanished enemy, and Europeans will no longer be prepared to brook the interference in their affairs that inevitably goes with such an arrangement. Over time, the American forces will come home or will move to new military bases in the third world. Whether the withdrawal is congenial or testy, by the year 2000 the Atlantic will be a wider ocean, from a defence and security perspective.

While the security question will be central to the U.S.–EC agenda, broader economic and political questions will be on that agenda as well. The broadest question concerns the exercise of leadership among the advanced industrial states. Since 1945, the United States has been the undoubted leader, able, in the final analysis, to determine the outcomes to key controversies more effectively than any other state. Although American hegemony has been based on the existence of critical economic, political, and military assets, what has been decisive in the global system has been the American ability to determine outcomes.

The completion of its economic and political integration will give Europe the potential to undermine the American ability to determine the outcome to key questions, and thereby to exercise hegemony. Alone among its potential competitors, Europe has the weight to challenge the position of the United States. The Soviet Union is rapidly losing its previous role as a giant regional hegemonic power, Japan simply does not possess the economic and political weight to push the United States from its position as hegemon, and China remains decades away from being able to mount its own challenge.

Europe's economic power and potential military power give it the capacity, though not necessarily the inclination, to mount such a challenge. Indeed, in the aftermath of the revolutions of 1989 and of the Gulf War of 1991, it is reasonable to project a period in which the United States will be, for a time, the only global hegemon. However, as Europe unites, American hegemony is likely to come into question. Although the present generation of European decision makers is so accustomed to American leadership that it would find it difficult to conceive of dispensing with it, the next generation may have fewer qualms as it discovers the vast power at its disposal.

THE NEW EUROPE

Finally, there is the question of where the European experiment will go in the future. Whether the post-national state will be a "cold monster" or an invention that brings forth a vital democracy is a challenge Europeans will face for decades. In this vast uncertainty, one thing appears clear, however. Transcending national sovereignty through the voluntary pooling of power to create a common state across an enormous region is an idea that fits with the pressures and historical forces of our age. Europe has travelled a very long way on its road to union. More important than all of the concrete achievements of the New Europe is the idea at its centre, the idea of a democratic union among peoples that allows each of them to cede sovereignty to the whole without giving up its national and regional personality. That idea, which has been reshaping Europe for over four decades, is now on the threshold of fruition, now at the point where it can become a world force of the first order.

The New Europe will be unlike any political entity the world has ever known. Around the solid core of the emerging post-national state, there will be a ring of concentric circles, each ring held in place by the magnetic power at the centre.[11] The New Europe will have fixed boundaries only on the north and west. Its eastern and southern flanks will be zones of turmoil, as Europe works out age-old conflicts. In spite of these zones of conflict on its eastern and southern perimeter, the New Europe will reach from the Atlantic to the Urals, from Northern Scandinavia to Turkey and North Africa. Its geopolitical heartland is now forming but, like molten lava, its final shape remains somewhat indeterminate. At the core will certainly be Germany, France, the Benelux countries, and Italy. Whether Britain will be in the innermost circle remains to be determined. If Britain opts in, a metropolitan heartland will form, bounded by lines drawn from Berlin to London, from London to Paris, from Paris to Milan, and from Milan to Berlin. All the outer rings in the New Europe will revolve around this metropolitan colossus. Within it dozens of languages and cultures, conflicting religions, and ideologies exist and will jostle for space, acting out ancient and novel conflicts within a new system of power. No single flag will fly over the whole of the New Europe, although the EC flag, with its twelve gold stars on an azure background, will fly over much of it, indeed over its privileged heart-land. Despite the zones of conflict that exist within it, the New Europe will constitute a single, giant constellation of geopolitical power. Its stellar mass is taking shape out of matter that formed parts of the empires of the two superpowers — the Soviet Union, which is being eclipsed by the New Europe, and the United States. The sinews that will bind the New Europe together are multifold and complex. Economic, historical, political, and cultural strands exist and are developing. Some of the sinews are exclusively European; others are global or partially extra-European in character. The New Europe, far from being an entity unto itself, will be a porous giant, penetrated from the outside by American, Japanese, and other multinational corporations, culturally attuned to American television, film, and music. Indeed, it will vibrate to the influences of many parts of the world. The porous giant will face outward as well, however. From it will radiate economic, political, military, and cultural energy. As the centre from which classical capitalism, fascism, socialism, and communism originated, the New Europe will continue to export models for social and political organization to the rest of the world. No one on earth will be immune to its gravitational pull.

ACKNOWLEDGEMENTS

★ ★ ★ ★ ★ ★ ★ ★ ★ ★ ★ ★

OVER THE LAST THREE YEARS, MANY PEOPLE HAVE PRO-
vided me with critical assistance in the conceptualization
of this book, in my writing, and in making it possible for
me to interview people in many parts of Europe.

While it is not my intention to list the names of all of those
interviewed for the book, since many people met with me on
condition that they not be named, there are a number of institutions and individuals to whom I must express my appreciation. I am
particularly grateful to the staff of the EC Commission in Brussels
for invaluable assistance in arranging interviews with members of
the commission staff. I am thankful to the staff members of the
European Parliament for assisting me in my work in Strasbourg and
in arranging interviews with members of the European Parliament
(MEPs). I must also thank those on the staff of the caucuses of the
European Parliament and those MEPs who helped me gain access to
caucus meetings and who set up meetings with MEPs and with
employees of the European Parliament. I would like to thank the
members and officials of political parties in a number of European
countries for their assitance and cooperation in setting up interviews
and in providing me with background and perspective on the positions taken by their organizations. I am grateful for the assistance
of businesspeople and trade unionists in many parts of Europe who
took time to explain how the onset of the single European market
has been affecting their enterprises and members. In particular, I
wish to thank the staffs of Airbus Industrie in Toulouse, Fiat in
Turin, Deutsche Bank in Frankfurt, and IBM in Portsmouth for their

generous assistance. I am grateful to Lord Cockfield for discussing with me his own personal role in the "1992" project.

I wish to express my gratitude to Catherine Yolles for her advice and encouragement over the past three years. David Kilgour has been the finest editor with whom I have ever worked. His thinking has been crucial to the shaping of the book from the proposal stage. I owe much to the late Peter Livingston for his invaluable assistance in working out the proposal for this project. I must single out for special thanks Malcolm Lester and Louise Dennys, two of the most distinguished figures in Canadian publishing, for their unfailing support throughout the life of this project, despite the distracting corporate difficulties that were confronting them for much of that time. I am grateful to my good friends Patsy Aldana and Matt Cohen for their advice and encouragement.

Because of the wide scope of this project and its duration, its completion has exacted more than the usual sacrifices from the members of my family. From my wife, Sandy, and my children, I can only seek forgiveness for having been a distracted and introverted presence in their midst for too much of the past three years.

NOTES

★ ★ ★ ★ ★ ★ ★ ★ ★ ★ ★ ★

CHAPTER 2

1 For a discussion of the strategic concepts on which American policy was based, see Stephen E. Ambrose, *Rise to Globalism: American Foreign Policy since 1938* (New York: Penguin, 1985).

2 Dominique Moisi, "The French Answer to the German Question," *European Affairs* (Spring 1990): 35.

3 Walter Hallstein, *Europe in the Making* (London: George Allen and Unwin Ltd., 1972), p. 21.

4 By American George W. Ball in his introduction to Monnet's memoirs: Jean Monnet, *Memoirs* (New York: Doubleday, 1978), p. 11.

5 Michael Burgess, *Federalism and European Union: Political Ideas, Influences and Strategies in the European Community, 1972-87* (London: Routledge, 1989), p. 49.

6 Ibid., p. 33.

7 Ibid., p. 29.

8 Ibid., p. 68.

9 Wolfram F. Hanrieder, *Germany, America, Europe: Forty Years of German Foreign Policy* (New Haven: Yale University Press, 1989), pp. 8, 9.

10 Simon Bulmer and William Paterson, *The Federal Republic of Germany and the European Community* (London: Allen and Unwin, 1987), p. 5.

11 For a discussion of functionalism, see D. Mitrany, *The Functional Theory of Politics* (London: Martin Robertson, 1975).

12 Monnet, *Memoirs*, p. 316.

13 Ibid., pp. 294, 295.

14 Ibid., p. 394.

15 For a discussion of the industrial policy embodied in the ECSC, see Dennis Swann, *Competition and Industrial Policy in the European Community* (London and New York: Methuen, 1983).

16 Monnet, *Memoirs*, p. 366.

17 Ibid.

18 Ibid., p. 417.

19 *Treaties Establishing the European Communities* (Luxembourg: Office for Official Publications of the European Communities, 1987), p. 119.

20 Hanrieder, *Germany, America, Europe*, p. 343.

21 Monnet, *Memoirs*, p. 496.

22 Willy Brandt, *In Exile: Essays, Reflections and Letters, 1933-1947* (London: Oswald Wolff, 1971), p. 8. As cited in Burgess, *Federalism and European Union*, 67.

23 For an insight into Spinelli's perspective on the EC, see Altiero Spinelli, *The European Adventure: Tasks for the Enlarged Community* (London: Charles Knight and Co. Ltd., 1972).

CHAPTER 3

1 European File, January 1988: the European Community in Diagrams, data from the consulate of the Federal Republic of Germany, Toronto, Canada.

2 Ibid.

3 Commission of the European Communities, "The Regions in the 1990s: Fourth Periodic Report," February 25, 1991.

4 European File.

5 *International Herald Tribune*, April 4, 1990.

6 Paul Taylor, "The New Dynamics of EC Integration in the 1980s," in Juliet Lodge, ed., *The European Community and the Challenge of the Future* (London: Pinter Publishers, 1989), pp. 7, 8.

7 Ibid., p. 9.

8 Commission of the European Communities, "Completing the Internal Market: White Paper from the Commission to the European Council," Milan, June 28 and 29, 1985.

9 Taylor, "The New Dynamics of EC Integration in the 1980s," p. 8.

10 *Treaties Establishing the European Communities* (Luxembourg: Office for Official Publications of the European Communities, 1987), p. 129.

11 Alan Butt Philip, "European Border Controls: Who Needs Them?" The Royal Institute of International Affairs, Discussion Paper No. 19, August 1989, p. 3.

12 Ibid., pp. 5, 6.

13 Ibid., p. 14.

14 Paolo Cecchini, *The European Challenge 1992: The Benefits of a Single Market* (London: Wildwood House, 1988), pp. 8, 9.

15 Scott Davidson, "Free Movement of Goods, Workers, Services and Capital," in Lodge, ed., *The European Community*, p. 114.

16 Cecchini, *The European Challenge 1992*, p. 29.

17 Ibid., p. 25.

18 Ibid., p. 52.

19 Ibid., p. 53.

20 Ibid., p. 55.

21 Ibid., p. 56.

22 Ibid., p. 58.

23 Ibid., p. 59.

24 Ibid., p. 61.

25 Ibid., p. 16.

26 Ibid.

27 Commission of the European Communities, "Completing the Internal Market...," p. 23.

28 Cecchini, *The European Challenge 1992*, p. 17.

29 Ibid., p. 19.

30 Ibid., pp. 19, 20.

31 Ibid., p. 37.

32 Commission of the European Communities, "Completing the Internal Market...," p. 27.

33 Ibid., pp. 38, 39.

34 Dick Leonard, *Pocket Guide to the European Community* (London: Economist Publications, 1988), p. 88.

35 Commission of the European Communities, "Completing the Internal Market...," p. 47.

36 Ibid., p. 49.

37 Leonard, *Pocket Guide*, p. 93.

38 Ibid.

39 Ibid., p. 89.

40 Commission of the European Communities, The Week in Europe, June 6, 1991.

41 Cecchini, *The European Challenge 1992*, p. xviii.
42 Ibid., p. 97.
43 *Time*, January 23, 1989.
44 *European Economy* 35 (March 1988): 164, 166.
45 *Time*, January 23, 1989.

CHAPTER 4

1 *International Herald Tribune*, March 9, 1990.
2 Ibid.
3 Ibid.
4 *The Guardian*, March 24, 1990.
5 A.J.P. Taylor, *The Struggle for Mastery In Europe, 1848-1918* (London: Oxford, 1954), p. 223.
6 For a discussion of the Italian Renaissance, see Denys Hay, *The Italian Renaissance in its Historical Background* (Cambridge: Cambridge University Press, 1987).
7 For a treatment of the history of Florence, see Marcello Vannucci, *The History of Florence* (Rome: Newton Compton Editori, 1986).
8 Colin Leys, *Politics in Britain* (London: Heinemann Educational Books, 1983), pp. 212, 213.
9 Ibid., p. 212.
10 *The Economist*, May 26, 1990, p. 19.
11 For the classical discussion of the rise of nationalism in Europe, on which I have drawn for perspective, see Hans Kohn, *The Idea of Nationalism* (New York: Collier, 1969).
12 Ibid., p. 82.
13 See E.L. Jones, *The European Miracle* (Cambridge: Cambridge University Press, 1988).
14 For a classical treatment, R.H. Tawney, *Religion and the Rise of Capitalism* (New York: Mentor, 1961).
15 John Lough, *An Introduction to Eighteenth Century France* (New York: Longmans, 1964).
16 For a critical perspective on these developments, see J.L. Talmon, *The Origins of Totalitarian Democracy* (New York: Praeger, 1960).
17 Kohn, *The Idea of Nationalism*, p. 418.

CHAPTER 5

1 Saxton Bampfylde International PLC, *The Search for the Euro-Executive* (London, 1989), pp. 4, 5.

2 Ibid., pp. 14, 15.

3 Ibid., p. 26.

4 *Harvard Business Review* (May/June 1989), p. 81.

5 *Elle*, September 26, 1988, p. 162.

6 Ibid., p. 166.

7 *Harvard Business Review* (May/June 1989), p. 89.

8 Ibid.

9 John F. Magee, "1992: Moves Americans Must Make," *Harvard Business Review* (May/June 1989), p. 78.

10 Ibid.

11 Ibid.

12 Sir Leon Brittan, Text of speech, March 1989, p. 9.

13 Ibid.

14 Ibid., p. 10.

15 For a discussion of the industrial policies of European countries, see Graham Hall, ed., *European Industrial Policy* (London: Croom Helm, 1986).

16 *The European Electronics Industry*, Industry Pamphlet, p. 13.

17 *The Economist*, April 7, 1990, p. 78.

18 *The European Electronics Industry*, p. 9.

19 *The Economist*, April 7, 1990, p. 78.

20 *International Herald Tribune*, September 17, 1990.

21 *The European*, April 26, 1991.

22 *International Herald Tribune*, September 19, 1990.

23 For an analysis of the German Greens, see Werner Hulsberg, *The German Greens* (London: Verso, 1988).

24 EC Commission, Text of Jacques Delors's speech at Bournemouth, September 8, 1988.

25 "Europe in 1994: Motor Vehicles," an EC position paper, p. 47.

26 *Fiat Group Facts and Figures* (Turin: Fiat, 1989), p. 7.

27 *Financial Times*, February 12, 1991.

28 Kenjiro Ishikawa, *Japan and the Challenge of Europe 1992* (London: Royal Institute of International Affairs, 1990), p. 75.

29 *Financial Times*, December 10, 1990.

30 "Europe in 1994: Motor Vehicles," p. 50.

31 Sir Leon Brittan, "A Single Market for Motor Vehicles: Why and When?" Partial text of a speech, printed by the EC Commission, p. 2.

32 Ishikawa, *Japan and the Challenge of Europe 1992*, p. 70.

33 Ibid.

34 Ibid., p. 75.

35 *Financial Times*, December 10, 1990.
36 For a discussion of the transformation under way in the global financial services sector, see Joyce Kolko, *Restructuring the World Economy* (New York: Pantheon Books, 1988), chapter 5.
37 Deutsche Bank Group, *Annual Review for 1989*, p. 8.
38 Ibid.
39 Commission of the European Communities, *Background Report*, October 31, 1990, p. 1.
40 Committee for the Study of Economic and Monetary Union, *Report on Economic and Monetary Union in the European Community*, p. 9.
41 Dick Leonard, *Pocket Guide to the European Community* (London: Economist Publications, 1988), p. 87.
42 *Report on Economic and Monetary Union*, p. 12.
43 Ibid., p. 13.
44 Ibid., p. 14.
45 Ibid., p. 18.
46 Ibid., p. 27.
47 Ibid., pp. 31-33.
48 Ibid., pp. 33-35.
49 Ibid., pp. 35, 36.

CHAPTER 6

1 David Marsh, *The Germans, Rich, Bothered and Divided* (London: Century, 1989), pp. 173, 174.
2 Ibid., p. 15.
3 Ibid., pp. 12-14.
4 Henry Ashby Turner, Jr., *The Two Germanies since 1945* (New Haven: Yale University Press, 1989), pp. 38, 39.
5 C.C. Schweitzer et al., eds., *Politics and Government in the Federal Republic of Germany: Basic Documents* (Leamington Spa: Berg Publishers, 1984), p. 119.
6 Ibid., p. 120.
7 Turner, *The Two Germanies*, pp. 95, 96.
8 Ibid., p. 79.
9 Ibid., pp. 68, 69.
10 Ibid., pp. 166, 167.
11 *The Guardian*, November 11, 1989.
12 Strasbourg Notebook, European Parliament, November 22, 1989, evening edition.

13 *Vanity Fair*, December 1990, p. 238.
14 *International Herald Tribune*, March 7, 1990.
15 *The European*, September 7, 1990, p. 17.
16 Ibid.
17 Turner, *The Two Germanies*, p. 39.
18 Gordon Smith, "Structures of Government," in Gordon Smith, William E. Paterson, Peter H. Merkl, eds., *Developments in West German Politics* (London: Macmillan, 1989), p. 31.
19 Schweitzer et al., eds., *Politics and Government*, p. 374.
20 Turner, *The Two Germanies*, p. 150.
21 Ibid., pp. 159, 160.
22 Simon Head, "The East German Disaster," *The New York Review of Books*, January 17, 1991, p. 43.
23 For citizens under sixteen years of age in the GDR, their first 2000 Ostmarks in cash or bank accounts were exchanged for Deutschmarks at a rate of one to one, while Ostmarks in excess of that amount where exchanged for DM at a rate of two to one; for those in the GDR aged sixteen to sixty, the first 4000 Ostmarks were exchanged at a rate of one to one, and additional Ostmarks at two to one; for those in the GDR who were over sixty, the first 6000 Ostmarks were exchanged at a rate of one to one, and additional Ostmarks at two to one; for people outside the GDR holding Ostmarks in private or commercial accounts as of December 31, 1989, Ostmarks were exchanged for DM at a rate of two to one; for those outside the GDR opening accounts after December 31, 1989, the exchange rate was one to one. (Consulate of the Federal Republic of Germany, Toronto, Canada, March 1991.)
24 Timothy Garton Ash, "Germany at the Frontier," *New York Review of Books*, January 17, 1991, p. 21.
25 Head, "The East German Disaster," pp. 42, 43.
26 Smith, "Structures of Government," pp. 24–39.
27 *The European*, October 5, 1990.

CHAPTER 7

1 For a discussion of the fate of the Jews in Vichy France, see Michael R. Marrus and Robert O. Paxton, *Vichy France and the Jews* (New York: Schocken Books, 1983).
2 *The European*, September 7, 1990.
3 *International Herald Tribune*, April 26, 1988.

4 Ibid.
5 Vincent Wright, *The Government and Politics of France*, 3rd ed. (London: Unwin Hyman, 1983), Appendix 8 (B).
6 Richard Bassett, *Waldheim and Austria* (New York: Viking, 1988), pp. 76, 77.
7 Wright, *Government and Politics of France*, pp. 169, 213.
8 Ibid., Appendix 8 (A).
9 Ibid., p. 211.
10 Howard Machin and Vincent Wright, "Economic Policy under the Mitterrand Presidency, 1981-1984: An Introduction," in Howard Machin and Vincent Wright, eds., *Economic Policy and Policy-Making under the Mitterrand Presidency, 1981-84* (London: Pinter, 1985), p. 1.
11 *International Herald Tribune*, April 26, 1988. For a further investigation of Mitterrand's political manipulativeness, see the celebrated scathing biography *Le Président* (Paris: Seuil, 1990), by Franz-Olivier Giesbert.
12 Wright, *Government and Politics of France*, p. 198.
13 OECD, *Historical Statistics, 1960-1984* (Paris: OECD, 1986), p. 47.
14 Dominique Moisi, "The French Answer to the German Question," *European Affairs* (Spring 1990): 35.

CHAPTER 8

1 *The Economist*, November 17, 1990, p. 74.
2 Bob Jessop et al., *Thatcherism: A Tale of Two Nations* (London: Polity Press, 1988), p. 18.
3 See ibid.
4 *The Economist*, November 24, 1990, p. 20.
5 Anthony Sampson, *The Changing Anatomy of Britain* (London: Coronet, 1983), p. 52.
6 Alan Sked and Chris Cook, *Post-War Britain: A Political History* (Harmondsworth: Penguin, 1984), p. 329.
7 Keith Smith, *The British Economic Crisis* (Harmondsworth: Pelican, 1984), pp. 80, 81.
8 OECD, *United Kingdom* (Paris: OECD, 1986), p. 65.
9 Smith, *British Economic Crisis*, p. 35.
10 Sked and Cook, *Post-War Britain*, pp. 324, 432.
11 Henry Parris, Pierre Pestieau, and Peter Saynor, *Public Enterprise in Western Europe* (London: Croom Helm, 1987), p. 157.

12 *The Economist*, November 24, 1990, p. 17.

13 Parris et al., *Public Enterprise*, pp. 160, 161.

14 *The Economist*, November 24, 1990, pp. 18, 19.

15 House of Commons, *Official Report*, May 18, 1989.

16 For a discussion of the evolution of the Labour party's position on Europe, see Kevin Featherstone, *Socialist Parties and European Integration: A Comparative History* (Manchester: Manchester University Press, 1988), chapter 3.

17 Asa Briggs, *A Social History of England* (Harmondsworth: Penguin, 1987), p. 266.

18 See Michael Heseltine, *The Challenge of Europe: Can Britain Win* (London: Weidenfeld and Nicolson, 1989).

19 Ibid., pp. 214, 215.

20 *The Guardian*, September 18, 1989.

21 Ibid.

22 *The Economist*, March 9, 1991, p. 21.

CHAPTER 9

1 *The European*, August 3, 1990.

2 Henrich Schneider, "Austria and the EC," The Royal Institute of International Affairs, Discussion Paper no. 24, 1989, p. 1.

3 For treatments of Soviet industrialization, see Alec Nove, *An Economic History of the U.S.S.R.* (Harmondsworth: Pelican, 1982) and David Lane, *Soviet Economy and Society* (Oxford: Blackwell, 1985).

4 Patrick Brogan, *Eastern Europe 1939-1989: The Fifty Years War* (London: Bloomsbury, 1990), pp. 136, 137.

5 Janos Kis, "Turning Point in Hungary," *Dissent* (Spring 1989): 235.

6 Ibid.

7 Ibid., 237.

8 For a fascinating portrait of official personalities of latter-day communism in Hungary, see Hans Magnus Enzensberger, *Europe, Europe: Forays into a Continent* (London: Hutchison Radius, 1989).

9 *The Economist*, April 14, 1990, p. 21.

10 Vaclav Havel, *Living in Truth* (London: Faber and Faber, 1986), p. 14.

11 For a critical perspective on Vienna, Budapest, and Prague, see Stephen Brook, *The Double Eagle* (London: Picador, 1988).

12 Brogan, *Eastern Europe*, pp. 50, 51.

13 Ibid., p. 59.

14 *The European*, November 16, 1989.

15 Ibid.

16 Ibid., December 7, 1990.

17 *Marxism Today* (May 1990), p. 23.

CHAPTER 10

1 *Financial Times*, April 16, 1991.

2 David Buchan, "Whither WEU," *European Affairs*
(February/March 1991): 70.

3 Ibid., 69.

4 *The European*, March 8, 1991.

5 *International Herald Tribune*, April 10, 1991.

6 *The European*, March 8, 1991.

7 *International Herald Tribune*, April 10, 1991.

8 For analyses of the contemporary global economic and political
order, see Robert Gilpin, *The Political Economy of International
Relations* (Princeton: Princeton University Press, 1987), and
Paul Kennedy, *The Rise and Fall of the Great Powers: Economic
Change and Military Conflict from 1500 to 2000* (New York:
Random House, 1987).

9 Ajit Singh, "The Long-Term Structural Disequilibrium of the
U.K. Economy: Employment, Trade and Import Controls," a
paper presented at the University of Modena, November 1982.

10 For an analysis of the shifting patterns of alliances in social-
democratic movements, see Gøsta Esping-Andersen, *Politics
Against Markets: The Social Democratic Road to Power* (Princeton:
Princeton University Press, 1985).

11 For a discussion of the relationship between the expansion of
the EC to include new members and the strengthening of EC
institutions, see Helen Wallace, "Widening and Deepening:
The European Community and the New European Agenda,"
The Royal Institute of International Affairs, Discussion Paper
No. 23, 1989.

INDEX

★ ★ ★ ★ ★ ★ ★ ★ ★ ★ ★ ★

European People's Party, in
European Parliament, 13
European Parliament (EP), 9, 10–16,
50–51, 67, 78, 88, 147, 292–93;
meeting schedule of, 16;
membership of, 13; relationship
with Council of Ministers, 12
European Political Community
(EPC), 39, 41
European Right, in European
Parliament, 13
European System of Central Banks
(ESCB), 174
European union: as a reaction
against fascism, 25–26; Britain's
response to evolution of,
24–25; Franco–German
relations and, 30–31, 33–34, 48
–50, 291–97; history of
evolution of, 23–43; inspiration
for, 25–26; role of United
States in evolution of, 23–24;
supranationalism and, 34
Eurotom. *See* European Atomic
Energy Community
Euskara, 106
Exchange Rate Mechanism (ERM),
19, 170, 173, 232, 291

Falklands war, 252
Fiat, 154–58
Fiscal barriers, removal of under
"1992" program, 66, 81–84
Financial services, in the European
Community, 162–68
Florence, Italy, 102
Ford, Glyn, 78
Ford Motor Co., 156, 159
Forrai, Dr. Istvan, 273, 274
"Foulard" issue, in France, 226–27
France: as model nation–state, 98;

"foulard" issue in, 226–27; French
Revolution, 224–25, 238; issue of
"who belongs" in, 229–31; Left
vs. Right in, 224–26, 233–35;
North African immigration in,
224, 225, 231; racism in, 221–24;
regionalism in, 98–102; relations
of with Germany, 30–31, 33–34,
48–50, 239–41, 291–97; statism
and, 144–45; under Socialists, 231
–33
Franco, Francisco, 106
Free Democratic Party (FDP), in
Federal Republic of Germany,
191, 196–97
Free Democratic Party, in Hungary,
272, 273, 275
Freedom Party, in Austria, 228
French, the, as viewed by other
Europeans, 91–92
French Revolution, 224–25, 238
Friedman, Milton, 247, 274
Front National, of France, 10, 93,
223–24, 226, 229, 230, 234
Frontiers, dismantling of under
"1992" program, 65–66, 67–73

Galicians, 106–07
Gambetta, Leon, 100
Gang of Four, in Great Britain, 252
Gaudi, Antonio, 105
Gdansk, Poland, 283
General Agreement on Tariffs and
Trade (GATT), 309–10
Genscher, Hans–Dietrich, 196
German Economic and Monetary
Union (GEMU), 163–64, 197
German Empire, under Bismarck,
178
Germans, the, as viewed by other
Europeans, 92–94